WALKER'S BRITAIN

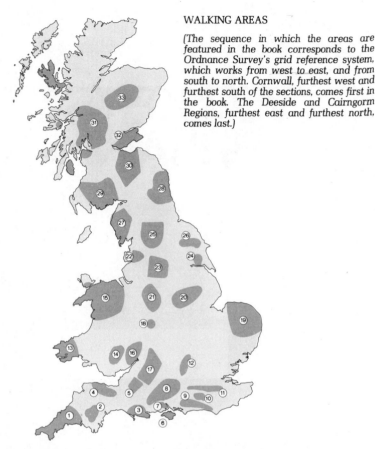

WALKING AREAS

(The sequence in which the areas are featured in the book corresponds to the Ordnance Survey's grid reference system, which works from west to east, and from south to north. Cornwall, furthest west and furthest south of the sections, comes first in the book. The Deeside and Cairngorm Regions, furthest east and furthest north, comes last.)

① Cornwall, page 14
② Dartmoor, page 24
③ Dorset, page 34
④ Exmoor and The Quantocks, page 42
⑤ Mendip Region, page 54
⑥ Isle of Wight, page 66
⑦ New Forest, page 72
⑧ The Wessex Downs, page 80
⑨ South Downs, page 92
⑩ Surrey, page 104
⑪ North Downs, page 112
⑫ Chilterns and Thames Valley, page 122
⑬ Pembrokeshire, page 132
⑭ Brecon Beacons and Black Mountains, page 140
⑮ North Wales, page 148
⑯ Welsh Marches, page 166

⑰ Cotswolds, page 172
⑱ Around Birmingham, page 182
⑲ Norfolk, page 188
⑳ East Midlands, page 196
㉑ Peak District, page 204
㉒ Lancashire, page 216
㉓ The South Pennines, page 222
㉔ Yorkshire Wolds, page 232
㉕ Yorkshire Dales, page 240
㉖ North York Moors, page 252
㉗ Cumbria and The Lakes, page 260
㉘ Northumberland, page 272
㉙ SW Scotland, page 282
㉚ South of the Forth, page 290
㉛ Highlands and Islands, page 298
㉜ Fife Region, page 310
㉝ Deeside and Cairngorm Regions, page 318

WALKER'S
BRITAIN

The Complete Pocket Guide
to over 240 Walks
and Rambles

Pan Books/Ordnance Survey

First published 1982 by Pan Books Ltd,
Cavaye Place, London SW10 9PG and
Ordnance Survey, Romsey Road, Maybush,
Southampton SO9 4DH.
Conceived, edited and designed by Duncan
Associates, 64, Fullerton Road, London,
SW18 1BX with Mel Petersen &
Associates, 5, Botts Mews, Chepstow Road,
London W2 5AG.

Pan ISBN 0 330 26611 X (Paperback)
ISBN 0 330 26853 8 (Hardback)
OS ISBN 0 319 00008 7

Printed and bound in Great Britain
by Morrison & Gibb Ltd.,
London and Edinburgh

Sections introduced by **Christopher Hall**
Illustrations **Tony Graham**
Special contributor **Marjorie Lampard**
Long Distance Section
compiled by **Jennifer Grafton**
Consultant **John Trevelyan**
Designer **Nigel O'Gorman**
Artwork to maps **Nigel O'Gorman**
Researcher **Trevor Dolby**
Editorial assistants **Fred and Cathy Gill,**
David Arnold
Picture research **Linda Proud**
Art Editor **Mel Petersen**
Editor **Andrew Duncan**
Invaluable inspiration and advice
was provided by Nigel Buxton.

As befits a national walking guide, this
book was created by a team of people all
round the country. Each is an expert on his
or her own area or areas; most are
authors of local walking guides (listed on
page 336 together with some biographical
details). Their knowledge, skill, enthusiasm
and energy – in all weathers – made the
enterprise possible.

Cornwall, **David Platten**; Dartmoor, **Liz
Prince and staff of the Dartmoor National
Park Office**; Dorset, Isle of Wight, New
Forest, The Wessex Downs, **Anne-Marie
Edwards**; Exmoor, **David Butler**; The
Quantocks, **C. Trent Thomas**; Mendip
Region, **E. M. Goold with G. Lane and S.
Franklin of the Mendip Ramblers' Asso-
ciation**; Surrey, North Downs, **Janet Spayne,
Audrey Krynski**; Chilterns and Thames
Valley, **Nick Moon**; Pembrokeshire, **Tom
Goodall and members of the Pembroke-
shire Ramblers' Association**; Brecon
Beacons and Black Mountains, **Chris
Barber**; North Wales, **James T. C. Knowles**;
Welsh Marches, **Donna Baker**; Cotswolds,
**Richard Sale, Nathan Sale and Mike
Rogers**; Around Birmingham, **S. G.
Wallsgrove, Denis N. Keyte, R. Pickard**;
Norfolk, **Jeanne le Surf**; East Midlands,
Brett Collier; Peak District, Northumber-
land, **Brian Spencer**; Lancashire, **Cyril
Spibey**; The South Pennines, Yorkshire
Dales, **Colin Speakman**; Yorkshire Wolds,
Geoff Eastwood; North York Moors, **Walter
Henderson**; Cumbria and the Lakes, **John
Parker**; SW Scotland, **Ken Andrew**; South
of the Forth, Fife Region, **Dave Forsyth**;
Highlands and Islands, **Bill Brodie, Charles
Target**; Deeside and Cairngorm Regions, **F.
C. A. Gordon**.

Another team of walkers strode hundreds of
miles checking and testing the walks. Of
these Anne Duncan, John Nolan, Fiona
Grafton and John and Caroline Sharpe,
Charles Target and Helen Alexander
deserve special thanks. We are also grateful
to Georgina Chichester, Hugo Charlton,
Clare and Julian Whately, Louise Hallett,
Paula Grant, Margaret Robertshaw, Lorne
and Bill Cobb, Adrian and Diana Dent,
Richard and Jane Clayton, Martin Mitchell,
Bill Chester, the Preston C.H.A. Rambling
Club, Alan MacPherson. Dr. and Mrs.
Wynne Willson and Linda Abraham.

CONTENTS

The book is divided into 33 sections representing the cream of Britain's walking. These are shown, with page numbers, on the map on the preceding, facing page. For ease of reference, the contents are also organized into six regional sections, with page numbers given below.

Using this book	page	6
Footwear and Clothing		8
The Walker, the Law and Safety		10
The South-West		12-63
South-east England		64-129
Wales		130-163
Middle England		164-213
Northern England		214-279
Scotland		280-327
Long Distance Walks: a briefing		328-334
Index of place names that are starting points, or near starting points of walks		335
Acknowledgements		336

All distances mentioned are approximate. Remember that the countryside changes frequently; landmarks disappear – especially stiles.

USING THIS BOOK

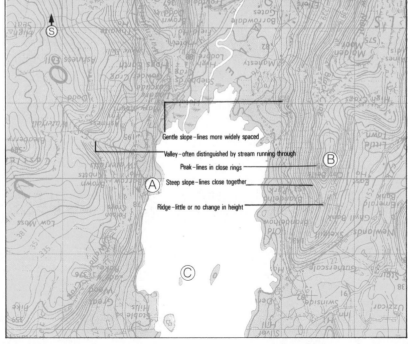

Gentle slope – lines more widely spaced

Valley – often distinguished by stream running through

Peak – lines in close rings

Steep slope – lines close together

Ridge – little or no change in height

You can do the routes in *Walker's Britain* just by following the directions linked to the numbers on the maps. However, some understanding of maps and map-reading will greatly add to your enjoyment.

The maps in this book were made by Ordnance Survey, the U.K.'s national surveying and map-making organization, usually referred to simply as O.S.

O.S. maps are the best available. They are based on detailed surveys: accurate measurements of the ground combined with aerial photography. No other maps are precision instruments in this sense.

The range of O.S. maps covers widely differing scales, for varying purposes. In this book are extracts from the 1:50,000 'Landranger' series.

To show the walking routes as clearly as possible, extracts from the monochrome versions of the 1:50,000 sheets have been used with a green tint overlaid. The route is 'windowed' to give a clear view of the mapping beneath.

1:50,000 maps are useful to walkers because, in colour, they show rights of way in England and Wales and are drawn to a scale giving enough detail for route-finding in most areas. For extra enjoyment of this book, use it with the relevant colour sheets. They open up limitless walking possibilities.

As a beginner, start by getting to know the meaning of the map's symbols (see inside front cover). Contour lines are the only complex ones. They are imaginary lines along which the ground is the same height, and show the way the land rises and falls (see map opposite).

Before starting to walk, 'set' your map. If walking due north, have the top of the sheet pointing north; if walking south (see opposite), have the sheet upside down.

Next, identify two or three points on the ground and find them on the map (see A, B and C). This confirms your position.

Next, understand the full implications of the map's scale. On 1:50,000 maps, one unit on the map; represents 50,000 units on the ground. This is equivalent to 1¼ inches (3 cm) on the map for every mile (1.5 km) on the ground. An average walking pace is 3 mph (5 km/h) on the flat – a mile for every 20 minutes'. In hill country, add 25%.

Finally do *not* put the map away when you walk. Always know your position. Cross-check it by estimating distance against time, observing landmarks as they pass and being aware of progress across contour lines.

● The O.S. mapping used in this book does not show all rights of way, but the routes as marked are on rights of way or land with open access.
● The **sheet numbers** refer to the relevant O.S. Landranger sheet.
● **The six-figure number** following the sheet number is the grid reference of the walk's starting point on the Landranger sheet.
● **Mud after rain** means the route has a chance of drying out. **Mud** means suitable footwear must be worn.
● **The number of climbs** is a broad guide only. Remember **stiles** are of widely varying construction. **Path** usually means a narrow way – sometimes just beaten-down grass; **track** is usually broader and better defined.

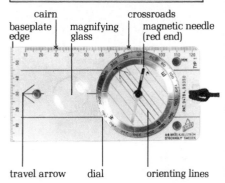

cairn

baseplate edge | magnifying glass | crossroads

magnetic needle (red end)

travel arrow   dial   orienting lines

In poor visibility or on featureless ground, you need a compass. The 'Silva' type is the easiest to use with a map; here is one of several ways in which it works.

Imagine being on moorland when the cloud comes down. You know your present position – a cairn. You want to make for a crossroads.

Place the compass baseplate edge on the map so it connects cairn and crossroads. Turn the dial so that the orienting lines on the transparent bottom are parallel with grid lines running N-S on the map. Then turn the whole compass, plus map, until the red end of the magnetic needle points to N.

Look up and distinguish a rock or clump of grass that lies along the line indicated by the travel arrow. Eyes on the landmark, walk to it. Repeat the procedure.

FOOTWEAR AND CLOTHES

You must have proper footwear for serious walking. Gum boots, gym shoes or kickers may be adequate for a stroll. Stout walking shoes will take you all day on country lanes. But if you walk regularly, and if you want to see the moorland and hill country – which means negotiating bogs and rough, stony ground, you need to protect your feet in leather walking boots.

Leather allows your feet to 'breathe' because it is porous. Ventilation is the key to comfortable feet because even if boots are sodden (as they will be – leather is no more than water-resistant), drying out can begin with the feet inside them. Rubber boots offer no such luxury: the feet are always slightly damp because the perspiration and condensation is trapped inside.

Only the stout construction of a walking boot can give the ankles the support they need to minimize risk of sprains. Only leather can mould itself to the feet, providing the fit that allows walking all day.

A genuine pair of walking boots costs at least £30.00. Beware of other people's boots: they can never mould to your feet.

Wear in new boots on short walks – a total of about 30 miles (48 km) does the job. After walking, wash off the mud and let them dry naturally – direct heat distorts their shape. Wash them especially well after walking in boggy country: acids in marshy water can damage leather and stitching. While the boots are still wet, apply a dressing.

Clothes

When choosing walking clothes, remember that wind is potentially a serious problem. It reduces body temperature dramatically because of the heat loss in evaporation. A walk which starts in a light breeze in the valley can, on the hill-top, be a battle with a gale. Plan accordingly: have layers of clothing that can be shed, or added to. Remember, too, that significant body heat is lost from the head: so wear a hat.

Waterproofs need choosing carefully because of the condensation problem: your body warmth causes water droplets to form inside a waterproof garment if it is tightly closed against the rain. Some new materials claim to minimize the slight dampness so-caused, but ease of ventilation is still important. The waterproof anorak that opens up the front allows this, whereas one-piece, knee-length cagoules do not. Capes give excellent ventilation, but blow around violently in strong wind.

Buying boots
● Go to a specialist who will let you take time over fitting ● Try on boots before midday – later your feet may have swollen ● Your big toe ought not to press against the boot's toe ● When laced, the boot should hold the foot back, so that it does not slide forward when going downhill ● Sides of feet ought to be firmly held, but not squeezed when boots are laced ● The boot's heel should cup your own ● Your heel will move slightly in a new boot, but soon the boot's heel and yours should move together ● The back of the boot should be stiff enough to support your heel ● The uppers should be one piece of leather – no seams to leak ● A padded tongue and padded sides give extra comfort ● The sole must have some flexibility and be at least ½ inch (13 mm) thick. 'Vibram' or 'Commando' composition soles are reliable ● The welts should not stick out too far: this looks clumsy and if scrambling on the points of the toes long welts can lessen your contact with the ground, impairing balance. ● Boots should have a scree cuff for gripping the ankle and keeping out small stones. ● Hooks or 'D' rings are intended to be easiest to tie with cold fingers ● Two pairs of socks should be worn even with the perfectly fitting boot, a thin pair next to the skin, a thicker pair on top. The result is a cushioning effect and warmer feet. Most reputable dealers have thick socks at hand for fitting purposes.

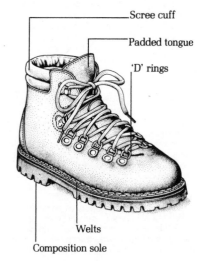

Scree cuff

Padded tongue

'D' rings

Welts

Composition sole

**Features of an efficient
waterproof anorak**

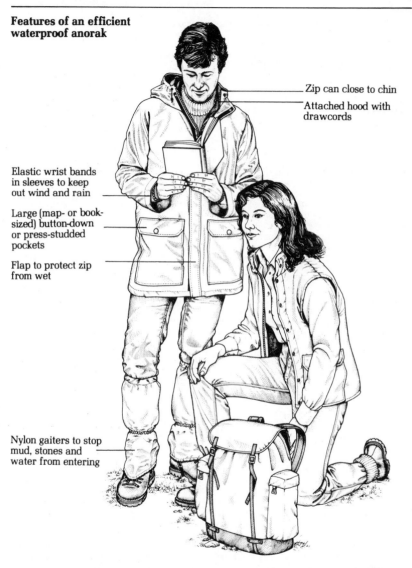

Zip can close to chin

Attached hood with
drawcords

Elastic wrist bands
in sleeves to keep
out wind and rain

Large (map- or book-
sized) button-down
or press-studded
pockets

Flap to protect zip
from wet

Nylon gaiters to stop
mud, stones and
water from entering

Jeans, despite their popularity, are not ideal
walking trousers. Wool or corduroy are
warmer, and provide some protection
against chilling wind even if wet through.
The most comfortable combination for hill
walking is knee-length breeches and socks.

The rucksack should contain waterproof
over-trousers. The most practical type can
be put on without taking the boots off.
Increasingly popular are light, padded
jackets to give body warmth with freedom
of arm movement.

THE WALKER, THE LAW AND SAFETY

WALKERS' RIGHTS, AND DUTIES

Great Britain has more public footpaths than any nation on Earth. The network in England and Wales is more than 120,000 miles long; in Scotland, where the law is different, walkers theoretically enjoy even more open access to the countryside.

Moreover, in England and Wales, the right to wander in the countryside is supported by an interesting principle of law, itself an embodiment of many of the principles of social freedom we take for granted.

In law, public footpaths can be born at any time, on anyone's land, by the process known as dedication. Dedication can be 'presumed', in which case, if a path is in use without a break for 20 years, it is presumed to be a right of way. Or it can be 'direct', in which case it is negotiated, or even compulsorily ordered. A landowner can prevent presumed dedication by closing the path just once during the 20-year period; but the principle, and the possibility, of creating new paths always exists.

A right of way is just what it says: a right of passage across someone's land. The landowner may rightly object if the walker does damage, or leaves litter. But he may not complain – legally – if the walker pauses on the path to enjoy the view, or to eat lunch.

Trespass

If a walker strays from the right of way, he is trespassing. In this case the landowner ought to insist that the trespasser returns to the right of way, or leaves the land. Should the trespasser refuse, the landowner may use the minimum possible force to make the trespasser do so.

It is not an offence, in itself, to trespass; if you are taken to court as a result of trespassing, the landowner will sue for damages. If you, the trespasser, are found guilty, you would pay these damages. They may or may not amount to much in terms of cash; but you would also have to pay the landowner's legal fees: never cheap.

Maintenance

If a public footpath is blocked by wire, machinery, indeed by anything, the landowner is at fault and the walker may go round the obstruction, or climb it, making every effort to cause no damage. Generally, local authorities have a duty to keep the surface of paths in good condition.

A landowner may plough over a footpath if it is not along a field boundary or headland provided the path is returned to usable condition within two weeks of starting to plough, or as soon as practicable if weather prevents this being done. Sometimes farmers leave an unploughed strip; if they do not, the walker is still entitled to walk across, provided he or she keeps to the right of way.

This has tended to be a source of worry and confusion for walkers. People instinctively feel that it is better to trespass, and thereby avoid damage to crops, than to keep to the footpath. But in legal, and practical terms, the best course is to keep to the right of way. The damage to a field under crops is minimal if the walker(s) keep in single file; the consequences of trespass may be worse.

The Ramblers' Association

All these privileges, which are all too often abused and neglected (especially where ploughing is concerned) are protected on our behalf by the Ramblers' Association.

This is a privately funded lobby group, and if you care about going on country walks, you should support it, too. It has many local branches, some of which helped to prepare this book. The address is on page 328.

Bulls

Do not let your country walk be spoilt either by being unnecessarily frightened, or foolhardy when there are bulls or cows around. Cows and bullocks (young bulls) may rush up to you in a field, but they are rarely being aggressive.

If you see a bull alone in a field where there is a public right of way, it is probably there illegally; if it is with cows, it is probably there legally. If you encounter a truly aggressive (ie, charging) bull in a field where there is a right of way, tell the police and the Ramblers' Association.

Stallions, boars and cows with calves should be treated with due caution.

The Landowner

Remember the landowner's point of view, whatever your feelings about private ownership of land. Farmers, rich or poor, provide employment. Possibly their chief objection to walkers centres on dogs, which can upset livestock and kill game. After that, damage to crops and property are the main causes of friction. Share the countryside: you have a right to be there, but it is not exclusive.

SAFETY ON THE HILLS

Britain's mountains and hills are not high, but they are dangerous. Because they are near the sea, their weather changes fast.

Much about modern life makes us especially vulnerable to their treachery. We are unfit, because we sit all day. We arrive at walks in the comfort of cars, from which it is doubly hard to imagine the potential nastiness of the serenely inviting hilltops. Once out of the valley, a perfect summer's day can turn, in minutes, to wintry ghastliness.

Almost all accidents, and tragedies, can be prevented by following these rules.

● Wear the right clothes (see pages 8-9) and footwear. Take spare clothing.
● Be equipped. The lunch box should contain some emergency rations – chocolate, dried fruit and biscuits. There should be a flask containing a hot drink. The prudent take a first aid kit, even on a day's outing. Learn first aid for frost bite, fractures, hypothermia and strains.

The same applies to a whistle, a torch and a spare battery. Know the distress signal: six blasts of the whistle, or shouts – in fact of anything – followed by a minute's silence, then repeated.

Take a map. The O.S. 1:50,000 sheet for the area (better, 1:25,000 sheets or the 2½-inch Leisure Map as well) and a compass.

● Say where you are going; or at least leave a note on the car windscreen. Report any changes of plan by telephone. When you are home, report in.

● Plan the route. Make sure it is within the capabilities of the weakest member of the party. Allow enough time to be home well before nightfall. Allow an extra hour for every 1,500 feet (457 m) to be climbed. Take a watch. Know what time sunset will be.
● Ring the pre-recorded 24-hour forecast, or the local met. office for a weather report.
● Do not go alone. Three is the minimum safe number. In an accident, one can go for help; the other stays with the injured.
● Move at the pace of the slowest. Never straggle. Never split up, unless to get help.
● If the cloud comes down, walk in single file with 20 yards (18 m) between each of you. The last man – or woman – uses the compass, directing the leaders.

If you are caught in poor visibility, and cannot find the way down, stop until the weather clears, find shelter or build a windbreak from branches or rocks. Put on spare, dry clothing. Sit on something dry. Eat part of the emergency rations and drink something hot. Build an emergency bivouac from anything suitable – a groundsheet, a plastic mack, a cape. If cold, keep the limbs moving. Stay awake. Loosen laces and cuffs; huddle close to companions.

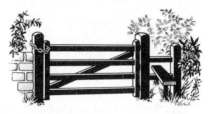

THE COUNTRY CODE

GUARD AGAINST FIRE Every year, carelessness costs thousands of pounds.
FASTEN GATES – even if you find them open. Animals will wander if they can.
KEEP DOGS UNDER CONTROL – on a lead wherever there is livestock.
KEEP TO PATHS – if they exist.
AVOID DAMAGING FENCES, HEDGES AND WALLS
LEAVE NO LITTER
SAFEGUARD WATER SUPPLIES Do not pollute streams or cattle troughs.
PROTECT WILDLIFE, PLANTS, TREES
GO CAREFULLY ON COUNTRY ROADS Keep in single file, facing on-coming traffic, on the right.
RESPECT THE LIFE OF THE COUNTRYSIDE

THE SOUTH-WEST

CORNWALL

If anywhere is Lyonesse, the lost land of Arthurian legend, it is Cornwall. However, the county has more real claims on our sense of the past. The narrow, illogically twisting lanes are a motorist's bane. But on foot one can see how, along with the sunken and often tunnel-like tracks which have never achieved tarmac, they are needed to link the scattered farms and hamlets. For this landscape was originally settled by the Celts. Here, the neatly centred villages of Anglo-Saxon England, and the relatively uncomplicated road pattern that goes with them, are rare.

It is an industrial landscape, too. All over the eastern part of the county are the crumbling engine-sheds and chimney-stacks of the once flourishing tin-mines. The waste of a newer industry, china clay, makes glistening white hills around St. Austell.

Inland, most of the county is a plateau. The exception is Bodmin Moor, a dome of carboniferous rock like its bigger brother, Dartmoor. Here are glimpses of a landscape little, if at all, changed since the Celts carved their scraps of fields from wilderness. Round all is an enchanting coast, nearly all of it walkable. But take your time: long indentations and steep cliffs make it surprisingly strenuous work.

Carn Brea

2 miles (3 km) Sheet 203 688413

Easy A panorama of industrial Cornwall, an Iron Age site and a castle-restaurant; comfortable strolling mainly on well-defined gravel paths. *Heath; one climb.*

Start From the A30 at Redruth turn on to the A3047. At hospital turn left and continue to crossroads. **Parking** up W arm of crossroads, on left just past garage; alternatively, on summit of Carn Brea (access via Carnkie) – start walk at ④.

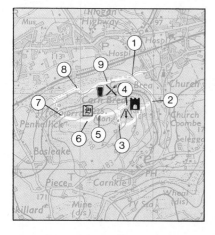

Carn Brea's summit: the hill was fortified in the Iron Age.

① Turn sharp left at junction of tracks where path emerges on to open heath and continue round edge of Carn, leaving castle up to right. ② Follow the bridleway, keeping right at path junctions, to meet gravel-surfaced road; follow this to top of Carn. ③ Where path meets road, turn right up to the castle. ④ At castle turn left along ridge and follow any of the paths towards the monument. ⑤ From monument, follow track to right of rocks and along ridge to farthest rock outcrop. ⑥ From outcrop, follow the most obvious path straight down ridge towards houses in distance. ⑦ Where path reaches edge of heath, with iron gate on left, turn right along field wall down to lane, where turn right. ⑧ At junction of lanes, take right fork on to footpath, keeping to moor side of houses. ⑨ Follow any of the paths alongside Carn, keeping parallel to ridge. All converge at ①.

🏰
✕ Carn Brea's 19th C. 'castle' houses a
🍺 restaurant with good home cooking.

⚒ A former tin and copper mining area: 15 mine chimneys can be counted to the S.

🏛 The Dunstanville Monument, in honour of Francis, first member of the old Cornish family of Basset to be ennobled. They grew rich from mining.

15

CORNWALL

Advent Church
5 miles (8 km) Sheet 200 108839

Moderate Typical agricultural Cornwall – mixed farmland with simultaneous views of moorland, lush valleys and the distant coast; and a church in a peculiarly remote setting. *Water meadow, farmland, woods, moorland; one climb; mud after rain.*

Start Camelford, on the A39 between Bude and Wadebridge. **Parking** in Church Field Car Park, on left just past traffic lights if driving N.

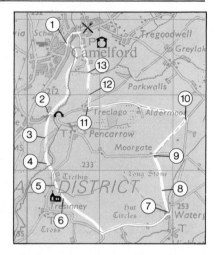

① From Fore Street, turn left under arch beside D.I.Y. shop. Plaque over arch reads 'River and Advent Church'. Follow river bank, crossing and re-crossing on footbridges. ② Where path emerges on to road by granite bridge, turn right uphill along road, to third gate on left with 'Public Footpath' signpost. Follow the path, crossing second field diagonally to mid-point of opposite wall, beyond which are woods. ③ At edge of field, cross stone stile and take path downhill through woods, and diagonally across water meadow. ④ At far corner of meadow, look for the footbridge hidden among trees. Cross the bridge and the stile in the wire fence, and leaving bushes to left, climb bank. Follow field wall up to road gate. ⑤ Just past Trethin Holiday Farm (clearly labelled) look for the overgrown stile leading off obliquely to the left. Beware of the wide gaps in the granite cattle grid in front of stile. Continue to ⑥ far edge of first field, where Advent Church tower is visible ahead. Head directly towards tower, arriving at gate into churchyard. Leave by small gate in E boundary, opening directly on to field (E is the altar end of the church). Follow the path alongside field walls to the road. Turn left and continue to Watergate. ⑦ At Watergate, just before stream, turn left at 'Public Footpath' sign, and follow partly paved track through rough meadows. ⑧ At edge of small pinewood, cross old stile and the newer one next to it. Cut diagonally uphill, following line indicated by the long, wooden step of the newer stile, to intercept well-defined path wandering across field towards trees around Moorgate Farm in distance. Follow this to Moorgate Farm and ⑨ join road by large, corrugated asbestos barn. Ignore 'Public Footpath' sign and steps in opposite wall; instead take rough track which branches left off road 10 yards (9 m) E of signpost. Follow track across patch of rough moorland, between field walls and on across more rough moorland. ⑩ At wooden road gate, turn left along wall to old iron gate. Follow the well-defined cart track downhill to entrance of Aldermoor Farm. Continue along lane to Treclago. ⑪ Just before reaching Treclago, turn right along lane. This becomes a track and ends at a gate into field. ⑫ Go through gate and follow hedge to small gate in bottom right corner of field. ⑬ Cross footbridge to stile in middle of hedge opposite and continue through next field to stile leading to lane. Car park is opposite far end of lane.

🏛 Camelford's North Cornwall Museum features a mock-up of a typical, 19th C. Cornish kitchen and many 19th C. farm implements.

⌒ This is known as a clapper bridge – one of the most ancient forms of bridge in the country.

🏠 Advent Church gives visitors a feeling of going back several centuries, indeed, its congregation is mainly drawn from the neighbourhood's farmers and shepherds, a community relatively unchanged by the 20th C. The tower with 8 pinnacles could be unique in Cornwall.

✗ Bridge Café; licence; take-away food.

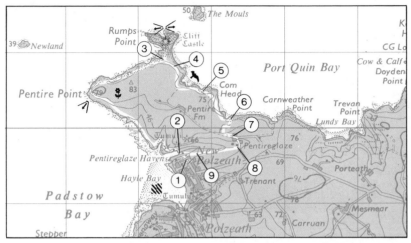

The Rumps and Pentire Head

3½ miles (5.5 km) Sheet 200 936796

Moderate Some of the most accessible, yet dramatic, North Cornish coastal scenery; exceptional for viewing seabirds; a substantial Iron Age fort.*Cliff tops, pasture; mud after rain.*

Start From Wadebridge take the B3314 (just past school at top of hill when driving E) and continue to New Polzeath. **Car park** at end of road into New Polzeath.

① From car park entrance turn right and right again into Gulland Road, past public conveniences. ② At end of road, carry straight on down path to beach, across top of beach and up wooden steps on to path leading up left on to cliff top. After descending through gully ③ turn left at meeting of paths to visit Rumps Point. ④ After retracing steps from Rumps Point to path junction, keep right, along highest path, crossing stile into fields. ⑤ At third stile, follow path as it swings right for 10 yards (9 m) and then back on to top of Com Head. Leave top on side nearest fields to intercept well-defined path leading round back of Com Head. Later descend and climb gully and ⑥ immediately before low slate stile, climb stile consisting of 3 posts driven into wall on right; follow round edge of field to next stile and the quarry car park. ⑦ From car park turn left down lane to farm, and right at road

junction down to barns on left side of road. ⑧ By second gate on right past barns, turn right along public footpath, over stile; continue through 2 gates and fields. ⑨ Where path forks, take left branch up past houses and turn left into Gulland Road.

🐌 Polzeath, an undistinguished holiday village with a fine surfing beach.

🌸 Humble and prolific, thrift or sea pink is nonetheless pretty when, as here, it flowers *en masse* in April-Aug.

↖ The tower (above Stepper Point) on the far side of the Camel estuary is The Daymark, a landmark for shipping.

🏛 The remains of the Iron Age fort on ↖ Rumps Point are not obvious, but 3 distinct ramparts can be made out. The views along the coast are famous; in a westerly gale, the sight of the seas breaking over Newland Rock and The Moules just as dramatic.

🐦 Several interesting seabird species breed on the cliffs, but the most captivating are the fulmars. They are grey-white, like gulls, but there the resemblance ends. They are supreme fliers, with long, narrow, stiffly held wings, perfect for gliding; watch them exploit the wind and cliff face for extraordinary feats of aerobatics.

CORNWALL

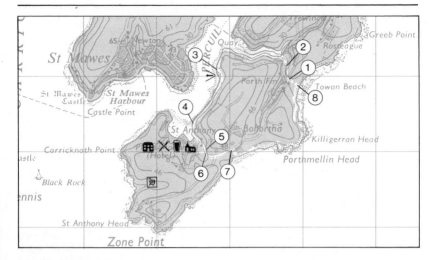

Roseland Peninsula
3½ miles (5.5 km) Sheet 204 868329

Easy Excellent views of St. Mawes waterfront, one of the south coast's great yacht anchorages, and a visit to Place Manor, open May to September. *Woods, cliff tops; one climb; mud after rain.'*

Start Porth Farm, near St. Anthony on the Roseland Peninsula – approach via Portscatho. **Car park** (National Trust) at Porth Farm; also a lay-by with limited space ¼ mile (0.5 km) up hill on left.

① From car park return to road and turn left downhill. ② Just before reaching head of creek, turn left off road and over footbridge by signpost reading 'Footpath to Place etc.' Turn right on other side of footbridge. ③ For uninterrupted views of creek, cross stile through hedge and continue to beach. To continue with walk, return to field. ④ Where concrete steps descend on right towards water, go through gate and along bottom edge of field to road. ⑤ At road, turn left if continuing walk without stopping at Place Manor Hotel. If visiting hotel, go through gate on to front lawn. ⑥ If visiting church only, walk past hotel along road. By iron gate and stile with signpost 'Coast Path and Public Footpath to St. Anthony Head' turn right for church. From church, retrace to road and continue. ⑦ At top of hill, by sign indicating right bend, climb stile and continue on footpath across field. At steps on far side of field turn left. (There is a beach at bottom of cliff – access by steps and path.) ⑧ Having walked over Killigerran Head, drop down to beach past white marker post and turn left up path towards road. Car park is at opposite end of path.

\ɫ/ The beach accessible from ③ gives the best views of the yachts in the Percuil River, and of St. Mawes, named after a Welsh prince of the 6th C. who became a monk.

🍴 The bar lunches at Place Manor, a family hotel, are delicious and excellent value. ✕ The present building is Victorian, but 🍷 there was a Tudor house here, and before that a monastery. Henry VIII and Anne Boleyn are reputed to have spent their honeymoon at Place, but its real fame is as the home of the naval family the Sprys, from whom the present owner is descended. Place means palace in Old Cornish.

🏠 The church butts right on to the house, giving rise to the claim that it is the only private church in England. Memorials to centuries of Sprys; the tower is 700 years old and there are some impressive Norman features.

🏛 'Roseland' evolved from the Old Cornish word ros, a spur or peninsula.

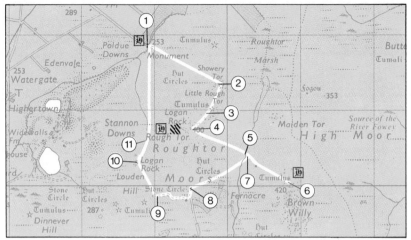

Brown Willy

5 miles (8 km) Sheets 200 and 201 138818

Energetic Cornwall's highest point, with views to the N and S coasts, and its nearest to hill walking. *Moorland, rocks, heather; 2 climbs; the heather and bracken can be extremely wet; the peat bogs, seen as dark brown patches, are easily avoided. Do not attempt in poor visibility.*

Start Take rough lane signposted 'Roughtor 2 miles' half-way up hill at N end of Camelford. **Car park** at end of lane.

① From bridge across stream below car park, follow faint, grassy path up to left end of ridge, where 3 giant boulders appear piled one above another. ② From the boulders (Showery Tor) bear slightly left along ridge to first rise (Little Rough Tor). ③ Approaching summit of Rough Tor, take any of the various paths winding between the rocks: all lead eventually to ruins of medieval chapel and memorial plaque on top. ④ From summit, identify stone wall on far side of moor below, leading off left from patch of trees. Scramble down over rocks and make for any point along wall. ⑤ Follow wall left, down to gate and bridge over stream, then up past ruins to trig. point just visible on summit of Brown Willy. ⑥ From the summit, it is safe to wander along the ridge, but do not pass the last rock outcrop. On return, retrace to gate and steps at ⑤. ⑦

Having re-crossed stream, follow wall round to track leading from Fernacre and turn right towards large, stone cricle. ⑧ From stone circle, regain track and follow past dead trees and ruined house to bridge over stream. ⑨ Leave track at bridge and, skirting left side of marshy area, head for far right end of ridge, where prominent boulder is perched on rocks (Logan Rock). ⑩ From Logan Rock, head for right end of stone wall ahead and follow stream back to car park. ⑪ After rain, area around stream can be marshy; bear right towards Rough Tor and intercept obvious grassy path from Rough Tor leading back to car park.

🏠 Charlotte Dymond's memorial: this serving girl's fate still captures the imagination of local people, who believe she haunts the moor where she was brutally murdered. Doubt remains as to whether her cripple lover was guilty of the crime, for which he was hanged.

🏠 A visitors' book hidden in a metal box near the summit commemorates the Queen's Silver Jubilee. The name Brown Willy is derived from the Old Cornish Bron Ewhela, meaning highest place.

🏠 There are weirdly eroded granite formations near the summit of Rough Tor, pronounced Row-ter. A plaque on the summit, the site of a medieval chapel, remembers dead of the 43rd Wessex.

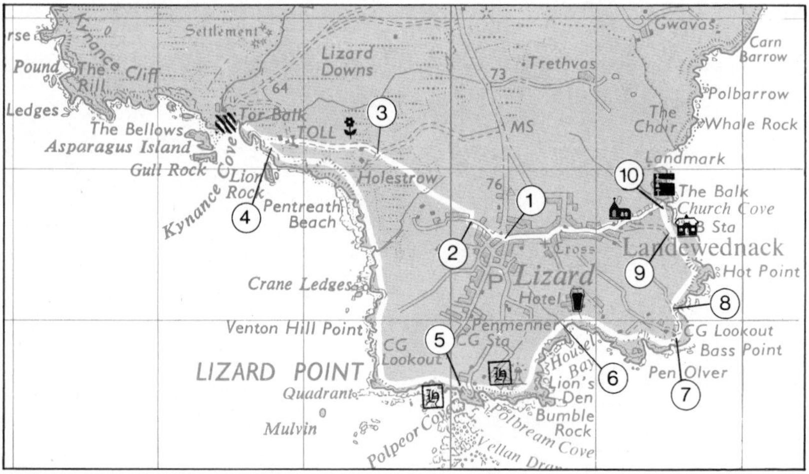

Round the Lizard

5½ miles (9 km) Sheet 203 703126

Easy The British mainland's southernmost tip: geology and botany; crowded in high summer. *Cliff tops.*

Start Lizard village, reached by the A3083 from Helston. **Parking** at centre of village on green.

(1) From car park turn right past public conveniences along lane signposted 'Public Footpath to Kynance Cove', etc. (2) By white chalet, fork right, up stone steps, on to footpath along top of wall. (3) Where path meets road junction by large National Trust notice-board, keep straight on past signpost for 'Kynance Cove and Car Park'. (4) From Kynance Cove, keep to seaward of buildings along grassy path at edge of cliffs. (5) At Polpeor Cove (by old lifeboat station) keep left above rocky beach, cross footbridge, go through hedge and climb steps alongside fence. (6) Where path meets track from Housel Bay beach up to village, turn left, then right after 50 yards (46 m), to follow coastline. (7) Where path joins lane back to village, keep right, along field side of hedge, towards Coastguard Look-out. (8) 100 yards past Bass Point House and Look-out, keep right at path junction by metal post. (9) From lifeboat station, continue on path round back of highest building, down first flight of steps and left past collection box. (10) At Church Cove, turn left past first house and up lane towards thatched cottage. Follow lane back to Lizard and car park.

The Lizard area harbours plants which thrive uniquely in the area's mild, sea-dominated climate, including large Lizard clover, sand quillwort and ciliate rupturewort.

Kynance Cove with its serpentine islets.

The cliff here is said to hold 700 unmarked graves of shipwreck victims.

Lizard Lighthouse, open to the public.

Housel Bay Hotel welcomes walkers.

Lifeboat station, open to the public.

In Church Cove is one of the many local establishments for cutting and polishing serpentine. The stone, seen everywhere in the cliffs and rocks, is a magnesium silicate formed by pressure and heat in the upheavals of the Earth's crust. The veins do look quite like serpent's skin.

Look for blocks of serpentine built into the tower of St. Wynalow's.

Looking E over Lizard Point (foreground) to the lighthouse and, beyond it, Housel Bay.

CORNWALL

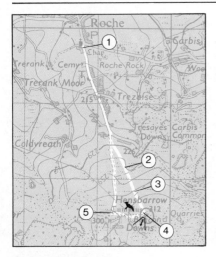

Hensbarrow Downs

2 miles (3 km) Sheet 200 990590

Easy The route goes through Cornwall's china clay mining area, showing workings in detail. *Downland; one climb; mud after rain.*

Start Leave the A30 6 miles (10 km) SW of Bodmin, taking the B3274 for Roche. **Parking** in lay-by, on right side of road, just past chapel, when going S.

① From car park walk S nearly a mile (1.5 km) and turn right into wide new road (unmarked on map) signposted 'Nanpean and Whitemoor'; immediately turn left on to old minor road, leaving prominent spoil heap on right. Branch left on footpath just past farm gate. ② Where paths cross, continue forward, skirting right edge of wide, shallow hollow. ③ The path peters out; head for highest point of hill straight ahead across open grassland. (An RAF beacon will appear ahead and slightly to the right.) ④ From trig. point on prominent mound at summit, head for conspicuous radio mast in distance. On reaching wide, gravel-surfaced road, ⑤ turn right and follow road back towards ①.

🐾 Dense population of skylarks: do not tread on their nests.

⚲ A weird landscape of white and grey spoil heaps: the waste is quartz sand. The tips seen SW are working.

Mount Edgcumbe

6½ miles (10.5 km) Sheet 201 454535

Moderate All-round views of Plymouth Sound and the waters radiating from it. *Woods, farmland; 2 climbs; mud after rain.*

Start Cremyll, on the B3247; buses (with connecting ferry) from Plymouth. **Car park** behind the Edgcumbe Arms, Cremyll.

① Turn right by telephone box next to Edgcumbe Arms, following public footpath signposted for Empacombe. Keep left past Cremyll Hall and right at junction signposted 'Footpath'. ② Where field-edge path joins gravel drive, turn right through entrance of Empacombe House and follow signpost to public footpath round edge of little harbour, across lawn and through wooden gate in far corner. ③ Where field-edge path meets road by iron gate and stone stile, cross road and go into field through gate opposite with signpost 'Public Footpath to Maker', etc. Follow the main cart track, roughly parallel to road. ④ At locked gates and chainlink fence, turn right uphill and follow fence to corner, where path leads off to left through woods. Cross stile into woods, turn sharp right, then left after 75 yards (69 m) by ruined gate. Continue up past 'Public Footpath' signpost. ⑤ Where path forks 50 yards (46 m) past signpost, turn left up bank and past wall on right. Cross road and join path signposted 'Maker Church ¼ mile', etc. ⑥ From W entrance of church (same end as tower), follow hedge along car park field. ⑦ Halfway along field, cross stile in left wall and follow hedge on other side to stile and iron gate. ⑧ On opposite side of lane, cross stile and follow path through 2 fields, turn right at lane beyond and left at signpost for Kingsand. ⑨ Just past road junction at Maker Heights, branch left along path signposted 'Kingsand ½ mile'. ⑩ Where path forks, keep left and continue through lanes of Kingsand to beach. ⑪ From E end of Kingsand, follow concrete/gravel paths along top of rocky beach past holiday chalets. ⑫ At ruined fortification with danger sign turn left along path through bushes into field and turn right to stone stile in top corner of field. ⑬ Where path joins road at gate and stile, turn right and immediately left up path indicated by 'Coast Path' sign. ⑭ At fork in bridleway 100 yards (91 m) into wood, take left, upper, way and continue, following coast path signs between banks of rhododendrons. ⑮ Pass stone arch and in 100 yards fork right to follow zigzag path down to lower level near water, emerging in clearing by half-timbered building (Lady Emma's Cottage) opposite Drake's Island. ⑯ Where path emerges again on to open parkland, with ruin to left, keep right and continue down to Barn Pool. Make way through formal gardens to Country Park entrance.

⛪ A leaflet available in Maker's church describes its remarkable role in war and peace, and much local history.

🏚 The twin fishing villages flourished because before the Plymouth breakwater was built the bay was an
🍺 anchorage for the Fleet – hence also the fine pubs.

🏛 See the official guide book, or leaflet, for
❀ Mount Edgcumbe House and park.

Access to the SW Peninsula Coast Path is generally easy in Cornwall, and most parts can be walked in short sections. Tintagel to Boscastle is a famous stretch; the rocks of Bedruthan Steps, 6 miles (9.5 km) N of Newquay, should not be missed and from St. Ives towards Zennor there are some lovely coves visited by seals.

There is a disused railway line walk from Bodmin via Wadebridge to Padstow, through the picturesque Camel Valley.

Poltesco Cadgwith Nature Trail, near Helston, covers 3 miles (5 km) of woods, cliff tops and caves.

The circuit of Tresco, Scilly Isles, is an ambitious and rewarding project.

St. Agnes Beacon is also worth climbing.

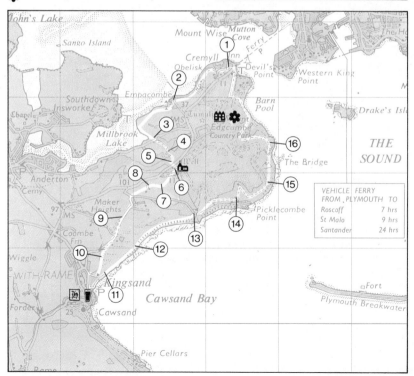

DARTMOOR

There are two Dartmoors. First, the heart of the 300-square-mile (121 ha) plateau: apparently endless, rolling moorland and hills broken only by the grotesque tors – contortions of granite – on the summits. Here is the nearest thing to wilderness in southern Britain.

Second, around this central area, and still within the National Park, lie the wooded valleys (cleaves is the local word), twisting lanes and grey farmhouses where the green fields begin.

In its isolation, Dartmoor has preserved an enormous number of prehistoric remains. There are hut circles, standing stones, burial chambers, stone rows and crosses, dating from any time after 1800 B.C., all in settings of loneliness and power. Relatively modern are the spoil heaps and gullys made by the tin miners who flourished in the 12th to the 15th centuries, though they were there in the Bronze Age and did not finally depart until the 1920s.

Height and the nearby coast combine to produce wet and swiftly changing weather. Winds can be fierce, and the fogs descend in minutes, adding to the danger of bogs anything from a yard to a mile across. To avoid the latter, watch for the tell-tale vivid green Sphagnum moss and keep well clear of where it grows.

Hardly a year goes by without a well-publicized case of exposure on Dartmoor; often enough, victims find they have spent their chastening night out within yards of a road which was nonetheless hidden by fog or snow. Anyone walking the area, with or without a planned route, is urged to know and heed the advice given on page 9.

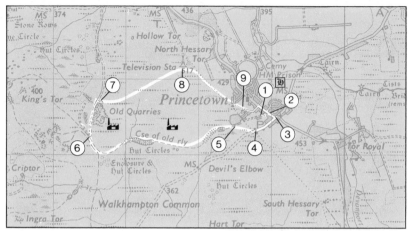

Princetown
4 miles (6.5 km) Sheet 191 587735

Moderate Much industrial interest, explaining why Princetown developed in such a remote, exposed position. *Moorland; one climb; do not attempt in poor visibility.*

Start Princetown, on the B3212 near centre of moor; infrequent, seasonal buses to Princetown from Plymouth, Yelverton, Tavistock and Moretonhampstead – special service – check times by ringing Plymouth 64014. **Public car park** at town centre.

① From car park almost immediately ② turn right passing prison officers' mess. ③ At road junction, turn right and follow main road to the toll houses (one each side of road) where ④ bear right; keeping wire fence to right, follow path to old railway line. ⑤ Turn left on to railway line and follow it 1½ miles (2.5 km). ⑥ Follow hard track leading off to right, in about ¼ mile (0.5 km) reaching Fogintor Quarry where ⑦ bear right, heading for North Hessary Tor, with mast on top. ⑧ At mast, turn downhill, keeping the wall on left. ⑨ Reach iron gate at end of track, turn left into lane and continue to Station Road; at end, turn right for town centre and car park.

🏰 Princetown Prison is part of a settlement founded in 1785 by Thomas Tyrwhitt and named in honour of the Prince Regent. It was first used in 1809 for French prisoners taken in the Napoleonic Wars. They were joined by prisoners taken in the 1812-14 war with the U.S. It became a convict prison in 1850.

🚂 In the old railway line to the Quarry there are granite sleepers.

🚂 Fogintor Quarry, now derelict and enclosing a quiet pool, produced granite for many local buildings, including the prison.

Dartmoor's rugged upland is a typical habitat for the buzzard, largest of the predators commonly seen in the SW. It is a bird with widely variable plumage, so much so that it is best identified on its size, and on its wheeling, soaring flight.

DARTMOOR

Widgery Cross
5 miles (8 km) Sheet 191 513848

Moderate A pilgrimage to one of Dartmoor's most deservedly famous monuments. *Lanes and moorland; 2 climbs; mud; do not attempt in poor visibility.*

Start Lydford, off the A386 S of Okehampton. **Public car park** in Lydford.

① From car park turn right along Lydford main street and at Y-junction bear right down Silver Street. ② At crossroads carry straight on, turn right at junction and continue to main road. ③ Cross main road with caution and take track opposite, then through gate on to open moor. Take upper track (faint and grassy), going over the shoulder of High Down and joining stony track leading diagonally down steep slope to remains of old tin mine by River Lyd. ④ It is normally easy to cross the river here, but after heavy rain a crossing can be found higher up. Go straight uphill, then make for Doe Tor (the tor without a cross), crossing the brook just above a small waterfall. ⑤ From Doe Tor cross to Brat Tor (NE), on which is Widgery Cross. ⑥ Take the grassy track down to river, where there is a choice of stepping stones or footbridge. Follow track over High Down to Dartmoor Inn on main road. Cross and follow road to Lydford.

🏭 Wheal Mary Emma tin mine, worked for a short time about 1850, was named

Widgery Cross.

after the young daughter of the then owner. ('Wheal' or 'weal' is the Cornish word for mine.)

🗓 Widgery Cross on Brat Tor was erected in 1887 by John William Widgery, a Dartmoor artist, to commemorate Queen Victoria's Golden Jubilee. The cross is unusual in that it is built of separate granite blocks: all the other stone crosses on Dartmoor – about 250 of them – were hewn out of single blocks. They were put up either to mark medieval boundaries or to guide travellers. Many marked paths linking monasteries.

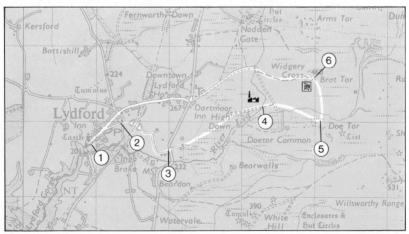

Grimspound and Challacombe Valley
6 miles (9.5 km) Sheet 191 699835

Easy Shows the 2 fascinating human faces of Dartmoor – Bronze Age dwellings and centuries of tin mining. *Moorland; mud after rain. Do not attempt in poor visibility 1:25,000 map and compass recommended.*

Start Car park on B3212 6 miles ·SW of Moretonhampstead; infrequent, seasonal bus service between Plymouth and Moretonhampstead – special service – check times by ringing Plymouth 64014. **Car park** (gravel surface, fine views) on right just after reaching open moor if travelling in Princetown direction.

① From car park cross road and walk uphill past hut circles and through low heather to scattered stone blocks of Hookney Tor. ② From Tor, turn right, heading downhill to road. Cross, and continue down track towards Headland Warren Farm. ③ Just before farm turn left, passing it on upper side. Go through wicket gate, cross drive diagonally and go downhill through farm gate. Follow grassy track down valley. ④ Through gate in fence and continue in same direction to end of field, then past front of farmhouse and buildings. Follow track uphill, over top and into next valley. ⑤ Climb stile and continue up valley between conifer plantations. Where tracks divide, keep straight on. ⑥ At Y-junction, bear right. Track soon narrows, winding through mining area. Follow it uphill to Bennett's Cross beside B3212, where ⑦ turn right back to car park.

▣ Grimspound's hut circles and village are thought to be Bronze Age structures. The hut walls are granite, which is why they have lasted so long. The roofs, in a wigwam shape, would have been of turf or thatch over poles laid up to a central point. The people who built these dwellings were both metal-workers and farmers, keeping livestock on the moors and protecting them in compounds.

⌂ Tin mining remnants; the gullies in the hillside above Headland Warren Farm date from the 16th C., when miners followed the rich seams of tin upward having exhausted the valley bottoms. The stone heaps are waste.

Tor comes from the Welsh word twr *meaning tower or heap.*

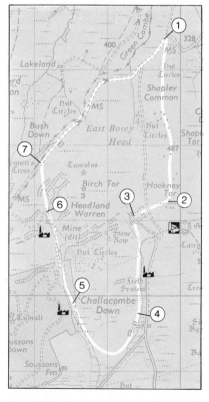

DARTMOOR

Becky Falls and the Bovey Valley
4 miles (6.5 km) Sheet 191 784794

Easy The comparatively lush, eastern fringe of Dartmoor; a fine waterfall, interesting plants and flowers. *Moorland, woods; 2 climbs; mud after rain.*

Start Parking areas on B3344 2½ miles (4 km) NW of Bovey Tracey. **Parking** 3 areas within 100 yards (91 m) of the cattle grid.

① From car park walk in direction of Manaton beside the B3344 to point where Yarner Wood ends (on left). Turn left and follow edge of wood up to higher road. ② Right along road to junction with B3344. Turn right. ③ Leave road after 120 yards (110 m). Cross bridge on left and follow path, keeping brook on right. To visit Becky Falls, take the railed steps; for the café, take the long footbridge. ④ Rejoin woodland path (waymarked by orange dots). Where well-defined path crosses, turn right. ⑤ Go steeply downhill and cross river by small stone bridge. Turn left along wide track. ⑥ Ignore next bridge. For views of Packhorse Bridge and Fairy Glen, go second left through gate. Rejoin track and climb to starting point.

Heath milkwort, unlike the other milkworts, has its lower oval leaves in opposite pairs. It usually flowers May-August.

☘ Trendlebeare Down is rich in plants, among them blue milkworts, yellow tormentil (its roots were used in tanning) and whortleberries (bilberries) with delicious blue-black fruits.

☀ Black Hill has prehistoric cairns.

🌊 Becky (or Becka) Falls drop 80 feet (24 m) into the River Bovey.

🍺 Kestor Inn, Manaton (the name comes from *maen-y-dun*, Celtic for 'hill fort').

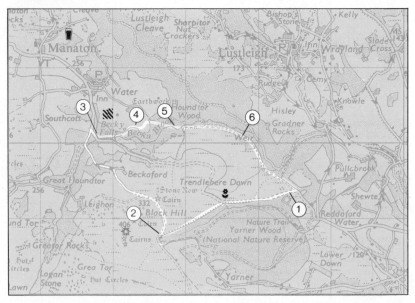

The blue-black fruits of the whortleberry (also called bilberry, huckleberry and whinberry) make excellent pies and jam.

Ditsworthy and Ringmoor Down
8 miles (13 km) Sheet 202 558666

Moderate Reveals the pretty Dartmoor, around the Plym. *Downland, moorland, riverside. Do not attempt in poor visibility.*

Start From the B3212 NE out of Yelverton, take road at Dowsland Cross signposted Sheepstor. In 2 miles (3 km), turn left on to road signposted Sheepstor and Burrator. In ½ mile (0.8 km) look for Ringmoor Cottage. **Car park** beside cottage.

① From cottage follow grassy track due W, climbing moor to Gutter Tor, at first out of sight behind horizon. Then drop to small slab bridge seen below at end of road. ② Cross bridge and take track past abandoned mine workings. Fork right after ruined buildings and follow narrow path down to River Plym. ③ Cross Plym at ford and go downstream to Plym Steps (stepping stones) keeping to ridge above river valley to avoid boggy patches. ④ Re-cross river at Plym Steps. Continue downstream past Bronze Age remains to Ditsworthy Warren House, where ⑤ continue in same direction, taking left branch of track to cross boggy patch. Cross moor to Legis Tor. ⑥ From Tor bear right, following path downhill to stepping stones near head of stream. Continue uphill over moor past stone circle until Ringmoor Cottage comes into sight.

The tin mine ruins are part of the Eylesbarrow complex.

Between Eastern Tor and Giants Hill are many Bronze Age relics.

Ditsworthy Warren House, mainly 16th C., was the centre of one of many warrens set up for breeding rabbits.

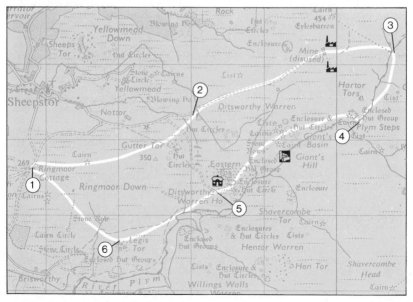

DARTMOOR

Highest Dartmoor
14 miles (22.5 km) Sheet 191 562917

Energetic Dartmoor at its most rugged and remote – the true wilderness; also has the spectacular Meldon Reservoir. *Moorland, woods; 3 climbs; mud; no definite path between ① and ②, but route easy to follow by landmarks except in poor visibility, in which case do not attempt. Compass and 1:25,000 map recommended. The route passes through Okehampton ranges and firing times must be checked; ring Plymouth 772312 or enquire at a local post office.*

Start Turn off the A30 about 3½ miles (5.5 km) W of Okehampton on lane signposted Meldon (not Meldon Quarry). **Parking** at Meldon Reservoir.

① Cross Meldon Dam. Climb directly to top of Longstone Hill, and on reaching level plateau bend right across to Black Tor. ② Spot the small, square army lookout hut perched on edge of Fordsland Ledge, and make for it with West Okement River in valley on right. ③ From hut look for top of High Willhays and make for it; from there bear left along army track to Yes Tor. ④ From the top of Yes Tor looking E look for 2 clumps of trees about 2 miles (3 km) distant. Aim for the right-hand side of the smaller clump, walking direct over open moorland, using grit tracks where useful. ⑤ Above clump of trees, cross East Okement River on track, then stay on track with river on left for 1¾ miles (3 km) to just beyond ruined cottage. Turn off track down steep hillside to

Okehampton Castle, the oldest parts of which date from late Norman times.

river. ⑥ Cross river on wooden footbridge, bear right on track up through woods, and cross 2 fields, continuing through Lower Halstock Farm to join metalled lane. Cross cattle grid and at T-junction turn right down larger road for about 200 yards (183 m) to waymarked gate. ⑦ Walk down middle of field, then take road to railway station. Turn left after bridge and continue along road with railway line on left. ⑧ At T-junction take footpath opposite which joins metalled road and leads to golf course. Just below clubhouse the path leads off across golf course. Follow it straight on for over one mile (1.5 km), through gate, fields, farm buildings, more fields to road. ⑨ Join road and just past viaduct turn down grassy track on right. Keep near the river and cross it at small footbridge. Turn left up track and after row of beeches slant up across field, following hedge on right back to car park.

🚣 The water supply for all North Devon.

💥 The cairn may be a Bronze Age burial place. Small stones from cairns were used for local road building in the 19th C.

🪨 High Willhays and Yes Tor, the highest points on Dartmoor; the ridge between them is called the 'roof of Devon'.

🦅 Typical buzzard country.

🏰 Okehampton Castle.

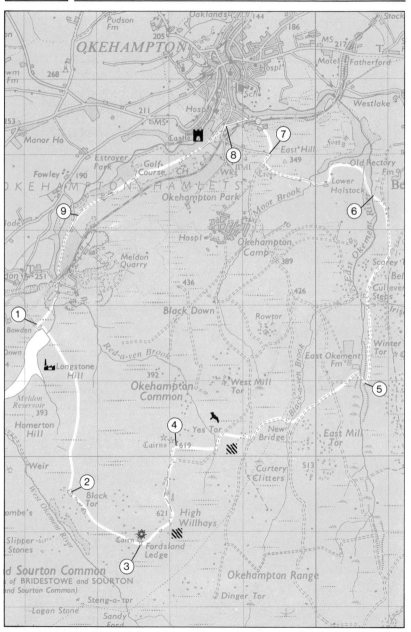

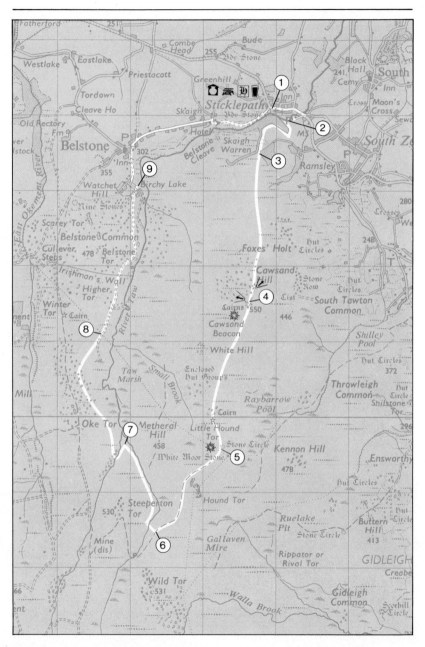

Cawsand and Taw Marsh
9 miles (14.5 km) Sheet 191 640942

Easy Introduces the bare, empty spaces of northern Dartmoor, and the impressive landscape of Taw Marsh valley. *Woods, moorland, river valley; one climb; mud; do not attempt in poor visibility.*

Start Sticklepath, on the A30 E of Okehampton; infrequent buses from Okehampton and Exeter. **Parking** The Devonshire Inn car park, opposite the Inn, using end farthest from road.

① Left out of car park and follow main road to bridge over River Taw. Walk upstream along footpath by river. ② Follow path into wood. It bears left uphill, then right and levels out. After gate, turn sharp left up field, keeping field edge on left; emerge on to moorland through gate in top left corner of field. ③ Walk up moor, aiming for the top (Cawsand Beacon) – a 1¼ mile (2 km) stretch. ④ From cairn on Cawsand Beacon continue on pony track in same direction downhill, then up the small rise of Little Hound Tor, from which make for the stone circle. ⑤ From stone circle retrace steps to slightly sunken track and continue in previous direction, bearing slightly right. Follow track along right side of next hill, Hound Tor. ⑥ Where track peters out, turn downhill, making for stream. Follow this downhill to where valley suddenly widens, where ⑦ curve left around base of Steeperton to meet River Taw. Cross river and continue downstream. Keep well left of river to avoid extremely boggy marsh. In 1¼ miles join ⑧ a stony track. Follow this to edge of moor where ⑨ continue on road to Belstone, ignoring left turns in village and following road downhill to A30 at Sticklepath; turn left to ①

⌂ Sticklepath's Finch Foundry Museum has a working display of the machinery and the processes used by 19th C. blacksmiths and foundrymen. All the machinery is water-powered by the River Taw. Free car park; picnic area.

🔟 Behind the Museum is a former Quaker burial ground. Sticklepath was a Quaker stronghold in the 17th C. Friends from the village sailed to America with William Penn, the founder of Pennsylvania, in 1682.

🍺 Devonshire Inn, good food.

☀ On Cawsand Beacon there is a good example of a Bronze Age burial cairn.

\↑/ The view W from the Beacon is to the peaks of East Mill Tor and Belstone Tor.

\↑/ Looking NE from Cawsand Beacon there is a clear view of the well-laid-out pattern of the strip fields of South Zeal – large fields sub-divided to grow different crops.

☀ White Moor Stone Circle is another Bronze Age relic. Circles of stone marked points of assembly and enclosed burial grounds. The standing stone (*menhir*) 200 yards (183 m) distant is also a memorial.

Wandering Dartmoor at will is for the experienced and well equipped, but there is some safe, introductory walking.

The Forestry Commission has laid out 2 short walks from Bellever Forest Car Park, 1½ miles (2.5 km) from the B3212 at Postbridge.

The banks of the Plym can be walked from near Cadover Bridge, approached by unclassified lanes from the A374 at Plympton or the A386 (Plymouth to Yelverton).

Round Burrator Reservoir is a spectacular circuit: access from Norsworthy Bridge Car Park at NE end of reservoir; several waymarked trails nearby.

A beautifully wooded path runs about 3 miles (5 km) through the Teign Valley from Steps Bridge to near Clifford Bridge. Approach from Exeter along the B3212; find path by crossing river from car park and turning left into woods.

Dr. Blackall's Drive, a grassy track following a ridge above the Dart valley, is an exciting, 2-mile (3 km) stroll. Park at Bel Tor Corner, at top of hill on unclassified road between Poundsgate and Dartmeet. Reach track by following stone wall seen on left when facing SW (back to the road). At the corner, bear left, then right between stone walls. On reaching open moorland, take the right (upper) fork.

DORSET

Geologically there are five different Dorsets, which means that this small and astonishingly unspoiled county embraces a great variety of scenery. Right across the middle runs a belt of chalk hills, starting on the coast around Lulworth and ending (so far as Dorset is concerned) in Cranborne Chase. North of their escarpment is the clay Vale of Blackmoor. The western end of the county is limestone and clay; while in the east Purbeck (a mix of chalk, clay and limestone) and the heathlands are separate areas again.

The best walking companion is still Thomas Hardy. Often it is hard not to think the charming, false names of the novels more apt than the real ones – for instance, Mellstock rather than Stinsford for the village churchyard where his heart is buried. Individual lanes, farms and footpaths can be traced from the stories, though, alas, this is not a county that respects public paths as it should.

On the hilltops there are the ancient resonances. The county is rich in burial mounds from the Bronze and Neolithic Ages which have survived because until recently the hills were not intensively farmed. To the Iron Age belongs Maiden Castle, perhaps the most numinous earthwork in all Britain and several hours of exciting walking in itself. The South West Peninsula Coast Path follows the entire coast to its terminus at Poole Harbour.

Studland and Old Harry
4 miles (6.5 km) Sheet 195 043825

Easy Dorset's finest chalk cliff scenery, justly popular walking. *Farmland, cliff top, downland; one climb.*

Start In Studland (on B3351) turn right for Middle and South Beaches, then right in front of Manor Hotel; car ferry from Haven Hotel, Sandbanks. **Car park** (South Beach) on right after hotel.

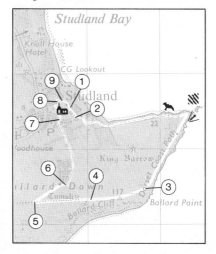

From the cliffs above Old Harry – Studland Bay, Poole and Bournemouth.

① From car park turn right and follow minor road past Bankes Arms Hotel. ② As road curves right, turn left to follow sign 'To Swanage via Old Harry. This is the Coast Path; follow the blue flashes and acorn symbols nearly 2 miles (3 km). ③ Bear right, keeping to main track which climbs the down and follows top of ridge. ④ Through gate, past Nat. Trust sign and straight on, following blue arrow as for obelisk. ⑤ At cross-track turn right through small wooden gate by Nat. Trust sign; follow direction of blue arrow to Studland. ⑥ Cross stile and continue down surfaced lane towards Studland, ignoring left turns. ⑦ Cross minor road leaving cross on right and take lane ahead 'To the Church'. Take path on left of the church through churchyard. ⑧ At road turn right and continue a few yards to ⑨ T-junction where turn right to ①.

🦅 Well-established cormorant nest sites.

𝔑 Old Harry, his (smaller) 'wife' and 2 more oddities of erosion, the Haystack and Pinnacle – stumps of rock 'like a skeleton's lower jaw' wrote Hardy.

\↑/ The Needles and Isle of Wight.

⛪ A superb example of a small Norman church – massive arches, vaulted roofs.

DORSET

Littlebredy
8 miles (13 km) Sheet 194 591889

Moderate Littlebredy is the essence of timeless Dorset, a place to linger in. *Downland, parkland, lakeside, woods; 2 climbs.*

Start From the A35 about one mile (1.5 km) W of Winterbourne Abbas take the road signposted Littlebredy. **Parking** close to village in lane to Littlebredy Farm.

① From parking walk a few yards away from village towards farm. ② Turn right in direction of sign 'Bridleway White Hill'. Bridehead House is on the right, and cricket ground on left. ③ Go through gate and continue uphill following terraced path round hillside. ④ Walk round edge of wood, fence on left and ⑤ continue due S leaving barns behind. ⑥ Go straight on along well-defined path. ⑦ Take care here: track turns left to join a lane; turn right through a gate (blue arrow waymark) and follow path (hedge on left). Ignore the other right of way, leading from farther round the corner to Gorwell Farm. ⑧ Cross stile on left to see the long barrow 200 yards (183 m) on far side of hedge. Retrace to path and continue ahead following signs to Kingston Russell Stone Circle. ⑨ Straight ahead through gate to Stone Circle. ⑩ With Stone Circle on left and copse on right, walk over the field to the fence ahead, then a few yards left to a gate (no path). ⑪ Go through gate and with ditches and mounds of earthworks on left continue ahead down steep hillside (no path) to pick up well-defined track heading N at the corner of the wood seen below. ⑫ Follow track – trees on right – until shortly seeing gap in fence ahead, slightly to the left. ⑬ Go through gap, turn left and walk to the NW corner of the field; then turn right to a gate at the foot of the field (no path). ⑭ From gate follow track seen as a faint line leading down next field (boggy after rain), through gate in hedge to small bridge over stream. ⑮ Cross stream, go through gate ahead, then left through another gate; turn right and continue up field (hedge on right) to road. ⑯ Cross and follow signposted bridleway up the hillside opposite (house on left). ⑰ Continue straight on – path curves round hill, dips, then climbs to skyline. ⑱ Follow 'Bridleway to Little Bredy' signposted right (lettering on reverse). ⑲ Continue straight ahead over the field, following line of burial mounds (tumuli). The Hardy Memorial is

seen ahead on skyline. ⑳ Continue along track to road by bridleway sign. ㉑ Turn right and follow road into Littlebredy. ㉒ At foot of hill bear right, then left through churchyard to church and gate into Manor grounds. Retrace to foot of hill and ①.

🏘 The 19th C. Bridehead House is named after the River Bride, which rises in the grounds. 'Brid' means roaring.

\¦/ Possibly the best of the walk.

⁂ The Grey Mare is the prehistoric burial chamber, her Colts the standing stones.

⁂ Kingston Russell Stone Circle, a ritualistic monument, dates from about 1500 B.C. Some of the stones may have been moved.

🏛 Kingston Russell House (about 1730), birthplace of Nelson's Admiral Hardy.

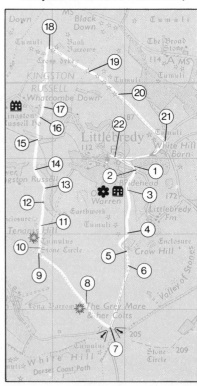

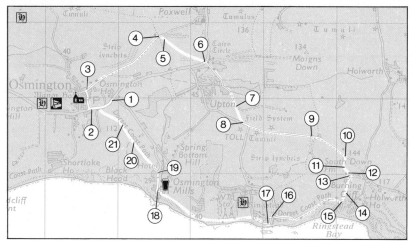

Osmington and the Seaward Downs
7 Miles (11 km) Sheet 194 729829

Moderate An enchanting Dorset village, and the grassy cliffs characteristic of the area. *Village, downs, low cliff tops; one climb.*

Start Osmington, off the A353; buses. **Parking** for modest fee at St. Christopher's Garage, Osmington, on the A353 almost opposite signpost to Osmington Mills.

Partially waymarked. ① From garage turn right and follow A353 about 300 yards (274 m). ② Turn right down lane into Osmington village. ③ Facing 'Cosy Cottage' the road bends left; turn right uphill and follow track for almost a mile. (1.5 km). ④ Pass barn on left to go through iron gate. Leave the main track (which continues to Poxwell) and turn right towards another gate uphill. ⑤ Through gate, cross field ahead heading towards highest electricity post. Then follow path to right of fence in dip a little to left, straight on towards house by road. ⑥ Cross and follow lane straight ahead downhill past farm buildings. ⑦ Continue straight on uphill to road. ⑧ Turn left along road and carry straight on (do not turn right for Ringstead). ⑨ Go through gate to keep on through Nat. Trust property. ⑩ At signpost turn right for 'Ringstead Beach' – narrow path. ⑪ The path divides; turn left to walk under 3-wire pylons. ⑫ Follow path slightly right to single-wire pylons, cross stile and turn right

downhill to stone track by signpost for Ringstead. ⑬ Follow track donwhill until it turns right; carry straight on in direction of 'Ringstead' signpost. ⑭ Where path curves left, look for stile on right (under power cable), cross, and follow path past Rose Cottage to join Coast Path, where ⑮ turn right and continue. ⑯ When Path meets lane at Ringstead, turn left towards the sea ⑰ Turn right, follow Coast Path a little over a mile (1.5 km) to Osmington Mills. ⑱ At road, turn right and continue 300 yards. ⑲ Turn left and follow path signposted 'Footpath Osmington Village'—lettering on reverse. ⑳ Cross stile on right and walk ahead, bearing a few yards to left of electricity post ahead; walk slightly uphill to stile seen ahead; can be difficult to spot-look for yellow arrow-heads. ㉑ Over stile, bear slightly left down field to stile to left of gate. Cross and turn right for ① .

🏠 Village and church are full of interest – see the leaflet in church. Constable honeymooned and painted here.

In *The Trumpet Major* Hardy describes 'forty navvies at work' on the chalk memorial to George III, visitor to nearby Weymouth. Locals were unimpressed: it shows him leaving.

The site of a medieval village.

🍺 The Smugglers Inn.

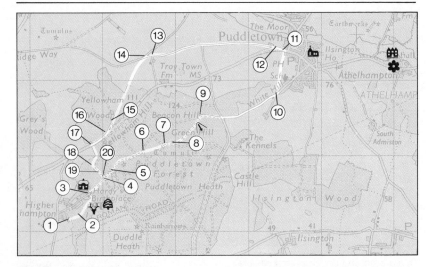

The Heart of Hardy's Wessex
5½ miles (9 km) Sheet 194 725921

Easy Much from the novelist's life and work. *Woods, town, downland; mud.*

Start From Dorchester take the A35 3 miles (5 km) towards Puddletown and turn right up lane signposted Higher Bockhampton. In about ½ mile (0.8 km) turn left for Hardy's Cottage. **Car park** signposted before Hardy's Cottage.

① From car park follow path signposted by red-tipped arrow 'Woodland Path to Hardy's Cottage'. ② Turn left, as signposted, for Hardy's Cottage following the red arrows. ③ Pass cottage on left and turn right to follow path into Forest. ④ Go straight over cross-track. ⑤ After a path joins from left, bear right a few yards, then left uphill. ⑥ About 300 yards (274 m) after top of hill turn along track half right, signposted 'Forest Walk'. ⑦ When path meets well-made track, continue along this. In about 200 yards (183 m) fork left on to smaller track through woods. ⑧ Track divides; turn left; ignore other paths. ⑨ Turn right, walk out of forest and down lane ahead towards Puddletown. ⑩ Turn left and follow path waymarked by yellow arrows over fields, keeping power cables on right. Continue to A35. ⑪ Turn left along A35 a few yards and cross to group of buildings on right, just past

bus stop. ⑫ In front of buildings take path on left signposted 'Bridleway Charminster'. ⑬ Track turns left twice; keep straight on and through gate ahead on to Ridgeway. ⑭ Leave Ridgeway almost immediately, turning left through gate to follow narrow track towards Yellowham Wood. ⑮ Path meets track; continue along this to A35. ⑯ Turn right along A35; continue about 60 yards (55 m) to lay-by on left where ⑰ turn left from its far end up narrow track just inside edge of wood. ⑱ At junction bear slightly right. ⑲ Path divides – bear right. ⑳ Turn right to walk down to Hardy's Cottage.

🏠 See the board and leaflet describing
⚲ Thorncombe Wood Nature Reserve.

🏠 Hardy was born here in 1840; it is the home of the Dewys in *Under the Greenwood Tree* (view by appointment – 0305 2366). Few paths and villages in the area do not feature in the novels. Egdon Heath is at the end of the lane.

⚲ Eustacia Vye stood here and looked at the Quiet Woman Inn.

🏠 St. Mary's has fine Jacobean, wooden fittings. Puddletown is Weatherbury in *Far From the Madding Crowd.*

🏛 Medieval Athelhampton House opens at
❀ various times; walks in the grounds.

St. Aldhelm's (or St. Alban's) Head
5 miles (8 km) Sheet 195 974776

Moderate – but strenuous in parts. This is a sensationally beautiful walk, along one of the Dorset coast's most dramatically rugged stretches. *Farmland, cliff tops; short, tiring climbs and descents.*

Start Worth Matravers, off the B3069.
Public car park on right just before village when approaching from Kingston.

① From car park turn right towards Worth Matravers and continue along road a few yards. ② Turn right opposite Square and Compass along 'Footpath to Church and Hill Bottom'. ③ Cross stone stile on left and continue down field. ④ Turn left through small swing gate and cross churchyard to visit church. ⑤ Leave church by S porch and turn right, following the road right. ⑥ Turn left along 'Footpath to Winspit'. Continue about 1¼ miles (2 km); explore quarry. ⑦ Turn right to climb over top of quarry, following direction of sign 'To St. Aldhelm's Head'. ⑧ The path divides – bear right, away from cliff edge, fence close on right, to climb to coastguard station and St. Aldhelm's Chapel. ⑨ Walk behind coastguard station and continue along cliff path (sign to Chapman's Pool). ⑩ Just before the slipway and boat houses, turn right to climb hill and bear left round top of Chapman's Pool. ⑪ After the Coast Path enters the river valley, leave it and fork right beside the waymarked post. Walk uphill a little, then follow the river valley with river on left (hidden by trees). ⑫ Go through gate, over bridge, and follow minor road for 150 yards (137 m). ⑬ For a short-cut back to ①, follow this lane via the farm back to Worth. To continue, turn left where the road turns right uphill, following 'Bridleway to Afflington Farm' (mud). ⑭ Turn right along 'Footpath to Worth Village' (quarry overspill on left). ⑮ Climb stone stile and bear right over field (hedge and overhead cables close on right). At road turn left to village.

🏚 At the 12th C. St. Nicholas is buried Benjamin Jesty, a local man who pioneered cow pox vaccination 'and who from his great *strength of mind* made the Experiment from the *Cow* on his Wife and two Sons'.

🍴 The Square and Compass Inn is named after the local quarrymen's tools; cream teas at the tea shop.

🔟 The furrows in this gorge, known as strip lynchets, were made by teams of oxen over 600 years ago, when strip farming supported a thriving Worth.

〽 The huge galleries of the marble quarries are supported by columns of Purbeck Stone. The recesses harboured another local industry, smuggling. When the East Indiaman *Halsewell* was wrecked here in 1786, killing 168, some escaped by being swept into the caves.

🏚 The Norman chapel is dedicated to the man who brought Christianity to this area in the 8th C.

⭦ W to Portland; E to the Isle of Wight.

⭧ Chapman's Pool.

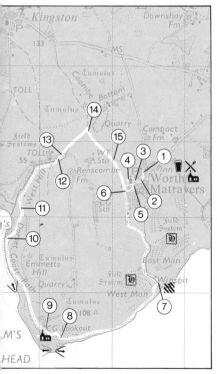

DORSET

The Giant of Cerne Abbas
6½ miles (10.5 km) Sheet 194 662017

Easy Dorset chalkland at its best; spectacular views for relatively little effort; great historical interest. *Village, hillside, ridge, downland, farmland; 2 climbs; mud after rain; slippery chalk after rain. Paths at ⑭, ⑯ and ㉑ may be ploughed out – follow directions carefully.*

Start From the A37 take the A352 and continue towards Cerne Abbas, which is off the road; frequent buses. **Parking** area just past village by a fork back to the village.

① From parking walk down road (giant on left) towards Cerne Abbas and soon ② turn left down lane. ③ Just before bridge turn right on to path along bank. ④ Turn left to cross stream and follow lane to Abbey Street. ⑤ Go down Abbey Street (church on left) to junction with road. ⑥ Turn left along road (Alton Lane). Continue about ¼ mile (0.5 km) after village. ⑦ Turn left along track towards Giant Hill (unsignposted). ⑧ Main track bears right – carry straight on to follow bridleway as it curves up side of Giant Hill (2 iron gates). ⑨ At top of hill carry straight on, fence/hedge on left. ⑩ Go through gate by bridleway sign, turn left and follow road about ¾ mile (one km). ⑪ Just past small wood on left, opposite bridleway on right, turn left through small wooden gate then right along top of field towards gate seen ahead. ⑫ Through gate, continue ahead, hedge on left. ⑬ Go through gate and turn left along ridge track. ⑭ After less than ¼ mile, watch very carefully for an iron gate, opposite a small gate, about 25 yards (23 m) past small wood on left. Turn left through gate, bear half right and walk down field to another gate (no path). ⑮ Through gate bear left down field to corner of small wood, where a double gate is seen. ⑯ Go through gate and straight over field ahead to gate. ⑰ From gate walk a few yards to join a well-defined track. Continue past Minterne House and the church to reach A352 by bridleway sign, and ⑱ turn left, continuing past right, then left bend, just after which ⑲ turn right through gate and go up track between trees. (Electric fence may obstruct gap at top – climb under.) ⑳ With low trees on left and hillside on right, turn left. The path is indistinct: walk half right towards the gate in the top left corner. ㉑ Through gate bear left round field, then right up field to

small wooden gate (partly obstructed by bushes) in top left corner (not large iron gate on left). ㉒ Through gate, turn left and continue a few yards along bridleway, then follow bridleway as it bears right down East Hill. ㉓ At junction with lane, turn left – Up Cerne Manor ahead. ㉔ In front of Manor turn right and follow lane as it bears left to A352. ㉕ Continue to ①.

ℹ️ Like most chalk figures, the giant is a mystery. He could be a Celtic fertility idol; and he could have been carved during the Roman occupation as a whim of the Emperor Commodus, who proclaimed himself a reincarnation of Hercules. Only this century was the grass removed from the phallus. Legends about him terrify local children.

❀ The earthwork behind the giant, the 'Trendle' or 'Frying Pan', has produced evidence of Stone Age habitation.

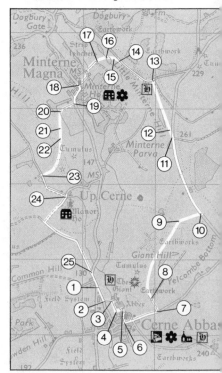

DORSET

 The ruins of the Benedictine abbey which gave the village the second half of its name are in romantic riverside gardens.

 The glorious glass in St. Mary's E window may have come from the abbey.

 On the right side of the churchyard is St. Augustine's Wishing Well. Its supremely clear water has, they say, never dried up. Drink it from a leaf, and wish.

 Hardy knew this ridge walk well, and brought Tess along here on her wanderings. Below, in 'the loamy Vale of Blackmoor', he set *The Woodlanders*.

 The gardens of Edwardian Minterne House are open in certain summer months.

 Up Cerne Manor, with its honey-coloured front, was built around 1600.

Hardy's Dorset can be further explored with the help of the Hardy Trail, starting from Dorchester (leaflet from the Tourist Information Office).

A rightly popular cliff-top walk is from Lulworth Cove to Durdle Door.

The Dorset Coast Path can be walked in sections starting at several points; a particularly interesting and lovely stretch begins at Kimmeridge.

There is easy access for walkers to several large areas of Dorset owned by the National Trust, in particular Golden Cap, Portesham Hill and Brownsea Island in Poole Harbour.

The enormous earth ramparts of Maiden Castle are reached from the car park signposted off the A354.

The virile giant of Cerne Abbas stands 180 feet (55 m) from head to toe.

EXMOOR AND THE QUANTOCKS

Exmoor is moorland at its most benign. A few miles off, across an intervening vale, the Quantocks are a separate range of low hills, some 40 square miles (104 square km) in extent, gently rounded and bracken-covered. Together they comprise the cream of North Devon's walking country.

During bad weather (rain drives in from the Bristol Channel), and with bad map-reading, it is possible to get lost on Exmoor, but the remaining areas of wide, open moor are now relatively small. Roads are frequent and one can park a car within 200 yards (183 m) of the highest point, Dunkery Beacon.

The three commanding attractions are the coast, the moors and the streams, and one can taste all three in a day's march. To the north there are the towering coastal cliffs which carry the South West Peninsula Coast Path on its marathon, switchback journey ending on the south coast at Poole. Inland, the main block of heather moorland extends South to Simonsbath in the heart of the former hunting forest. Between the moors, the enchanting streams tumble through deeply cut combes (hollows) with steeply wooded slopes.

Paths are plentiful. There is thorough signposting by the Exmoor National Park and a number of 'permissive' paths exist, opened by the owners as a special concession, to supplement rights of way.

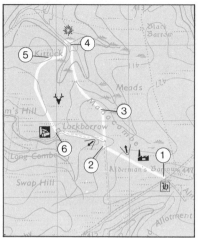

Near Larkbarrow: a wistful, scarcely changing landscape.

Exmoor Forest
3½ miles (5.5 km) Sheet 181 835423

Easy Gives an impression of Exmoor's past appearance – modern farming methods make only a muffled intrusion. Once discovered, the tranquillity of Three Combes Foot is long remembered. *Moorland; one climb; mud; best appreciated in at least fair visibility.*

Start From the A39 at top of Porlock Hill, take the Exford road. In 2½ miles (4 km), at Lucott Cross, turn right and continue ¾ mile (one km) to cattle grid. **Parking** by roadside E of cattle grid.

① Go through gate in direction signposted for Doone Valley and continue straight on for 500 yards (457 m) to gate opening on to farm track. ② Turn right on to track through next gate to follow boundary bank on right. ③ As trees appear half left about ¼ mile (0.5 km) away, veer off towards them across open moorland, passing through gap in crumbling boundary bank and arriving at trees, part of the 'stell' at the foot of Three Combes. ④ Cross footbridge immediately below trees to right, then cross another bridge 50 yards (46 m) farther on, and another 30 yards (27 m) to left, which crosses Chalk Water. Climb track (re-passing stell down to left) and in 150 yards (137 m) fork right, climbing steeply. As path levels out, a small barrow and some standing stones are reached.

⑤ Veer left towards old boundary bank, avoiding boggy ground to left and heading for trees surrounding Larkbarrow ruins. Walk through ruins to farm track. ⑥ Turn left to follow track to gate at ②, and retrace steps across moor, heading for right end of trees on skyline.

🏛 The route is through the former Exmoor Forest or royal hunting ground, sold in 1818 to the Knight family, who planted most of the mature trees seen today.

🚂 The remains of the unfinished 19th C. railway from Simonsbath to Porlock.

\↑/ The Bristol Channel and Wales beyond.

\↑/ Across the heart of Exmoor with Chains Barrow 6 miles (9.5 km) away.

※ The stell, a round, stone-faced earthen bank surmounted by beeches, was built as a shelter for sheep.

🦌 Red deer abound in this part of Exmoor.

🏚 Larkbarrow Farm is now a pile of stones because it was in the centre of a gunnery range in the 1939-45 war. The area was finally cleared of unexploded missiles only in 1981.

EXMOOR AND THE QUANTOCKS

Selworthy Beacon
5 miles (8 km) Sheet 181 897481

Energetic Shows some of Exmoor's spectacular coastal scenery, and gives access to some of the historic Acland family walks on the Holnicote Estate. *Hillside, coastal path, woods, riverside; one climb.*

Start From A39 one mile (1.5 km) E of Porlock, and continue to Bossington. **Car park** (Nat. Trust) at centre of Bossington.

① From car park cross bridge over Horner Water, then fork right on footpath signposted Selworthy. In 30 yards (27 m) fork left to go uphill, keeping straight on through narrow gate with stone wall on right. Turn left on reaching level, grassy path and continue 150 yards (137 m) to wooden seat. ② Turn right and climb steep, grassy path to another wide path at a higher level. Turn left on to this to skirt Bossington Hill, then keeping straight on to follow coast path towards Minehead, which is waymarked with an acorn symbol. ③ Where coast path forks left, carry straight on to Selworthy Beacon, then turning sharp right to follow path down to road. ④ Cross road and follow signposted footpath through woods to Selworthy. ⑤ Go through gate by church and turn right into Selworthy Green. Take path signposted to Bossington, skirting edge of woodland and crossing a wide track signposted to Allerford (passing 'Katherines Well') and forking left here to keep to edge of wood. One hundred yards (91 m) after fork, veer right under large, leaning pine trees and follow signs to Bossington until reaching a T-junction after the House of Lynch. ⑥ Turn left to follow lane across bridge to road, then right to follow road to car park.

🌳 Examples of holm (evergreen) oaks.

🏚 The paths in Selworthy Woods once totalled 40 miles, and were cleared of branches, even swept, by estate pensioners.

🏠 The cottages on Selworthy Green, built in 1828 for Holnicote Estate pensioners, are a picturesque monument to the old landowner's benign paternalism.

✗ Tea shop – cream teas a speciality.

🏠 One of the finest half-dozen on Exmoor.

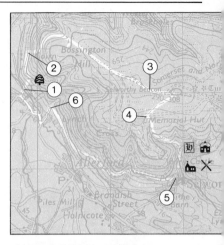

The Barle and Exe Valleys
12½ miles (20 km) Sheet 181 874325

Moderate These beautiful, unspoilt valleys are the dominant feature of southern Exmoor; splendid views from the moorland between. *Woods, farmland, moorland, riverside; 3 climbs; mud after rain.*

Start From the B3223 (Dulverton-Exford) crossing Winsford Hill, follow signs to Tarr Steps. **Public car park** between Liscombe and Tarr Steps.

① From car park walk to Tarr Steps Bridge. Turn right to follow path with yellow waymarks along riverside to Withypool, passing wire debris trap and Bailey Bridge; after about 3 miles (5 km) pass the stepping stones below South Hill Farm. Continue to Withypool road. ② Turn left, and in 100 yards (91 m) right to follow path with red waymarks towards Exford. After stiff climb, 6 stiles and 4 gates, reach the Dulverton-Exford road. ③ Cross road and through gate on to Room Hill. Follow hedge on right, and as head of combe appears ahead, veer slightly left to descend the combe on wide, stony track to River Exe. Turn right to follow path with yellow waymarks to Nethercote Bridge. ④ Continue straight on along farm road for 50 yards (46 m), then fork sharp right uphill, following hedge on right. At top of hill, go through gate on right and carry on in same direction on boundary of grass and bracken. Go through next gate and carry straight on where wide track forks off left downhill. Follow the red waymarks until the path emerges on the Withypool-Winsford road. ⑤ Turn left and follow road into Winsford. Turn right after ford and follow road passing Royal Oak. ⑥ Turn left 150 yards (137 m) after 'Karslake' and follow path with yellow waymarks signposted Tarr Steps. Cross stream at Yellowcombe, and climb again through conifers to gate leading to grassland at Summerway. ⑦ From disused quarry continue in direction of sign to Tarr Steps, rejoining yellow waymarks in far corner. In 200 yards (183 m), path emerges on to open moorland of Draydon Knap. Follow it around boundary to the left arriving at the Exford-Dulverton road. ⑧ Cross road and follow Liscombe road to cattle grid. Here fork left to follow path with yellow waymarks across Varle Hill and Ashway Side back to Tarr Steps.

Ⓗ Tarr Steps, an ancient causeway over the Barle, may be prehistoric, but is more likely to be 500-600 years old. Reconstructed many times, it is protected by the wire hawser upstream.

⋎ The Barle is an excellent sporting river. Trout are seen in pools at many points. Otters, though rare, have been sighted downstream from South Hill Stepping Stones. Do not confuse otters with the smaller, more plentiful mink.

⤙ A heronry. The Exe upstream from Nethercote Bridge has dippers.

▯ Both are excellent village inns; real ale.

⛪ Winsford church's list of vicars starts in 1280. Ernest Bevin was born opposite the Methodist chapel.

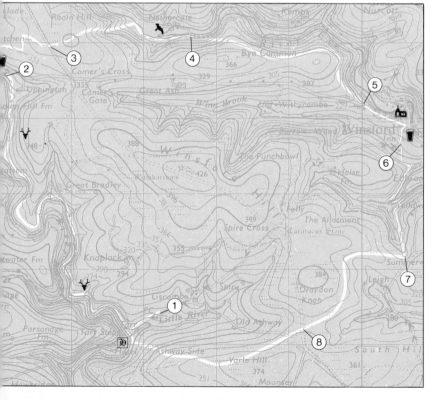

EXMOOR AND THE QUANTOCKS

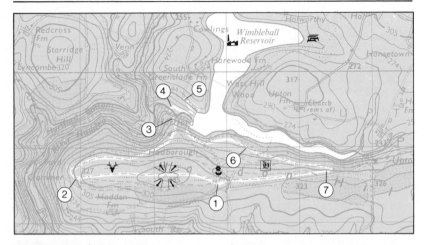

Haddon Hill and Wimbleball
7 miles (11 km) Sheet 181 969285

Moderate Shows that man-made beauty can compensate for the loss of wilderness – something local people found hard to believe when the Wimbleball Reservoir was proposed. Offers fine views into the heart of Devon, with hundreds of square miles of rich pasture and few signs of human habitation. Best in May and June, when the greens of the woods and moorland are in strongest contrast, and the reservoir's blue most striking. *Moorland, woods; 2 climbs.*

Start Leave the B3190 at the right-angle bend 1½ miles (2.5 km) W of Upton. Cross cattle grid and follow signs to car park. **Public car park** (free) with lavatories.

① From car park make for Haddon Hill (signposted), following wide track passing trig. point at summit to where track ends under power cables. Carry straight on through heather to boundary fence. ② Turn right to follow track beside fence. Continue to follow fence line as track leaves woodland and narrows to path through rhododendrons. Pass under power cables again and keep straight on, diverging from fence. Fork left down a gulley and turn left to cross stile over fence and head downhill into trees. ③ After crossing another stile and descending steep stone steps, turn left on to the reservoir road and then right to cross wooden bridge over River Haddeo. ④ Turn

right at top of bridge approach to follow sunken track towards dam, turning sharp left, steeply upwards, just before dam. ⑤ At top of climb turn sharp right on to concrete road which crosses dam. Turn left at end of dam, and after climb fork left on to track signposted to Upton. Just after entering oak woods, join an old coach drive. ⑥ Turn half right to follow drive; turn right just before next gate, leaving drive. ⑦ After short climb, reach gate leading on to B3190. Turn right before gate to follow path inside the boundary towards start.

♣ Haddon Hill's fine heather moorland was threatened by agricultural 'improvement' until Exmoor National Park and the owner agreed to own and manage it jointly.

\t/ Clockwise: the Quantocks; the Wellington Monument and Blackdown Hills; Yes Tor, Dartmoor's highest point; Winsford Hill and Dunkery Beacon.

↓ A herd of pure-bred Exmoor ponies was founded here by Exmoor National Park in order to preserve the breed.

↳ Wimbleball Reservoir and Dam, landscaped to preserve the place's beauty and atmosphere.

ⓗ The drive – 'Lady Harriet Acland's' – was constructed in the 18th C. for carriages.

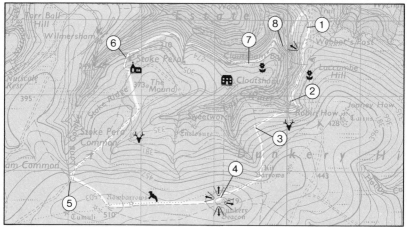

Dunkery Beacon
6½ miles (10.5 km) Sheet 181 903438

Moderate Exmoor's highest point; views of some fine, coppiced oak woodland, most colourful in autumn. *Moorland, combe, woods; 2 climbs; mud after rain.*

Start From the A39 (Minehead to Porlock), take the Horner or Luccombe turning and follow signs for Dunkery until road forks at Webber's Post for Cloutsham and Wheddon Cross. **Car park** at Webber's Post.

① From car park walk along Cloutsham road to start of nature trail and follow trail to stone no. 2. ② Turn left to climb through carpet of whortleberry plants with stream below to right. At well-worn path turn right to cross stream. A quarter mile (0.5 km) after stony trail emerges from wooded combe on to open hilltop, it is crossed by a grassy path. ③ Turn left to climb through heather, veering right around head of another plunging combe, then forking left uphill to summit of Dunkery. ④ Turn right to follow ridge path to Rowbarrows (check direction with viewpoint indicator). Pass one barrow, then turn right to pass to left of the next. Take right fork to pass rainfall gauge and walk down to Cloutsham road. ⑤ Turn right to walk on, or parallel with, road to sign for Dicky's Path on right. Turn left and head for right corner of plantation and continue in same direction across heather to Stoke Pero road. At road turn left to church and

farmhouse. ⑥ Turn right to follow 'Priestway'. Continue on this path (signposted) into oak woodland, then follow signs to Webber's Post along boundary of wood with fence on right. As fence changes to wall and path emerges into open, the starting point at Webber's Post is seen half left. ⑦ Veer left away from wall by seat and nature trail stone no. 5, and fork left to follow track turning right at next sign to continue downhill to East Water. ⑧ Turn left to cross water, then take steep path on right up to Webber's Post; turn right through narrow gap in gorse near top to ①.

⑂ The Horner and East Water valleys.

🌸 Parts of the walk coincide with the Cloutsham Nature Trail (guide published by Exmoor National Park) on the National Trust-owned Holnicote Estate.

🦌 Red deer may be seen all round the walk.

🦃 A likely stretch of heather for spotting grouse, a few of which remain.

⛪ At 1,013 feet (309 m) above sea level, this is one of the loneliest churches on Exmoor, and still lit by candles only; once used by couples who wanted quiet weddings.

🏠 Cloutsham Farm's 'Swiss' extension was built and used by the Acland family, owners of the Holnicote Estate.

EXMOOR AND THE QUANTOCKS

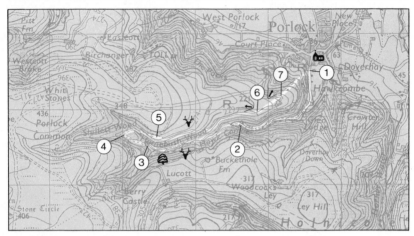

Hawk Coombe and Homebush Wood
4 miles (6.5 km) Sheet 181 885465

Moderate A route with several good examples of man conserving his immediate environment. *Streamside, woodland; 3 climbs; mud, especially in hunting season.*

Start At centre of Porlock, turn off by church. **Car park** in Parsons Street.

① From car park follow road with steam on right, passing disused mill and following signs indicating valley path and public bridleway to the head of Hawk Combe, passing 'Owls Barton' to end of surfaced road at 'The Stables'. ② Go straight on along woodland track, cross footbridge, take right-hand track at fork and cross another footbridge. Stay on the right side of the stream, passing dammed pond and tree nursery. ③ At ford, cross stream and follow main track to 4-way signpost and ④ turn right to follow path with red waymarks. Climb steeply and turn off right immediately before cattle grid. ⑤ Follow path with red waymarks along top edge of wood and through conifer plantation. ⑥ At end of plantation, leave waymarked path and turn half left through gate to follow hedge on right through 2 more gates to drive leading to house on right. ⑦ Cross drive and fork slightly left to follow sharply descending bridleway. Turn sharp right towards Hawk Combe. Veer left, then right downhill to path 'T' junction. Turn left and continue to ①.

England's last substantial herds of red deer – largest of the deer – inhabit Exmoor.

⛪ An interesting Early English church, with a beautiful arcade of 5 bays, pieces of a Saxon cross and some outstanding monuments.

ⱴ Red deer, seen frequently.

🌲 Many of the oaks have been coppiced: the heads lopped off, usually to provide winter feed or 'browsing' for the deer. The practice produces the many slim stems, with various uses, including charcoal burning.

ⱴ Hawk Combe Head.

ⱴ Porlock Bay, Hurlstone Point, Bossington Hill and Selworthy Beacon.

Nutscale Reservoir
5½ miles (9 km) Sheet 181 848419

Moderate Open spaces and superb moorland views; best from April to October – there is considerable bird activity in spring and, from summer onwards, the glory of the heather. *Streamside, hillside, farmland, moorland; 3 climbs; mud after rain.*

Start From the A39 at top of Porlock Hill take the Exford road, looking for car park in 3 miles (5 km). **Car parks** on the Exford side of the bridge over Chetsford Water.

① From car park cross bridge and turn right to follow Chetsford Water. ② Cross Chetsford Water at ford, where there are large rocks in midstream. Climb wide track immediately opposite, veer left and follow track uphill through heather. Go straight

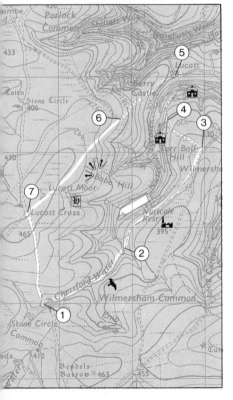

across access road to reservoir, and join minor road for 200 yards (183 m) to edge of open moorland. ③ Turn left to follow farm track with wire fence on right descending through gorse and turning right through gate. In 100 yards (91 m) where road turns sharp left to descend to valley ④ go straight on through gate to join metalled track, which descends to an isolated cottage on right. Then follow the path down to Nutscale Water, cross the footbridge, turn right and then immediately left through a gate. Climb steep, stony track to Lucott Farm, turning left as the farm access road is reached. ⑤ At Lucott Farm turn left to take wide track which passes to the left of the farmhouse. This has yellow waymarks and climbs steadily with fields on both sides. ⑥ As the track goes through gate on to open moorland, go straight on, skirting the top of the deep combe which descends to Nutscale on left. Go through the next gate on to grassland and veer slightly right towards a marker in the middle of the field. Continue straight on through next gate on to open moorland again and head for the right end of a row of trees on the skyline. The path becomes a grassy track through heather and reaches the Exford-Porlock road at Lucott Cross. ⑦ At Lucott Cross turn left and follow road to ①.

🦅 The valley of Chetsford Water is the local quiet spot for bird-watching – relatively rare species seen include the merlin, smallest of the falcons, and the ring ouzel, resembling a blackbird with a white gorget (neck patch).

🚰 Nutscale Reservoir, formed by damming Chetsford Water, is the water source for Minehead and District.

🏠 Sympathetic conversions of old country dwellings for modern needs.

\𝑡/ Dunkery Beacon; North Hill and Selworthy Beacon; the Bristol Channel and Welsh Coast.

🅱 Most of the route is on the delightful Holnicote Estate, now National Trust, which came into the Acland family in the 18th C. The 12,500 acres, mostly open to the public at all times, includes such landmarks as Selworthy Beacon and Dunkery Hill, and there is much of architectural interest. In the Aclands' day, the stag hunting was greatly prized.

EXMOOR AND THE QUANTOCKS

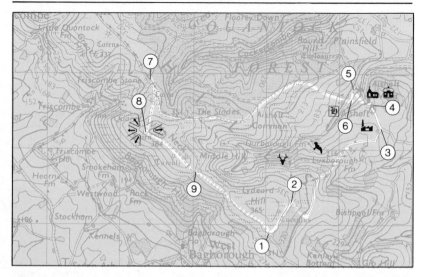

Wills Neck
5½ miles (9 km) Sheet 181 181338

Moderate An introduction to the woods and valleys of these hills, with a climb to their highest point for superb 360° views. *Hills, lanes, moorland; 2 climbs; mud.*

Start From Kingston St. Mary, N of Taunton, pass through village and up Buncombe Hill. Turn left at garage on corner for Bishops Lydeard. In one mile (1.5 km) turn right at a house. In ¼ mile (0.5 km) look for car park sign. **Car park** at foot of Lydeard Hill.

① From stile at NE end of car park take broad track along side of wood. ② Turn right through gate and woods. Turn left along unpaved lane, soon descending, and. in ¼ mile becoming unpaved. After ½ mile (0.8 km) ③ at T-junction join road, passing old lime kiln on left. Continue ¼ mile to village and church of Aisholt. ④ Continue from church steeply downhill for 100 yards (91 m) to Old School House. Cross bridge over stream and go uphill for 200 yards (183 m) to ⑤ a sharp U-turn. Turn left at the 'No Through Road' sign and continue ¼ mile. ⑥ Turn right before reaching farmhouse and continue up lane past cottage on right. Reach open moor and take right fork to climb hill track for ¼ mile to a picnic area. Turn left along path close to

wood and continue (W) uphill, with ridge of hill on skyline ahead. Continue along path by woodside for one mile then alongside Slades Wood. At top of hill turn right and keep alongside wood for ½ mile to car park at Triscombe Stone. ⑦ Retrace steps for 50 yards (46 m) and take the broad track on right away from wood uphill over moor. In ⅓ mile (0.5 km) reach trig. point at Wills Neck. ⑧ Continue along ridge path (SE).·In ¼ mile keep to left of wood. ⑨ Aisholt church comes into view below to the left. Continue alongside wood to stile and gate, cross, and keep to this path, reaching car park in one mile.

ʮ Red deer may be seen all along route.

🦅 Buzzard country.

🏚 The lime kiln was last used in the 19th C.

🏘 Aisholt village (with a 15th C. church), where the poet Coleridge wanted to live – but his wife thought it too remote.

🏡 The poet Sir Henry Newbolt lived in the Old School House during the 1930s.

\|/ Notably: E and SE, the Mendips; NW to Minehead; W, the Brendon Hills; SW, the length of Dartmoor; S, the Blackdown Hills and, SE, Pilsdon Pen.

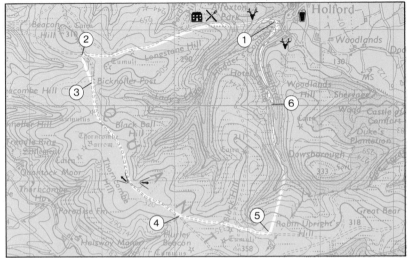

Wordsworth's Quantocks
5½ miles (9 km) Sheet 181 155411

Moderate *Reveals a variety of beautifully changeable scenery. Wooded combe, moorland, ridge, woods, streamside; one climb; mud.*

Start In Holford on the A39 turn left for Alfoxton and Hodder's Combe, continuing ½ mile (0.8 km) to Holford Green. **Car park** on left of Holford Green.

① From car park follow Y.H.A. sign on cottage wall in direction of Alfoxton Hotel. In 300 yards (274 m) leave road and turn left at bridleway sign. Continue up hill on stony track for ¾ mile (one km) to open moor. Continue straight ahead on broad track uphill towards ridge, going left at fork and meeting ridge walk on top of hill, where ② turn left at crossways along ridge path. In 300 yards (274 m) pass ③ Bicknoller Post on left (large stake in ground). Continue 100 yards (91 m) on main path and fork left, continuing along main path. In ¼ mile (0.5 km), pass through open, grassy area and keep to main path (on right) uphill. Continue along winding ridge path. In one mile (1.5 km), pass a small white post on right marked 'V gas'. After 100 yards (91 m), leave ridge path and ④ fork left along double track round side of hill. Keep to this (passing

4 tracks on left) for one mile. After passing solitary tree on left, go up steep rise to grassy, stony open space, where a path crosses. ⑤ Turn left, and descend wide, grassy path towards wooded area in valley below, changing direction from E to N. Continue downhill into woods (stony path) to reach stream. Continue left of stream on broad path for 100 yards (91 m), cross another stream by stepping stones and immediately turn right. In 100 yards, cross main stream by stepping stones, and continue along path on right side of river. In ¾ mile, reach picnic area. ⑥ Continue straight ahead on broad lane and in ¼ mile (0.5 km) pass cottage and Combe House Hotel on left. After more cottages, on outskirts of Holford, turn left past pillar box, then sharp left; Car park in 100 yards on left.

🍺 The Plough Inn: snacks or full meals.

🏨 Alfoxton Park, an 18th C. manor house now a hotel and restaurant, where
✕ Wordsworth lived for a year in 1797 and produced poems about the Quantocks.

\†/ Hinckley Point Nuclear Power Station; the barrow on Thorncombe Hill, itself a vantage point worth a detour.

⩔ Red deer are seen regularly around Holford and in Alfoxton Park.

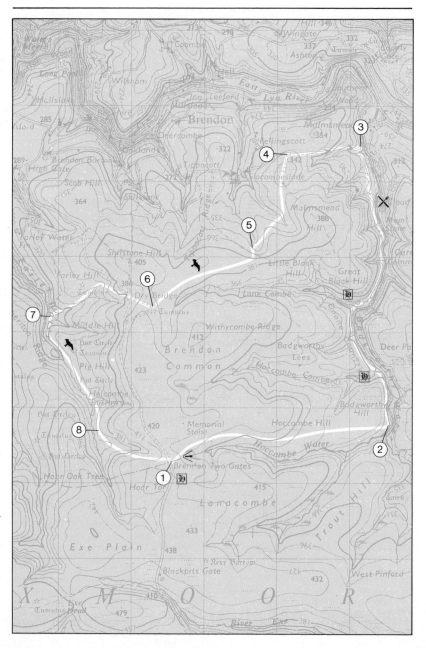

Doone Country
11 miles (17.5 km) Sheet 180 763433

Moderate Shows that Exmoor is a romantic moor, despite appearing less desolate and lonely than other moorland tracts. The *Lorna Doone* story is a true picture of these parts, and reading the book adds another dimension to the walk's enjoyment. *Moorland, streamsides, woods; 2 climbs; mud after rain.*

Start Brendon Two Gates, on the B3223 between Simonsbath and Lynton. **Parking** on wide verges immediately S of the cattle grid at Brendon Two Gates.

① Cross cattle grid. Turn right to follow track running parallel to Hoccombe Water, passing through one gate and eventually descending sharply to Badgworthy Water at footbridge below junction with Hoccombe Water. ② Turn left to follow path (yellow waymarks) towards Malmsmead, crossing bridge over Hoccombe Water and bridge over Lank Combe with Water Slide to left. Then make for Blackmore Memorial Stone, then Cloud Farm, where waymarked path veers left away from water. ③ At road turn sharp left to climb to brow of hill (over cattle grid, under power cables). ④ Turn left to follow gravel track, turning right across shallow stream after some isolated beech trees. As track peters out, fork left to make for head of next combe. ⑤ About 100 yards (91 m) after combe, leave track to fork left across 200 yards (183 m) of heather to join a distinct track from Malmsmead Hill. Turn right to follow this W, passing a 4-way and a 3-way signpost. ⑥ 350 yards (320 m) past 3-way sign, by tumulus (with Star of Bethlehem) fork right to dry bridge on the Lynton Road. Cross road to follow stream, criss-crossing at will, to stream's junction with Farley Water. ⑦ Turn left and continue upstream, again using either bank, passing large mounds of Holcombe Barrows after about 20 minutes' walking. ⑧ Where wide track descends to the valley from the right, veer left away from water to follow continuation of this track up combe. Go straight on from head of combe to hit road at ①.

🏠 Brendon Two Gates, a once-important entrance to Exmoor's royal hunting ground, had a combination of self-closing gates to prevent animals straying.

The grey wagtail – grey upperparts, bright yellow beneath – favours flowing water.

⅄ Dunkery Beacon, 8 miles (13 km) distant.

🏠 Site of the medieval settlement which was probably R. D. Blackmore's model for the Doone stronghold in *Lorna Doone*. The novel features several Exmoor locations, in degrees of imaginative transformation.

🏠 Blackmore's probable model for the terrible Water Slide in *Lorna Doone*.

✕ Cloud Farm's café, and Malmsmead café, open seasonally, the latter licensed.

🐦 The occasional red grouse, and the last of Exmoor's black grouse may be seen.

🐦 Dippers and wagtails.

Exmoor is hospitable to the walker who wants to improvise; its bogs are harmless and the paths well signposted.

Porlock and Selworthy are useful starting points, the first for moorland routes, the second for the network of paths through Selworthy Woods, leading to Allerford, Bossington and beyond to Hurlstone Point.

There is nearly 20 miles (32 km) of the North Devon Coastal Path between Lynmouth and Minehead. Less ambitious coastal strolls can be devised using the paths on North Hill (access from Lynmouth) with spectacular cliff-top passages. (See pages 328-334.) Booklets describing the National Park's waymarked walks are available from Exmoor House, Dulverton (send S.A.E.).

MENDIP REGION

The Mendips (plain Mendip to the expert) are a modest range of hills, never higher than a thousand-odd feet 305 m), and running a mere 30 miles (48 km) from the Bristol Channel to Frome; but they are massive, constituting, for most of their length, a solid, unbroken wall rising abruptly from the willows and water of the Somerset Levels.

To explore the hills properly takes a little trouble: there are relatively few footpaths. On a fine weekend, the area's maze of lanes may be crowded, for this is Bristol's playground. On quieter days, the flat-topped Mendip plateau is extraordinarily lonely.

Some of the villages almost have a look of the industrial north in their grey limestone, and quarrying has taken ugly bites from the hills. To compensate, there are the natural wonders. The limestone here is soluble; rainwater gradually seeps downwards, eating away the rock, making great caves. Sometimes the roof falls in to produce a canyon like Cheddar Gorge.

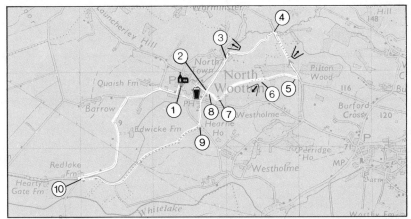

North Wootton
2 or 5 miles (3 or 8 km) Sheet 182 564417

Easy Away from the main Mendip tourist area in the vineyard country, agreeably dominated by views of Glastonbury Tor. *Woods, farmland; one climb; mud.*

Start North Wootton, SE of Wells. **Parking** outside the church or in adjacent road.

① From church cross bridge and turn right to road along which turn left; take first left and follow lane to its junction with the Worminster road. ② Left on to road and continue to No Through Road sign. ③ At sign turn right, following lane past Mill House. Continue (later through wet section) to junction with Worminster–Pilton road. ④ Turn right, walking uphill to top. As road flattens, ⑤ turn sharp right (before reaching Y-junction). Take track (actually a bridleway) into wood, shortly keeping to main path close to edge of wood. ⑥ Continue ahead, pool to right, in a few yards leaving wood under wire on right. Continue in same direction (as through wood) using faint path along field edge. Continue through second field with hedge on right. Cross third field diagonally, leaving through gate into lane. ⑦ Follow lane downhill, looking for small brick building (pumping station) in field on right. Just past it, look for stile at top of bank on right. Cross into field, walking below pumping station, after it turning left, dropping to stile in field corner by shed with corrugated metal roof. Cross into road. ⑧

Left on to road, in 150 yards (137 m) meeting crossroads at Crossways Inn. Turn right back to church if not continuing. Otherwise straight over crossroads, leaving pub to right. Straight over next crossroads, ⑨ entering bridleway. Follow it to gate and overhead cables, continuing straight on along bank of stream to Redlake Farm. ⑩ Over bridge at farm and right along lane, following signposts back to North Wootton.

⌂ The church contains a Norman font. The pub at the crossroads – The Crossways **🍺** Inn – was a cider press.

\⫯/ Passing Mill House there is a clear view of some of the vineyards flourishing in the area. The centre of local wine-making is the nearby Pilton Manor Vineyard (The Manor House, Pilton), with an exhibition of wine-making and a wine bar with the local wine on sale.

\⫯/ The harmonious scene looking back NE from Stoodly Hill is Worminster Sleight, Dungeon Farm and Church Hill.

\⫯/ From the top of the hill, and frequently on the return to Wootton, Glastonbury Tor is in view. The tower itself is the remains of a 15 C. church; the town, with its ruined abbey and associated buildings, a formerly great religious centre and subject of legends going back to King Arthur. Beyond it spread the Somerset Levels, the low-lying area which was impenetrably marshy until drained for farmland.

Flax Bourton, Backwell and Bourton Combe
6½ miles (10.5 km) Sheet 182 507693

Easy Excellent vantage points and varied scenery close to Bristol; less used than the nearby Brockley and Goblin Combes. *Pasture, arable farmland, combes; 2 climbs; mud; path may be overgrown between ⑭ and ⑬.*

Start Flax Bourton on the A370 SW of Bristol; buses from Bristol and Weston. **Parking** near church in Flax Bourton main street.

① From Church walk E and turn up Bourton Combe. ② At top of lane bear left towards Barrow church, crossing stile and fields uphill to Barrow Court. Follow wall of Court, over stile in 'wire fence and out of drive leading to church. ③ Turn right on to road along estate wall and ④ at first stile on left at top of hill go through field adjoining Home Farm. Continue straight on over stile, downhill through gate and uphill over 2 further stiles. ⑤ In next field turn right and go uphill through gate. Bear right across next field and exit to a short lane. ⑥ Straight across at end of lane into field (by Slade Lane sign) and uphill, through gate. Continuing in same direction, follow fence with wood on right and track, going through 3 gates. At gate immediately on left, ⑦ turn left and follow track along side of 'the Plantation'. Turn sharp right into field and then bear right across it, leaving Jubilee Stone on right. ⑧ Look carefully for gate leading out to lane where wall makes a right angle. Follow lane to crossroads. ⑨ Turn right, later first left, and in 80 yards (73 m) ⑩ take the narrow track on the right leading to Backwell Jubilee Stone. Continue past this downhill (left of stone) to an iron stile. ⑪ Over stile and bear left across field looking down on to Backwell church, left. Take gate on right in corner and in a few yards turn right ⑫ where path bears to left. Walk up Farleigh Combe and exit to road over stile in left corner. Turn right along road for 50 yards (46 m). ⑬ Go through first gate on left, following well-defined, stony track and continuing along narrow path through gate into wood. Go straight ahead, slightly uphill, and continue to end of track past farm buildings. ⑭ Turn sharp left and follow the buildings right round, almost doubling back behind farmhouse, to find a gate into wood. (This is

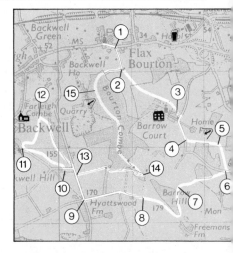

the NW of the 3 gates.) Through it, continue about ¼ mile (0.5 km), then bear left towards large clump of yew trees. Follow track to 'the Plateau'. ⑬ Where 'plateau' narrows, about half-way along, take track to right through wood and downhill to lane which leads to Bourton Combe lane and point ①.

🏛 Barrow Court is a restored Elizabethan house on the site of a Benedictine nunnery built in 1211. The 12 statues ranged round the lawn represent the months of the year.

\↑/ A good view of Barrow Gurney, the valley and the old mill.

\↑/ View of Long Ashton, the fruit research station run by Bristol University; beyond, Christchurch, Clifton and Bristol. Nailsea, noted for glass-making, is straight ahead across the valley.

🏛 Backwell church has a Norman font, a medieval screen, a 15th C. chapel, and the tomb of Sir Walter Rodney.

\↑/ View of Backwell church in the valley and the coast at Clevedon. Clevedon Court, built in 1320 with later additions, is a National Trust property within easy reach.

🍺 Jubilee Inn.

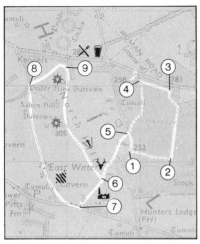

Adders (proper name, black adders) are brown with a black zigzag band on the back. Bites require hospital treatment.

Mendip Forest and Priddy Barrows
2 or 5 miles (3 or 8 km) Sheet 182 548512

Easy Enchanting coniferous plantation route, with a contrasting hillside section for the energetic. *Woods, pasture; one climb; mud.*

Start From A39 NE of Wells take unclassified road to Priddy, turning right at Hunters Lodge Inn. After first (major) right bend, stop at roadside area and gate into woods (NB, *not* at main entrance, marked by Forestry Commission boards). **Parking** by road.

① Through gate and along grassy track, ignoring the first left; at crossways ② turn left downhill. Continue, ignoring first left and bearing left where track joins from right. ③ *Within sight* of–about 100 yards (91 m) *from*–gate on to road, turn left along faint path through trees, soon continuing on obvious path, parallel and close to road. After about ⅓ mile (0.5 km) ④ left on to broad track, continuing straight on to road. ⑤ Cross, taking track opposite to pool with lead mine workings ahead. Continue to view mining remains, then retrace to pool and take path through trees on left. Follow it to road at farm. ⑦ Turn right along road passing Fairladywell Cottage. In 100 yards (91 m) enter field on right over bars. Cross field to stone stile just visible apparently left of farm buildings. Exit on to lane, turning right. Follow this uphill, in ½ mile (0.8 km)

continuing on possibly swamp-like, usually muddy path. ⑧ Where path meets road, turn right through small gate and, bearing left, make for brow of hill. From brow, head for gate in gap between trees in far corner. ⑨ At gate turn right, aiming for barrows (mounds). Walk between barrows, continuing ahead to gate in wall which soon comes in sight. Through gate, keep straight ahead along crest of North Hill in direction of TV mast. Cross stile and bear right through long, coarse grass a few yards until reaching path. Follow this left downhill towards pool. At track retrace to ①.

ᗄ The area is well known for adders, the only poisonous snake species in Britain.

🗴 St. Cuthbert's lead mines (closed) contain Roman remains. Records of mining here go back to the 12th C.

〰 The gully contains the entrance to East Water Swallet, the deepest known cleft in the Mendips.

✳ Priddy Nine Barrows and Ashen Hill Barrows are Bronze Age burial mounds.

\↑⁄ To the E Mendips, and the Tower of Cranmore, above Cranmore Hall.

🍺 The Miners' Arms, once a lead miners' inn, is now a restaurant famed for ✕ Mendip snails; brews own ale.

MENDIP REGION

Yarley and Hembury Hills
3½ miles (5.5 km) Sheet 182 514453

Easy Fine vantage points for viewing the Somerset Levels. *Farmland; one climb; mud; the District Surveyor has been asked to clear the obstruction at* ⑦.

Start The Pheasant Inn, near Worth on the B3139; buses from Wells and Burnham stop near the Pheasant. **Parking** behind the Pheasant Inn where the lane to Fenny Castle meets the B3139.

① Walk along the lane below Ben Knowle and fork right. ② Take first lane on right, following it uphill, then gradually downhill to T-junction by cottages. Turn right. Continue to next T-junction and ③ turn left uphill. Almost immediately turn right through gate of Keeping Cottage, continuing straight ahead through 2 gates along bridleway. Where bridleway stops, continue straight on uphill, across the field, through gate and straight on over brow of hill. Cross field to metal gate opposite. ④ Turn sharp left on to narrow track, becoming a bridleway, and follow to end. ⑤ Turn right towards Callow Hill, following the road round and turning left. ⑥ Where the road bends sharply left, go through gate on right and climb straight across the field, continuing in same direction through 2 gates on to ridge of Hembury Hill. Continue down the ridge (Glastonbury Tor ahead) and ⑦ near the hedge bear left to the end of the hill. Exit under wire near woodland unless obstruction at ⑦ has been cleared. Alternatively, make towards road to the right and continue along it into village. Past the hedge, bear right across the field to the gate near the cross and exit into lane where ⑧ turn left and continue to starting point.

\↑/ Former peat cutting areas, of which the most significant were Meare and Shapwick Heath. The latter is now a nature reserve.

\↑/ To the Abbot's Fish House at Meare (459418), quarters of the Abbot of Glastonbury's personal fisherman, who worked the substantial lake or mere before the Levels of which it was a part were drained for farmland.

※ The site of an ancient, wooden, possibly Anglo-Saxon fortification.

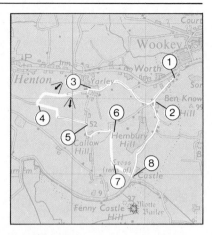

Across the Mendips above Wells
7 miles (11 km) Sheet 182 549463

Moderate An introduction to the Mendips, with Wookey Hole and the great cathedral town of Wells. *Arable farmland, pasture, grassy slopes; one climb; mud.*

Start Mountery Road, off New Street, Wells; frequent buses from Bristol and Street – alight at Walcombe Lane near point ①. **Public car park** in Union Street – reach point ① via Chamberlain and New Streets; parking in Mountery Road is limited.

① From junction of Mountery Road and New Street walk up the main road in the Bristol direction, and just beyond the crossroads ② turn left along Walcombe Lane. Continue to a small cluster of houses and ③ bear right past 2 garages along a short lane and take first gate on right by hydrant. Cross field to right-hand corner and enter public bridleway. Follow this (it narrows after gate on left and later becomes a metalled road) to its exit near the Pen Mast. ④ Walk past entrance to mast and cross 'Peggy Marriott' stile. Follow path bearing right away from mast, turn left at first gate and continue over waymarked stiles to the road above Rookham. ⑤ Turn left and walk down road to top of Rookham Hill. ⑥ Turn right along drove road and follow this nearly to Higher Pitts Farm. ⑦ Turn left into waymarked field and continue through 2 fields to crest of ridge. Then continue straight ahead downhill towards Wookey Hole, through 2 gates, then bearing diagonally left across next field to iron gate. Through this, continue straight ahead to the village school. ⑥ Downhill past old paper mill and straight ahead through Wookey Hole towards Wells. ⑦ Turn into field on left signposted 'West Mendip Way' and follow signs and waymarks whole way to its end at New Street, Wells. Turn right downhill to reach Union Street car park or walk a few yards uphill to Mountery Road.

✿ The garden and combe of Milton Lodge are open occasionally in spring/summer to raise money for charity.

🏠 The railway coach was converted about 1904 into a summer bungalow by H. E. Balch, distinguished local figure, pioneer of Mendip caving, and the first curator of Wells Museum.

↟ To Glastonbury Tor; Hinckley Point Nuclear Power Station; Brent Knoll, the National Trust property with earthworks and church, and, in clear conditions, the Quantock Hills about 12 miles (19 km) distant.

❀ Bee orchids flower in June and July on the slopes above Wookey Hole.

📷 Wookey Hole Cave, operated by Madame Tussaud's with a variety of additional attractions to the cave itself; a waxworks storeroom, Lady Bangor's fairground collection and the paper mill, with a demonstration of paper-making. All of them can be viewed in an inclusive tour.

🍺 Wookey Hole Inn.

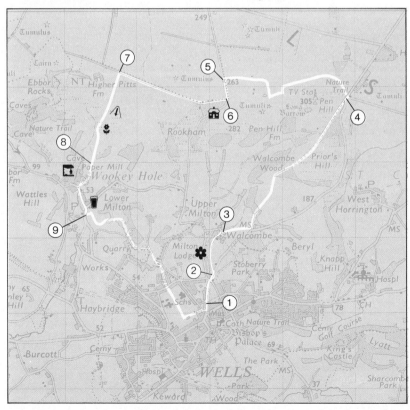

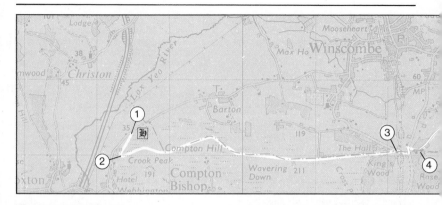

The West Mendip Way
14 miles (22.5 km) Sheet 182 385563

Energetic A section of the long-distance route from Weston-super-Mare to Wells, covering some of the finest Mendip scenery; passes above Cheddar Gorge. *Grassy uplands, drove road, farmland, woods; 4 climbs; mud.*

Start The West Mendip Way guide post by the quarry on the Barton road, close to the M5 SE of Weston; buses from Weston and Wells stop at Winscombe, 2 miles (3 km) from start. **Parking** in the disused quarry.

The West Mendip Way is waymarked by fingerless oak posts at each major change in direction, with ample repeater signs.

① From post by quarry go uphill along track. ② Turn steeply uphill at post labelled Shute Shelve. Continue in same direction across Compton Hill and Wavering Down. (Divert from Compton Hill to summit of peak if desired.) Keeping to left of trig. point, go straight ahead and downhill through King's Wood to road. ③ Through gate and straight ahead to the A38. Turn left and in a few yards cross road to take drove road uphill. ④ Where tracks meet, bear left and continue along drove road. ⑤ Turn left along lane to Winterhead Farm. ⑥ Opposite farm enter field on right and make straight for stone and wooden stile. Continue straight ahead, dropping steeply to track. Cross it, and descend steeply to small stream. Then uphill. ⑦ Bear left uphill, cross stile and continue to road. ⑧ Turn right, cross road and take track uphill following Cheddar sign. Straight ahead through gate. ⑨ At private gate take small gate adjoining it and follow track across mining area. ⑩ Bear left along track and over stile. ⑪ Turn left down lane and out to metalled bridleway. ⑫ Turn right along bridleway uphill. ⑬ Where bridleway turns left, go straight ahead down narrow (often muddy) track to Rowberrow Warren. Continue in same direction, cross stream and follow main track through Forestry Commission ground (labelled 'Public Bridleway to Blackdown'), through gate and on to Tyning's Farm. ⑭ Follow path out of farm and turn left along toad to Charterhouse for about ½ mile (0.8 km). ⑮ Take metalled track on right to Charterhouse Farm and keep to right of farm buildings. Continue straight ahead across 2 cattle grids to top of field. ⑯ Turn left along top edge of field, follow wall and hedge downhill, over stile and down track to Long Wood. ⑰ Cross stile opposite Long Wood entrance and continue along track to Cheddar Gorge. Go straight across road and steeply uphill. ⑱ At top, turn left in a few yards away from Gorge. (To visit Cheddar, follow track running parallel with Gorge.) ⑲ Where paths meet take care to cross over junction and bear left uphill. Follow narrow path downhill looking towards Cheddar church. ⑳ At post part way down, bear left towards wood and keep along path outside wood to entry to Nature Reserve. ㉑ Turn left along track into Nature Reserve and go straight ahead, continuing on track between market gardening fields. ㉒ Bear right, then turn left on to metalled road. Just before junction with main road, ㉓ turn left along grassy track, through gate and up track. ㉔ In a few yards bear left, taking narrow,

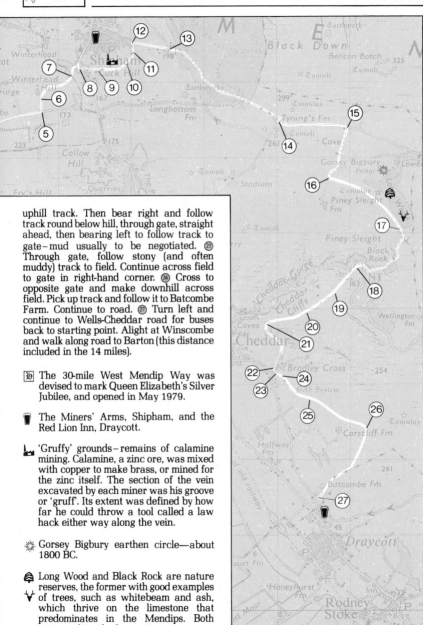

uphill track. Then bear right and follow track round below hill, through gate, straight ahead, then bearing left to follow track to gate – mud usually to be negotiated. ㉕ Through gate, follow stony (and often muddy) track to field. Continue across field to gate in right-hand corner. ㉖ Cross to opposite gate and make downhill across field. Pick up track and follow it to Batcombe Farm. Continue to road. ㉗ Turn left and continue to Wells-Cheddar road for buses back to starting point. Alight at Winscombe and walk along road to Barton (this distance included in the 14 miles).

⑲ The 30-mile West Mendip Way was devised to mark Queen Elizabeth's Silver Jubilee, and opened in May 1979.

🍺 The Miners' Arms, Shipham, and the Red Lion Inn, Draycott.

⛏ 'Gruffy' grounds – remains of calamine mining. Calamine, a zinc ore, was mixed with copper to make brass, or mined for the zinc itself. The section of the vein excavated by each miner was his groove or 'gruff'. Its extent was defined by how far he could throw a tool called a law hack either way along the vein.

❋ Gorsey Bigbury earthen circle—about 1800 BC.

🌲 Long Wood and Black Rock are nature reserves, the former with good examples ⩣ of trees, such as whitebeam and ash, which thrive on the limestone that predominates in the Mendips. Both reserves have badger setts.

MENDIP REGION

Some N Mendip Villages
8½ miles (13.5 km) Sheet 172 633557

Easy Gentle scenery in an interesting and unvisited former mining area. *Pasture, arable farmland, woods; 2 climbs; mud.*

Start Church Lane, Farrington Gurney, at the junction of the A39 and A362; buses from Wells and Bristol. **Car park** in Church Lane.

① Left out of car park; follow road towards church. Through gate, leaving church to left, cross field, over old railway line and straight ahead. ② Half-way across, bear left over stile. Make diagonally across the next stile. Keep near left hedge to next stile; cross and continue slightly uphill, bearing right to far end of field. ③ Through gate, bear left to stile in corner and in next field cross stone 'plank' and stile on left. Turn right, over 2 further stiles, then straight on to gate and on to road. ④ Turn left, then first right into Wells Road, then turn right across river. ⑤ In a few yards turn left along public footpath between houses. Cross stile into copse, over another stile and straight ahead into Greyfields Wood. ⑥ Bear left through wood, cross flat, stone bridge and continue uphill. ⑦ Bear right over stile, cross field into wood again and follow uphill path in same direction to end of wood. ⑧ Turn right along lane, then first left, continuing straight ahead to Maynard Terrace, Clutton. ⑨ At main road turn left over stile (Public Footpath sign), cross stream, cross field to stile by sewage plant, bear slightly right and follow line of telegraph poles. Go through gate on right, across old railway line and straight ahead towards Clutton church. ⑩ Out through gate at Bendall's Bridge and turn right. ⑪ At church car park, turn left into field, go straight across through kissing gate and uphill through 2 further fields to reach the A37. ⑫ Turn right and shortly find footpath sign on left. Follow path through garden. ⑬ Uphill through 3 fields, making for top right-hand corner of third. (Ignore obvious stile in top hedge.) Cross stile near top of right-hand hedge, then across to gate on left. Turn right along edge of field and make for gate. Through it, bear slightly left across field uphill to the farthest corner. Find stile, bear left across corner of next field and keeping along ridge exit into lane at extreme end. ⑭ Turn left down lane. ⑮ At end of lane turn right uphill. ⑯ Left at Coley – Litton

How the colliery at Greyfield (near point ⑤) looked in its heyday: the area had several coal-mines, and some unsightly tips.

signpost and continue to Hinton Blewett green. ⑰ Take the Litton road from Hinton Blewett. ⑱ Take first lane on left and continue to its end. Into field, and straight ahead to footbridge. Straight ahead to stile into wood; cross, follow path through to field and turn right. ⑲ Exit into Pitway Lane and continue to the A37. Turn left, cross and continue along Church Lane to car park.

🏠 The Old Parsonage (about 1700), one of the Mendips' finest houses, now a hotel.

⛪ Clutton's church is 12th C. John Wesley, founder of Methodism, was refused permission to preach inside, so performed from a stone in the graveyard. It is unusual for the staircase leading to the gallery to be outside. The church has a connection with the famous actor Sir Henry Irving – his grandparents William and Elizabeth Brodripp are buried here..

\†/ To Cameley church and fish tanks, with Downside Abbey about 6 miles (9.5 km) beyond. Some of the monks of this Benedictine foundation are schoolmasters at Downside, the Roman Catholic public school associated with the Abbey. The community was started in 1793 by monks from the famous monastery at Douai in France.

🍺 The Ring of Bells – Wadsworth beer.

✗ The Farrington Inn – restaurant.

Cheddar Gorge's limestone cliffs winding 2 miles (3 km) through the Mendip plateau.

The banks of the Bradford-on-Avon to Bath Canal make an intriguing expedition, easy to navigate. The whole length is a substantial day's outing.

Three miles (5 km) N of Congresbury there is a waymarked trail in Brockley Combe, famed for its trees, including an outstanding avenue of limes; leaflet from the Brockley Combe Fruit Stall.

There are 2 waymarked walks in Ebbor Gorge, one through the gorge, one through the woods. Start from the picnic area just off the unclassified road between Easton and Wookey Hole, or from the entrance to Wookey Hole.

Starting on the road E out of Wells, to Dinder, there is a fine waymarked route via Dinder back to Wells.

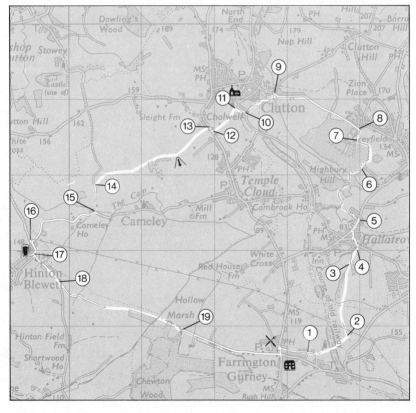

SOUTH-EAST ENGLAND

ISLE OF WIGHT

First-time visitors to the Isle of Wight – locals call it 'the Island' – can be surprised at how well it has survived as a world apart; as a miniature, with cosier neater proportions, of the real-life England across the Solent.

Charles I was imprisoned at Carisbrooke, but the Island's royal connections did not begin in earnest until Queen Victoria bought Osborne. Lord Tennyson settled at Farringford, other Victorian notables followed, and the Isle of Wight became fashionable. The Victorian flavour still lingers, not only in the architecture of the seaside terraces, but in the tempo of life, which moves, even in holiday season, at the tempo of yachting ports and steam trains, against a background of farm- and woodland.

That is the Island's peaceful walking country, crisscrossed with well maintained, energetically signposted footpaths. Because the bus service is so good, it is terrain for the walker who likes improvising; no necessity for circular routes here.

For exhileration, there is the chalk ridge which forms the Island's spine. Walking it has been compared to flying low over the whole landscape, only more exceptional, because of the wild flowers, birds and butterflies.

Godshill
4 miles (6.5 km) Sheet 196 527819

Easy The Island's gentler charms – a picture-book village and impressive 18th C. remains. *Woods, downland, farmland; 3 climbs (one optional); mud after rain.*

Start Godshill, beside the A3020, W of Shanklin; frequent buses. **Public car park** opposite Griffin Hotel.

① With Griffin Hotel on left, follow lane a few yards, then left at footpath sign. Cross

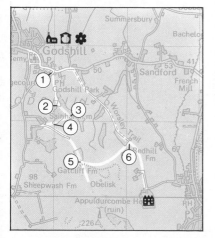

Godshill, probably the most charming and commercialized, of the Island's villages.

field and go along wooded valley. ② Just inside the wood, the path divides. Turn left and follow path uphill, keeping inside the wood. ③ Turn right along cross-track. Go through wood to gate opening into field. ④ Path is not clear, but make across field for farm buildings (Sainham Farm), leaving them to right; cross stile to join lane. Turn left following path signposted 'Gatcliff and Stenbury'. Continue on track across field, then through gate into wood. ⑤ To visit obelisk, go through gate and follow path (unsignposted) to right. To continue, go through wicket gate and take path signposted 'Wroxall and Godshill', following it along stone wall to Freemantle Gate. ⑥ Turn right if visiting Appuldurcombe House, which is about one mile (1.5 km) on. If not visiting house, turn left at gate.

🏠 The church has a rare wall painting of the Crucifixion.

🏠 Two museums – toys, natural history.

✿ Gardens to visit at Old Vicarage (with model village) and Old Smithy (aviary).

🏛 Ruin of Appuldurcombe House, with an elegant 18th C. exterior. Home of the Worsley family, one of whom publicly accused his wife of immorality. She denied taking 34 lovers, claiming it was only 27.

ISLE OF WIGHT

Yarmouth to Freshwater
4 miles (6.5 km) Sheet 196 355895

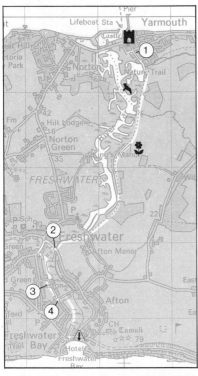

Easy A rewarding introduction to a considerable range of the Island's varied scenery with a happy contrast of bustling town and peaceful woods. *Seaside town, riverside, woods, farmland; mud after rain.*

Start Yarmouth; frequent car ferries from Lymington (on the mainland); frequent buses. **Public car park** at corner of Tennyson and River Roads. **Return** to start by bus – frequent services from Freshwater Bay.

① From car park into River Road, then first right into Mill Road, where there is shortly a footpath sign. Follow this path nearly 3 miles (5 km) ignoring all other signs until ② turn right on to the A3055, crossing bridge, then left into Stroud Road. About 150 yards (137 m) on, follow footpath sign pointing left. Path runs close to a cottage and appears to lead through garden. ③ Cross stile, join road and bear left. ④ Take Blackridge Road a few yards, then path signposted to right, which leads to bay.

🏰 Yarmouth Castle, built in the 1540s by Henry VIII against French raids; grandstand views from the gun platform.

🦅 Wetland birds, including curlews.

🌺 Three fern species grow close to the Wilmingham signpost – hart's tongue, soft shield and broad buckler fern.

\ɬ/ The cliffs are hung with samphire, the plant once popular for relish.

The Island's Roof

12 miles (19 km) Sheet 196 347857

Moderate An easily managed section of the Tennyson Trail, with views giving a superb overall impression of the Island; butterflies and plants at best in summer. *Downland, woods, farmland; 2 climbs.*

Start Freshwater Bay; frequent buses. **Public car park** on bay opposite beach or, if full, off A3055 on Afton Down. **Return** to starting point by bus – frequent service.

From road on top of East Afton Down the walk is waymarked by red flashes on posts and 'Tennyson Trail' signs. ① From car park follow beach towards East Afton Down. Climb wooded steps up cliff and take cliff-top path to road (A3055) where ② cross and take path signposted 'Bridleway'. ③ At gate bear right a few yards along road (B3399) to gate on right. Take path signposted 'Bridleway Newport'. ④ Go through gate into woods and follow wide, grassy track. Keep straight on at next cross-track to gate on to Mottistone Down. ⑤ From car park, bear left along road, then left into lane rising to summit of Brightstone Down. ⑥ Turn left into Brightstone Forest. ⑦ Cross lane and follow path signposted 'Bridleway'.

♣ Chalkland species including clustered bellflower, whose mauve flowers (May-Sept.) are in a distinct cluster.

↟ From Brightstone Down, views in clear conditions of whole island, from Culver Cliff (635854) to St. Catherine's Point (498754) to Freshwater Bay (347856).

✀ At least 5 species of butterfly can be distinguished in this conserved area.

▣ Carisbrooke Castle, probably dating from the late 11th C., and best known as Charles I's place of imprisonment in 1647 – 8 after defeat in the Civil War.

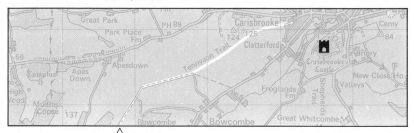

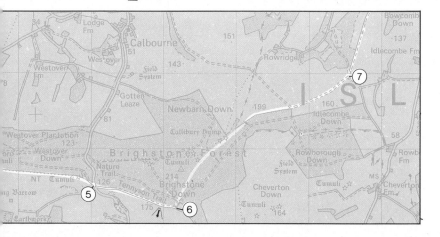

ISLE OF WIGHT

Tennyson Down and the Needles
7 miles (11 km) Sheet 196 347857

Easy The Island's chalk ridge at its most dramatic, with sweeping views of Solent and Channel. *Downland, cliffs, farmland; one climb; keep clear of cliff edge and do not attempt if misty.*

Start Freshwater Bay; frequent buses. **Public car park** in bay opposite beach.

① Leave car park facing sea and turn right along road. After 150 yards (137 m) take path signposted 'Tennyson Down'. Make for the monument, which soon comes into sight. ② Follow path straight on (due W) from monument. It bears slightly right, then through a gate. Continue about 1½ miles (2 km) to fenced areas. ③ Follow signs round fencing to Needles viewing platform. Last few hundred yards is along concrete road. ④ Retrace steps along concrete road to point by coastguards' cottages where road joins from left. Take path signposted 'Alum Bay', leaving road, crossing flagstones and climbing stile by sign. Path curves round grassy cliff, then downhill to road. Follow road to Alum Bay. ⑤ If not visiting bay, continue by path leading right, signposted 'Freshwater Bay' before road drops steeply. Freshwater is about 1½ miles (2 km) on. with Farringford signposted on way. For shorter version, frequent buses run in summer only from Alum Bay to Freshwater Bay.

🌸 Freshwater Bay and St. Catherine's.

'Heads' and stems of the bee orchid (left) and autumn lady's tresses (right).

🦅 Tennyson Down to Alum Bay is a bird sanctuary. At dusk in summer, listen for the weird, dry trills of nightjars – strange birds with moth-like camouflage. Uncommon sea birds nest on the cliffs, including guillemots, razorbills, fulmars and (remarkable for southern England) puffins.

🌸 Orchids found on the chalk downland include bee orchid and lady's tresses.

🏖 Alum Bay's famous sands, coloured by minerals.

🏖 The Needles, chalk eroded by the sea.

🏨 Farringford, now a hotel, where the poet Tennyson lived 40 years from 1853. He wrote several of his most famous works there, including *Idylls of the King,* and loved walking the downs where, he said, 'the air was worth sixpence a pint'.

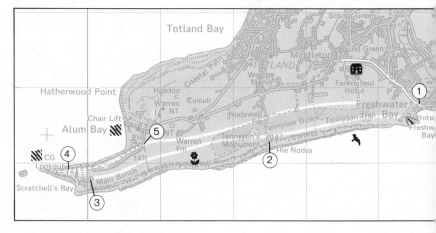

Havenstreet Steam Railway and Arreton

6 miles (9.5 km) Sheet 196 547919

Easy Takes in the Island's authentic steam railway and one of the several fine manor houses; best in May-Sept. – railway run-ning. *Wooded creek, farmland; one climb.*

Start Wootton Bridge, on the A3054 E of Newport; frequent buses. **Parking** in front of Sloop Inn, Wootton Bridge. **Return** to starting point by bus (not possible by steam railway)—frequent service from Arreton to Newport, changing for Wootton Bridge.

① Take the 'Bridle Road' signposted opposite Sloop Inn, with creek on left. Where track divides, bear right on to gravel track. Continue about 1¼ miles (2 km), crossing railway line and farmyard. ② About ¼ mile (0.5 km) past 'Keeper's Cottage' take care to turn left, ignoring track branching right. ③ Pass pond, continuing through gate ahead (not left through farmyard). ④ Turn left at road, continuing about 500 yards (457 m) to visit Steam Railway Centre. Retrace steps to ⑤ track signposted 'Public Bridleway Downend'. Follow this about 1½ miles (2.5 km). ⑥ At Combley Farm fork left leaving farmhouse to right. Track climbs Arreton Down. ⑦ Turn right on to road, then left at Hare and Hounds. ⑧ Take path signposted 'Public Footpath Arreton' on left after quarry. Path is unclear, but make for over-head cables, turning right beneath them. Drop steeply to stile (to right). Cross, go down steps, follow path towards manor.

▌ The Sloop Inn.

🚂 Havenstreet Steam Railway Centre is a well-restored steam-age station with at least one train in running order. Round trips to Wootton take about 30 mins. Open Easter and Sundays, May-Sept., but check–times vary.

⅄ Robin Hill Country Park.

▌ Hare and Hounds.

🎪 Arreton Manor, early 1600s, with 3 ghosts (one a little girl in a blue dress), 🏠 doll's house collection and National ✕ Wireless Museum. Tea room serves lunches. Country Craft Workshop.

🏠 St. George's, dating from pre-Norman Conquest, enlarged in the 12th C.

In addition to the Tennyson Trail, the Isle of Wight County Council has waymarked and signposted 6 other medium to long distance routes: the Worsley, Stenbury, Nunwell, Bembridge, Hamstead and Shepherds Trails. Leaflets describing them are available from local bookshops and stationers.

The Isle of Wight Tourist Board publishes a leaflet describing 6 interesting nature trails.

O.S. Sheet 196 covers whole island.

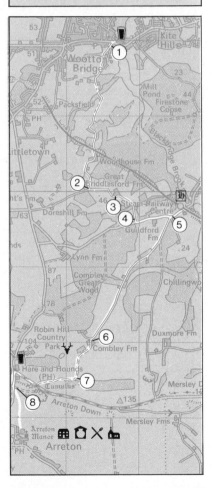

NEW FOREST

A 'forest', yet with wide-open views; dry, adder-haunted heaths and bogs juxtaposed; ancient common rights and the Court of Verderers coexisting with management by a public corporation, the Forestry Commission. The contradictions make this a singular and lovely place, of continually changing colours and shifting centres of interest.

'Forest' means a royal hunting ground, as opposed to a chase, which is a hunting ground, but owned by someone of lesser rank. The New Forest has served the Crown not only for recreation, but militarily: it was a vital source of oaks for the navy. There are plenty of beeches, too, and more recently, for quick profit, the Scots pines and sitka spruce. But the Forest is managed for amenity, rather than profit, and local conservationists are continually on guard against felling of the hardwoods.

Among and around the woodlands are the grassy Forest 'lawns' and the spreading, heather-clad heaths. There is much mud, too (it rarely dries out under the trees) and bogs occupy some 7,000 of the Forest's 92,000 acres (37 ha). They cannot dry out because they lie on top of impermeable geological deposits. The distinctive danger sign of these areas is cotton grass, which has whispy, white tufts in summer.

Under the trees, ones sense of direction departs rapidly; and because the Forest has been lived and worked in for so long, there is a labyrinth of tracks. Careful map-reading is essential. The Ordnance Survey 2½-inch Leisure Map provides much helpful detail.

Rufus Stone
3 miles (5 km) Sheet 195 271125

Easy Peaceful walking close to one of the Forest's most well-known historic sites. *Woods, Forest lawns, heath: one climb; mud.*

Start The Rufus Stone, signposted from the A31 about 1¼ miles (2 km) W of the Cadnam roundabout; frequent buses from Ringwood or Southampton – stop is on A31 near Rufus Stone turning. **Car park** at Stone.

① Leave car park by track marked 'access to cottage'. ② At cottage and shed turn right and make through woods (no obvious path), keeping fence on bank in sight to left. In about 500 yards (457 m), cross the stream and make for houses shortly in view. ③ By houses, bear left along gravel track. ④ Turn left down grassy track, passing house named 'Woodpeckers'. Continue about ½ mile (0.8 km) to ⑤ T-junction, at which turn left along road. At corner skirting garden of 'Walter Tyrell Inn' look for ⑥ Car Free Area barrier on right. Past this, make for track to left of inclosure far right of open ground. Continue straight ahead. ⑦ Path dips to cross stream. Do not cross, instead turning left entering wood where ⑧ just inside, turn left (away from stream), following fringe of trees. After crossing narrow stream and clearing, ⑨ turn right, following overhead cables uphill. Where cables bear right, continue uphill bearing slightly left, through gorse, in about 300 yards (274 m) meeting well-defined track, on to which ⑩ turn left. ⑪ Where

Forest ponies, the well-worn, but apt symbol of these woods, heaths and 'lawns'.

path divides, fork left. When it divides again, bear half left downhill to Stone and car park, at first hidden by trees.

🏦 The Rufus Stone.

🏦 The ancient hamlets of Canterton, which means settlement of the Kentish folk. They were in fact Jutes, the first Saxons to settle the Forest in the mid-5th C.

🍴 The 'Walter Tyrell' contains a mural depicting the killing of Rufus.

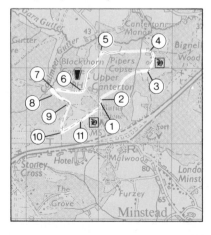

THE NEW FOREST

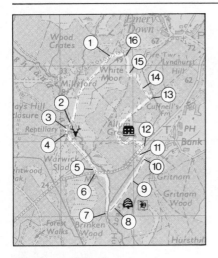

The Heart of the Forest
4 miles (6.5 km) Sheet 195 278081

Easy Reveals the extensive old woods at the Forest's centre; fine glades and a glorious streamside section; best if trees are in full leaf. *Heath, woods, streamside; mud.*

Start near Emery Down, off the A35 W of Lyndhurst. At New Forest Inn (conspicuous in village) take minor road signposted 'Bolderwood, Linwood, Fritham'; frequent buses to Emery Down. **Car park** White Moor Car Park, about ½ mile (0.8 km) from the turning by pub.

① Leave car park by barrier marked Car Free Area. Follow footpath ahead, ignoring all cross-tracks, for about ¾ mile (1 km). ② In sparse wood, path dips, becoming unclear. Continue about 100 yards (91 m) through muddy patches (may be flowing water), looking for ford through large stream. Cross, and make for gate at near right corner of fenced field. ③ Before gate, turn left, following fence to Hollidays Hill Keeper's Cottage. (Reptiliary other side of cottage.) ④ At barrier in front of cottage turn left on to gravel track. Continue through camp site to main road (A35). ⑤ Cross road and through stile by gate opposite, where ⑥ turn left and continue about 200 yards (183 m) to the large stream (Highland Water). Turn right, following bank until ⑦ a footbridge. Cross and bear left following

well-defined track which ⑧ shortly forks – bear left. ⑨ The track forks again – bear left. Continue on main track, which ⑩ turns left, crossrs a stream and meets the A35. ⑪. Cross, turn right and continue 50 yards (46 m) on verge to gate with cattle grid. ⑫ Through gate make for house, walking to left of it, then turning right with gravel track to skirt garden and 2 cottages, soon meeting a high wall. Continue to end of wall, then straight ahead for about ¼ mile (0.5 km). ⑬ About 30 yards (27 m) before bridge over small stream, take faint track on left up a wide, grassy ride. Path soon becomes clearer. ⑭ Where path divides, bear left. ⑮ Cross over intersection. ⑯ Keep left to cross White Moor to car park.

The tiny Dartford warbler, one of the Forest's relatively rare bird species. It has a long, dark tail and frequently perches on gorse, bouncing away erratically when disturbed.

ᛉ Reptiliary; adders and other snakes.

🌲 The oak and beechwoods of Brinken and Gritnam are among the Forest's finest. Until this century they supported several trades – charcoal-burning, woodcutting, swineherding and snakecatching. The most celebrated snakecatcher was Brusher Mills, at the height of his career in the 1890s. He was so-named because he swept snow from Brockenhurst Pond for skaters, but his real living was snakes, sold to zoos, and for medicine. He inhabited a hut in Gritnam Wood made of branches overlaid with turf, and died brokenhearted after finding it destroyed one night.

🏠 Allum House, typical of the pleasant houses built after the railway came.

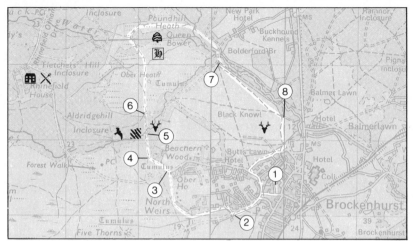

The Queen Bower
6 miles (9.5 km) Sheets 195 and 196 298024

Easy Shows how lush the Forest can be; unforgettable oaks in the Queen Bower, which may be busy in summer. *Village, heath, woods, streamside; mud.*

Start Brockenhurst, on the A337; frequent buses; trains from Southampton and other stops on the London-Bournemouth line. **Public car parks** signposted at village centre.

① From car parks turn into village street, passing shops to reach footbridge and ford. Cross and turn left along the Burley-Ringwood road. ② Take gravel road right, signposted North Weirs. ③ At minor road, turn right for a few yards, then left over the car park at Beachern Wood. ④ Where the gravel track bends right, take path straight on through lightly wooded area. ⑤ Cross footbridge, ignore red waymarking and go through gate a few yards to right. After gate, follow path which bears right. ⑥ Go through gate by Aldridge Hill Cottage. Ignore obvious paths leading to camp site, turning left in front of cottage, crossing a small water course, then right over heath following a well-defined path with water course to right at first. At far side of heath, cross footbridge, climb track edged with shrubs, then cross 2 more bridges and a patch of heath. Go through woods to meet stream (Highland Water); follow it to Boldreford Bridge. Cross

and bear left on to open heath where ⑦ follow edge of wood, striking out across heath when the prominent white building (Cloud Hotel) is in sight on far side. ⑧ Follow minor road in front of hotel right, tracing way back to Brockenhurst centre and car parks.

〰 Oberwater, a typical stream of the central part of the Forest, its water tinged red-brown by the soil's iron content. This and other streams on the walk are typical kingfisher habitats.

⩇ Fallow and roe deer may be sighted.

🏛 Rhinefield House, built 1885 in the then-popular pseudo-Gothic style – battlements, arched doors and mullioned windows. Open to the public; restaurant.

🏠 The Queen Bower owes its name to Queen Philippa, wife of Edward III (died 1377). She admired the oaks' fantastic shapes.

⩇ The ponies graze this heath, as they do others all over the Forest, making the grass characteristically smooth, hence the term Forest 'lawns'. The ponies are descendants of a wild breed peculiar to the Forest and are owned by farmers, breeders and individuals with Common Rights. These are usually attached to houses, date from medieval times and permit grazing and fuel-gathering.

THE NEW FOREST

The Dark Water
2½ miles (4 km) Sheet 196 437017

Easy Unexpected remoteness at the SE edge of the Forest; best in spring for wild flowers. *Heath, woods; mud after rain.*

Start near Blackfield, off the A326 (Southampton-Fawley); take road signposted 'Exbury' near the Hampshire Yeoman pub; frequent buses to Blackfield, stopping near Hampshire Yeoman. **Car park** Blackwell Car Park, ½ mile (1 km) from turning at pub.

① Turn left out of car park onto road, following it over heath towards line of trees. Cross bridge and walk a few yards uphill to car park on right, where ② turn right, walking through parking area, bearing left through the fringe of trees. Look for well-defined path running to right of wire fence. Follow this NW, the Dark Water stream (hidden by trees) in valley to right. ③ Through gate to where path divides, and go straight on, ignoring several paths branching left and continuing ahead at cross-tracks until ④ bear right with track downhill (just after another track joins from left) to bridge over stream. Cross and continue uphill to ⑤ where, just inside inclosure, 4 tracks intersect. Turn right to return on other side of Dark Water valley. ⑥ Leaving the wood, keep ahead for a few yards, then bear right past the small-holding. Walk over heath to road, where ⑦ turn left towards car park. (It is unwise to attempt short cut over heath – boggy patches.)

❧ In late spring this hillside is carpeted with wild flowers, notably violets. The common dog violet predominates: it is relatively large – up to 8 inches (20 cm) high – and may occur in large clumps with 20-30 flowers (April-July), which vary in colour from the typical bluish-purple to white. There are also some of the smaller sweet violets, which have the real, violet scent. Their flowers (Feb.-April) are white through to purple-blue.

📖 The Dark Water stream and valley were a favourite haunt of the naturalist and novelist W. H. Hudson, whose books on the English countryside inspired many during 2 decades from about 1910. His was the apt description of some New Forest streams as being 'the colour of old sherry' – on account of the iron.

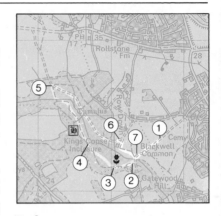

Burley
8 miles (13 km) Sheet 195 212031

Easy History and fine views on the Forest's SW fringe; follows part of a smugglers' way. *Heath, woods; 3 climbs; mud.*

Start Burley, off the A31; frequent buses. **Car park** by the Queen's Head.

① From car park turn right past Queen's Head, bearing right through village along road to Ringwood. ② At footpath sign pointing right join raised path beside road. When it meets road again, cross and continue a few yards. ③ Left over cattle grid and up lane following footpath sign. Near top, follow sign right into wood. ④ Leave wood by stile and turn right along lane. ⑤ Raised circular banks of Burley Hill Fort come into view. Just before it, *look carefully for path running left downhill to right of a gully.* Follow it, keeping gully to left. ⑥ At cross-track turn right and follow this to road from Burley Street to Crow. ⑦ Left along road (crossing stream); in 50 yards (46 m) ⑧ leave road, turning on to first track leading right. ⑨ At choice of 3 ways, take the one bearing right. ⑩ Path divides. Turn left up the hill to a cross-track, where ⑪ turn right and continue to meet a wide grassy track. ⑫ Turn right along this and continue to minor road from Burley Street to Picket Post. ⑬ Cross road and straight on down track ahead. ⑭ At cross-tracks turn right. Follow path down to bridge, then uphill into Ridley Wood. ⑮ Entering wood, look for sunken track on right. Follow it ahead. When it rises to ground level, continue straight on through

Ridley Wood. ⑯ At edge of wood path divides; go straight on over small area of heath, through small wood and over bridge. ⑰ Path divides; keep straight on, then bear left with path to edge of Berry Wood. ⑱ At cross-tracks turn right and walk through edge of Berry Wood. ⑲ A jumble of paths. Follow the one bearing right over the heath towards Turf Croft Cottage, plainly visible ahead. Turn left past cottage and follow track to road over Burley Moor. Here bear right for Burley Street. ⑳ Over crossroads and right past post office. ㉑ A few yards on, turn left over green and walk up Randalls Road. ㉒ Turn left along wide crossing track on top of ridge. ㉓ Track divides; bear right to walk over banks of Burley Hill Fort; rejoin outward route.

In smuggling days, contraband, brought form the coast under Forest cover, was distributed at the Queen's Head.

✕ 16th C. Manor Tea Rooms – cream teas.

The hill fort is Iron Age. Views W to the Avon valley; NW to the Wiltshire Downs and SW (clear days) to Christchurch Priory (160925) and the sea.

The ridge was part of a smugglers' way.

Sunken track: a smugglers' *rendez-vous*?

Magnificent, pollarded beeches: pollarding is cutting off the tops, and produces the many sprouts.

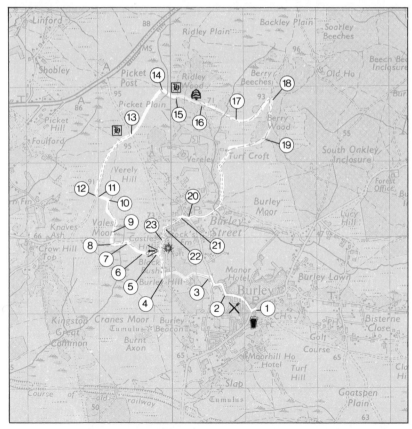

THE NEW FOREST

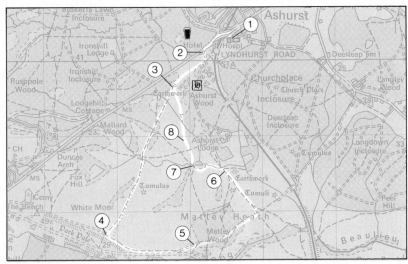

Matley Heath and Wood
6 miles (9.5 km) Sheet 196 336104

Easy Many features of the Forest landscape in quite a short circuit. *Woods, heath, 'lawn', streamside; mud.*

Start Ashurst on the A35; frequent trains to Lyndhurst Road Station, by point ①. **Parking** area near Ashurst Hospital Gates.

① Leave parking area turning right; cross railway bridge. Left down the A35, in about 100 yards (91 m) turning left through gate. After 50 yards (46 m) ② turn right parallel to A35. Soon join poorly-defined track into wood on right. ③ Cross lane leading to Ashurst Lodge, and make for Car Free Area barrier (no distinct path), then keep straight on. ④ At far side of heath, turn left. Continue parallel to road, in about ½ mile (0.8 km) joining gravel track at Forestry Commission 'Denny Wood Chemical Closets' etc. sign. ⑤ Enter wood past barrier, and continue along main track. Leave wood after ½ mile. In 400 yards (366 m) continue over crossing tracks. In 150 yards (137 m) turn left on to smaller crossing track. Continue with track until ⑥, turn left before bridge and follow path parallel to stream over footbridges. Continue 500 yards (457 m) over green, looking for footbridge in trees on right. ⑦ Cross bridge and go straight on with path for 400 yards

Deer can be sighted on most Forest walks, typically where woods or nearby cover meet open heath or grass. Most are fallow deer (left), but there are also roe deer (centre), and, S of the railway, Sika (right). A few red deer remain near Burley.

until ⑧ path divides. Bear right. Continue to meet Ashurst Lodge lane by barrier.

🍴 New Forest Inn; restaurant adjacent.

🏛 Blending of woodland, glades and heath is the essence of Forest scenery. A remarkable survival of medieval landscape into the 20th C., it has changed little since William the Conqueror declared it his personal hunting ground or 'Forest'.

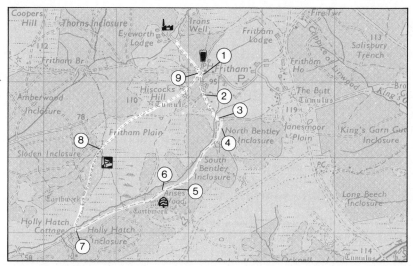

The Valley of Dockens Water
8 Miles (13 km) Sheet 195 232142

Easy Reveals the northern Forest – hilly. *Woods, streamside, heath; one climb; mud.*

Start Fritham, N of the A31 – approach from Cadnam roundabout – other access from A31 blocked. **Car park** past Royal Oak.

① From parking return to Royal Oak and take lane on right leading past houses. ② Where track branches left and path right, carry straight on. ③ Cross green and footbridge, then take the right-hand of the 2 tracks into wood ahead. In about 50 yards (46 m) bear right. Continue about 250 yards (228 m) to locate gate into inclosure on left. ④ Turn right opposite gate and make way through trees, over clearing to stream. Cross and locate inclosure fence on left. Follow fence, bearing right, soon joining fairly well-defined wide path. Continue ¾ mile (1 km). ⑤ *Be extra careful to halt in first sizeable clearing* (after inclosure fence has borne away left, and passing 2 square posts on left). In clearing, path peters out. Cross bearing right to locate narrow, gravel path other side of trees, climbing a few yards. Follow it on to sparsely wooded hillside. Continue to Anses Wood, ahead. ⑥ Several paths in wood but continue with Dockens Water to right. Cross small stream, then locate inclosure fence to left. Follow it, along grassy path, to Holly Hatch Keeper's Cottage. ⑦ Cross footbridge, follow track uphill and through Sloden Inclosure. ⑧ Leave inclosure to follow track over heath to car park. ⑨ For extension to Eyeworth Pond, left along road.

🌳 Gigantic beeches with ingrowths – branches growing back into the trunk or each other.

▧ Evidence of a Roman Pottery.

🍺 A typical old Forest pub.

⚒ Eyeworth, once site of gunpowder works.

O.S. 1:25,000 Tourist maps give helpful detail of this often confusing area.

Waymarked by the Forestry Commission: 3 walks from Bolderwood Car Park; 3 from Rhinefield Ornamental Drive Car Park; one from Puttles Bridge; one from Wilverley Inclosure on the A35.

Also try the Riverside Walk from Beaulieu to Bucklers Hard (leaflets from newsagent in village street); and walking beside the railway, leaving the car at a station, returning by train.

THE WESSEX DOWNS

Four chains of chalk hills are united in this section. From the east come the North and South Downs, from the south-west the chalk hills of Dorset and from the north-east the Chilterns. They all merge into, or closely adjoin, the chalk hills of either Hampshire, Berkshire or Wiltshire – the central chalkland of the country. In the physical sense, it is as close as anywhere to perfect walking. The turf is springy underfoot. The hills are not too high, but high enough to open spreading views. The slopes are not too steep, but steep enough for the walker to appreciate the good sense of the prehistoric folk whose tracks stick firmly to the tops and so provide mile on mile of ridge walking.

Of these tracks the Ridgeway is only the best known. It can be traced all the way to the Dorset coast in the south and to Norfolk in the opposite direction. Ridgeways were the usual routes of these old cultures, as is indicated by the monuments of Avebury, Stonehenge, the White Horse above Uffington and a mass of tumuli.

Then there are the valleys, whose chief charms are the chalk streams, admirably blending all the best qualities of rivers – hurrying sometimes, and at others slowing contemplatively.

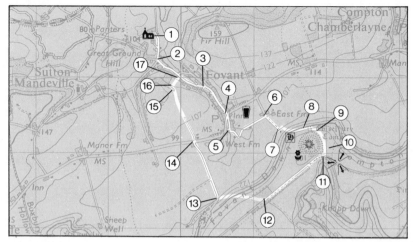

The Nadder Valley
4 miles (6.5 km) Sheet 184 997296

Moderate A delightful village, with the chance to visit others; majestic ridge walk with grand views from Chiselbury Hill Camp; regimental badges carved in chalk hillside. *Farmland, downland; one climb; mud after rain.*

Start Fovant, signposted from the A30 W of Wilton; in village turn left at Y-junction and right along lane to church; frequent buses. **Parking** near church.

① Walk away from church following lane towards Fovant. ② Bear left through village towards A30. ③ Turn right to the A30. ④ Cross the A30 and follow the lane ahead, just to the right of the Cross Keys Hotel. ⑤ Walk a few yards down lane on right to see lake where the Fovant stream rises. Retrace to original route. ⑥ The lane curves left towards the grey stone house (East Farm); immediately past house turn right down short track to go through iron gate. The route ahead (to Chiselbury Hill Fort) can be seen clearly here – from ⑧ it is obscured. Continue straight ahead towards the down, hedge on the right, then left to side of Chalk Pit. ⑦ Bear left round the Chalk Pit. ⑧ Path peters out. Continue uphill a few yards to fence and embankment of Chiselbury Hill Fort beyond. ⑨ Get on top of embankment and follow it to the left. ⑩ Where

embankment curves right, go straight on over grass to opening in fence. ⑪ Go through opening and turn right to walk along ridge track. In about ½ mile (0.8 km) ⑫ turn right to cross stile beside gate. Continue along path down grassy clearing, through a thicket to a steep grassy track which descends. ⑬ Cross stile and turn right along lane leading to A30. ⑭ Cross road and continue on track straight ahead. ⑮ Path divides – bear left. ⑯ Turn right to cross stile and walk down field to gate. ⑰ Through gate and continue along lane. Turn left to rejoin outward route and continue to ①.

🛉 Fovant's beautiful 15th C. church contains several delights, including a memorial brass recalling the building of the tower by Sir George Rede, rector in 1495. The priest's doorway is exquisitely carved.

🍺 The Cross Keys.

🔲 The famous military badges were carved by troops training in the area during the 1914-18 War; details on noticeboard in Fovant village.

Chiselbury Camp, a particularly fine example of an Iron Age Hill Fort, dates from about 800 B.C., but its site, the Ridgeway, is up to 2,000 years older. In early summer the embankments are golden with cowslips; views all round.

THE WESSEX DOWNS

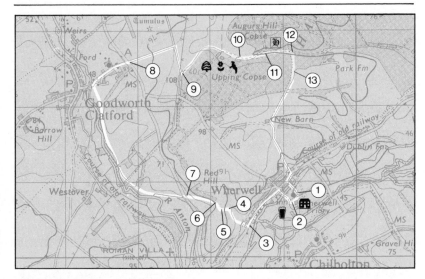

Wherwell, the Test and the Anton
5 miles (8 km) Sheet 185 392408

Easy Access to the Hampshire chalk streams is not always straightforward, but this route takes in some characteristically lovely stretches: also some remote woods. *Stream- and riversides, downland.*

Start Wherwell, off the A303. From war memorial take lane to church; buses. **Parking** area near church entrance.

① From parking turn left through church gate to walk round church, church on right. ② Go through gate, turn right up lane, then next left. ③ Turn right under railway arch, following direction of bridleway sign. (Ignore footpath sign just before it on right.) ④ At top of field follow path left. ⑤ Follow path as it bears right between hedges – Anton valley on left. ⑥ Go through gate and continue over side of down (path indistinct), woods to the right, fence on left until reaching bridleway sign. Follow its direction downhill to gate leading to A3057. ⑦ Cross road and go through gate opposite. Follow direction of bridleway sign. Turn right at road, passing church. ⑧ Cross A3057 and take the straight track immediately ahead. Turn right at T-junction. ⑨ Take care, just before reaching wood, to leave the broad track and turn left along footpath running beside the wood

(wood on right). ⑩ Just past cottage on the right, join concrete track. ⑪ Where the concrete track turns left, follow path as it bears slightly right following direction of footpath sign along valley. ⑫ Just before the gate, turn right up the hill. ⑬ Leaving the wood, turn right, then follow path round the wood (wood on right). Continue to village.

🏛 The 17th C. house to the left of the churchyard stands on the site of Wherwell Priory, a Benedictine nunnery. It was founded in 986 by Queen Elfrida, widow (and second wife) of King Edgar, to amend for the murder of her stepson King Edward. Her motive, it is assumed, was to make way for her son by her previous marriage.

🍺 The White Lion.

🌳 Harewood Forest has spacious glades of oak and beech where the scent of bluebells can be almost overwhelming in April–June. Nightingales nest here, particularly in thickets at the fringes of the wood. They generally sing at night, but it is possible to hear them by day, too.

🗿 The obelisk records a connected murder, that of Earl Athelwold by King Edgar; Athelwold 'perfidiously' married Elfrida, Edgar's intended bride.

Burghclere
2½ or 4½ miles (4 or 7 km) Sheet 174 471611

Easy For little effort, an excellent introduction to much that is typical of the gentle, rolling Wessex countryside; also, a chance to see the Stanley Spencer murals in Sandham Memorial Chapel. *Woods, farmland; mud.*

Start Burghclere, off the A34 5 miles (8 km) S of Newbury: frequent buses. **Parking** turn right at the war memorial and park on left in a few yards just before village hall.

① Walk away from village hall past war memorial to minor road ahead. ② Cross and follow path through trees, over stile and across field. Cross stile and turn left along track to minor road. ④ Turn left and continue to crossroads. ⑤ To see Memorial Chapel turn right, cross bridge and continue a few yards to brick building on right set back from road. Retrace to crossroads. ⑥ Continue down road signposted Ecchinswell. After 300 yards ⑦ turn right through gate.⑧ Through gate turn left to walk along disused railway track. In about ½ mile (0.8 km) ⑨ where lane runs close to track, turn off track to lane, leaving a house to the left. ⑩ Turn right and follow lane to Y-junction where ⑪ bear left for a few yards crossing stream and going uphill (as for Ecchinswell). ⑫ Turn left along the track opposite road junction. ⑬ Turn left and follow the track as it approaches Earlstone Manor Farm. ⑭ Turn right through gate, leaving farm on left, cross field and go through gate to rejoin track; follow it one mile. ⑮ Cross road and follow road signposted Highclere back to ①. For a 2-mile (3 km) extension, do not leave railway track but follow it to Old Burghclere. Then follow bridleways to rejoin route at ⑪.

🏠 Stanley Spencer called on his experience as a private soldier in the 1914-18 War to conceive this moving and important wall painting sequence. Private generosity enabled the chapel to be purpose-built to house the work, which was completed in 1923-32. The canvas had to be woven in Belgium: no English loom was large enough. The name Sandham recalls the donor's brother, who died after serving in Macedonia, a landscape depicted in several of the murals. Keys are obtained from either of the almshouses.

'Filling Waterbottles' – one of the 19 Stanley Spencer murals in the Sandham Memorial Chapel. They show the ordinary soldier's experience of war.

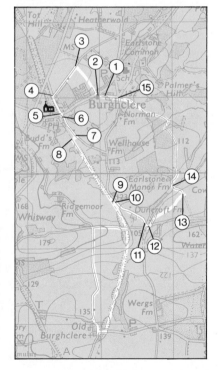

THE WESSEX DOWNS

Inkpen
6 miles (9.5 km) Sheet 174 370620

Easy Apart from the obvious attractions – fine old houses and churches, spectacular views, ancient woods, the highest chalk hill in England – this area has a wealth of folklore. Best on clear days for long views. *Downland, farmland, woods, village, one climb; mud after rain.*

Start From Inkpen follow signs for Combe and Linkenholt. After climbing steep hill, the road divides (left for West Woodhay, straight on for Combe); frequent buses to Inkpen. **Parking** where road divides, by hill fort. If full, there is another parking area 50 yards (46 m) up track to Combe Gibbet. Alternatively, the landlord of The Swan Inn, Inkpen, allows walkers to use his car park if it is not full – 'phone first, Inkpen 326.

Smooth, rolling Wessex chalkland, from the ridge path near Walbury Hill Fort.

① From car park follow direction of sign for 'Wayfarers' Walk' along gravel track. (It crosses the fort.) ② Where track meets metalled lane, keep straight on. ③ Turn left following lane signposted East Woodhay. ④ At cross-track turn left and follow path at first straight ahead down field, then curving right past farm. ⑤ At road turn left for West Woodhay. ⑥ At T-junction turn left for Inkpen and Combe. ⑦ Just after lane turns left round Great Farm, follow track on right. ⑧ Track meets road (Crown on left) – go straight across. ⑨ Follow path ahead as it bears slightly left. ⑩ In about 50 yards (46 m) path divides at a large stone. Continue leaving stone to left – no obvious path but keep straight ahead, crossing 2 streams. ⑪ Emerge from wood on to road. Cross. ⑫ Follow track straight ahead ⑬ Turn right along lane and walk past old school to meet road. ⑭ Turn left and follow road (Weaver's Lane) into Inkpen, turning left – Upper Inkpen/Gibbet. ⑮ Turn right – Inkpen church. ⑯ Turn left

THE WESSEX DOWNS

– sign for Ham. ⑰ Turn left at footpath sign towards the down and follow drover's road straight ahead. ⑱ At foot of down cross stile and bear slightly right uphill. ⑲ Meet ridged track and turn left to follow this to top of down. ⑳ Go through gate and turn left along track running along ridge top. Pass over Inkpen Hill (or Beacon) past Combe Gibbet to ①.

⁂ The magnificent Walbury Iron Age hill fort: 80 acres (32 ha) of hill top lie within its mile-round ramparts.

☘ Look for the corner of delicate white and silver plants in the charming memorial garden beside the church.

🏠 The gardens of the rectory beside the church garden were designed by Le Notre, who laid out the gardens of Versailles for Louis XIV. The terraces to the W are probably the site of the original Saxon settlement, Inga's Pen.

The rectory itself was built by Colwall Brickenden in 1695.

🏠 Inkpen's church was probably founded in the 13th C. by Roger de Ingpen, whose ancestors may well have received their lands from Hardicanute, son of the famous Canute. De Ingpen's tomb can be seen N of the high altar. Above the 13th C. font is a sculpture by the New Forest artist, Ron Lane.

🍺 The Swan – real ale.

⁂ Clear traces of Wansdyke, the great earth wall which ran 80 miles (129 km) from here to the Bristol Channel.

\!/ On clear days 9 counties may be seen.

⑲ Combe Gibbet: the original was erected in 1676 to hang George Broomham and his mistress, who murdered Broomham's wife.

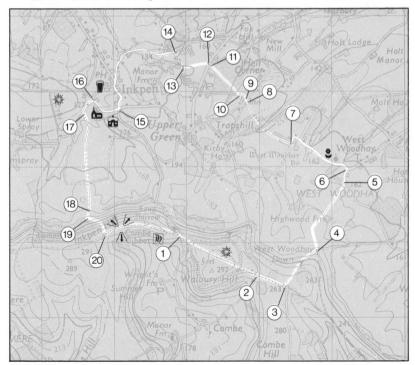

THE WESSEX DOWNS

The Ridgeway
6½ miles (10.5 km) Sheet 174 265851

Easy An introduction to the Ridgeway long-distance path and some of its most famous features. The Ridgeway is popular, so choose an off-peak time if possible. *Downland, farmland; one climb; the chalk is slippery after rain and sticks to footwear.*

Start Ashbury, on the B4000. In village turn on to the B4507 and look for Rose and Crown; frequent buses. **Parking** Rose and Crown car park.

① From car park turn right and walk along road to its junction with the B4000 (Lambourn Road) where ② turn right and continue a few yards. ③ Turn right at Ridgeway sign and follow the path through the gate up the hill. ④ At the double lines of quickset (small thorn trees) bordering the Ridgeway, turn left and follow the wide track for just over 2 miles (3 km). ⑤ Pass the embankments of Uffington Castle on left, ignoring first footpath sign on left. Turn left at the second footpath sign towards the Castle. ⑥ Follow the embankment round (grassy area of Castle centre on left) but do not descend the hill. ⑦ When the embankments turn left, leave them and turn right (past 2 isolated thorn trees) and walk a few yards along the down for a magnificent view of The Manger and Dragon Hill; also portions of the White Horse. ⑧ Retrace steps along Ridgeway about one mile (1.5 km) until reaching the cross-lanes just before Wayland's Smithy. ⑨ Turn right along the metalled track. ⑩ Cross the B4057 (The Icknield Way) and carry straight on following the sign to 'Compton Beauchamp at foot of hill'. ⑪ Turn left along the lane to the right of Compton House leading to the church. ⑫ Go through wicket gate just to right of church gate and walk up field to farm gate ahead. ⑬ Go through gate, turn

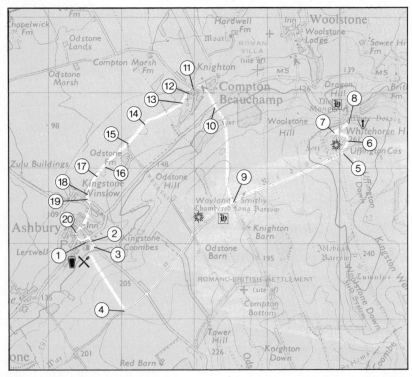

half right and cross next field, leaving corner of wood on right and clump of trees on hilltop well over to left. Continue on this line diagonally to cross 2 fences, looking ahead for small gate in corner of second field. (Path is indistinct.) ⑭ Go through gate, and with fence on left, follow field edge to cross stiles either side of a bridge. ⑮ Pass farm leaving it to left and continue through all gates, going straight ahead until line of power cables comes into view. ⑯ Bear left to follow line of power cables, crossing 2 stiles to fence on left. ⑰ Go straight on, fence on left, power cables on right; the path soon becomes a wide, fenced way. ⑱ Cross track by 2 stiles and continue round slightly left to go through a gate (marked with yellow diamond footpath sign) to join lane running through Kingstone Winslow. ⑲ From the gate turn left, then almost immediately right down small lane crossing a stream and rising to Ashbury. ⑳ Turn left, then left again for the Rose and Crown.

▮ Rose and Crown – try the home-made steak and kidney pie or mussels with ✕ shrimps and garlic.

※ Wayland's Smithy, a Neolithic barrow or burial mound; legend told that Wayland, smith to the Saxon gods, would shoe a horse left with a coin by the tomb.

🔟 The Ridgeway (see pp. 328-34), possibly the oldest road in Europe, could date from before the last Ice Age – about 11,000 B.C.

※ Uffington, a fine hill fort – 500 B.C.

\†/ The early chapters of *Tom Brown's Schooldays* are set among these downs.

🔟 Where St. George killed the dragon.

The White Horse's date and manner of carving remain a mystery.

THE WESSEX DOWNS

The Avon Valley and Stonehenge
5 miles (8 km) Sheet 184 149411

Easy An exciting, unusual way to approach Stonehenge: the monument is directly ahead for more than a mile (1.5 km), growing in stature constantly. Visits other Neolithic remains, too, which add to the picture of this awe-inspiring centre of the great prehistoric culture of North Wessex. Best out of holiday season – fewest crowds. *Town, wooded riverside, downland; one climb; path may be overgrown between ⑦ and ⑨ – easily trodden down, but footwear to protect the ankles against nettles is advised.* Stonehenge is open 15th March-15th October, 9.30-6.30; 16th October-14th March 9.30-4.00. Sundays vary. Closed Christmas Eve, Boxing Day, New Year's Day, May Day. Modest entry fee.

Start Recreation Road, Amesbury, which is a lane leading from the corner of Church and Stonehenge Roads; frequent buses – from bus station turn left, left again past church and abbey, then cross river. First left is Recreation Road. **Car park** off Recreation Road in front of playground. *Optional return to start from Stonehenge by bus, last one leaving at 4.30 p.m.*

① From car park turn left and follow lane to cross Avon by 2 bridges. ② At cross-tracks keep straight on in direction of sign for Durnford. ③ Go through iron gate *but do not follow obvious track straight ahead.* Turn right and walk around edge of field, passing mound on left, reaching gate on right. ④ Turn left (back to the gate) and follow the valley (do not go uphill) with stream, then wider expanse of water, on right. ⑤ Straight on through small wood of willow trees. ⑥ Turn right over small wooden bridge. ⑦ From bridge follow path as it bears right for about 50 yards (46 m) (may be overgrown). ⑧ Follow path left to cross bridge over Avon. ⑨ Cross stile and follow path ahead a few yards then left to pass house. ⑩ Go through gate and turn right to follow lane to minor road. ⑪ Turn left and follow road for ¼ mile (0.5 km) until just before Wilsford church. ⑫ Turn right up well-defined track between 2 thatched cottages. ⑬ Follow track, passing Springbottom Farm on right. ⑭ Follow wide, grassy way which leads uphill between fences – Stonehenge directly ahead. ⑮ Turn right and follow A303 to junction with A344. ⑯ Turn left and continue to car park for entry to the monument. Either walk back to Amesbury following footpath beside the A303, taking the first right which leads to Recreation Road; or take a bus.

🏛 The church is mainly Norman and Early English, with a well-carved roof.

🏛 There is nothing quite like Stonehenge anywhere else in the world. Exactly why these massive stones were transported, carved and set upright in these formations remains a matter for speculation. Some of the stones come from the Preseli Hills in S Wales – 135 miles (217 km) away. The place seems to have been devoted, at least partly, to sun worship. On midsummer's day the sun rises in line with the axis of the avenue leading into the monument. Recently experts have shown that the circle's positioning may have made it useful for certain astronomical observations. It was probably a burial place, too.

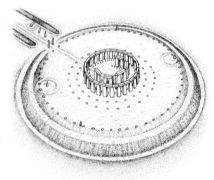

The majesty of Stonehenge now, and how it may have looked to those who used it as a cathedral, burial place, observatory and landmark up to 4,000 years ago. Its age is uncertain, but some authorities put its earliest form, a simple, circular, wooden building surrounded by a ditch and a few stone posts, as early as 2800 B.C. Around 800 years later, it could have looked more or less complete; but it seems that reconstruction and refinement took place over a further 900 years. The largest stone upright is 21 feet (6.5 m) high and sunk 8½ feet (2.5 m) below the ground. The larger blocks are sarsen sandstone, the smaller granite 'blue' stones.

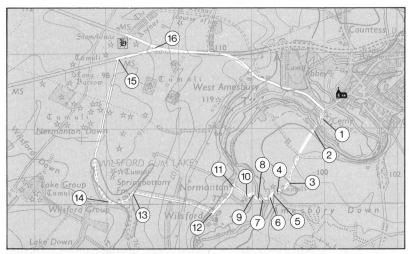

THE WESSEX DOWNS

Cranborne Chase
9 miles (14.5 km) Sheet 184 944178

Moderate With its hanging woods, the Chase has a special charm. A historic village and some fine ridge walking; one magical path descending from the Ridgeway between arms of woodland. *Village, downland, woods; one climb; mud.*

Start Tollard Royal on the B3081; seasonal buses. **Parking** area just past left bend of B3081 (when approaching from Ringwood), on right.

① From parking area follow bridleway on right (no sign) uphill, wall at first on left, thatched cottage on right. ② Continue straight on to signpost at top of down, ignoring all side tracks – not quite 2 miles (3 km). ③ For optional extension to Win Green (highest point of Chase: fine views) follow direction of the sign along the grassy track ahead; retrace to this point, then continue straight on along minor road 25 yards (23 m) beyond sign on left. ④ If not visiting Win Green, turn right at signpost and follow road along top of down. ⑤ Where road turns left continue straight on in direction of sign for 'Rushmore only – past 'No Through Road' sign. ⑥ Where road bears right (slightly downhill) continue straight on along grassy track. ⑦ Straight on along Ridgeway for about 1½ miles (2.5 km). ⑧ Look for large, derelict building on right at head of a valley. Turn right and follow the track just past it, dipping towards woods. ⑨ At iron gate and joining track on left keep to main track as it bears slightly left at first. ⑩ Track divides – continue straight ahead along valley bottom. ⑪ Pass house on left and just before reaching road *turn right* to follow path uphill. ⑫ Path divides – bear slightly left along edge of wood. ⑬ Follow track into woods. Keep to main track, straight on over all cross-tracks. (Occasional waymarks – yellow blobs on trees.) ⑭ Cross beech avenue and follow track ahead (yellow dot on beech to left). ⑮ Cross over well-defined track and keep straight on. ⑯ A more open area to the left, wood on right. ⑰ Turn left at cross-tracks (not on map) – yellow blob on trees to left. ⑱ Cross over track, go through iron gate and go straight on over field – hedge close on right. ⑲ Leave gate into park on right and cross over track to walk along edge of field (trees on right) for a few yards. ⑳ Turn left at

corner of field and follow edge of field (trees on right). ㉑ Where path bears left, look carefully for gate into wood on right (marked by yellow blob). Turn right through it. ㉒ Ignore first path on left and continue to cross-track. Turn left and follow path slightly downhill (yellow blobs). ㉓ At cross-track (not on map) bear left. ㉔ Cross metalled lane and go over stile into field ahead. (No path here.) Turn half right to cross avenue of beeches. Continue down field towards power cables (on right) to iron gate. ㉕ Go through gate and follow wide drive to B3081. ㉖ Turn left for ①.

⛪ Contains a startlingly detailed effigy of a crusader knight, Sir William Payne.

🌂 Over Dorset and Hampshire.

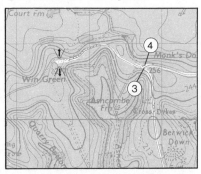

Combe Hill, 5 miles (8 km) SE of Hungerford, is a focal point for several downland walks.

The prehistoric barrows on the downs just N of Lambourn are an easy and satisfying objective.

Some 5 miles N of Romsey on the A3057 the area around Horsebridge and Marsh Court gives some easy walking in the Test Valley.

Postern Hill, among the beech avenues of the Savernake Forest (off the A346), offers secluded paths and nature trails; and of course the whole of Savernake Forest is an honoured strolling ground.

There are several interesting trails around the prehistoric hill fort of Cadbury Castle. Approach via A303 7 miles (11 km) NE of Yeovil.

Cranbourne Chase was formerly a thickly wooded royal hunting ground of about 100 square miles (259 square km). The rights passed from James I to the Earls of Salisbury to the Earls of Shaftesbury and finally the Pitt-Rivers family, who lived at Rushmoor House.

An avenue of 500-year-old beeches. They are pollarded – meaning the heads were cut off to provide, among other things, feed for deer. The practice produced the many sprouting branches.

A museum of chimney pots at Chase Cottage opens on Saturdays and Sundays. Opposite is a 300-year-old well.

King John's Arms.

King John's House (13th C., restored 1889) was a hunting lodge and suggests why the village is 'Royal': King John frequently came here to take advantage of the hunting.

About a mile S of the village are the Larmer Tree Grounds, so-named because of the larmer tree or wych elm growing there which was a favoured meeting place for the hunt and for the administrative and judicial assemblies known as court leets. The tree blew down in a storm in 1894, to be replaced by an oak. More recently, the late General Pitt-Rivers turned the area into a public garden, with an entertaining collection of follies in the oriental style and an impressive little theatre.

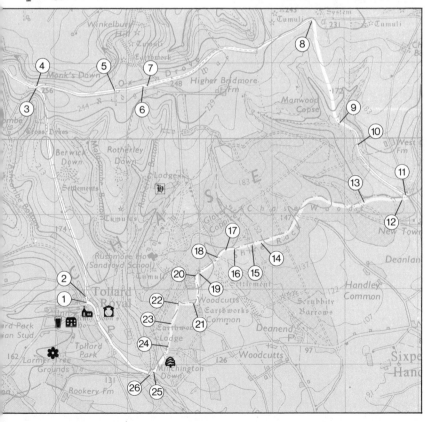

SOUTH DOWNS

The dimpled, chalk hills of the South Downs stretch in a
nearly unbroken chain a full 60 miles (97 km) from Old
Winchester Hill in Hampshire to the sea at Beachy Head
in East Sussex. Once they were mown short by sheep but
today the ploughs creep far up the slopes and often right
over the spine (carrying the South Downs Way) so that
walkers are as likely to be threading a thin path through
wheat as treading springy turf.

This is walking with wide views. To the south, the
Channel, and the north, what Kipling called the 'wooded,
dim, blue goodness of the Weald'. Walkers who find the
downland chalk sticky in winter need only try the
Wealden clay for something that really clings to the
boots.

- While the Weald was still waste, the Downs were
being settled, as testified by the Neolithic flint mines (for
example at Cissbury and Findon) and the earthworks of
'beaker' and later folk. Millions of the flints are now
embedded in the walls of the area's villages and
churches. But note how very few of these settlements are
on the downs. Nearly all lie crushed between the hills
and the sea, or along the spring line to the north. The
result is that, despite trains from London, these downs
offer the loneliest walking in the south-east.

Eartham and Stane Street
5½ miles (9 km) Sheet 197 940106

Easy For a change with ancient sites, there is plenty to see on the ground. *Downland, woods; mud; path across field on Long Down between ③ and ④ may be ploughed out.*

Start About 4 miles (6.5 km) S of Duncton on the A285 take the minor road to Eartham, in ½ mile (0.8 km) looking for car park on left; buses along A285. **Car park** the Eartham Wood Forestry Commission car park.

① From car park turn left on to road and in 150 yards (137 m) turn right across stile at corner. Head SW along Stane Street. ② Turn left along A285. In 275 yards (251 m), turn back left along woodland track. ③ At end of wood bear *slightly* right over open downland, crossing low summit. ④ Through swing gate. Follow line of conifers to Eartham. ⑤ Turn left, then right at George Inn. In 100 yards (91 m) fork left on downhill track. In ½ mile turn left, walking on inside edge of wood. In 150 yards (137 m) turn right. In another 150 yards turn right to join bridleway path. In 200 yards (183 m) turn left. Soon join farm track. ⑥ With folly in sight to left, turn left, and continue uphill, keeping left of reservoir, following fence to

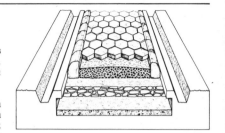

Roman road construction: a typical width, as of Stane Street, was 25 feet (7.6 m).

ruined folly ⑦ and trig. point. ⑧ Bear left into wood and follow forest ride, ignoring side tracks. ⑨ Fork right downhill by massive tree stump. ⑩ Turn right. ⑪ Where woodland ends, turn left. ⑫ At meeting of 6 ways, turn left; follow Stane Street to ①.

🔲 Stane ('Stone') Street was the Roman road running from Chichester to London in just 4 straight sections.

⛪ Eartham church has a memorial to William Huskisson, the famous M.P. for Chichester killed at the opening of the Liverpool-Manchester Railway – the first rail death.

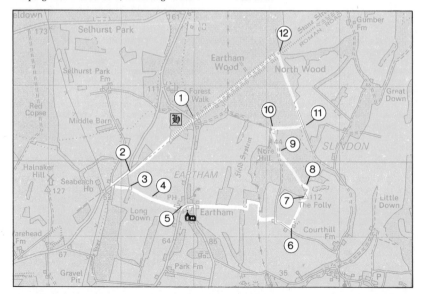

SOUTH DOWNS

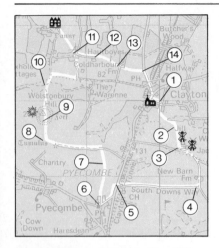

Clayton Mills and Wolstonbury Hill
5 miles (8 km) Sheet 198 300140

Moderate A pleasant variation of down and weald. *Downland, farmland; one climb; mud.*

Start Clayton, off the A273 N of Pyecombe; **Cark park** at Clayton Green – entrance 150 yards (137 m) E of Clayton church.

① Go through farm gate opposite car park entrance. Follow boundary on left uphill, continuing in sunken track bearing left. ② On emerging on to open downland, bear half left between clumps of trees, then follow sunken gully uphill to gate into Clayton Mills car park. ③ At far end of car park turn left on to rough track (bridleway) and at 2 forks keep right, continuing to top of rise beyond New Barn Farm. ④ Turn right following South Downs Way downhill to A273. ⑤ Cross road and turn left on to path behind hedge, then turn right on to road to Pyecombe church. ⑥ At road junction near church turn right on to rough track becoming enclosed bridleway and follow it to crest of hill. ⑦ Ignore crossing path, then turn left on to crossing track and, ignoring left fork, follow track to top of ridge. ⑧ Just over top, turn right on to signposted footpath to stile on to Wolstonbury Hill. ⑨ Bear half left through bushes to triangulation post then bear half right to join path descending steeply into wood towards Danny House. ⑩ In wood, bear half right for stile, then go straight on, turning right in 100 yards (91 m),

eventually reaching road and turning left. ⑪ To inspect Danny House, turn left by Victorian post box on to footpath through copse and go straight on across field to house.) To continue walk, retrace to road. A few yards further, turn right on to concrete drive. ⑫ At Hautboyes, keep left of outbuildings and go straight on across 2 fields to reach track. ⑬ Turn sharp right on to track, then immediately left to follow hedge to A273. ⑭ Turn right along A273, then left into Underhill Lane.

🏠 Clayton's church, listed in Domesday Book, has murals painted about 1150.

✠ The mills – 'Jack and Jill' worked to 1908.

✺ The earthwork is Iron Age.

♨ The 1918 Armistice agreement was drawn up at Danny House.

Cissbury and Chanctonbury
9½ miles (15 km) Sheet 198 179112

Moderate Visits the South Downs' 2 most famous historic sites, and Steyning, well worth exploring. *Downland; one climb; mud.*

Start Steyning, on the A283; frequent buses. **Car Park** in Church Street.

① From White Horse at S end of Steyning's main shopping street, take road signposted to police station straight on out of town. ② Leave road at Pepperscombe House and take path straight on into copse. Go straight on uphill ignoring all forks to right, then just past top of quarry join bridleway bearing slightly right. ③ At seat, turn right, then, by clump of bushes, follow fence straight on to 5-way junction. ④ Turn right crossing South Downs Way on to fenced track and follow it to bottom of dip. ⑤ Turn left on to track down valley bottom and follow it for one mile (1.5 km) to T-junction. ⑥ Turn right on to rough track and follow it to car park at top of rise. ⑦ For the Ring, turn left and climb. ⑧ Retrace steps to car park, take track straight on through it and continue for ⅔ mile (one km) ignoring crossing bridleway. ⑨ At second crossways, turn left on to track and in 200 yards (183 m) fork right and follow enclosed bridleway straight on for ¾ mile (one km) passing house. ⑩ One hundred and fifty yards (137 m) past house turn right through gate and bear half left, soon crossing road and continuing straight on to join chalky lane. Follow this straight on to ridge-top crossways. ⑪ Turn right on to wide track and follow it straight on, later joining South Downs Way for 1¾ miles (3 km) to Chanctonbury Ring. ⑫ Continue straight on for further ½ mile (0.8 km) to track junction. ⑬ Bear half left and follow South Downs Way for ⅓ mile (0.5 km) to right bend. ⑭ Turn left on to signposted bridleway following fence on left to wood, then turning right to follow edge of wood to second signposted path into it. ⑮ Turn left on to path down through wood to open hillside, keeping straight on to reach Steyning.

✻ Cissbury Ring is a massive Iron Age hill fort on the site of Neolithic flint mines.

🅱 The (restored) dew pond is an example of the ponds made to water sheep and replenished by dew and mist.

Chanctonbury Ring is an oval, Iron Age rampart dating from 300 B.C. which once enclosed a camp. The beeches inside the rampart were planted by a local landowner, Charles Goring, in 1760.

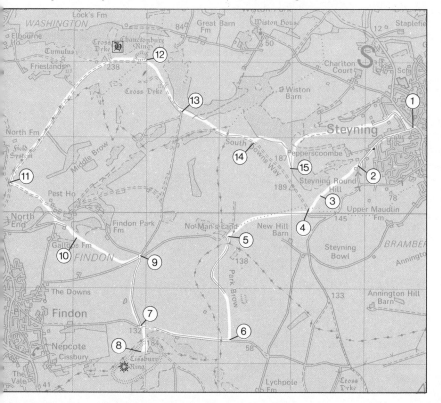

SOUTH DOWNS

Ditchling Beacon and High Park Woods
5½ miles (9 km) Sheet 198 333130

Moderate An outstandingly beautiful and varied walk starting from one of the Downs' highest points; superb mature beechwoods. *Downland, 'bottoms', woods; one climb; mud; section between ③ and ④ often ploughed out – alternative route indicated.*

Start Ditchling Beacon, on the B2116. **Car park** on top of Ditchling Beacon.

① From car park, head E along ridge on South Downs Way. ② Cross road to Streathill Farm. In a few yards, turn right to follow track S past farm buildings. ③ Just before reaching bungalow, go through gate and continue S on opposite side of fence. About 200 yards (183 m) beyond last building, go through gate and bear half right SW across large field (may have crops, but right of way exists). Over brow of hill make for stile in fence to left of copse ahead. (Alternative route from ③: instead of going through gate by bungalow, bear slightly left, following track. In ½ mile (0.8 km) at end of plantation (by gate across track), turn right through plantation, cross stile and continue ahead beside plantation. Then follow hedge and fence to stile already mentioned. Cross stile and small field to bridleway gate. ④ Through gate and follow track downhill to bottom; make for stile in fence across valley. Cross, and climb slope on right to gate in trees. Through gate, follow track uphill to crossroads under overhead cables. Turn right and follow track through beechwoods. ⑤ At buildings on right fork left and go over crossing track. Follow path through wood to rejoin track at gate. Through gate, turn sharp right to road, where ⑥ turn left, and in a few yards go through gap in fence on right. Continue downhill, through bridleway gate, turn right and follow line of fence on right to gate leading to enclosed track. Follow this one mile (1.5 km) to meet South Downs Way, where turn right for Beacon and car park. The walk can be shortened by cutting from ④ back to the South Downs Way.

🏛 Ditchling Beacon, at 800 feet (244 m) the second highest point of the Downs, \↑/ where one of the great chain of fires was lit to signal the coming of the Spanish Armada. Views: N to the Surrey Hills and North Downs; SE to the chalk mass

The harebell, left, flowers July-Oct; the aromatic, common wild thyme in June-Sept.

of Seaford Head beyond Newhaven Harbour; W to Wolstonbury Hill and Pycombe; SW to Chanctonbury Ring and Devil's Dyke.

🏛 Westmeston church, attractively restored, has a 17th C. porch incorporating 14th C. timbers and a shingled bell turret.

❀ Typical downland flowers include the blue harebell, small scabious, sweet-smelling wild thyme and various orchids.

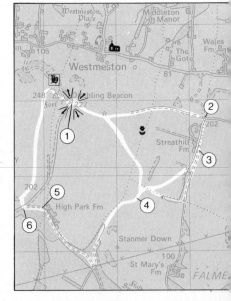

Chilgrove and the Devil's Jumps
5½ miles (9 km) Sheet 197 828144

Easy The Devil's Jumps are particularly striking earthworks. A mostly sheltered route, suitable for poor weather. *Woods, farmland; mud.*

Start Chilgrove, on the B2141 N of Chichester. **Parking** opposite The White Horse.

① Facing away from pub, walk along left edge of green, parallel to road. ② Thirty yards (27 m) short of the telephone box, turn left over stile and follow field edge. ③ After mound on left, bear slightly left, heading across field to right of nearest pylon. Continue on road bearing slightly right, passing cottage. Down and up hill. ④ Bear left off road (ignore right fork) and pass flint cottages. Follow track. In 400 yards (366 m) ignore left fork. ⑤ Continue down to buildings of Monkton Farm. At bottom, bear left and leaving barn on left, climb gently with path along valley floor, later turning left and entering wood. In 50 yards (46 m) ⑥ stop at cross-tracks. To visit Devil's Jumps, turn right and in 400 yards (366 m) look carefully for access to Jumps on left. Retrace to cross-

tracks and continue downhill on principal track in same direction. In about ¾ mile (one km) ⑦ turn left opposite Royal Oak and follow well-defined track along valley floor. After 500 yards (457 m) ⑧ fork left into wood on waymarked (yellow arrows) path. Continue on waymarked path, climbing gently. ⑨ Leave wood over stile and bear half right to cross second stile. Climb through strip of woodland and follow field edge under cables. Continue on enclosed track, soon bearing right and right again for Chilgrove.

🍺 The White Horse, Chilgrove, and The Royal Oak, Hooksway, serve real ale.

⁂ The Devil's Jumps are Bronze Age barrows (burial mounds), reminders of the people whose 'period' began about 1800 B.C., and who used weapons and implements first of copper and later of bronze. Their way of life seems to have merged with that of the Neolithic people, the first farmers, who date from 3000 B.C.

The Devil's Jumps were thoroughly excavated in 1854, but later became overgrown. Since 1978 the Society of Sussex Downsmen's clearance work has achieved the worthwhile object of exposing their contours again.

SOUTH DOWNS

Alfriston, Jevington, The Long Man
9 miles (14.5 km) Sheet 199 521033

Moderate An ideal introduction to the E end of the Downs, with superbly varied countryside. *River valley, woods, heath, downland; 4 climbs; mud.*

Start Alfriston, S of the A27 between Eastbourne and Lewes; buses from Eastbourne and Seaford. **Public car park** at N end of Alfriston.

① Turn right from car park exit. ② Turn left at village cross then right following W bank of River Cuckmere to Litlington. ③ Cross bridge, follow macadam path to village street, then go left to church. ④ Just past church turn right then immediately left through farmyard. ⑤ By gated field entrance turn right into stony lane uphill and follow it straight on, ignoring all crossing or branching tracks, for more than 2 miles (3 km), crossing 2 ridges. ⑥ After passing through wood, fork right then left for Jevington church. ⑦ Turn left through churchyard to road, then straight on along it. ⑧ Opposite 'Old Post Office', turn left on to rough track. ⑨ Near foot of hill fork right into enclosed bridleway to Folkington. ⑩ At end of right-hand road by Folkington church, bear half left on to cart track and continue straight on for more than ½ mile (0.8 km). ⑪ At far end of second wood where track descends, fork left up through gate and take defined path straight on, following contours of hill for one mile (1.5 km), passing Long Man to reach gate. ⑫ Go through gate and

The Long Man of Wilmington, cut into Wendover Hill, is 226 feet (69 m) high.

follow fence straight on to stile, then turn left and in 50 yards (46 m) right on to chalk track, descending to road. ⑬ Cross road, take track straight on, then, after 100 yards (91 m) turn left over stile and bear half right across 2 fields heading for church. ⑭ Cross stile then turn right through gate and go straight on to road. ⑮ Cross road bearing slightly right and take path over 2 bridges back to Alfriston.

🏠 Alfriston church, the spacious late 14th C. 'cathedral of the South Downs'.

🏠 Alfriston Clergy House, 14th C., timber-framed and thatched, was the first building bought by the National Trust.

🏠 Charleston Manor – 'a perfect house in a perfect setting' – gracefully blends Norman, Tudor and Georgian elements.

🏠 Jevington church has a strange Saxon carving of Christ fighting a wild beast.

🏠 Wilmington church, 11th C., has a curious 'insect window', depicting St. Peter in the midst of bees, butterflies and moths. In the churchyard is a giant, twin-trunked yew, possibly 1,000 years old.

📖 The Long Man of Wilmington is a total mystery. No one knows when it was carved, or why. One theory states it is Woden, the Norse God of War.

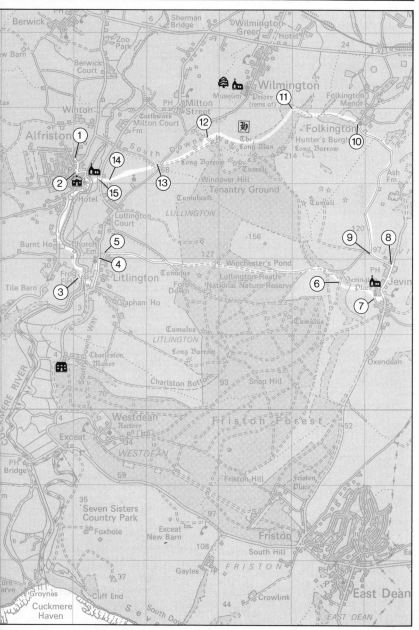

SOUTH DOWNS

Bow Hill and the Mardens
15 miles (24 km) Sheet 197 787105

Energetic A substantial ramble with superb views, visiting 3 remote and beautiful churches. *Downland, woods; mud.*

Start Walderton, off the B2146 NW of Chichester. **Parking** just after turning off B2146, on open space beside stream.

① Follow stiled path SE from road junction climbing with fence to right in second and third fields to edge of wood, then turn left into rough lane. ② Where lane turns left by Forestry Commission notice, turn right and follow woodland bridleway uphill to reach field. ③ Fork right and in 30 yards (27 m) turn right through gate and follow fence to barn, then left heading for far right corner of field. ④ Go through gate into woodland, then straight on. After about 150 yards (137 m), fork left and ignoring tracks to right go straight on to gate leaving wood. ⑤ Go straight on along edge of wood subsequently re-entering it. ⑥ At far side of clearing, turn sharp left uphill, leaving wood. ⑦ At kink in track, turn right on to forest ride and go straight on for 2¼ miles (3.5 km) crossing Bow Hill, ignoring all crossing or branching tracks. ⑧ After re-entering woodland, about 300 yards (274 m) beyond far end of felled area on left, fork left. ⑨ At edge of wood, turn right on to track to B2141, then left along it. ⑩ Just after right bend, turn right through iron gate, then immediately left to follow left side of tree line to stile, then straight on to stile on to farm road. ⑪ Cross farm road and another stile, then straight on left of second tree belt to reach track. ⑫ Turn right on to track and follow it through gates into wood. ⑬ At right bend, take lesser track straight on along edge of wood to road at Hooksway; turn left on to it. ⑭ At far end of right-hand wood, turn right into rough lane. ⑮ Soon after sharp left bend, fork left on to enclosed path to B2141. ⑯ Cross road, go straight on to another road, then turn right. ⑰ At bend, turn left into rough lane, then fork right and, at farm gate, turn right along path to church. ⑱ Go through gate left of church, then resume direction to New Zealand (barbed wire) gate and follow hedge on right downhill. ⑲ At bottom, cross 2 stiles and go half left to third stile, then take path uphill beside hedge, later in belt of trees, to reach field. ⑳ Turn left and follow hedge to road junction. ㉑ Take Up Marden road

straight on for 50 yards (46 m), then left over stile. Keep left of beech strip to next stile, then half right to cross stile in distant belt of trees, then continuing to far right corner of field. ㉒ Turn left on to track then, at road, go straight on into East Marden. ㉓ About 100 yards (91 m) before centre of village (thatched well), turn right over stile then half right across field to stile. ㉔ Cross stile and follow fence on left round 2 sides of field to belt of trees, then turn left and follow right side of tree belt into wood. ㉕ Climb steeply, ignoring crossing path, and at top, follow hedge, then lane straight on to road. ㉖ Turn left along road past farm, then right on to rough track. About 80 yards (73 m) beyond second black barn, turn left and follow hedge on right. ㉗ By corner of wood, cross stile and follow edge of wood zigzagging downhill to stile. Cross this and continue to stile into wood. ㉘ Turn left into wood and in 150 yards (137 m) turn left on to track downhill and up again, ignoring branches to right. ㉙ At T-junction, turn right leaving wood and later re-entering it. ㉚ Ignore track to right, then at T-junction turn right following track veering left, then ignore crossing track and leave wood. ㉛ At right bend after cottages, bear half left into hedged lane, and follow it straight on into and through wood. ㉜ Where field becomes visible to right, turn right following outside edge of wood until it turns sharp left. ㉝ Turn right into wood, then immediately left, soon leaving wood and following track straight on, eventually reaching road. ㉞ Follow road straight on to junction, then take bridleway straight on. ㉟ By back of house turn left on to bridleway parallel to road. ㊱ At T-junction turn right and follow bridleway for ½ mile (0.8 km), then turn left and left again on to road to Walderton.

※ On Bow Hill the 2 Bronze Age barrows (burial mounds) are a clear landmark. The area has a number of other prehistoric sites, including an Iron Age farmstead and Goose Hill Camp.

\↑/ From the top of Bow Hill the view N is to the Downs between Beacon Hills.

\↑/ The view S from Bow Hill takes in Chichester, the coastal plain and, in the distance on a clear day, the Isle of Wight.

⬧ Kingley Vale is a nature reserve and the oldest yew forest in Europe. There is a

SOUTH DOWNS

legend that the forest began in AD 900 with 60 trees, planted to mark the defeat of Viking marauders. A field centre provides information about the reserve.

 North Marden's Norman church, one of the smallest in Sussex, is little more than a room, simple and unspoiled.

 East Marden's tiny 13th C. church has a chamber organ from St James's Palace in London and beehives in the churchyard.

 In Up Marden, too, there is a small, remote 13th C. church. Its simple candlelit interior has been described as one of the loveliest in England.

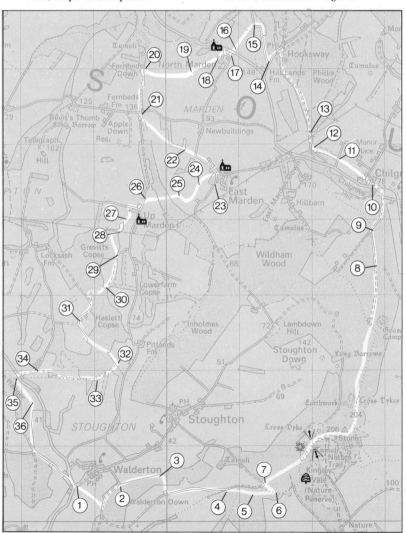

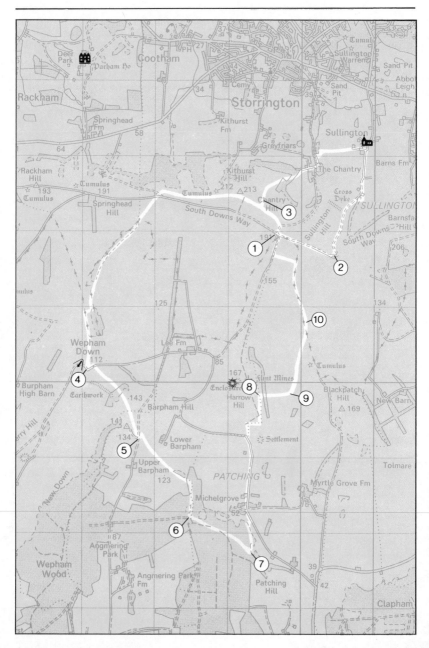

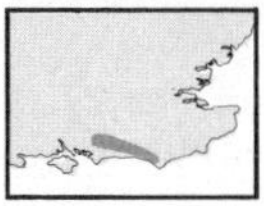

Chantry Hill, Michelgrove and Sullington

10 or 7½ miles (16 or 12 km) Sheets 197 and 198 087120

Moderate Has several of the Downs' best vantage points. *Downland, woods; one climb; mud; path between ⑧ and ⑨ may be ploughed out.*

Start From the A283 ¼ mile (0.5 km) E of Storrington's centre follow Chantry Lane to top of Downs. **Car park** on Downs ridge.

① From car park head E along South Downs Way. (For 7½-mile version, follow track W which begins shortly back down road, to join main route in about one mile [1.5 km].) ② Fork left by barn and in 70 yards (64 m) turn left downhill and follow well-defined track to Sullington church. From church, turn W and continue to road (Chantry Lane), turning left uphill. Turn right along drive opposite ponds. Beyond belt of trees fork left uphill with trees to left. ③ Fork left and follow fence to head of combe. Beyond gate turn back sharply right along top of ridge. Continue one mile (1.5 km) to meet South Downs Way at parking area. Cross, leaving ridge to bear left down slope. Follow bridleway to Wepham. In just over a mile turn right before gate into wood and make for gate across field. Through it, turn left. Continue ½ mile (0.8 km) to ④ where 30 yards (27 m) beyond double gate turn left and in 100 yards (91 m) right to climb Wepham Down. ⑤ Beyond gate into field turn left, cross farm track and in 30 yards turn right through gate by telegraph pole. ⑥ At T-junction turn left between gateposts on woodland track. In 100 yards, at meeting of 4 ways, fork left. ⑦ At cross-track, turn left downhill. Continue one mile. Leave road where it bends sharply left, joining bridleway through gate on right. After 20 yards (18 m), turn left to climb hill. Where the ground dips away steeply into the combe, go down path to left. ⑧ Turn right and cross floor of valley, keeping to right of fence line and bearing away from it to gate at ⑨, beyond which turn left and climb shoulder of hill veering away from fence line on left. Head just E of N for barn seen intermittently on summit – path may be ploughed out. ⑩ Go through gate and follow fence almost due N, later turning left and right, also following fences, for point ①. *This final leg is permitted by Highway Authority pending official investigation.*

Skipper butterflies, typical of downland, are brownish, and aptly named.

�︎ Sullington's church has a Saxon tower, but was built mainly in the 13th C. The effigy of the knight inside may be the oldest of its kind in Sussex.

🏛 Parham House, begun in 1577 by Sir Thomas Palmer, who sailed with Drake to Cadiz.

\†/ The view SW is of the valley of the River Arun, Arundel Castle and Park, with Chichester Cathedral beyond, and, on a clear day, the Isle of Wight.

☀ On the NE slopes of Harrow Hill there are remains of Neolithic flint mines, one of which had a gallery 50 feet (15 m) long. The hill is also the site of an Iron Age fort or fortified cattle compound.

This area has 2 notable tracts of land with public access, ideal for improvised walking and rambling: the Seven Sisters Country Park, near Eastbourne, with the clifftops of Beachy Head; and the 183-acre (74 ha) Ditchling Common, N of Ditchling.

Off the Downs, the old railway line between Groombridge and East Grinstead is a country park.

The South Downs Way (see pages 328-334) is one of the most clearly waymarked and well-maintained of the long-distance footpaths, ideal for day trips because of easy access to short sections gained from the many roads cutting across it, principally the A286, A285, A24 and A23.

SURREY

A geological sandwich; historically insignificant; architecturally and scenically undistinguished: that would be an accurate but misleading description of Surrey. It is a county of intense variety – cosy farmland, heaths and woods – all within a half day of London. Indeed, for a Londoner seeking a short winter day's walk with the certainty of fast, frequent electric trains home, it is ideal.

There are three principal landscape belts: the North Downs, on chalk; to the south, a parallel line of hills, of which Hindhead, Holbury and the Leith Hills are the chief, lying on greensand; and between and around the rest, clay.

Two special pleasures are the commons, many in public or National Trust ownership, and the woods. In fact about 12 per cent of Surrey is covered with trees – more than enough to offset suburbia.

Leatherhead and Fetcham Downs
4 miles (6.5 km) Sheet 187 163559

Easy A stretch of the Mole valley. *Farmland, parkland, riverside; mud after rain.*

Start Leatherhead, on the A24; frequent buses and trains – bus garage and railway station ½ mile (0.8 km) from point ①. **Public car park** at Leatherhead Leisure Centre, signposted from town centre – turn left just before railway bridge.

① Facing away from road, with Leisure Centre on right, make for kissing-gate. Turn right. Cross railway. Bear left. Cross stile and bear right. At top of hill turn left. ② At road, cross to drive of Bocketts Farm and continue in same direction with field on right. To avoid mud, take parallel path in trees on left. In ½ mile (0.8 km) ③ turn left on crossing track. Keep left at fork. Turn right at next fork to drive. ④ Turn right at Norbury Park drive. At end of fencing turn left. At corner of fence bear right to viewpoint seat. Retrace steps. Pass Norbury Park House. ⑤ One hundred yards (91 m) past end of fence on right, turn left downhill, later passing under bridge. ⑥ At cottage on right turn left on track. Follow river under road bridge back to Leisure Centre.

🏚 Local landowners long resisted the railway, but it hardly spoilt the scenery.

🏚 18th C. Bocketts Farm and Great Barn.

The view from Norbury Park of the Mole valley and village of Mickleham.

↟ Deer may be sighted.

🏛 The house (1774) is noted for its painted room, with scenes dovetailing into views from windows. London is seen NE.

\↟/ E side of Mole valley; Mickleham.

〴 The Mole is said to get its name from disappearing underground in drought.

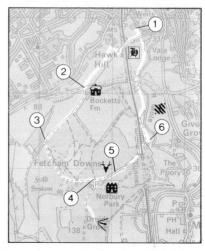

SURREY

Friday Street and Broadmoor
3½ miles (5.5 km) Sheet 186 126458

Easy Friday Street is one of the most popular
Surrey 'backwaters', but still serene; lovely
views from earth bridge in Tillingbourne
valley. *Wooded hills, plantations, farmland,
river valleys; 3 climbs; mud after rain.*

Start Friday Street, S of A25, signposted
from Wotton Hatch. In 1½ miles (2.5 km)
turn left to **public car park** before lake at
Friday Street.

① Turn right out of car park parallel with
road. Pass lake on right. Bear right uphill.
Continue over 2 roads. Carry straight on,
later bearing right. Finally turn left downhill.
② Turn left through Broadmoor. Opposite
last house fork right for 200 yards (183 m) to
waterfall. Retrace to house. Go left a few
yards to path on left, soon bearing left on to
track. Pass house on right, carrying straight
on uphill. After path flattens out continue
over crossing path. Cross wide, sandy track.
Forward, then downhill to junction of paths.
Take second on left, still downhill. Turn left
at crossing track, which later turns left. ③
As track bears right through farm maintain
direction through gate on left. Cross stream.
Through gate on right. Follow path to lane. ④
Turn left. After buildings, continue uphill on
bridleway. Fifteen yards (14 m) beyond field
end on left, turn left. Bear right uphill to stile.
Cross field. ⑤ Over crossing track down to
stile. At main track turn left. Shortly turn
right over stile. Cross Tillingbourne. Go
uphill through woods. ⑥ Cross road to
footpath. As field on left ends, turn left on to
path edging wood. Later bear left to cross
stile. Right on to Kempslade Farm drive.
Continue to car park.

🚩 Stephen Langton, born in Friday Street,
was the Archbishop of Canterbury
instrumental in Magna Carta.

🏛 In pre-Christian times, Friday Street
seems likely to have had a shrine to Frig
or Frigga, the Norse goddess of Earth
and Love, who is invoked in the day of the
week, and the village's name.
   The lake, or Silent pool, is one of many
mill or hammer ponds in Surrey and
north Sussex, a reminder that the area
was rich in iron foundries or 'hammers'.

ⓨ Deer may be seen all round the walk.

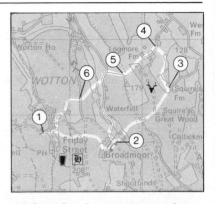

Winkworth Arboretum, Hascombe and Dunsfold
11 miles (17.5 km) Sheet 186 990411

Moderate A fine arboretum, 2 picturesque
villages and a vineyard; arboretum at best in
autumn or spring. *Parkland, farmland,
woods, tree plantations; one climb; mud.*

Start Winkworth Arboretum, on the B2130
about 2 miles (3 km) SE of the A3100. **Car
park** on road at Arboretum entrance.

① Leave car park with Nat. Trust collection
box to right. When path starts downhill, soon
turn right along contour for ½ mile (0.8 km),
finally dropping to road. Continue in same
direction for ½ mile. ② Turn left on to
signposted bridleway. Shortly turn right on
crossing track. When this turns right
continue in same direction on path. Later
bear left with path. At T-junction turn right
through Hascombe. ③ Turn left beside inn.
After ⅓ mile (0.5 km) continue on hedged
bridleway for ½ mile. Go through gate and
continue up sunken bridleway. ④ When
bridleway ends turn right, skirting tennis
court, later continuing in same direction
across hillside for ½ mile. Turn left at drive.
At gate in crossing lane take footpath
diagonally right. Pass pond on left. Continue
half right to stepped stile and road. ⑤ Cross
to footpath opposite, making for free-
standing tree. Continue across farm track.
Go diagonally left, making for second set of
bars in hedge. Turn right on to road through
Dunsfold. ⑥ Immediately after Hawk and
Harrier turn right on to footpath. At house
entrance continue on path on right. At road
turn left. Left again at signpost to 'Church

Green'. Facing away from church, take left lane to road. Turn left. ⑦ Opposite Hook House Farm, turn left on to signposted footpath. Diagonally right to stile. Continue with woods on right. Right over stile into woods. Just before field ahead, turn left and immediately right through woods. Turn left on to track. Later, at junction, keep left on bridleway. ⑧ Turn right at road, continuing up Upper Vann Lane for over ½ mile. At Maple Bungalow turn right on to track. After ¼ mile (0.5 km) turn left at signpost, later bearing right with woods on left. ⑨ Turn left on to crossing path. Shortly keep right at fork, ignoring side turnings. Continue through plantation to road. ⑩ Cross to track opposite. After 80 yards (73 m) as path goes

downhill take small path on left. Finally drop to valley bottom. Forward through gate. ⑪ Soon fork right uphill, later going downhill. Follow track to T-junction. Turn right to road and car park.

🌲 The Arboretum is noted for its fine collection of maple and Pyrus species.

🍺 The White Horse and Hawk and Harrier.

⛪ Dunsfold church, described by William Morris as the 'most beautiful country church in all England'. A rarity, it was built entirely during the period 1260-1320: a masterpiece of medieval craftsmanship.

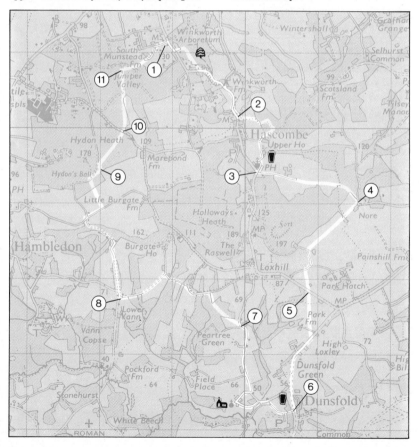

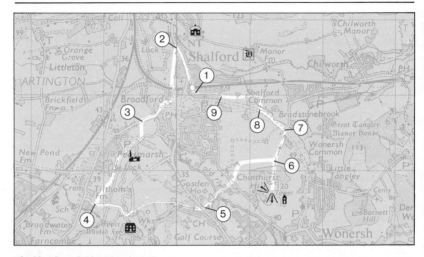

Shalford and Chinthurst Hill
6 miles (9.5 km) Sheet 186 001471

Easy A good example of Surrey river walking, with fine views from Chinthurst Hill. *River- and canal-sides, farmland, wooded and open hill; one climb; mud.*

Start Shalford, at the junction of the A248 and A281 S of Guildford; frequent buses; frequent trains (Tonbridge-Reading line) – Shalford Station is adjacent to point ①. **Parking** near Shalford Station.

① From station right past the Queen Victoria for ¼ mile (0.5 km) to footpath on right signposted Shalford Mill. ② From visiting mill, retrace to main road, turn right, cross and almost immediately left on to signposted bridleway, soon bearing left. Cross railway. Bear right past cottages, continuing over green to main road. Bear right over River Wey. ③ Left on to towpath. In one mile (1.5 km) ④ turn left at road bridge. Left at T-junction. Shortly, after old barn and manor house, turn right and follow track, passing sewage works, continuing on narrowing footpath to road. ⑤ Cross diagonally to left and continue on marked footpath to Gosden Green. At end turn left and cross river and disused railway bridges. At T-junction straight across to signposted bridleway on left, at first with hedge on right, later between hedges. At next field bear right with hedge on right, later continuing on hedged track to crossing path. ⑥ Turn right, soon up steps, following zigzag path to open hilltop. Retrace to steps. Continue on path to road. Turn left, passing road junction. ⑦ At postbox bear right to signposted footpath; Through gate, cross stream over stile, forward towards house and lane. Over second stile turn left. Continue in same direction over Shalford Common. ⑧ As common ends, bear right along Station Road, later turning right on to marked footpath between industrial buildings and over footbridge to station.

🏛 Shalford had an important fair in medieval times, possibly the model of Vanity Fair in *Pilgrim's Progress*. The stocks and whipping post remain outside the churchyard wall.

🏠 Shalford Mill, open to visitors, is early 18th C. It operated until 1914, and most of the machinery is intact.

🛥 A section of the Wey Navigation Canal (opened 1754), built to avoid bends in the Wey between Guildford and Godalming.

🏢 Unsted Manor House and barn are listed buildings, the house part-14th C.

\t/ Among views from Chinthurst Hill, with its folly, are NW, the Hog's Back,
🛆 Guildford Cathedral on its hill and S, Hascombe Hill.

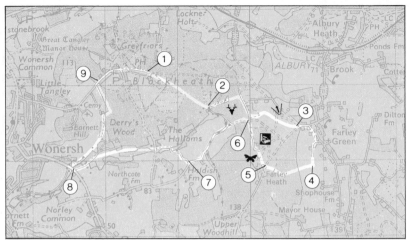

Blackheath and Farley Green
7 miles (11 km) Sheets 186 and 187 036462

Easy An example of Surrey's greensand heath walking; panoramic views; the heather is out in August, and the bluebells in May. *Sandy heath, forestry plantations; one climb.*

Start From the A248 at Chilworth Station turn off opposite Percy Arms and continue ¾ mile (one km) to crossroads where turn left continuing to end of road; frequent buses stop at Chilworth Station; frequent trains to Chilworth Station. **Car park** on Blackheath.

① Facing away from road, leave car park at far right corner; later downhill over crossing path to continue in same direction on wider track. ② Opposite first cottage on right, turn left, immediately taking 2 successive right forks. Pass cottage on left. Turn right on to crossing track. Left at next crossing track, immediately forking right. At hilltop maintain direction over crossing track. Soon left on to crossing path. ③ At road turn left into Farley Green, turning right at green, touching road and forking right again. After barn ignore stile on right. ④ Shortly right, up to stile. Cross field and stile into woods. Continue straight ahead, keeping left at choices. Through holly hedgerow. Immediately turn right with plantation on left. When path turns left, turn right avoiding right fork. ⑤ Cross road to track forking left.

At T-junction turn right, soon keeping left at junction of paths. (Sound parallel path at higher level on right.) ⑥ Turn left on to crossing track. Soon left at lane; continue ½ mile (0.8 km). ⑦ Turn right on path, later between lakes to road. Turn right and continue 100 yards (91 m). ⑧ Take rising path on right continuing over drive and several crossing paths. Maintain direction and at crest of hill keep forward along edge of cricket field on left. Continue on lane with line of houses on left. Turn right for car park.

ψ Roaring heard in this valley sounds like, and is, a pair of lions kept in the garden of a local house.

ψ To St. Martha's, the church on the downs that was a popular stopping place for pilgrims on the way to Canterbury. It remains a famous landmark.

✘ By the path, at shoulder level, there is a wood ants' nest in the tree trunk growing out of the embankment.

▨ Archaeologists think the temple which stood on this site consisted of a sanctuary 18 feet (5.4 m) square with an outer colonnade about 46 feet (14 m) square, standing in 10 acres (4 ha) of grounds. Both Roman and Celtic (ie native British) gods seem to have been worshipped, following the Roman policy of integrating their religion with that of their subjects.

SURREY

Reigate and Leigh
8 miles (13 km) Sheet 187 255499

Easy On the flatter land below the Surrey hills – a pleasant variation; rewarding in late winter – snowdrops in profusion along the river near Wonham Mill. *Parkland, farmland, heath; mud.*

Start Reigate, on the A217; frequent buses – Reigate bus station is close to point 1; frequent trains – Reigate Station about ½ mile (0.8 km) from point ①. **Public car park** at entrance to Priory Park in Bell Street.

① From car park, Priory on right, cross grass to gap in trees ahead. Later fork right uphill. Continue along top of ridge. Downhill to steps. At road turn left. ② Soon turn right on to footpath. Continue with garden on left. At signpost forward diagonally over 2 fields. ③ Right on to road. Left at junction. Right beside house. After farm, bear left round field. Cross stile and turn right into lane. ④ At road turn left and continue ¼ mile (0.5 km). Opposite signpost on right turn left on to footpath. Cross bridge. Turn right. As field edge turns right, bear diagonally left to cross stile at end of line of trees. Over bars, making for stile near far right corner of second field. Turn right, and immediately right again to cross bridge. Bear left to churchyard path. ⑤ Bear right round church. Turn right on to road. Soon turn right on to footpath. Cross 2 stiles. Soon left over footbridge and field to road. ⑥ Cross to track opposite. After ⅓ mile (0.5 km) bear left past barn. Soon turn right over stile. Diagonally left to bridge. Bear right round field. ⑦ Right over stile. Cross River Mole. Left on to bridleway. Just before farm, turn left over stile. Turn right. Later cross stream. Later over stile and footbridge to road. ⑧ Turn right. Soon turn left on to footpath between pond and mill house. Turn right on to footpath. At gate to wood on right, turn left and shortly right to farm track. Turn right, follow track to heath. ⑨ Bear left to pass windmill on right. Bear right past house to downhill path. Cross road and green. Pass cottage on right. Continue to footpath (path avoiding mud higher on left). At lane turn left. ⑩ Left on to footpath. Cross road to footpath. Bear left round Priory Park lake. Continue in same direction to point ① and car park.

🚩 Skimmington Arms.

Reigate Heath's windmill, and the round house used as a chapel.

🏚 Reigate Castle grounds contain the remains of the moat, keep and excavations of a castle reputed to have belonged to William, Earl of Warren. It was surrendered to Louis, the Dauphin of France, in 1216 and French coins are said to have been found in the moat.

Under the court is the curious Barons' Cave, a long, curved crypt with a pointed roof cut from the hard sand. Tradition has it that the Barons conferred there prior to signing Magna Carta at Runnymede, in the Thames valley.

🏛 Reigate's Old Town Hall dates from 1728.

🏢 Reigate Priory, built in the 13th C., stood in these grounds until Henry VIII turned it into a house. Little of the Tudor building remains; the existing house is mainly late 18th C.

🏢 The Priest's House is actually a row of medieval, timbered buildings, with additions and renovations, and no overall theme; but nonetheless attractive.

🌱 Snowdrops, flowering Jan.-March; they are uncommon in the wild.

🎏 The windmill dates from 1765 and the brick-built round house is a chapel, still
🏚 used for services on some Sundays.

The Priest's House: Horsham slate and large chimney stacks add to the charm.

Hindhead Common, Frensham Common, Witley Common – Surrey is the county of sandy heathland, the essence of convenient strolling. To vary the theme, try exploring the dramatic combes which occasionally puncture it, notably the Devil's Punchbowl on the A3. A nature trail is marked on the S rim.

The Forestry Commission have waymarked some trails from the Green Dene car park near Horsley.

A straight line route using the Pilgrim's Way: from Dorking station, go up Ashcombe Road and continue ahead when it ends, joining the Pilgrim's Way. Descend to Westcott and take the bus back to Dorking.

River walking: from Guildford, follow the River Wey to Godalming, taking a bus or train back, or vice versa.

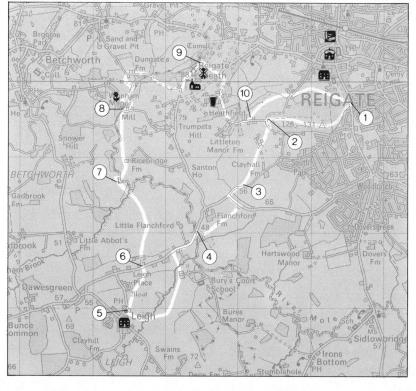

NORTH DOWNS

Although the North Downs have a long-distance footpath of their own, the North Downs Way, this 100-mile (161 km) chain of chalk hills has never quite achieved the public identity of the South Downs or the Chilterns: a pity.

The Surrey end of the Downs comprises some of the most accessible walking in Britain, close to London and crossed at short intervals by train and bus routes. Here, local authorities, at their most enlightened, have built an estate of continuous public open spaces out of commons, land bought for green belt preservation and adjoining National Trust properties. Walkers have – for the Home Counties – the unusual experience of being free to wander, not confined to paths only, over many square miles of easy, wooded hills.

In Kent, as the Downs curve gradually towards Dover, there is greater restriction; but this is historic walking. Scholars dispute whether the Pilgrims' Way marked on the maps is any such thing, but there is no doubt that for centuries men and women went on foot and horse along these hills to Canterbury.

Gomshall and Hackhurst Downs
4 miles (6.5 km) Sheet 187 089479

Easy A pleasant way of climbing Hackhurst Downs, with some of the finest viewpoints between Dorking and Guildford. *Farmland, wooded and open hillsides; one climb.*

Start Gomshall, on the A25 between Dorking and Guildford; frequent buses; frequent trains stopping at Gomshall on the Tonbridge-Reading line. **Car park** at station.

① From station cross A25. Left under railway. Right on Wonham Way, later bearing left. As lane bears right, turn left beside house. Immediately right through gate. Continue in same direction over stream. After houses bear left to road. Turn left. ② Opposite Fish Farm turn right up lane. After about 200 yards (183 m), turn right up path bordering woods. Continue to lane. Turn left through farm. Cross railway. Continue uphill. As track narrows, turn right through opening. Climb open hillside. ③ At crossing track turn left. After ¼ mile (0.5 km) continue over clearing to seat. Fork right on crossing track. Follow main path, later through posts, to turn left on droveway, continuing ½ mile (0.8 km). ④ Twenty yards (18 m) before static water tank on right, turn left. As path bears left up to viewpoint seat, turn right to join main path downhill. Continue down Colekitchen Lane to A25. Turn left for station.

The North Downs in high summer – rich, rolling country, with Gomshall at the centre.

☙ Gomshall village is famous for its beauty, its watercress beds and a tannery dating back at least to the 11th C.

⌒ A 16th C. packhorse bridge.

▣ The droveway on Hackhurst Downs – part of the North Downs Way – is an ancient track.

☙ Bee and fly orchids.

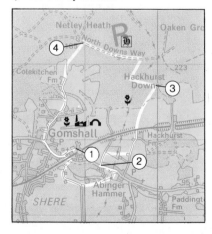

113

NORTH DOWNS

Puttenham and Wanborough
3 miles (5 km) Sheet 186 932483

Easy Through 2 typical and charming villages on the N and S sides of The Hog's Back; shrub path at ④ best in spring. *Hillsides, golf course, farmland; 2 climbs.*

Start The Hog's Back, along which the A31 runs W from the Guildford by-pass. **Car park** ¼ mile (0.5 km) W of the B3000 turning.

① From car park entrance turn towards Guildford, continuing 250 yards (229 m). Turn right on to bridleway, continuing for ⅓ mile (0.5 km) to road. Turn left to Puttenham. Passing church, continue to main road. Turn right. ② Opposite Jolly Farmer turn left on to North Downs Way, continuing for almost one mile (1.5 km). ③ Immediately past Monksgrove Cottage and Farm House, turn left alongside garden. Continue, ignoring side turnings, to gate. After woods, cross field, bearing slightly left to gate into lane. Cross lane and grass area to gate. Cross field to another gate into another lane. Cross to stile and go up side of field to A31. ④ Cross to bridleway to Wanborough church. Turn left. Left at road. ⑤ At bend, turn right over stile. Go diagonally right uphill to A31. Cross to car park.

🏠 Puttenham's church of St. John the Baptist dates from about 1160, but was much restored in 1861. The well in the churchyard 'reappeared' in 1972 when a cypress tree subsided into it; it had been filled in more than 200 years earlier.

🏠 Puttenham village has many attractive tile-hung and timber-framed houses, some built in the 14th and 15th C.

🏠 Puttenham Priory (1762) is a fine Palladian mansion and the site of a much earlier house, part of the manor of Puttenham. This came into the Prior of Newark's possession in 1248, hence the house's name. There was never a monastic foundation here.

🏠 Wanborough, a beautiful hamlet which seems to grow naturally from the hillside, has a tiny church (interior measurements 44½ by 18 feet [13.5 by 5.4 m]); a manor house and an ancient tithe barn worth a visit.

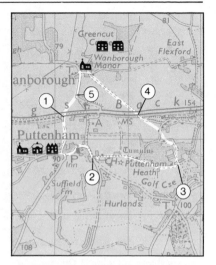

Headley Heath, Brockham Hills, Juniper Top
7 miles (11 km) Sheet 187 205539

Moderate Little-used paths in an over-visited area of the North Downs; an incomparable path over Juniper Top, with magnificent views. A summer walk – especially troublesome mud in winter. *Heath, wooded hillside, chalk downland; one climb; exceptionally steep downhill path between ② and ③ best not attempted if wet.*

Start Headley, by the B2033 SE of Leatherhead. **Car park** (National Trust) on Headley Heath opposite the cricket pitch.

① Leave car park with Jubilee Plantation on left, walking parallel to road. As plantation ends, take third path on right. After continuing in same direction over crossing track, keep left at fork. At picnic area, bear left with pond on right. Cross bridleway to track doubling back on left. At crossing track go right for 150 yards (137 m). Take second of 2 paths forking off on left. Soon turn right on to crossing track. Over crossing track. Through gate ahead. Forward on path to road. Turn right. ② Turn left on to signposted footpath. At T-junction in clearing turn left. Soon, at sign on tree, turn right downhill. At lane, turn right, then left. ③ Soon turn right on to North Downs Way, continuing uphill and over bridge. After passing old chimney stack, turn left steeply downhill. Soon turn right on to track, keeping left at fork. Ignore side turnings. After ½ mile (0.8 km), a narrow-gauge railway track is visible on left. Continue through Brockham Museum Trust area. After stile keep left at fork. When path divides into 2 parallel paths, the right one is preferable. ④ When paths rejoin at pillbox and pylon on left, turn right uphill. Turn left up steps at North Downs Way sign. Right on to track. Later left downhill on North Downs Way, soon turning right. Later, at crossing track, turn right to road. ⑤ Cross to track opposite with fenced caravans on right. Turn right with fence. Take first path on left. Continue over crossing track. Later emerge on open hillside of Juniper Top. Continue downhill. ⑥ Near bottom of slope turn right on path doubling back into scrub. Later keep left at fork. Over stile and right on enclosed path. Continue in same direction over 3 more stiles, with fence on left. After next stile go

downhill to turn right up drive. ⑦ After passing through brick gate posts, turn sharply left downhill. Soon bear right on track down to main bridleway. Turn left. Soon, at junction of paths, forward through fence on left to path going diagonally uphill. After passing seats, rejoin bridleway on right. Go straight ahead over junction of paths back to car park.

🏠 Brockham Museum Trust area has a collection of old railway rolling stock.

\†/ Views from Juniper Top are magnificent. One takes in Norbury Park House, an 18th C. mansion, once the home of Dr. Marie Stopes, feminist and reformer.

❧ Wild orchids in early summer.

❧ The profuse heather on Headley Heath is at its best in late summer. Sweeping views in most directions.

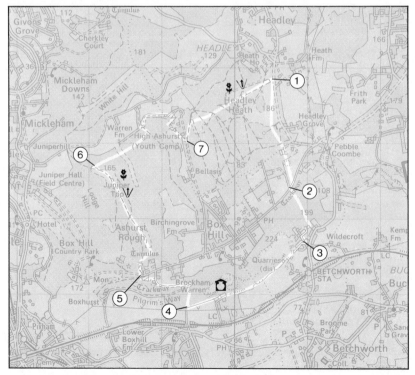

NORTH DOWNS

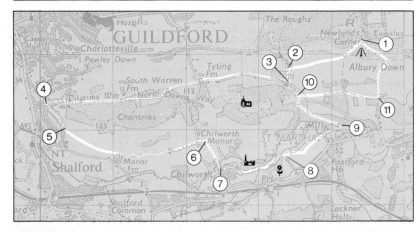

Newlands Corner and Albury Downs
7 miles (11 km) Sheet 186 044492

Moderate Varied walking with superb views from one of the Downs' key points. *Hillsides, farmland, woods, lakesides; 2 climbs.*

Start Newlands Corner on the A25 W of Guildford. **Public car park** at Newlands Corner.

① From car park go S downhill. Turn right on path keeping trees on right. After ½ mile (0.8 km), fork left downhill. Soon enter woods. Bear left to road. ② Cross to steps. Turn left on to roadside path, continuing for ¼ mile (0.5 km). ③ At lodge turn right, continuing for ¾ mile (one km). After Tyting Farm, cross road to track. Keep on main track as it bears left, then right. ④ Turn left round Chantry Cottage on track. Continue for a few yards on road before turning left over stile. ⑤ Straight ahead on footpath with upward slope of Chantries on left. After ½ mile (0.8 km) bear right opposite farm and immediately left, continuing in same direction on track for ¾ mile. ⑥ At road turn right. In a few yards turn right on to path. At road turn right. ⑦ Soon turn left through gate beside West Lodge. Follow main path through woods for ½ mile. Through high bank of earth, and follow river to lane. Turn right and continue for a few yards. ⑧ Left over stile. Cross field diagonally to stile. Go along edge of 2 fields with ditch on right. Continue along garden boundary to lane. Turn left, with lake on

right. Bear left with next lake on right. ⑨ Turn left beside Millstream Cottage. Follow path for ½ mile to heath. Bear right towards pine trees, going through posts, then left to road. ⑩ Cross to footpath opposite. Later cross track and right round field edge. Turn left at corner. Later through gate. Continue to lane. ⑪ Turn left, continuing for ⅓ mile (0.5 km). Bear right with lane. At pillbox on right turn left on track rising over Albury Downs. Ignore side turnings. Through posts to car park.

\⫟/ The rightly popular view from the crest of the Downs at Newlands Corner.

⛪ St. Martha's Chapel, near the walk route and on the Pilgrims' Way to Canterbury, dates from Saxon times. Damaged by a gunpowder explosion in the 18th C., it was left derelict for a long time, but rebuilt in 1848.

⚒ Chilworth, being a good site for a water-wheel, was a centre of industry for centuries. In 1625 the East India Company set up mills making gunpowder and cordite; in Queen Anne's reign they manufactured bank notes, too. By the end of the 17th C. there were 16 mills at work and they were still in use until the end of the 1914-18 War.

🌿 Jewel-weed – orange balsam – grows in the river. It was first found growing wild in England on the River Wey in 1822, by John Stuart Mill.

Woldingham, Marden Park and Tandridge Hill
5 miles (8 km) Sheet 187 360563

Easy Rewarding views for comparatively little effort. *Parkland, farmland, woods; mud.*

Start Woldingham, off the A22 E of Caterham; frequent buses; frequent trains to Woldingham. **Car park** at Woldingham Station.

① Through door on upside platform of station to drive. At lodge turn left, continuing for nearly one mile (1.5 km). ② Opposite school buildings turn right on to signposted footpath up steps. After ½ mile (0.8 km), at open field, pass line of trees on left, re-entering woods at telegraph pole. Soon pass waymarked stile on right. Cross next stile and go steeply downhill to lane–part of North Downs Way. ③ Turn left. Follow North Downs Way waymarks to T-junction at top of Tandridge Hill. Turn right. ④ At signpost on right, turn left into woods. Soon take middle of 3 paths, later passing large hollow on right. After stile, go downhill to drive. ⑤ Turn right, soon bearing left uphill. After ¾ mile (one km), pass Marden Park Farm ⑥ Turn right over railway and left on track to station.

🏠 Marden Park, now the Convent School of the Sacred Heart, stands on the site of several earlier houses. One was a feudal manor, left derelict after the Black Death wiped out the village of Marden in 1348-49. On the same site, in the mid-17th C., Sir Robert Clayton, wealthy merchant and Lord Mayor of London, built a mansion. The present Tudor-style buildings date from 1880. The modern buildings erected for the purposes of the school have fortunately done little to damage the valley's scenery.

🌿 The rare leopardsbane flowers here from late March into April. A member of the great Compositae (daisy) family it has a bright yellow, daisy-shaped flower, similar to that of the celandine.

🌿 The broad-leaved helleborine, another uncommon plant, grows in the woods. It is a member of the orchid family and its flowers–reddish mauve–appear from July to September.

Broad-leaved helleborine (left) is native to the British Isles. Leopardsbane (right) was introduced from elsewhere.

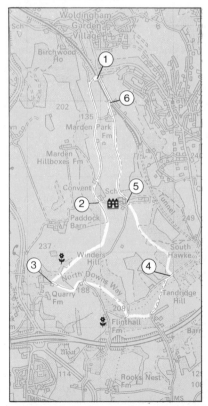

NORTH DOWNS

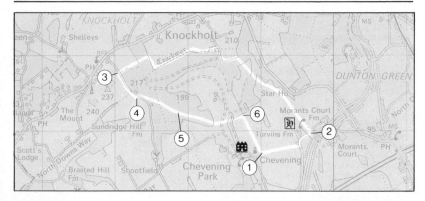

Chevening
5 miles (8 km) Sheet 188 489578

Easy Fine views over the Weald of Kent; a
well-known house in a gracious setting. At
the end of February, the snowdrops could be
mistaken for snowdrifts. *Farmland,
parkland, woods; one climb; mud after rain.*

Start Chevening, N of Sevenoaks. **Parking** on
grass verge near church.

① From church turn right and go through
churchyard. Continue straight ahead on
hedged path. At road turn left. In a few
yards ② turn left uphill on North Downs
Way. Follow the waymarks, later crossing
drive by house and eventually reaching a
minor road. ③ Turn left and continue for
⅓ mile (0.5 km). ④ At Keeper's Cottage turn
left. At end of woods bear left downhill with
fence on left. ⑤ Through kissing-gate, then
left following waymarks across estate to
where path crosses, forming T-junction.
⑥ Turn right to Chevening church.

🏛 Chevening House, mid-17th C., was
probably designed by Inigo Jones. It was
the birthplace of Lady Hester Stanhope
(1776-1839), the famous eccentric and
traveller. Her father, the 3rd Earl, an
amateur inventor, launched the first
small boat to be powered by steam on the
lake in the park. The family bequeathed
the house to the nation in 1959, and it is
now used for official entertaining.

🔟 This, and several walks in the section,
use a length of the North Downs Way, an
offical long-distance path. See pp.328-334.

Lullingstone Park and Shoreham
7½ miles (12 km) Sheet 188 506646

Moderate The attractive village of
Shoreham and fine views from the hills.
*Parkland, farmland, forestry plantations;
one climb.*

Start Lullingstone Park, signposted from
Well Hill, off the A21 N of Sevenoaks;
frequent trains to Shoreham, where the
walk can be joined in ½ mile (0.8 km)
between ⑤ and ⑥. **Public car park** at
entrance to Lullingstone Park.

① Bear right out of car park on track. Soon
turn right by trees to cross green into woods.
Continue over green and uphill. Turn right
over ladder stile to road. ② Turn left. Soon
turn right on to signposted footpath. Right
over stile. Later, diagonally left downhill.
Turn left at road. ③ Right at T-junction,
continuing for just over ½ mile (0.8 km),
ignoring left turning. ④ Opposite Timberden
Farm Cottage, turn left on signposted
footpath. Uphill into woods. Over crossing
track. Continue downhill out of woods. Cross
stile. Downhill to road. ⑤ Turn right, and
shortly left. Cross bridge. Left at riverside
path. ⑥ Left over bridge. Bear right beside
river. Cross stile and continue in same
direction along field. At next field bear
slightly left. Maintain direction between
cultivations. ⑦ Right on road for ¾ mile
(one km) to main road. Cross, turn left on to
path above embankment. (Easier access to
embankment about 30 yards [27 m] to right.)
⑧ When path drops to road, cross to track
opposite. At Roman villa turn left along
private road. ⑨ Just past gate towers of

Lullingstone Castle, turn right on to track into Lullingstone Park. Avoid left fork. Follow track for 1½ miles (2.5 km) back to car park.

Shoreham's 1914-18 War memorial is a white cross cut in the turf of the chalk hillside to the W of the village.

At Water House, Samuel Palmer, the visionary painter, lived for some years. He used the village as a background in his strange and touching pastoral paintings. William Blake often came to visit him here.

Shoreham's parish church of St. Peter

and St. Paul, dating back to the 15th C. but much restored in 1864, has one of the best examples of a medieval carved rood screen in England.

At Lullingstone Castle – in fact, an 18th C. house – the first game of lawn tennis was played in 1873. In the grounds are a herb garden and a 14th C. church.

Lullingstone Roman villa is one of the finest in the country. In about AD 370 the owner and his family became Christians and built a chapel in the house above a room which was probably used for pagan rites. No other Roman house in Britain is so-equipped.

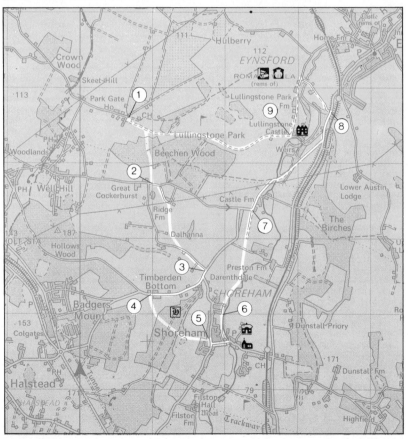

Otford, Knatts Valley and Romney Street
11½ miles (18.5 km) Sheet 188 524594

Moderate Knatts Valley offers the impression, at least, of remoteness, surrounded by over-populated Kent. *Open and wooded downland, farmland, open valleys, wooded hilltops; one climb; mud after rain.*

Start Otford, on the A225 N of Sevenoaks; frequent trains to Otford station. **Car park** at Otford station.

① From station turn right uphill. Right at T-junction. Soon turn left up North Downs Way path. Later continue in same direction with fence on right. ② At road junction, forward on road. Shortly right over stile. Go diagonally to corner of wood. Continue with woods on right. Cross drive and forward through gates of Hildenborough Hall. ③ Left over stile, continuing in same direction. Later bear left over 2 fields, through woods and diagonally left over field. Continue with woods on right. ④ Turn right at road, later turning right. Left on North Downs Way track. Continue in same direction, later with fence on left. Cross stile on left into woods to path on extreme right. Continue along field with fence on left. ⑤ Left through gate and up track. Left between barns. Go diagonally down field, keeping fence on left. Maintain direction over next field. Continue with woods on left. At farm, bear left to road. ⑥ Turn left for a few yards. Right over stile. Follow track past buildings to road. Turn left. Soon turn right on footpath. Keep hedge on right. Continue over stiles. Turn left on crossing path. Shortly go steeply downhill. Right at road. ⑦ Right at T-junction for 1½ miles (2.5 km) through Knatts Valley. ⑧ At road junction on right turn left up track. Turn left with track. At gate at top of track turn left on path. Ignore left turning. After ½ mile (0.8 km) straight on over clearing through gate with house on left. Continue in same direction for ½ mile. ⑨ Turn right over stile. Continue half right over 2 fields to stile into woods. Continue straight ahead to road junction. Turn right with house on right. ⑩ Opposite Fox and Hounds turn left over stile, bearing right to stile. Turn left over another stile. Keep trees on left until field ends. Over stile beside telegraph pole and down to road. ⑪ Left for a few yards. Right over stile. Follow garden fence to

Otford's Tudor remains, a pleasant end of walk stopping and picnic place with seats and a stream close by.

second corner, then ahead to stile in trees. Downhill and up to stile. Follow to road. ⑫ Turn right, continuing 300 yards (274 m). Left over stile and forward on track. Pass pylon. Downhill to open hillside. Turn right. Re-enter woods. Over stile and downhill initially with fence on left. ⑬ At road, left. Shortly right on footpath crossing railway. Forward, then diagonally left over field. Left on track. Left at road. Pass pond. Cross to church on left. (Diversion on path signposted Sevenoaks to visit Tudor palace.) Retrace to churchyard path signposted Kemsing. Pass wall on left. Continue to car park and station.

🖼 Otford has the remnants of a 16th C. palace, one of the residences of the Archbishops of Canterbury. It had been rebuilt from a manor house belonging to Archbishop Warham (1518), who also owned Knole, and was acquired in 1537 by Henry VIII.
Brickwork from the old palace has been incorporated in the row of cottages between the tower and the gatehouse. The latter was used as a dovecot in the 19th C.

⛪ In Otford church, by the green, there is a 17th C. timbered porch and an 11th C. nave. One of the monuments in the church is in remembrance of Elizabeth Polhill, granddaughter of Oliver Cromwell and daughter of General Ireton. The Church Hall was designed by

Edward Lutyens, whose brother was vicar of Otford.

🏠 In Otford's main street there are 16th and 17th C. houses, including the attractive 'Pickmoss'.

🍺 In the Bull Inn there is panelling which may have come from the old palace.

🏛 Broughton Manor has a medieval hall and a 16th C. gable.

❀ Flowers of the area include common milkwort, with its delicate blue, pink or white blooms, rich yellow rock rose and salad burnet, with its cucumber scent and petalless flowers.

Colley Hill, Box Hill and Newlands Corner are the North Downs' time-honoured contribution to Sunday afternoon strolling. Remember there is a road to the summit of Box Hill, and miles of heath behind it.

A delightful, waymarked 'greenway' starts from Hollingbourne on the B6213 one mile (1.5 km) N of the junction of the M20 and A20 E of Maidstone. The route goes to Harrietsham, turns left at the church there and climbs to the Pilgrims' Way, along which one can return to Hollingbourne.

The Alice Holt Forest, 4 miles (6.5 km) S of Farnham has trails.

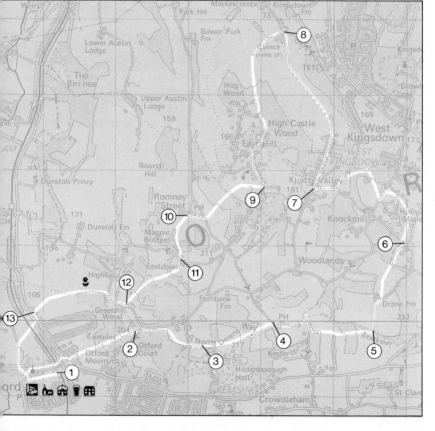

CHILTERNS AND THAMES VALLEY

For the walker, the Chiltern Hills and the eastern end of the Thames Valley have two great pluses: accessibility and scenery.

Train and bus services crossing the hills at intervals along their 50-mile (80-km) length enable Londoners to travel out by one route, tramp across country and return by another. At their disposal is a dense network of public footpaths – more than four miles (6.5 km) to every square mile (2.5 square km) – twice the national average. What is more, the paths are kept in excellent shape by the Chiltern Society. Signposting, waymarking and even restoration after ploughing are all above the norm.

The Chilterns are classic chalk country, hung with beechwoods, under which there is relatively firm going all the year round. In this terrain a typical route means slipping in and out of the woods and across the small intervening fields of the valleys.

Modestly dramatic country with wide views of the south midland plain can be enjoyed on the hills' escarpment, to the west. The ancient green road, the Icknield Way, runs along the scarp-foot, and behind, the hills drop gradually to the Thames in a series of winding valleys. Those marked on the map as having few roads can seem amazingly remote in atmosphere from London, less than 40 miles (64 km) away.

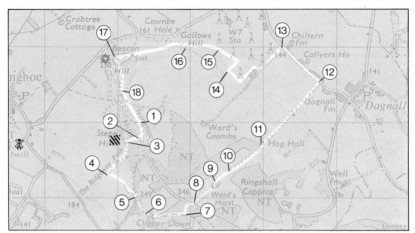

Ivinghoe Hills

6 miles (9.5 km) Sheet 165 963160

Moderate The spectacular north Chilterns downs – wide views and prehistoric sites. *Downland, farmland, woods; 3 climbs; mud after rain; between ⑬ and ⑯ the path, although a public right of way, may be ploughed out or under crops; route is obstructed between ⑯ and ⑰ by wired-up gate, which can be climbed.*

Start Ivinghoe Beacon, signposted from the B489 SW of Dunstable; infrequent buses (Luton to Aylesbury service) stop at foot of Ivinghoe Beacon, from where take path uphill to join route between ⑯ and ⑰. **Car park** signposted on Ivinghoe Beacon.

① Turn left out of car park on to road. ② Take first gravel entrance on right and go straight on past military warning sign referring to former use through scrub to fence at top of steep slope. ③ Left on to Ridgeway Path, soon crossing stile and continuing downhill to stile at next fence. ④ Just before stile, left along fence line to cross stile into scrub rising to wood. ⑤ At crossways, straight on, then at T-junction turn right for top of Clipper Down. ⑥ At fork, go left, leaving cottage to left and fields on right. ⑦ About 200 yards (183 m) beyond end of last field, left into slightly sunken track, then, by double-trunked tree on right, half right to road. Then right to entrance of Ward's Hurst Farm. ⑧ Turn left up farm

drive. ⑨ At farm, left then right through yard, emerging by silos. Then straight on along track downhill, keeping right of fence. ⑩ Follow right side of tree belt straight on downhill, crossing fence through scrub at bottom end of wood, then left passing Hog Hall. ⑪ Join drive, then straight on to A4146 at Dagnall. ⑫ Left along road to corner of radio station fence. ⑬ Left into hedged bridleway beside fence, continuing around back of radio station, turning right, left and right again until emerging through bridle gate into field. ⑭ Right, then left, still following radio station fence line to far right corner of field. ⑮ Through hedge gap and bear half left through field (which may be under crops) to top of Gallows Hill. ⑯ Half left over top of next hill to summit of Beacon. ⑰ Left, heading for bend in road left of small hillock. ⑱ Just before bend, slightly left on to worn path parallel to road back to car park.

〰 Incombe Hole, 250 feet (76 m) deep, possibly the most spectacular combe in the Chilterns; it was cleared of scrub by volunteers organized by the Chiltern Society, famed for its footpath work.

✕ Pitstone windmill (1627) is the oldest of its kind in Britain.

✳ The Beacon is topped by traces of an Iron Age fort, probable date 600 BC. Views include Mentmore (902197), the Rosebery house now a meditation school of the Maharishi Yogi.

CHILTERNS AND THAMES VALLEY

Turville Valley
5½ miles (9 km) Sheet 175 747910

Moderate Turville Valley is popular but comparatively unspoilt, the village a beautifully harmonious collection of buildings. *Heath, woods, farmland; 3 climbs; mud after rain; indistinct path at ③ has been waymarked.*

Start Turville Heath, off the B480 between Henley and Watlington. In village take cul-de-sac to Turville Grange. **Parking** within 15 feet (4.5 m) of road edge.

① Facing Grange gates, turn right through scrub along back of heath. ② Left on to road, then half right at junction on to path, keeping left of tree. ③ After 250 yards (228 m), just before large oak on right, bear left of hawthorn tree, then straight on to edge of wood, and follow left-hand waymarked path to stile at its far side. ④ Half right across field, then follow fence on right to stile at Southend. ⑤ Cross stile and turn left along concrete lane to farm, then straight on downhill to crossroads at Dolesden. ⑥ Straight on across field towards windmill, then take bridle lane into Turville. ⑦ Turn left passing church, then, opposite black barn with turret, right up 'Barn Cottage' path. At stile, half left uphill across field, through corner of copse, then hillside scrub to hilltop wood. ⑧ Along edge of wood, then, at T-junction, left on to track to a road. ⑨ Uphill along road, bearing right. ⑩ At second road junction, left on to path across field into wood. ⑪ About 30 yards (27 m) into woodland, turn right, following path straight on to road at Gray's Barn. ⑫ Left on road. At its end, take woodland bridleway straight on downhill. ⑬ At left bend, go straight on over stile, then half left downhill. ⑭ Straight on across next field to road. ⑮ Straight on along bridleway, climbing to Turville Heath. ⑯ Turn left along back of heath to Grange.

🌲 The avenue is of old lime trees.

🏠 18th C. Turville Grange.

🏠 Turville Court and estate belonged to Bysshe Shelley, grandfather of the poet. The house was built in 1847.

🍺 Both pubs serve real ale.

⛪ The church is Norman, its tower 16th C.

In warmer weather, Turville's Bull and Butcher is popular for lunch in the garden. The pub is one of the village's several timber-framed cottages and houses, mainly dating from the 16th to the 18th C.

🌀 Cobstone Windmill is an 18th C. smock mill, i.e. with a revolving top to bring its sails in line with the wind.

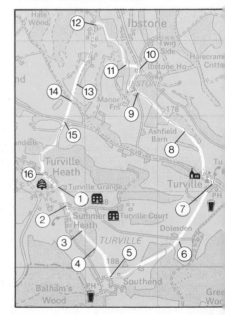

Great Kimble and Whiteleaf
4½ miles (7 km) Sheet 165 826060

Moderate The central Chiltern escarpment, with its wooded slopes, patches of downland and picturesque villages below. *Woods, farmland, downland; 2 climbs; mud after rain; may need clearing between ⑰ and ⑱.*

Start Great Kimble, on the A4010 S of Aylesbury; frequent buses. **Parking** in unsignposted lay-by S of church.

① From church take lane into village. ② Just past thatched cottage, left over stile and straight on to gate, then slightly right to stile by pylon. ③ Straight on, crossing drive, then half right across field to stile. ④ Beyond stile, left, then straight on, keeping right of hedge, to Askett. ⑤ Right, then left along Askett Lane to stile. ⑥ Straight on to stile on left, then sharp right to stile in corner of field. ⑦ Straight on, after marsh turning half left to footbridge, then on to road at Monks Risborough. ⑧ Straight on, heading for church tower, then left to village side street. ⑨ Left, then right to A4010. ⑩ Take path left of school to road, then right to T-junction in Whiteleaf. ⑪ Left, then right on to path

climbing past thatched cottage. ⑫ Right at fork, climbing steeply. At crossing path, straight on uphill through wood to clearing above Whiteleaf Cross. ⑬ From looking at view over plain, turn round and go through squeeze stile in larch fence, then straight on downhill to the Plough, Cadsden. ⑭ Left then right on to path between 2 beer gardens, then left at fork. ⑮ At further fork, turn right up gully, then left following fence on left to far side of wood. ⑯ Left along bridleway, crossing road to track behind lay-by car park. ⑰ By noticeboard for riders, fork right on to narrow, terraced path to stile on far side of scrub. ⑱ Straight on to stile right of far corner of field, then left down bridleway to Great Kimble.

🏛 'Kimble' derives from Cunobelinus or Cymbeline, the ancient British king.

⛪ Hampden signed his refusal to pay Ship Money in a former church on this site.

🍺 All 3 pubs marked serve real ale.

🏛 Experts cannot agree the age of Whiteleaf Cross, or its purpose; but it may be a marker on the Icknield Way.

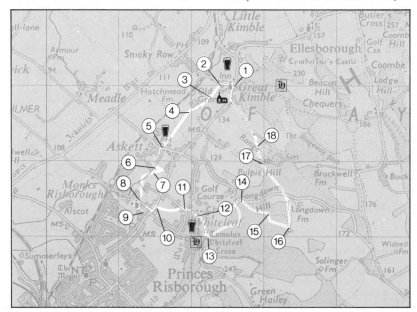

CHILTERNS AND THAMES VALLEY

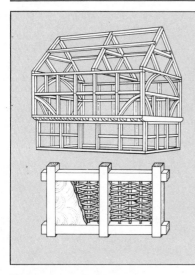

The timber-framed buildings characteristic of the Chilterns area (and elsewhere) were built by several methods, the most 'woody' appearance being given by the box-frame construction (top). The wooden frame carries the whole load of the roof, with the walling material acting simply as weather-proof filling for the gaps. As such, it was originally made of the simplest material, typically wattle and daub (below). This was flexible strips of wood woven around stiffer uprights, and coated with suitable 'daub', often mud mixed with clay. When it deteriorated, it was almost always replaced by brick panels, properly called brick nogging.

The Lee and Little Hampden
8, 4 or 3½ miles (13, 6.5 or 5.5 km)
Sheet 165 900043 and 858040

Moderate (8-mile route) or **easy** (4- and 3½-mile routes). Typical of the best central Chiltern countryside. *Farmland, ridges and 'bottoms'; one climb on each; mud after rain.*

Start (of 8- and 4-mile routes) The Lee, E of the A413 between Amersham and Wendover; (of the 3½-mile route) Little Hampden, W of the A413. **Parking** along S side of The Lee green – do not block entrances or use pub car park without landlord's permission. At Little Hampden, on common land opposite the Rising Sun (not pub car park). If full, return to foot of hill, then left and left again to Cobblers Hill Road. In 1¼ miles (2 km) stop at Cockshoots Wood Picnic Area, beginning walk from there.

For 8-mile route, walk ①-㉗; for 4-mile route, walk ①-⑫, then ㉔-①; for 3½-mile route, walk ⑲-㉓, returning by ⑬-⑲.

① Leaving green by memorial take road to copse on left. ② Turn left into copse, crossing stile. Cross second stile by black barn, then follow hedge on left until entering wood. ③ At far side of wood, left along track to road. ④ Cross road and follow hedge on right, passing through copse. ⑤ Beyond copse, slightly left to stile, then straight ahead along drive to stile in trees at bend. ⑥ At far side of pub car park, left up track to stile in hedge on right, then straight on to second stile. ⑦ After stile, right, then half left heading just right of right-hand of 2 distant cottages. ⑧ Straight on through garden, then slightly left towards left end of wood on horizon, arriving at stile in hedge at bottom of field. ⑨ Straight on to stile just right of Durham Farm. ⑩ Cross road, then half right to stile right of old farm, then straight on along road to A413. ⑪ Turn left, then, crossing road, right at lay-by on to signposted path across 2 fields. ⑫ If doing 4 mile route, sharp left along signposted path to A413; if continuing, straight on over railway bridge, then right. ⑬ Follow fence on right for 300 yards (274 m), then diagonally left to pick up corner of another fence. Bear left, keeping right of this fence to road. ⑭ Cross road, then uphill to gate under tree, then left, following hedge on right, leaving field through gate. ⑮ Right through second gate on right, soon entering lane. ⑯ At edge of wood, right for Dunsmore crossroads. ⑰ Left passing pond, then left over stile and half right downhill to farmyard. ⑱ Left into bridleway, then in wood half right uphill to Little Hampden. ⑲ If starting 3½-mile route, head down road. Otherwise left on to road. ⑳ Just past church and Manor Farm, left on to bridleway across valley, then uphill through wood and farm to road. ㉑ Take bridleway left of post box, then,

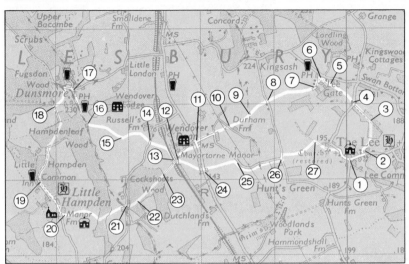

just beyond house, left into wood and follow waymarks. ㉒ At first fork, left; at second fork, right. At cross-tracks, straight on to stile. (If starting 3½-mile route here, take waymarked path from rear of picnic area, then at fork left to stile out of wood.) ㉓ Straight on towards railway bridge. If doing 3½-mile route, left just before railway. Otherwise over bridge and 2 stiles, then half right on to signposted path on right to A413. ㉔ Turn left, cross road and in a few yards turn right, following hedge on left. Continue uphill to gate. ㉕ Just before gate, turn right, walking parallel to road to join it at road junction. ㉖ Left, then right over stile and follow hedge on right to far side of field. ㉗ Right, then slightly left over several stiles to road, where turn right for green.

🏠 Church Farm is partly 13th C., and with the village's 2 churches stands inside the remains of a prehistoric fort.

🏛 The Lee green was created by Sir Arthur Liberty, founder of the Regent St. store, and owner of the Manor House.

🏛 18th C. Mayortorne Manor (spellings vary), once the home of the local writer, H. J. Massingham.

🏛 Halton House, a late 19th C. Rothschild mansion now used by the R.A.F.

Little Hampden, and Great Hampden across the valley, bear the name of the family that produced Buckinghamshire's most honourable politician. The Hampdens had been the most influential landowners in the county since before the Norman Conquest, when in 1635 the 'reigning' squire and M.P. for Wendover, John Hampden, refused to pay the arbitrarily levied tax called Ship Money. As much a gesture in defence of democracy as a deliberate challenge to the king's authority, it remains one of the most famous incidents of the years leading to the Civil War. Hampden died of wounds early in the war. His great-grandson lost much of the family fortune in speculation, but retained Hampden House, now a girl's school. It contains some interesting Hampden associations, but the nearby parish church has more: a relief of Hampden falling wounded from his horse at the Battle of Chalgrove Field, portraits and inscriptions.

⛪ The church is 13th C. with a 15th C. porch and some good medieval murals.

🏠 Manor Farm is 16th-17th C.

🍺 All 5 pubs marked serve real ale. The Rising Sun, Little Hampden, does not welcome muddy boots.

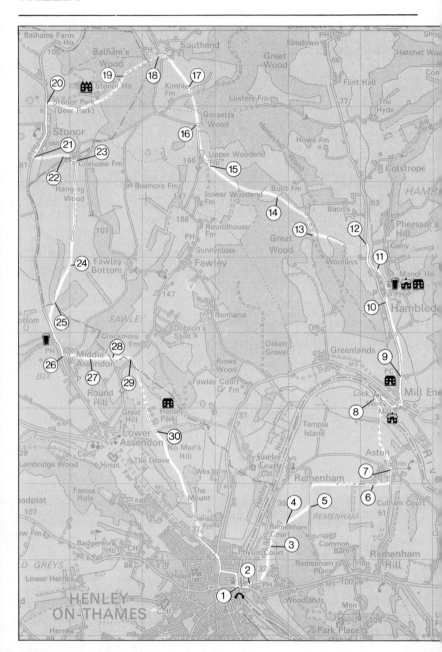

Henley, Hambleden and Stonor
13 miles (21 km) Sheet 175 763826

Energetic The Thames Valley Chilterns, with the beautiful Hambleden Valley and superb Stonor Park. *Farmland, hills; 6 climbs; mud after rain; path between ③ and ④ may be overgrown.*

Start Henley, on the A423; frequent buses from High Wycombe and Reading, infrequent services from London and Oxford; by rail, the London–Reading line, changing at Twyford. **Public car park** in King's Road, Henley, or use station car park.

① From Henley church, cross bridge and turn left through white gates to path on right to meadow. ② Turn right, cross road to stile right of iron railings, then half left through meadow, golf practice area and up through scrub. ③ By corner of fence on left, half right to stile (under second conifer from corner), then straight on through wood. ④ Half right across field to hedge gap near single tree. ⑤ Left along road, then, before copse, right on to farm track. Continue to far end of copse on left. ⑥ Straight on through hedge gap and downhill to road, then left. ⑦ At 'Flower Pot' turn left, then right on to track to Hambleden Lock. ⑧ Cross lock, weir and A4155, then take Hambleden road. ⑨ At Rotten Row Turn, go through kissing-gate and follow path parallel to Hambleden road. ⑩ Right into village, then left by post office into back lane. ⑪ After bridge, fork right over stile to far corner of field, then continue along road to left bend. ⑫ Left into lane, then at corner of wood slightly right up inside edge of wood, then along track into second wood. ⑬ At crossways turn right, then left at track junction, ignoring right forks. Continue downhill to valley bottom. ⑭ Cross track, bearing half right. Following waymarks, leave wood and take lane to farm. ⑮ Join concrete track, forking right through farm, then right along road to junction. ⑯ Take path straight on downhill, then up again. ⑰ Slightly left across field to tree clump on horizon, then to gate into lane to Southend. ⑱ Cross road and take track straight on downhill through wood. ⑲ By first row of pines on right, fork left on to path through plantation and Stonor Park to road. ⑳ Turn left and continue to far end of Stonor village. ㉑ Just past farm, left over stile and straight on uphill. ㉒ Near hilltop, straight on along farm track. At 3-way fork take centre route

to Coxlease Farm. ㉓ Just past second barn, sharp right through double gates on to track past farmhouse and along ridge-top. ㉔ At end of track, over stile, then right, shortly entering wood. ㉕ Straight on across field to road, then left. ㉖ Just past 'Rainbow', left on to Fawley road, then right on to track (Oxfordshire Way) uphill to field. ㉗ Slightly left over 2 stiles to gap in trees. ㉘ Half right across field to stile left of cottage. ㉙ Cross road and take track opposite. ㉚ At sharp left bend, through kissing-gate. Cross park, downhill to A423, left into Henley.

∩ Henley's elegant bridge was built in 1786. The famous regatta is in July.

🏠 Hambleden Mill, a 17th C. water mill.

🏛 15th-16th C. Yewdon Manor.

🍺 The Stag and Huntsman, real ale.

🏠 Hambleden's charmingly clustered cottages date from the 16th C. The manor
🏛 house is 17th C.

🏛 Stonor Park, famous for its Roman Catholic connections: Edmund Campion, the Jesuit martyr, sheltered here during the Tudor religious persecutions. Mass has been celebrated in the chapel for 8 centuries.

🍺 The 18th C. Stonor Arms, real ale.

🏛 Henley Park dates from the 18th C.

For more beechwood walking, try Burnham Beeches, off the A355 N of Burnham, or the beechwoods of Ashridge, approached across Berkhamsted Common. On the Ashridge Estate (Nat. Trust) there is a marked walk starting from the Information Centre at the Bridgewater Monument, outside Aldbury.

Chenies Valley competes with those of Turville and Hambleden for wholly delightful walking.

The Thames towpaths are the basis for many easy routes. An attractive stretch can be reached from Cookham.

Walking the escarpment W from Wendover over Coombe Hill is rightly popular.

WALES

PEMBROKESHIRE

The county of Pembrokeshire that was – now but a corner of Dyfed – is a distinct walking entity. It sits on the oldest rocks in Wales. The coastline is correspondingly fretted, indented and studded with bays. It is the only one in Britain to be made a National Park, and the path which follows its cliffs and headlands is truly one of the walking wonders of the world. Its beauty catches the breath despite the gross interruption of Milford Haven, now a major oil terminal, and a pox of caravan sites which cluster as thick as the puffins and guillemots.

Go waterproof, for this is Wales. On the weather maps, the coast shows up as a thin strip of relative dryness – less than 40 inches (102 cm) a year. Locals say the precipitation rises by an inch (2.5 cm) a year for every mile (1.5 km) travelled inland. On top of the Preseli Hills, 70 inches (178 cm) is not uncommon. Inland Pembrokeshire – if you can call it that, for nowhere is more than ten miles (16 km) from salt water – is not always a distinguished landscape. Early daffodils and potatoes flourishing in a warm, moist climate, together with the small farms, remind many of Cornwall. Perhaps the best echoes come from the Preseli Hills, and the line of Norman castles which marks what was formerly the English south from the Welsh north.

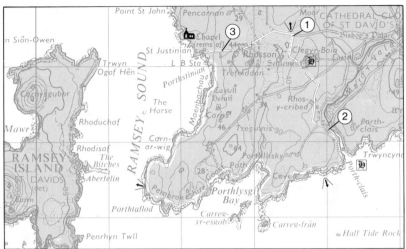

Ramsey Sound
6 miles (9.5 km) Sheet 157 735254

Moderate A magnificent, and comparatively trouble-free, section of the Pembrokeshire Coast Path; chance to view the rip tide sweeping through Ramsey Sound, making white water at The Bitches Rocks. From late April to late summer there is a succession of wild flowers. *Sunken lanes, cliff tops, beach, coastal scrub; several short, steep climbs; mud after rain.*

Start From St. David's take the unclassified road signposted 'Lifeboat Station/St. Justinian's. **Parking** on hard shoulder of left verge past T-junction.

Partially waymarked. ① Walk S along the unclassified road, Treffeiddan Moor on the right, continuing straight ahead at crossroads to Porth-clais Harbour. ② Climb the Coast Path, signposted behind the hut, and follow it for about 4½ miles (7 km). ③ Follow the road to ①.

\t/ Carn Lidi has a Stone Age burial chamber on its N slopes.

🏚 Boia's Rock, the base of Boia, an Irish pirate who operated in St. David's time.

🏚 Porth-clais was the harbour for St. David's, up the River Alun. There are

The black and white razorbill, among the most handsome of this coastline's sea birds; the sharp beak can hold several fish for the young.

some well-reconstructed lime kilns at the harbour head.

\t/ Skomer Island, a nature reserve noted for its puffins; beyond, out of sight, is Skokholm, famous for its huge Manx shearwater colony.

\t/ The treacherous Bitches Rocks.

🏚 The ruins of St. Justinian's Chapel, reputedly the 6th C. saint's burial place after his murder on Ramsey Island. Friend and confessor of St. David, he retired there, by tradition because mainland monastery life became too lax.

PEMBROKESHIRE

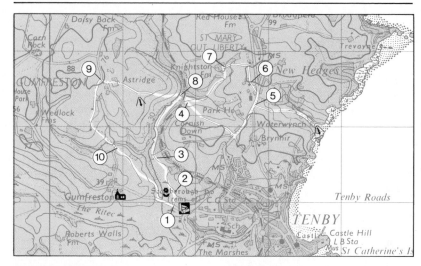

Scotsborough Woods
4 or 6½ miles (6.5 or 10.5 km)
Sheet 158 118009

Moderate A rewarding woodland walk, much of it using a sound earth track under trees – ideal for dull or wet weather. *Woods, farmland; 2 climbs; mud.*

Start From Tenby take the B4318 and continue ½ mile (0.8 km) to lay-by at Causeway Mill. **Parking** in lay-by; if full, use car park at swimming pool complex at junction of A4319 and B4318, ¼ mile (0.5 km) from ①.

Mostly waymarked. ① Enter Scotsborough Woods by waymarked stone stile or gate and continue on track. ② After ruins of Scotsborough House, turn left (waymarked) into poorly drained area. The track is distinguished by small banks and mature trees. ③ Follow the 3-foot (one km) wide earth track for ¾ mile (one km) through trees to the railway viaduct. ④ For 4-mile route, turn sharp left and follow ⑧ to ⑩. Otherwise pass under railway and go right, following uphill track to A478, passing Woodville Cottage. At road turn left and continue to ⑤ road signposted to Waterwynch Bay: sandy beach at low water, ideal for a picnic. To continue, walk as far as ⑥ caravan site entrances, where take lane leading to Knightston Farm. ⑦

Enter woods on left immediately before farm buildings. ⑧ Pass under bridge again and take track on right, continuing to brook by folly ruins. Cross stile and continue left uphill, joining track (wire gates) to Astridge Farm. ⑨ Turn left downhill on stony track beyond farm buildings. ⑩ Go through metal gate and cross middle of first and second field, using waymarked stiles. After second, continue along wood edge over 3 stiles to join B4318 200 yards (183 m) from ①.

The ruins date from the Middle Ages; the former owners, the Ap Rhys family, have a memorial in St. Mary's Church, Tenby. The house was once approachable from the sea by a creek.

The colony of flowers like white bluebells are triangular-stalked garlic flowering May-June.

Lundy Island, 30 miles (48 km) out in the Bristol Channel, appears as a low, dark rectangular shape on the horizon.

The skyline of Tenby, formed mainly in the 19th C. when the town was developed into a seaside resort.

The primitive, but interesting church at Gumfreston can be visited by going through the metal gate and continuing via Gumfreston Farm.

Preseli Top

5 miles (8 km) Sheet 145 075289

Easy A quick route to the roof of the Preseli Hills, with astonishing views; heather, gorse and whortle-berries, at their best in late summer, early autumn. *Heather hillside, woods; one climb; soft peat.*

Start Rosebush, on the B4313. **Parking** in lay-by SW of village.

① Take track signposted 'Unsuitable for Motor Vehicles' on right side of cottage. ② Use detour towards plantation to avoid marshes. ③ Go through metal gate and stock fence. ④ From cairn and trig. point strike out for the small 'cairns' (tumulus). ⑤ Aim NW towards the plantation corner and turn left to follow edge of plantation for ¾ mile (one km). ⑥ Turn left into plantation over wooden fence and follow signposts for Rosebush back to ①.

Three commonly planted conifers seen in Pantmaenog Forest: Norway spruce, left; Japanese larch, centre, and Sitka spruce.

⚒ The Preseli Hills are well known as the source for some of the smaller stones at Stonehenge, some 140 miles (225 km) away on Salisbury Plain. Experts think that 2 different types – dolerite and rhyolite – came from 3 separate sites. Among the most ingenious theories on how they were transported such a distance involves the glaciers of the successive ice ages. They could have penetrated far into England, providing a surface on which to haul sledges.

ⓑ This is a section of the ancient route to and from Ireland used by the prehistoric peoples centred on Salisbury Plain. The objective was the Wicklow Hills, with their gold and copper. Preseli, a sacred area (as the many cairns, hut circles and burial mounds suggest), must have been an important 'staging post' before the embarkation at Whitesand Bay.

🚩 The pub clad in corrugated metal is the sad reminder of attempts to give Rosebush a tourist trade in the late 19th C. Because of the slate mining, the village was already connected with the outside world by railway. To attract visitors, the metal building was erected as a hotel. Two lakes were dug, and advertised as spa waters. The public was not convinced of their curative powers, and the mines failed to prosper.

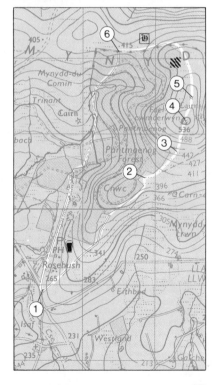

135

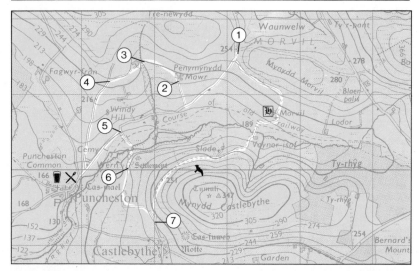

Afon Angof Valley
4 miles (6.5 km) Sheet 145 031316

Moderate Ideal for the solitary walker, mostly on hard surfaces, but with virtually no traffic. *Farmland, valley; one climb.*

Start From Fishguard or Narberth take the B4313 and continue to its junction with the unclassified road signposted Puncheston. **Parking** on verge by road junction.

① From parking walk downhill in direction of Puncheston and take the access track to Penymynydd Mawr Farm. ② From the farmyard go through gate between house and buildings; this leads to a track, which should be followed, hedge on left, past barn to reach metal gate into field. Go through and follow footpath round edge of fields to arrive at stream. In absence of bridge and stile, cross the wire. ③ Take the sunken access track left of the buildings to cross concrete cattle pound. At farm access drive, cross and continue 150 yards (137 m) by track to field gate. Through it, turn right (uphill) and continue to where gate gives on to grassy track. Continue on this past field intersections (3 gates) to junction with wider grassy track. ④ Turn left downhill and continue on lane to village. (There is a short cut to ① through the cemetery.) ⑤ At junction of Green Lane and metalled road,

Common buzzard attitudes: gliding (top), gaining height (left) and soaring (right).

turn left and continue on road to Glyn Helyg Farm. Turn right on to track and go through gate leading to bridge over river. Cross and ⑥ take track along valley. After starting to climb hillside, at sharp left bend go through gate on right to follow track across 2 fields and reach farm. Continue on surfaced track leading uphill to road at metal gate. ⑦ Turn left and continue on road to ①.

🍺 Drover's Arms; bar food.

🪶 Buzzards likely to be seen: habitual soarers, as many as 20 may wheel together in great circles.

🏛 The graveyard of the neglected Morvil church contains an early Christian stone with a cross and circle symbol.

PEMBROKESHIRE

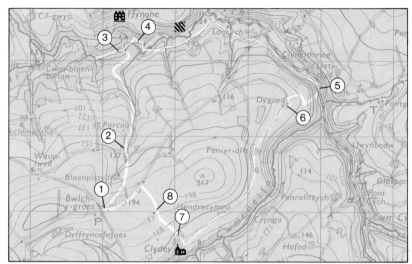

Cych Valley
6 miles (9.5 km) Sheet 145 240360

Moderate Comparatively sheltered in contrast to other walks in this section but still with a feeling of space. *Farmland, plantations, woods, hillside; one climb.*

Start From the A478 at Crymmych or the B4332 at Boncath, take the road to Bwlch-y-groes. **Parking** on verge by village sign 150 yards (137 m) E of crossroads.

① From crossroads go through ornamental gate-posts and follow track downhill towards Blaenpistyll Farm. Continue past farm access by grassy track to road. ② Enter Economic Forestry Group plantation by small gate. After ¾ mile (one km) take right fork to reach lake. ③ Continue round to lakeside cottage. Walk behind house to see waterfall; continue by house access track to road. ④ Turn right downhill on to minor road, taking left fork to Cych Valley road. Turn right and continue ¾ mile to reach Bridge Cottage, under trees. ⑤ Go through metal gate by side of house, and at rear of house cross bar stile to follow track through woods. Turn right at metal gate to farm. ⑥ Go through farmyard (may be temporary gates) to sunken lane; continue by road to Clydey church. Turn right and ⑦ go through farmyard to the centre of 3 gates and

continue uphill, following left side of hedge through 2 fields. ⑧ Pass ruined cottage on left and bear slightly right across field to fence. Then cross gate stile to join road by village school. Turn left for ①.

🏰 Ffynone House is an example of the early work of John Nash, one of a few houses he designed in Pembrokeshire. It was built in the early 1790s for the banker Sir Benjamin Hammett, some 20 years before Nash reached the height of his fame working for the Prince Regent on Brighton Pavilion and, among other famous London landmarks, creating the palatial terraces of Regent's Park.

Ffynone is not obviously the architect's work: the S front was redesigned in the early 19th C., and there was extensive remodelling in 1904. But his characteristic elegance is preserved in the hall and vestibule ceilings, the staircase and the drawing room. (House not open to the public.)

〰️ The Afon (River) Dulas joins the Afon Cych downstream, which later flows into the Teifi, which, with the Tywi, is the Pembrokeshire area's main river.

⛪ The tower of Clydey's church is Norman; there is a splendid font and a stone carved with a very early script.

PEMBROKESHIRE

Gwaun Valley

4 or 8½ miles (6.5 or 13.5 km)
Sheet 145 035350

Moderate Dramatic changes of mood as the route changes sides of the valley. *Plantations, moorland, woods; 2 climbs; mud; soft peat.*

Start Take the unclassified road running through the Gwaun valley. **Car park** (Forestry Commission) at Sychbant.

Partially waymarked. ① From rear of picnic site follow path uphill along right side of stream. After ½ mile (0.8 km) enter plantation by waymarked stile. ② Turn right immediately; continue on path with fence on right, ignoring left-hand track after 100 yards (91 m), by Forestry Commission signpost, to stile at limit of plantation – about ½ mile. Then follow grassy track to

fence and metal gate at roadside. ③ Continue E along rear of Bedd Morris Stone Car Park, with fence on right. Follow fence across Carningli Common, turning left at waymarked post, then right. At second small metal gate, with Carnedward Rocks on right, locate ④ poorly defined animal track immediately to left of rocks. Continue on this downhill through 5 fields and gates to bridleway at Pen-rhiw, where ⑤ turn right through waymarked gate downhill, with stream – likely to be wet. Exit on to road. For shorter version, turn right back to ①. To continue ⑥ enter wood by waymarked metal gate and follow well-defined path. ⑦ Climb steeply by cascades to metal gate and continue straight ahead along right edge of field. Turn right along road, crossing bridge over stream. Immediately after bridge ⑧ turn on to access track to Gernor and cross river by ford or footbridge, uphill. ⑨ Skirt farm anti-clockwise, cross stream and go

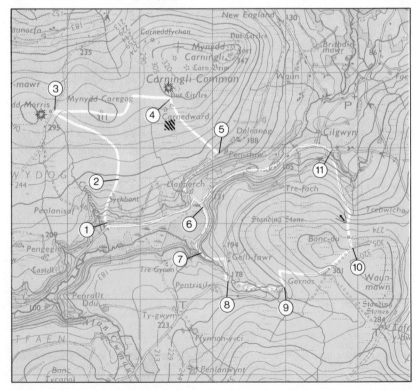

through gate (waymarked on reverse side of tree). Continue straight up sunken lane and cross waymarked gate. Turn right immediately; after ½ mile cross gate and continue on farm track. Go through farm; bear slightly left on to moor to corner of field. Continue 100 yards (91 m) with fence on left and ⑩ cross fence at junction with second fence leading up from valley and ruins. Follow this fence downhill. At ruins, join well-defined grassy track downhill to road. ⑪ Turn left and continue to ⑫.

Bedd Morris, a ritual standing stone.

The hut circles date from about 200 B.C.

Carnedward Rocks, raised volcanically.

The slopes of Carningli feature a stone hill fort and hut circles.

Below, the hill fort on Carningli.

The rocky promontory of Dinas Head, 4 miles (6.5 km) E of Fishguard, has some fine coastal paths and a wildlife trail. Access via village of Rhos Dinas.

West of Fishguard there is walking over the Pen-caer Peninsula to Mathry, where buses run back to Fishguard.

A few miles SW of Tenby there are trails at Penally and Lydstep, the latter with caverns to visit.

A trail for industrial enthusiasts showing wool manufacture up to the 1930s is at Dres-Fach Felindre off the A484 E of Newcastle Emlyn.

There are 3 forest trails round the Hafod Estate, 2 miles (3 km) SE of Devil's Bridge.

Bosherton's tranquil ponds, 5 miles (8 km) S of Pembroke off the B4319, are the start of several routes.

BRECON BEACONS AND BLACK MOUNTAINS

There is no finer mountain profile in all Britain than the firm but gentle tilt of the Brecon Beacons' three chief peaks, Pen y Fan and its slightly lower neighbours, Corn Dû and Cribin. As crows, or rather buzzards, fly, little more than a mile separates the three summits. They thus provide a classic ridge walk, but a tough one with hundreds of feet dropping and climbing between the high points. Don't try it in bad weather. The north face of these mountains is scooped out into great *cwms*; the one between Pen y Fan and Corn Dû is called King Arthur's Chair. To the south the slopes of these red sandstone mountains decline more gently towards the coal valleys of South Wales.

The Black Mountains are separated from the Beacons proper by the valley of the Usk. They face north-west on to the deep and winding valley of the Wye. Lovely as that river is, many find the little streams that hurry down the slip slope of these hills even more attractive. All this is set within the protection of the Brecon Beacons National Park, which also embraces mountains stretching west into what used to be Carmarthenshire and the easy strolling of the towpath beside the Monmouthshire and Brecon Canal.

Ysgyryd Fawr – the Holy Mountain
2½ miles (4 km) Sheet 161 329164

Moderate An isolated hill – one of the 3 dominant peaks of Abergavenny – with an unusual shape, fine views and strange legends. Offers a splendid ridge walk, over a mile (1.5 km) long, leading gently to the summit. *Farmland, woods, ridge, rocky valley; 2 climbs; mud.*

Start From Abergavenny take the B4521 NE. Continue 3 miles (5 km). **Car park** (small) on road.

① From car park cross stile and follow side of field to reach a stile. ② Follow path via steps through plantation to reach stile. ③ Turn right to reach waymarked path leading to ridge above. Follow crest of ridge to reach trig. point. ④ Descend the steep N slope with care to reach valley below. ⑤ Turn left and follow path through valley and woods to join outward route at ③.

🏚 On the W side of Ysgyryd Fawr there are steep cliffs where a massive landslip left a deep cutting. Local legend has it that this was made by Noah's Ark passing over the mountain, or by an earthquake at the time of the Crucifixion.

☼ To the S of the summit there are traces of the defensive ramparts of an Iron Age hill fort.

The Holy Mountain, its S ridge leading off to the right.

\⫮/ The Black Mountains, through the Vale of Usk towards Herefordshire and across Gwent to the Bristol Channel.

🖼 The site of the medieval Chapel of St. Michael, with 2 upright stones marking the entrance. It was used until the 17th C., and is the most likely explanation of why the mountain is called Holy.

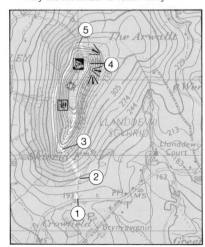

BRECON BEACONS AND BLACK MOUNTAINS

Crib y Garth – the Cat's Back
5 miles (8 km) Sheet 161 288328

Moderate An easy walk with a big mountain feel and superb views for little effort; an interesting section where the ridge narrows, becoming a series of rocky steps. *Ridge, plateau, valley; one climb; mud.*

Start From Longtown take the road to Llanveynoe and then up the Olcho Valley. **Car park** at foot of Cat's Back.

① From car park cross stile and head up slope. Soon reach the ridge. ② Continue along ridge, where the gradient is easier. It becomes rocky and narrow for a few hundred yards, then broadens into Black Hill, marked by a trig. point, where ③ follow well-worn path NW and descend to the head of the Olcho Valley. ④ Turn SE and descend the valley to reach road. ⑤ Follow road to ①.

This short E ridge of the Black Mountains is known locally as the Cat's Back, and from a certain angle it does vaguely resemble a sleeping cat. The narrow ridge is similar to that of Ysgyryd Fawr (see page 141).

The Black Mountains are so-called because from the Hereford side they almost always seem black. Like the Beacons they are made of Old Red Sandstone; it can be glimpsed through the screen of gorse and heather.

To the W is the long Hatterrall Ridge which carries Offa's Dyke Long Distance Path over 160 miles (257 km) from Sedbury to Prestatyn in N Wales (see pages 328-334). E are the plains of Herefordshire and NE, in the far distance, the Clent Hills, near Birmingham.

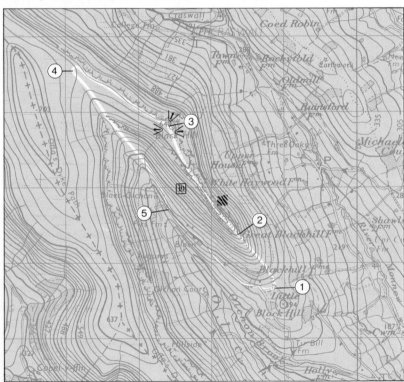

Waun Fâch and Pen y Gader-Fawr
9½ miles (15 km) Sheet 161 251286

Moderate Right into the heart of the Black Mountains, with quite a gradual ascent to their 2 highest peaks; pick a clear day – dramatic views. *Farmland, reservoir, mountain paths, high plateau, streamside; 3 climbs; mud. If inexperienced in hill walking, do not attempt in poor visibility.*

Start From Abergavenny follow minor road to hamlet of Forest Coal Pit, then continue straight on to enter Grwyne Fawr Valley. Follow road to picnic site about 2 miles (3 km) below reservoir. **Parking** in marked picnic site/car park.

① From near the picnic site follow a wide track leading up to the Grwyne Fawr Reservoir. ② Continue past the reservoir following a path near the Grwyne Fawr stream to reach the N escarpment of the Black Mountains. ③ Turn left to follow track leading over Pen y Manllwyn and on to the summit plateau of Waun Fâch. ④ Continue about one mile (1.5 km) along well-worn path to the hump of Pen y Gader-Fawr, where the summit is marked by a cairn. ⑤ Descend to the edge of a forestry plantation on the left and follow track down beside a stream to the valley below. Follow the Grwyne Fawr river to the right to reach a wooden footbridge. ⑥ Cross and return to ①.

🏚 Foundations of a village built to house those who constructed the Grwyne Fawr Reservoir, started 1912.

🌊 The reservoir, with its graceful dam, holds 376m. gallons (1,709m. litres).

🌿 Waun Fâch – meaning small bog – is the highest point of the Black Mountains.

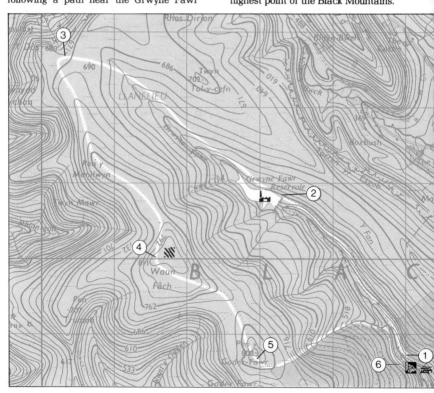

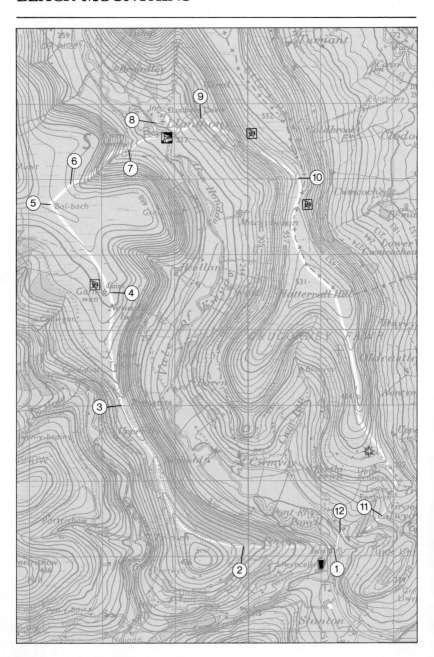

The Llanthony Circuit
12 miles (19 km) Sheet 161 312222

Energetic Varied walking with fine views taking in 2 ridges of the Black Mountains and some historic ruins. *Mountain ridges; mountain valley; 2 climbs; mud.*

Start From the A465 at Llanfihangel Crucorney take the B4423 for Llanthony. In 2 miles (3 km) stop at the Queen's Head Inn. **Parking** near Queen's Head.

① From the Inn take lane leading uphill to reach a metal gate giving access to open hillside. ② Continue along track to reach Dialgorreg stone. ③ Follow crest of ridge to reach the tall cairn of Garn-wen. ④ Continue on this track until reaching another cairn at Bal-bach. ⑤ Turn right and shortly ⑥ take the right-hand track leading down into Cwm Bwchel. On reaching stile ⑦ follow waymarked path past farmhouse and down through a dingle to reach a metal footbridge. Cross and continue into Llanthony village. ⑧ Follow lane up to Llanthony Priory and cross stile by Abbey Farm. Continue around rear of Priory beside long, stone wall to reach a stile. Go diagonally up through field to reach stile near right corner. Continue uphill through woods to stile. Go straight up field to another stile. ⑨ Turn right to follow well-worn track, soon gently climbing the hillside. On reaching crest of ridge ⑩ turn right and follow Offa's Dyke over Hatterrall Hill, past

Llanthony: the South Tower and the Prior's House contain a hotel.

a trig. point and down to the embankments of Pentwyn fort. On reaching metal gate ⑪ take road downhill to cottage on left, from which take track on right leading down through trees. At road turn right. At next junction ⑫ turn left and follow road back to ①.

🍺 The Queens Head, some 300 years old.

🔟 The tall, beautifully symmetrical cairn is craftsman made.

📷 Llanthony Priory, an Augustinian house, was founded in the early 12th C. In the 15th C. the monks tired of the harsh local weather and built a second Llanthony in Gloucester. The poet Walter Savage Landor bought the ruin in 1802 with romantic dreams of restoring it – but did not succeed.

🔟 This path was christened *rhin crw* – beer track – because monks may have used it to transport beer between the Priory and Longtown.

🔟 A section of Offa's Dyke long distance path (see pages 328-334); here, it does not follow the earthwork built in the 6th C. by King Offa of Mercia.

🌟 Iron Age Pentwyn Fort; fine views.

145

BRECON BEACONS AND BLACK MOUNTAINS

The Brecon Beacons Horseshoe

8 miles (13 km) Sheet 160 032179

Energetic A satisfying day's walking, particularly for those visiting the area for the first time: it takes in the Beacons' highest and most shapely summits. By any standards this is dramatic walking with an impressive traverse of Corn Dû, Pen y Fan and Cribin. Possibly best in autumn, when the route is less crowded and the colouring highly attractive. *Ancient way, mountain ridges, plateau, escarpment; 3 climbs; mud. Do not attempt in poor visibility without a 1:25,000 map and compass.*

Start From the A465 at Cein-coed-y-cymmer take the minor road via Pontsticill to the Neuadd Reservoirs. **Parking** near Taf Fechan Water Board buildings.

① From parking area follow fence to right to reach a track. Turn left, cross stile and follow path beside fence. By metal gate head upwards to join Roman road. ② Turn left and follow this ancient way to its highest point, known as The Gap. ③ Climb path on the left leading to summit of Cribin. ④ Descend the W slopes to a col and then climb steeply to the summit of Pen y Fan following well-worn path. Cross the summit plateau to reach the trig. point. ⑤ Follow path to the SW, descending at first, then climbing to the summit of Corn Dû. ⑥ Descend on the SW side of Corn Dû to Bwlch Duwynt and follow escarpment via Craig Gwaun-taf and Craig Fan-ddu to the trig. point at Twyn Mwyalchod. ⑦ Retrace steps and follow track steeply downhill to left edge of plantation. Follow side of plantation to more gentle ground below. Head across to a wooden gate giving access to right of way across the dam. Follow path up to metal gate and return to ①.

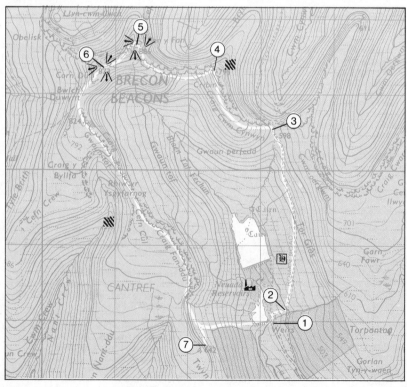

🔼 The twin reservoirs are fed by Taf Fechan.

ⓑ This ancient route crossing the Beacons may be of Roman origin.

⚠ Cribin is a shapely peak, sometimes called the Welsh Matterhorn – a title shared with Cricht in Snowdonia. The steep N ridge is known as The Snout.

⚠ Pen y Fan: see opposite page. (Take care on the edge of the NE face.)

⚠ Corn Dû: see opposite page. A Bronze Age burial mound was excavated here some years ago.

⚠ The long and beautiful valley passed on the W side of the 'Horseshoe' is Cwm Crew. Notice the moraine – glacial debris – near its top end.

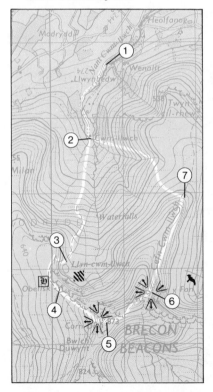

Pen y Fan from Cwm-llwch
6 miles (9.5 km) Sheet 160 007247

Energetic One of the most interesting ways of climbing this famous mountain – the highest in S Wales. The beautiful lake of Llyn-cwm-llwch comes as a pleasant surprise for those who have not been this way before. *Wooded valley, open mountainside and ridges; 4 climbs; mud. Do not attempt in poor visibility without a map and compass.*

Start Take the Ffrwdgrech road opposite the Drovers' Arms on the W side of Brecon. At fork take the middle road of the 3 and after crossing stream bear left off road; go straight over the crossroad and on to the track. **Parking** in clearing after gate.

① Follow track to reach a stile near Cwm-llwch Cottage. ② Continue on track uphill, forking left at cairn, to reach lake. ③ Ascend track on right to gain ridge and obelisk. ④ Follow ridge to summit of Corn Dû. ⑤ Continue NE to reach summit of Pen y Fan. ⑥ Continue about one mile (1.5 km) along ridge and ⑦ descend from crest of ridge over open country to reach outward route near Cwm-llwch Cottage.

⚠ Llyn-cwm-llwch, created by glaciation, is reputed to be bottomless: in fact it is 60 feet (18 m) deep at the centre.

ⓑ The Tommy Jones Obelisk tells a tragic and mystifying tale.

⚠ Corn Dû and Pen y Fan are the highest peaks of the Beacons, and of S Wales. Views range from the nearby Black Mountains to the Preseli Hills in the W to Cader Idris (NW) and Exmoor (S) – but conditions have to be near-perfect.

🐦 Dozens of ravens frequent the summit. Distinguish them from crows by their massive size and slightly pointed tails.

Hay-on-Wye is a starting point for walks N into the Black Mountains and S into Radnor Forest.

At Ystradfellte, 6 miles NE of the A465 at Glynneath, a popular walk starts from the car park; waterfalls.

The Brecon-Abergavenny Canal is beautiful walking.

NORTH WALES

This is no mere region, but a nation in miniature. For here is the stronghold of the Welsh language; a coastline which arguably includes the finest estuary in Europe (the Mawddach); fertile farmland (Anglesey and the Vale of Clwyd) and, above all, range upon range of mountains. It is pointless to name them all, but there is one for everybody.

There is Snowdon itself, whose summit, with some justice, has been called the highest slum in Europe; for the inexperienced, the railway climbs almost to the top *and* there are five paths to walk up. At the other extreme of difficulty are the tough, rough Rhinogs, running south towards Dollgellau. Beyond them is Cader Idris, and running north-east from that lovely mountain are the Arans and the Berwyns, also held in highest regard by connoisseurs of upland beauty.

Next to Snowdon across the Llanberis Pass are the Glyders and fierce Tryfan, and then beyond Llyn Ogwen are the Carneddau, a superlative range extending almost to the north coast, unbroken by pass or road and thus the preserve of those on foot. Carnedd Llywelyn is only 80 feet (24 m) lower than Snowdon. From it survey the country eastwards beyond the Conwy Valley, the Denbighshire Moors, and the Clwyd Hills, nearly in England.

Mawddach Estuary
3 miles (5 km) Sheet 124 636142

Moderate A short but fairly energetic walk with views of the Mawddach Estuary and Barmouth, also the Rhinog mountains. A short detour takes in Llynnau Cregennen, a small lake held by the National Trust. Best views are obtained when the trees are bare. *Woods, farmland; one climb.*

Start Going from Tywyn on the A493 to Dolgellau, about ½ mile (0.8 km) past the toll road to Barmouth look for a lay-by at Arthog; buses. **Parking** in lay-by close to school.

① The route is signposted from the parking area. Follow the clearly marked track up through woods, passing some remote cottages and eventually reaching ② a single-track lane. To extend the walk, bear right and follow the lane past the farm. Just beyond farm a track leads down to the left; follow this to Llynnau Cregennen. To continue, turn left at the lane and go steeply downhill. ③ At the main road turn left and shortly take the marked footpath to the right. Follow it ½ mile (0.8 km) across the Arthog bog. At edge of estuary follow track and footpath to road; at road turn left and return to the car park.

\!/ From the railway and footbridge there is a sweeping view of the estuary which William Wordsworth called 'sublime'.

The Mawddach Estuary and, inset, a reminder of the Welsh for public footpath.

🦅 The woods above Arthog are a home for many warblers, including the little chiffchaff, which gets its name from its song; the green and yellow wood warbler; and the black cap, often called the northern nightingale.

\!/ Inland from Llynnau Cregennen the heights of Cader Idris are seen: Cader means Chair of; Idris was a legendary warrior-bard.

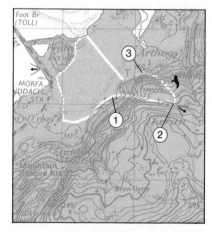

NORTH WALES

Nant-y-Gamar Woods

3½ miles (5.5 km) Sheets 115 and 116 795821

Easy A rich and varied section of countryside, still unspoilt though close to Llandudno. Fine views of coast, town, mountains and of Anglesey. Much interest – the old tracks are largely 15th C. or earlier; there are rare limestone flowers, butterflies in profusion and plenty of birdlife. *Farmland, woods, heath; one climb; mud.*

Start Take the A546 from Llandudno to Craig-y-don, in Colwyn Bay; frequent buses. **Parking** on seafront, close to County Hotel.

① Walk down Queen's Road, past shops and a small park. ② Past entrance to North Wales Medical Centre turn left up stony track. ③ Turn right then left along track at bottom of wood. ④ Go through gate on to limestone pasture, and continue alongside the stone wall. ⑤ Go through gate and follow track through oak woods past Gloddaeth Hall. ⑥ Bear left along path up through Nant-y-Gamar woods. ⑦ Emerge on to Nant-y-Gamar hill. Turn right along wall. ⑧ At end of wall go through gate and turn left past small farm. Walk down farm road. ⑨ Take path leading down through woods down to Bodafon Road, then follow road to seafront.

🐛 The woody plants in the hedge show that the track is from 400 to 500 years old. Since each species takes about a hundred years to become established .

🏛 In 1980, silver coins, minted in Chester and dated 1034, in Canute's reign, were found by the path and valued at £20,000.

🦋 Many butterfly species (spring, early summer) including speckled woods, gatekeepers and meadow browns.

🌳 The trees beside the track are holm oaks, the evergreen variety, with small, dark green leaves, bright green acorns and tassels of tiny yellow flowers.

🏢 Gloddaeth Hall, a 15th C. building, was once the home of the Mostyn family, still large landowners in the area.

🐦 Birds in the open country include the ring ouzel, with its white half-collar, and the stonechat, whose alarm call sounds like pebbles knocking together.

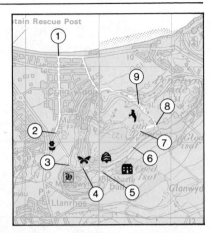

Conwy Mountain and the Sychnant Pass

10½ miles (17 km) Sheet 115 783774

Moderate Magnificent views, prehistoric interest, birdlife, plants and marvellous air – a unique blend of sea breezes and mountain winds. Best in spring to autumn – the upland areas really are bleak in winter. *Town, moorland, farmland; 2 climbs; mud after rain.*

Start Conwy, on the A55; frequent buses; trains to Llandudno Junction, about one mile (1.5 km) across river. **Car parks** in Conwy.

① Take the A55 (Bangor road) out of Conwy, passing through arch in town walls. After 150 yards (137 m) cross railway bridge and turn right. Turn into Mountain Road which runs off to the right around a bend in the road. ② At end of terrace of cottages take the footpath uphill. ③ Follow the path on the inland side of the ridge. At end of ridge follow path round small hill, then inland. ④ With farm on right, head downhill and keep straight on until the Sychnant Pass road is reached. ⑤ Cross road and take signposted footpath. Past the lake bear right until stony track is reached. Follow this round to the right, and continue on it as it wanders across the hills, eventually ⑥ reaching point where wooded ravine can be seen ahead, together with small farm at edge of wood. Keeping farm to the right, follow track to left up a small valley. ⑦ This track meets another from the left; turn right. Follow the grassy track beside a stone wall across the hills. After ¾ mile (one km) ⑧ go through a couple of gates on to metalled, single-track lane. Continue downhill. ⑨ At telephone box, turn left downhill. ⑩ Turn right at T-junction (signposted to Henryd). ⑪ In the village turn left. In ½ mile (0.8 km) ⑫ take the lane to the left. ⑬ At Groesffordd post office turn right. ⑭ Take the track marked 'Unsuitable for Motor Vehicles' which leads left at a small row of terraced cottages. ⑮ Having climbed steep hill this track eventually crosses the Conwy-Penmaenmawr road. Cross and go down the track opposite which runs into the valley. ⑯ Bear right along the bottom of the valley until reaching Mountain Road.

Castell Caer Seion, covering 10½ acres (4 ha), is one of the many Iron Age forts in the area.

The view encompasses Anglesey and Conwy Bay.

On the wilder sections of the route there is a chance of seeing peregrines, the rarest of the U.K.'s resident falcons. Its blue-grey plumage and black 'moustache' give it a dignified look. Most notable of its characteristics is the dramatic 'stoop' after prey, a near-vertical dive during which it reaches speeds of as high as 250 mph (402 km/h).

Bronze Age stone circles, standing stones and burial chambers are seen close to the route.

The castle, now a splendid ruin, was built in 1283-6 by Edward I, part of a chain intended to pacify the Welsh.

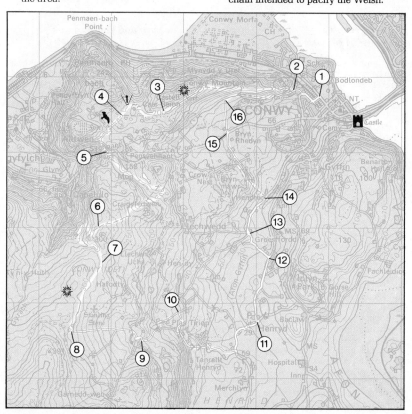

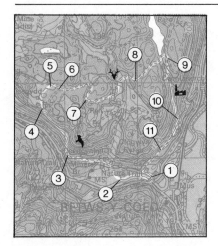

In the thickest parts of the Forest lives the goldcrest, 3½ inches (9 cm) long, the smallest British bird, with willow-green plumage and a gold crown bounded by black stripes. There are also black grouse, which, when roosting, look like small turkeys perched in the fir trees.

The Forest has a rare inhabitant, the pine martin, distinguishable from the squirrel by its slim build, bushy tail and light under-parts. Other mammals include the polecat, much commoner, not such a climber and looking like a short-legged black cat; also red squirrels.

Aberllyn mine, worked for much-needed lead ore in the Napoleonic Wars, is now disused. It is possible to find small quantities of the ore – cubic in shape and silvery in colour – in the spoil heaps.

Gwydyr Forest
3½ miles (5.5 km) Sheet 115 792568

Easy Fine views of Snowdonia; woodland with a variety of interest from rare birds to disused lead mines. *Riverside, woods, meadow; 2 climbs; mud. If inexperienced in hill walking, avoid in poor visibility.*

Start from the A5 turn on to the B5106 (Betws-y-Coed to Llanrwst road); trains to Betws-y-Coed, ¼ mile (0.5 km) away from start. **Public car park** past bridge on left, very shortly after turning on to B5106.

① From car park take path beside river. ② At massive rock, just before end of wood, bear away from river and follow path diagonally uphill through fir wood. Continue to bungalow seen ahead. ③ At metalled forest road turn left and carry on past farm. In about ½ mile (0.8 km), at bend in road, take path running to right. (If you reach Forestry Commission parking notices you have gone too far.) ④ Cross stile in meadow and bear left along stone wall. Follow path across 2 stiles. ⑤ At Forestry road turn right. ⑥ At T-junction go straight on. ⑦ At next T-junction bear left. Go straight across crossing road, past Forestry gate. ⑧ At Y-junction go left, passing end of Llyn Parc. ⑨ Turn right at next T-junction, then bear right down path after 25 yards (23 m). Follow stream into ravine, past Aberllyn lead mine workings. ⑩ Take lower path, with Conwy valley on left. ⑪ Return to car park.

Porth Ysgo and Hell's Mouth
9 miles (14.5 km) Sheet 123 207627

Moderate A walk for viewing coastal scenery, some of it wild. Goes through an area covered with an ancient pattern of small, well-enclosed fields. Particularly spectacular with a westerly gale blowing, driving the sea into Hell's Mouth. *Cliffs, shore, farmland, common; one climb.*

Start From Aberdaron take the steep road signposted Rhiw. At crossroads with telephone box turn right and drive down lane to Ysgo Farm. **Car park** marked at Ysgo Farm.

① From car park take path marked to Porth Ysgo. From beach retrace to Y-junction where ② take the path straight on up cliff. This joins the lane at a T-junction. Turn right. ③ At next junction turn right and follow the road up to Rhiw village. ④ Turn left at the crossroads. Take the next left, then ⑤ turn right up the metalled track leading past transmitting station. ⑥ Go through the gate and follow the track to the summit of Mynydd Rhiw. From the summit follow the track down to the lane and ⑦ turn left. ⑧ At the T-junction turn left and continue to bear left. After more than one mile (1.5 km), ⑨ turn right then a few yards on turn left and immediately turn left. Continue along this lane past Felin Uchaf and ⑩ turn left at the next T-junction. Follow this lane down to ⑪ the road junction with the telephone box, cross the lane and return to the car park.

〰 Hell's Mouth has been the scene of many wrecks during SW gales.

👁 From Mynydd Rhiw there is a fine view of the bay of Hell's Mouth and the whole Lleyn Peninsula, with Bardsey Island at its tip, reached by boat from Aberdaron. Bardsey is called the Island of a Thousand Saints: it was a place of pilgrimage from about the 5th C., when St. Cadfan founded its first monastery. It is a bird sanctuary (rare migrants) and nature reserve – good views of seals.

🦌 Many hares, stoats and weasels.

🍺 At Aberdaron there are 2 agreeable pubs, the Ship and Ty Newydd Hotels.

Turf-covered stone walls of the Lleyn Peninsula create a landscape unlike any other in North Wales.

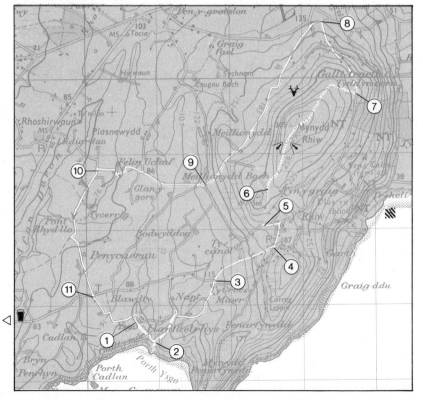

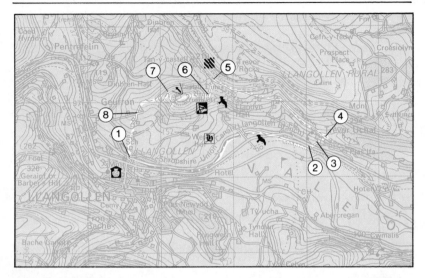

Vale of Llangollen
5 miles (8 km) Sheet 117 215423

Easy Aspects of Wales not covered by the other routes in this section: part of the Telford Canal towpath, and glimpses of early Welsh history. *Canal-side, hillside; 2 climbs.*

Start Llangollen, on the A5; frequent buses.
Parking in the centre of Llangollen, preferably near the bridge.

① At the N end of the bridge walk up to the Canal Museum, then walk E along the towpath, past stone bridge and pass under road bridge. ② Walk up beside next stone bridge and cross canal. ③ Cross road and follow lane up beside Sun Trevor Hotel. A few yards on take signposted public footpath to left. At junction of paths go right, up to the lane and ④ turn left following lane uphill, along edge of Creigiau Eglwyseg escarpment. After belt of trees, reach a gated lane ⑤ and follow this left. In about 150 yards (137 m) ⑥ cross stile and follow path as it crosses meadow and rises steeply to Castell Dinas Bran. ⑦ On far side of ruins follow zigzag path downhill to end of wooded lane. ⑧ Follow path down to Llangollen.

⚑ Canal Exhibition Centre, with horse-drawn canal trips.

Thomas Telford and one of his greatest civil engineering feats, Pont Cysyllte aqueduct.

🏛 The Shropshire Union Canal was one of Thomas Telford's greatest engineering feats. The famous aqueduct carrying it over the Dee 3½ miles (5.5 km) to the E is more than 1,000 feet (305 m) long.

🦅 Kingfishers are seen around the canal.

〰 Eglwyseg Rocks – limestone terraces.

🦅 The woods are notable for flycatchers, redstarts and woodpeckers.

🏰 Castell Dinas Bran was first an Iron Age hill fort, then a wooden castle, in the 13th C. a stone building, and a ruin by the late 1500s. The view is of Valle Crucis Abbey.

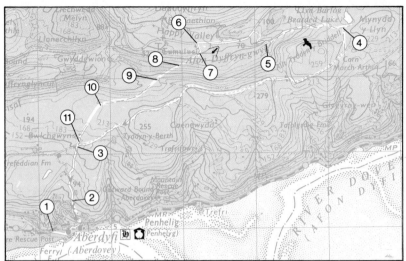

Aberdovey

7½ miles (12 km) Sheet 135 613959

Moderate Covers one of North Wales' most beautiful estuaries, with terrain akin to downland that contrasts to other routes in this section. Spectacular on fine days with the shadows of clouds sweeping across the hills; grand views of the coast towards Aberystwyth with the sea rolling in. *Hillsides, lakeside, farmland, woods, upland grazing; 2 climbs; mud after rain.*

Start Aberdovey on the A493; frequent buses; trains – Aberdovey is on the Cambrian coastline. **Car park** on the front.

① From car park walk up past church. ② Follow the steep lane running inland. ③ Turn right at crossroads and follow road across hills. In about 2 miles (3 km) go through gate and continue on well-defined track about one mile (1.5 km) to Llyn Barfog. ④ Going down to the lake take the track which runs to the left. ⑤ Follow the path down to lane in valley, past farmhouse dated 1741. Turn left along the lane and continue to group of houses on left, where ⑥ go down drive past houses and through gate. ⑦ Cross footbridge and immediately turn right up through oak wood. ⑧ Follow path up side of hill, along edge of wood and across open pasture. ⑨ At point where stony track does a

hairpin bend carry straight on along grassy track. Climbing steeply ⑩ pass between 2 old, wooden gateposts and continue upwards. At top of hill follow path across pasture, through gates, down to sunken lane. ⑪ Continue down lane to reach outward route and return to ①.

🏛 Aberdovey, popular today for small boat sailing, was a ship-building centre in the days of the sailing ships. These are recalled in the Outward Bound Sailing Museum on the waterfront.

🏔 From the hills there is a splendid view of the Dovey Estuary, one of the most beautiful in Wales, and of the long sweep of the coast towards Aberystwyth.

🐦 Birds conspicuous in the area during summer include skylarks, wheatears and redstarts. The skylark is often no more than a speck in the sky, pouring out song, but when it is at close range, starting up suddenly from the ground, it shows its white outer tail feathers and even its crest, though this is often flat. Grey-brown wheatears catch the eye by flirting their black and white tails. Their colours are much more subdued than those of the beautiful male redstart, with his blue-grey back, black throat and russet-orange breast and tail.

NORTH WALES

Bala Lake and Glyn Gower
5½ miles (9 km) Sheet 125 903322

Easy Provides a picture of the country round Bala, the largest natural lake in Wales. Valley, hillsides, plantations, lakeside; one climb; parts of the forest are wet.

Start From Bala take the B4391, turning right on to the B4403. Continue about 3 miles (5 km) to Llangower; lake train to Llangower from Bala, summer only. **Public car park** at Llangower.

① From car park turn left along road; 100 yards (91 m) past the church ② turn right. Follow the road all the way up the valley to the farm. Bear left past front of ruined cottages, following track as ③ it swings round behind cottages and uphill. Through gate follow track as it zigzags uphill, following course of rush-filled road. ④ Make for the old barn that can be seen ahead. Walk around edge of enclosure and follow the old wall, keeping to its right side. ⑤ Go through gate into plantation and follow path straight ahead. ⑥ At corner of older plantation climb stile and walk beside fence. ⑦ At hollow with stile leading back into plantation follow firebreak (gap in trees) over rough ground until a clearing is reached. Keep to the firebreak on the left. At edge of wood walk down until remains of old gate come into view. ⑧ Turn through gate into woods and follow path which runs down another firebreak. In about 250 yards (229 m) a ruined farm is seen through trees on the right. ⑨ Walk past front of this farm and join the paved track which goes left through the forest. ⑩ Continue on farm track. Eventually reach the original route up Glyn Gower, and in about ½ mile (0.8 km) the B4403. Cross the road and follow the track ⑪ to the lakeside. Walk to the left along the lake until reaching a stream. This can be crossed in summer, in which case continue by lake. If it is full, walk beside stream to the road and return to ①.

🔌 Bala Lake is the largest natural lake in Wales, 3¾ miles (6 km) long and ½ mile (0.8 km) wide. The River Dee flows out of it, giving it – and the town nearby – their name, for *bala* is the Welsh word for 'outlet'.

🚂 The Lake railway (opened 1972) follows the course of the old line from Ruabon to Barmouth, which closed in 1965.

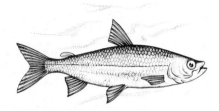

Though a distinct species, the Bala gwyniad is one of the whitefish family, with 7 other roughly similar members in various U.K. lakes and lochs.

↯ The lake contains its own, distinct fish species, the gwyniad. Its ancestors are likely to have been sea-freshwater migrants of the salmon family, landlocked by ice during the glacial eras.

↯ There are sweeping views from the top of the Glyn Gower hills.

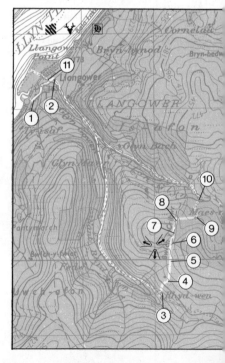

Newborough Warren and Llanddwyn Island

6½ miles (10.5 km) Sheet 114 423656

Easy A stretch of remote coastline on Anglesey with magnificent views of Snowdonia; geology and natural history. *Village, forest, shore, dunes; short stretches among the dunes may be boggy.*

Start Newborough, off the A5, along the A4080 at the S corner of Anglesey; buses. **Parking** in Newborough village.

① From crossroads at centre of village take the road marked to 'Beach and Llanddwyn Island'. ② Immediately before the church take the path to the right, then follow the path running behind the church. ③ Follow the path through the forest out on to the beach. ④ If tide permits, walk across the beach to Llanddwyn Island. If water is high, it drops after about one hour sufficiently to cross. Follow the path to the lighthouse and point. ⑤ Retrace steps to ④ , then turn right

to walk along the beach until level with the end of the forest. (Do *not* go up to the car park area half-way along this stretch.) ⑥ Walk along the edge of the Forest with the warren on the right; follow the path until it reaches a narrow lane running down from the higher ground on the left. ⑦ Walk up this to ⑧ the road. Return to village.

📖 Newborough's charter and its English name were conferred by Edward I.

〰 The island's rocks are some of the oldest in Britain – Precambrian, formed about 600 million years ago.

🔨 Shags and cormorants nest on the island, and terns and gulls are plentiful. Ringed plovers nest on the beach – if not disturbed. In the Warren are harriers and short-eared owls.

🌱 The Warren, which is a nature reserve, comprising forest, marsh and dunes, fosters orchids, sea plants and grasses.

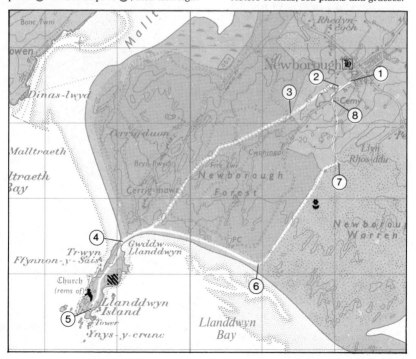

The Roman Steps and Llyn Cwm Bychan

12 miles (19 km) Sheet 124 622299

Energetic Crosses the Rhinogs, whose rocky, shattered terrain is unique in Snowdonia. *Wooded lane, lakesides, rocky mountain terrain, forest, moorland, farmland, riverside; one climb; some sections are extremely boggy – strong waterproof footwear essential at all times; dress well – passes through exposed country.*

Start In Harlech turn into the steep, narrow road beside Barclay's Bank. Continue ¾ mile (one km) to crossroads (telephone box). Go straight across and continue 2 miles (3 km). Turn left and continue to marked **car park** and picnic place.

① From car park turn right and follow lane uphill past Llyn Cwm Bychan. ② At far end of lake take the signposted path to the right. ③ Follow track, first through oak woods, then across open country. ④ After climbing Roman Steps the summit is reached. Ahead a large forest is seen; go down into gully, where follow well-defined path through heather into the trees. ⑤ Cross stile over Forest fence and follow path through dense trees, crossing stream and walking parallel to it down firebreak (gap in trees). The original path has been lost in the boggy ground. Keep to the firebreak. ⑥ At Forestry Commission road turn right and continue. ⑦ Take the left fork at the junction. Turn right at the next T-junction. ⑧ On sharp left bend, keep straight on down another firebreak. Follow path to forest gate on to moor. Follow the clearly defined path seen leading across the hills and through a pass. On this path eventually ⑨ reach farm at head of Cwm Nantcol. Take the road down into the valley, going right at the fork. ⑩ At the hamlet, cross the river and turn right. Continue more than 2 miles up the single-track lane to ①.

🌿 Among unusual plants in the area are sundews, which trap their insect food on the sticky hairs on their spoon-shaped leaves, and twayblades, their stems of greenish yellow flowers rising from 2 opposite stem leaves.

🦅 Beside the lake and the rivers, sandpipers perch on banks and stones, bobbing their rounded white-edged tails up and down.

🦋 Marsh fritillaries may be seen.

🏛 The Roman Steps may have been laid by Roman, British or medieval builders. They are broken flights of 'stairs', formed of flat slabs of unhewn rock, buttressed at the sides by upright blocks, and were once part of a trade route between Bala and the coast.

⚠ The heather conceals rocks and fissures – keep to the path.

🏛 Harlech Castle, about 3 miles (5 km) along this road, was built by Edward I between 1283 and 1289. It was besieged by the Welsh in 1294-5 and held by a garrison of only 37 men. It was the last stronghold to fall in the Wars of the Roses, and among the survivors was a boy of 12, who was to become Henry VII, founder of the Tudor dynasty.

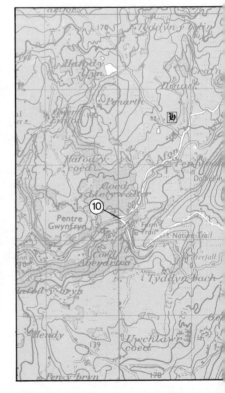

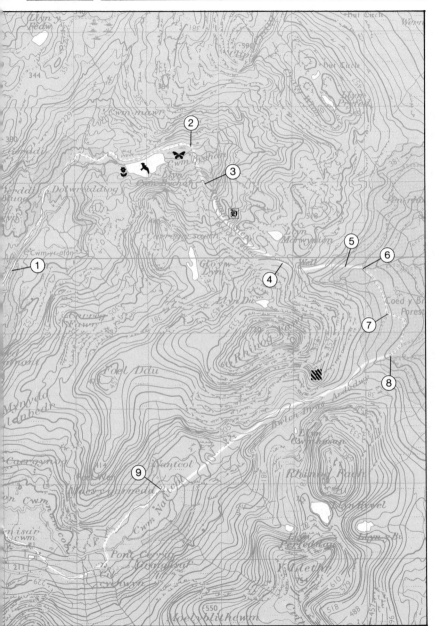

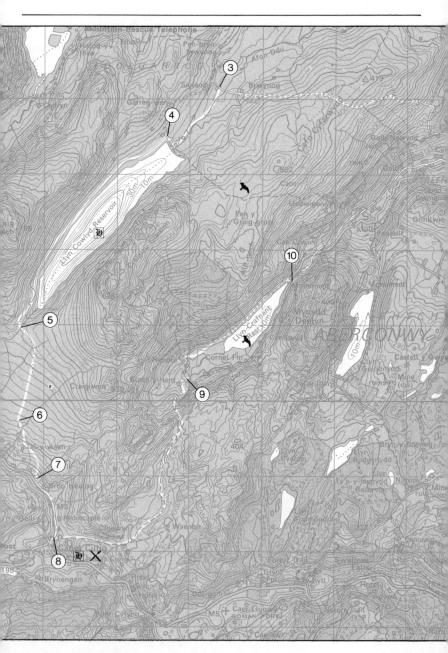

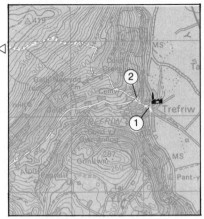

Water from Llyn Cowlyd supplies Colwyn Bay and a power station at Dolgarrog.

Two Lakes Walk
13 miles (21 km) Sheet 115 783630

Energetic Excellent hill walking across some safer slopes of Snowdonia, covering a wide variety of terrain typical of northern Snowdonia. Some exposed upland country: dress appropriately in winter. *Rough pasture, heather hillside, woods; 3 climbs; some sections boggy at all times. Do not attempt in poor visibility.*

Start Trefriw on the B5106; buses; Llanrwst Station is about one mile (1.5 km) from Trefriw across the river. **Public car park** at Trefriw opposite the Woollen Mill.

① From car park cross road and go over bridge to right. Turn left up first road on left and climb steeply to signpost ② pointing right to Cowlyd. Follow this road uphill past small village cemetery. It climbs steeply for 2 miles (3 km) – ignore all side turnings. On top of moors follow road as it drops down to deserted farms. ③ Take path to the left and walk to Llyn Cowlyd. At the dam turn right and ④ follow the edge of the lake for 1¾ miles (3 km). Climb track at far end of lake and ⑤ cross the second of the 2 footbridges. ⑥ Follow the wide, grassy and boggy track down to the stile and past cottage in trees. ⑦ At A5 walk down to Capel Curig. ⑧ Take signposted footpath beside the church (opposite the couple of shops). Follow path – clearly marked – 2½ miles (4 km) to Crafnant. As the path reaches the road beside the lake, ⑨ bear left along a stony

track. Pass cottages in the woods and before reaching house called 'Hendre' take marked footpath which runs off right across meadow. On reaching Forestry Commission road turn right and follow the road to the far side of the lake. ⑩ Turn left at end of lake and take lane down through woods to ①.

Trefriw Woollen Mills have made Welsh cloth since the early 19th C., when they were powered by water from the River Crafnant. They are open to the public, and have a shop attached to them.

The area abounds in birds: buzzards, ravens and grouse in the open country, dippers, grey wagtails and sandpipers on the rivers; pied flycatchers, redstarts, wood warblers in the woods in summer.

Llyn Cowlyd, a man-made lake in a flooded valley, provides local people with water. When a dam burst below the lake in 1925, there was a serious flood. In winter wild swans may be seen here, otherwise the lake lacks wildlife.

Capel Curig is a notable climbing centre, and E down the A5 there are several cafés.

On Llyn Crafnant, another reservoir, there is good trout fishing. The lake is a habitat, too, for wild duck and heron.

Llyn Dinas and Aberglaslyn Pass

9 miles (14.5 km) Sheet 115 588483

Moderate This is one of the most beautiful parts of Snowdonia: south-facing, it is always warmer and lusher than the N, and it has rugged mountain scenery. Superb variety – mountains, woods, rivers. In May and June the hills are covered with wild rhododendrons in flower. *Riverside, meadows, lanes, hillsides, mountain pass; one climb; some wet meadows – waterproof footwear is essential.*

Start Beddgelert, on the junction of the A498 and the A4085; frequent buses. **Car Park** at the Porthmadog end of the village.

① From car park walk down village street away from Royal Goat Hotel. ② Before road bridge over river turn right along road beside river. Cross footbridge at end of this road and bear left beside river. ③ Follow path which keeps to the course of the river. ④ Across the meadows keep to the footpath notices and gates. The path is clear if one follow where others have walked. ⑤ Follow path through farm – it is clearly signposted. ⑥ On reaching single-track lane at end of farm drive, turn right and follow lane about 3 miles (5 km). Follow lane past quarry then (on bend) a farm. Shortly a wooden footbridge comes into view on right. ⑦ Pass through a gap in the low stone wall and walk across the meadow to this bridge. ⑧ Cross and walk to the left end of the barn seen ahead. Follow the track up through the oak woods. ⑨ At the top of the hill keep to the wall, go through gate and follow the old cart track. ⑩ Passing ruined farm buildings follow the stony track up the hill. At brow of hill a gate is seen to the left across the meadow. Make for this, go through and follow the paving stones up the hill. ⑪ Go through the farmyard and join the farm road running downhill. (If the llamas are here, they are harmless if left alone.) ⑫ Where the farm road meets the lane turn right. Go through village of Nantmor and ⑬ just before right bend follow course of old railway, turning right. ⑭ The track enters a tunnel, which is dark. The ground is even but this route can be avoided by diverting left to a path which rejoins at the far end of the tunnel. ⑮ Cross the footbridge and turn

The River Glaslyn roars beside the road through the Aberglaslyn Pass.

right. Follow the marker posts across the water meadows to Beddgelert.

⑲ Beddgelert means 'grave of Gelert'. Gelert was the hound of Prince Llewellyn, who one day left the dog to guard his baby son. When he returned the child was missing and the dog horribly bloodstained. Llewellyn killed the dog on the spot, only to find his son asleep, hidden by bedding, and beside him the huge body of a dead wolf. Gelert had saved the child's life, and in remorse for killing his faithful dog, the Prince built a memorial to him. This is in a meadow on the S side of the village.

🛕 A Celtic priory was founded in Beddgelert in the 6th C., followed, in the 12th or 13th C., by a small Augustinian

(i.e. following the rule of St. Augustine) priory. All that remains of it is the village church, once the priory chapel.

🏭 Mine workings remain from the time when Beddgelert was the centre of a thriving copper mining industry

♣ There are uncommon plants and flowers in the meadows and lanes: it is worth taking an identification guide.

🦙 The Llamas sometimes seen grazing here are kept for their wool.

🔦 From detour around tunnel go to bridge for fine view of gorge.

🚂 A section of the former Welsh Highland Railway.

An interesting agricultural trail 3 miles (5 km) W of Capel on the A5 demonstrates hill farming methods.

A nature walk through oak woods begins at the car park on the B4410 2 miles (3 km) W of Maentwrog.

The market town of Corwen on the Dee is a starting point for paths along the river and into the Berwyn Mts.

Llangollen is another departure point for Dee-side walks. The aqueduct at Pont Cysyllte is to be found 3½ miles (5.5 km) to the E off the A5 or A539.

The Lleyn Peninsula's coastal paths offer considerable scope.

About ¾ mile (one km) N of Llanallgo on Anglesey there is a peaceful, historical trail with a Bronze Age tomb.

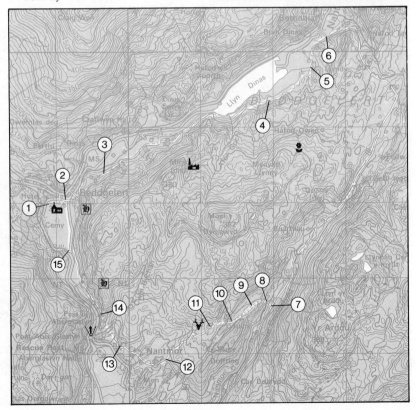

MIDDLE ENGLAND

WELSH MARCHES

Borderlands are places of mystery and anomalies, and it is these qualities which make the area where England and Wales meet a paradise for walkers. In the south, the Forest of Dean is an ancient woodland sitting on top of a coalfield, with Foresters exercising unique and ancient rights. Through it flows the River Wye, having left Wales by the flank of the Black Mountains: a river of great beauty, and not only at the over-visited Symonds Yat.

Herefordshire (now joined with Worcestershire), is one of the last remaining great farmscapes of England, far less damaged by contemporary agriculture than most; but you must pick your paths with care as few are well-walked and obstructions are frequent.

On the eastern side of Herefordshire the Malvern Hills rise to nearly 1,400 feet (427 m) – a miniature mountain range. From end to end it is an easy 9-mile (14.5 km) walk with spectacular views. A truly clear day may produce almost unbelievable sightings: Plynlimmon in the north-west, the Mendips in the south and the Wrekin in the north.

The Southern Malverns
3 miles (5 km) Sheet 150 758368

Easy A comparatively unpopulated and unknown area of the Malvern Hills, but characteristically beautiful. *Hillside, woodland; one climb; mud.*

Start From Ledbury take the A438 in direction of Tewkesbury and continue 5 miles (8 km). **Parking** on left of A438 (going from Ledbury) at the road's highest point – the foot of Midsummer Hill, near cottages.

① Walk down to crossroads and turn right on to minor road. ② Leave road at lodge (small toll payable at times) and walk along the estate track, entering beechwoods and continuing one mile (1.5 km). ③ Leave wood by iron gate and continue straight on with track for 200 yards (183 m); turn right through gate and cross field to gate and road. Turn right along road to Whiteleaved Oak. ④ Immediately after postbox, where road bends right, take track to left. In 100 yards (91 m) bear right on to grass track, through gate, and follow path along side of hill back to road at ①.

☀ Midsummer Hill's twin peaks are the site of an ancient hill fortress.

🏠 Between Midsummer Hill and Swinyard, 2 of the South Malvern Hills, lies the lovely wooded valley unpoetically named the Gullet.

Midsummer Hill, at the least conserved, some say prettiest end of the Malverns.

🏠 Raggedstone Hill, S of Midsummer Hill, looks bare and bleak. Local legend says it is haunted, and that its shadow carries a curse. To the S of it is the beautifully named Valley of the Whiteleaved Oak.

↘ The Black Mountains, in Wales.

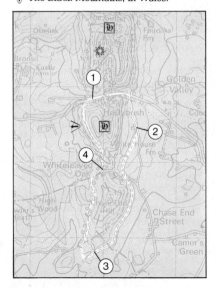

WELSH MARCHES

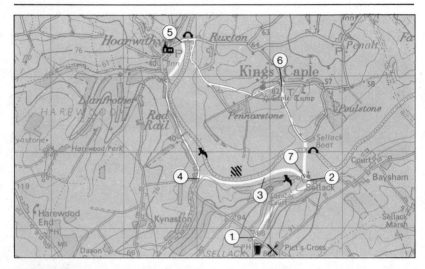

Wye Meadows
5 miles (8 km) Sheets 149 and 162 557268

Easy Typical, lesser-known Herefordshire countryside – a pleasant walk for an evening or half-day finishing at Love Pool Inn. *Meadows, woods, riverside; one climb; mud after rain.*

Start From Ross-on-Wye take the A49 in direction of Hereford, going second right after the roundabout, left at T-junction and right at fork. **Parking** at Love Pool Inn.

① Cross awkward stile opposite Love Pool Inn and follow path across meadow to gate, through further meadow past pools and woodland, and through 2 more gates. Go up slope to lane by cottages and Sellack church. ② Take track to left immediately before church, cross stile, and follow path bearing left to river bank. ③ Continue on river bank for ½ mile (0.8 km) past wood, then turn left through field gate to road. ④ Turn right and follow road for one mile (1.5 km) (signposted 'Hoarwithy/Little Dewchurch'). Take signposted public footpath just after 'Hoarwithy' arrival sign. Return to river bank and follow this to bridge at Hoarwithy. ⑤ Cross bridge, take path on right, leading to lane into King's Caple. ⑥ Turn right at crossroads, leaving road to cross suspension bridge at Sellack Boat, and follow path back to church. ⑦ Retrace to ①.

🐦 Game birds are bred in the woodlands here – keep dogs on leads.

〰 The River Wye (in Welsh *Gwy*) rises on Plynlimon in the Cambrian Mountains of central Wales. Five rivers have their source on that one mountain: the Severn, the Wye, the Dulas, the Llyfnant and the Rheidol. The Lower Wye, winding from Ross, takes in some of the most peaceful and beautiful country in Britain. (Parts of this stretch can be explored by boat.)

🐦 The Wye is a notable salmon-fishing river and the home of many water-birds, including kingfishers, wagtails and redshank. The latter are recognized in flight by the white triangular patches on the rump and the trailing edge of each wing.

⛪ Hoarwithy church, of an unusual Italianate design, contains a number of mosaics.

⌒ Over this stretch of the river there are two suspension bridges: an iron one at Hoarwithy and a wooden footbridge at Sellack Boat.

🍴 The Love Pool Inn, an old timbered building, serves an imaginative range of snacks and meals. Its bright log fire in winter is a welcoming sight at the end of the walk.

Tintern Abbey and the Devil's Pulpit
7 miles (11 km) Sheet 162 539012

Moderate A section of Offa's Dyke long-distance path; opportunity to visit Tintern Abbey (short detour); particularly fine views; atmospheric in autumn and winter. *Riverside, crags, farmland; 2 climbs; mud after rain.*

Start From Chepstow take the A466 in direction of Monmouth and stop ½ mile (0.8 km) N of Tintern Parva. **Parking** in lay-bys on A466.

Partially waymarked. ① Cross bridge and turn right by the New Inn, Brockweir, then right along footpath signposted Tintern, following beside river and veering left up slope to cross stile. ② Turn right on to track, climbing above river, and left up well-defined track to fork right for Devil's Pulpit. Signs do not continue whole way. ③ Turn left up steep, rocky path to wide track. ④ Turn right, *keeping on main track*, passing below Shorn Cliff. Follow track 1¾ miles (3 km) round loop to meet Offa's Dyke path, marked with an acorn sign. ⑤ Turn left along Offa's Dyke, following acorn signs, to Devil's Pulpit. Continue downhill through meadow to Brockweir and ①.

🟥 Brockweir has a pottery.

🍺 The Anchor Inn at Tintern, part 13th C.,
✕ serves good food and real ale.

🍺 New Inn.

♠ Tintern Abbey, now a venerable ruin, was a Cistercian house, founded in 1131 by Walter FitzRichard, Lord of Chepstow, although what remains belongs to buildings of a later date.

📖 The Devil's Pulpit acquired its name
\↓/ from the story that Satan preached from it to the Abbey monks to entice them from their work.

❋ Traces of Offa's Dyke, constructed in about 784 by the Mercian king Offa to mark the frontier between Celt and Saxon. The great earth rampart stretched 100 miles (161 km) from near Prestatyn to the mouth of the Wye. An official long-distance footpath runs along most of its course – see pages 328-334.

The otter, rare in England now, but still occasionally spotted on the quieter stretches of the Wye. It should not be confused with the (smaller) mink.

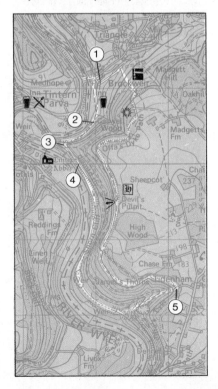

169

WELSH MARCHES

British Camp and Eastnor Park
6 miles (9.5 km) Sheet 150 764404

Easy Views E and W over the Cotswolds and over Herefordshire into Wales. *Ridge, parkland; one climb; mud after rain.*

Start From Great Malvern take the A449 S and continue 5 miles (8 km). **Car park** (for British Camp) at foot of Herefordshire Beacon.

① Climb path signposted at front of car park to British Camp. Continue S along ridge path, then bear right down slope to stone marker. ② Take the track straight from Swinyard Hill to the gate of Eastnor Park. ③ Go through gate and follow marked path to obelisk; continue across park to Ridgeway. ④ Turn right on to Ridgeway and continue 2 miles (3 km) to A449 (occasionally waymarked with white-topped stakes). Ignore right turn to Netherton, also later right turn. ⑤ Return right along A449 to car park.

The views from Herefordshire Beacon are magnificent, but the hill is chiefly famous as the site of the huge British Camp, one of the best examples of an ancient hill fort in Britain. It commanded the only pass existing at that time through the Malvern Hills, and is thought to have held about 20,000 men. According to tradition, Caractacus was captured here in A.D. 75.

On the S side of the Beacon is a recess known locally as the Giant's Cave, but marked on the map as Clutter's Cave. It is man-made, but for what purpose no one knows.

The grounds of Eastnor Park, skilfully laid out, contain some exotic trees, and also shelter a herd of deer. The obelisk is a memorial to the Somers family, owners of Eastnor Castle, built in 1810-17, in the elaborate 'Gothick' style, by Robert Smirke.

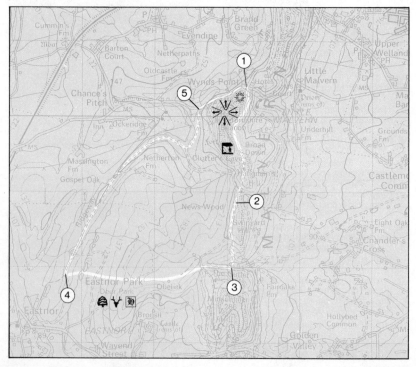

Arthur's Cave
6 miles (9.5 km) Sheet 162 564158

Moderate A popular but unspoilt walk with exceptional views over the Wye and Forest of Dean; archaeological interest. The punt ferry used between ① and ② does not operate some winter months. Check at Forestry Commission Hut, point ① and if necessary return direct from suspension bridge to ①. *Woods; 2 climbs; mud.*

Start From the A40 5 miles (8 km) N of Monmouth, take the B4229 for Symonds Yat and turn right after one mile (1.5 km). **Parking** at Symonds Yat Rock.

Partially waymarked with yellow arrows. ① From car park, walk down road under footbridge to footpath on left signposted 'Wye Rapids & Ferry'. Follow this to river, and cross by punt ferry. ② Go up road from ferry landing, turning right, and on bend take rocky steps to left leading behind Wye Rapids Hotel. Follow path to join wider track and continue about ¼ mile (0.5 km) to open space, where ③ fork right to follow path through young trees, continuing to cross a forest road. Follow waymarked path to Arthur's Cave. ④ From cave, follow waymarked path to Seven Sisters Rocks (each rock is off the path), then descend following waymarks steeply to river bank, turning left to walk beside river to suspension bridge. ⑤ Cross bridge and turn left to walk beside river to punt ferry; after crossing turn left to continue beside river to point above rapids, where fork right up track. Continue ¼ mile to ①.

[𝔥] Symonds Yat Rock, over 500 feet (152 m) above sea-level, took its name from
\†/ Robert Symonds, a 17th C. High Sheriff of Herefordshire. ('Yat' or 'yacht', in the Forest of Dean, mean 'gate' or 'pass'.)

[📷] In Arthur's Cave – according to legend a refuge of the hero-king – there were fossil remains of hyena, mammoth, rhinoceros and flint tools.

\†/ More fine views of the Wye and the Forest of Dean from Seven Sisters Rocks.

⌒ At the Biblins there is a swing bridge
🚣 over the Wye and a picnic area.

✕ Refreshment hut at Symonds Yat.

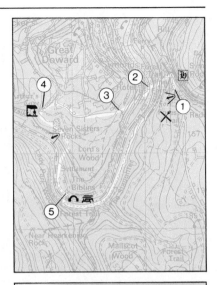

The Forest of Dean is widely regarded as this area's centrepiece. Many of its paths are waymarked (yellow arrows), and it is easy to improvise routes taking in the great rocks. One starting point is the lay-by near Staunton on the A4136 just over 2 miles (3 km) out of Monmouth. Walk along the road towards Staunton, take the forestry track on the left, forking right to reach Suck Stone. From there climb the path to the top of Near Hearkening Rock – unforgettable at sunset.

Paths from Great Malvern, 7 miles (11 km) SW of Worcester on the A449, find their way easily to the tops of the Malvern Hills.
Signposted 5 miles (8 km) SE of Hereford on the Mordiford Woolhope road, a car park and picnic site give access to woodland walks with fine views of Hereford and the Welsh mountains.
From New Radnor (on the B4362 from Presteigne at the foot of the Radnor Forest Hills) there are walks around the town's Norman ruins and paths into the surrounding hills.
Knighton, in the Teme valley, is a centre for walks into the nearby border country, and along Offa's Dyke.

COTSWOLDS

Here – perhaps more than in any other part of Britain – beauty depends on the built environment. The towns and villages, despite all the mistakes and horrors of recent decades, reflect the earth itself by the uniformity of their building stone. That stone is, of course, the limestone of the Cotswolds and it comes in a score of subtly varying shades of grey and gold. Out in the countryside the uplands of the wolds are, however, somewhat bleak, not least because the fields are separated by stone walls which, though once joys of skilled craftsmanship, are now mostly crumbling and in ruin.

The wolds, today almost all arable, were once vast sheep-walks which provided the wealth for the gracious town houses and churches of the area. The rivers of this region are all quite exquisite and their meanders link strings of little settlements. On the western side of the hills is the escarpment, bold and in places cliff-like. In geological time it has retreated, leaving behind outliers of the same limestone such as Bredon Hill. The 100-mile long (160.9 km) Cotswold Way – a walk of great views – runs along this escarpment from Chipping Camden to Bath.

Ozleworth Bottom
2 miles (3 km) Sheet 162 794928

Easy Ozleworth is the most delightful of the bottoms – the valleys cut back into the escarpment – that are so distinctive of the Cotswolds around Wootton-under-Edge. Some marvellously quiet open meadowland. *Woodland, farmland; one climb.*

Start From Wootton-under-Edge take the road for Alderley, Hillesley and Hawkesbury. In about one mile (1.5 km) turn left at the Ozleworth signpost. Continue about 2 miles (3 km) to the obvious sharp left bend with house opposite. **Parking** with care in vicinity of the left bend.

① At the sharp left bend walk down the lane that leads off right. ② Where the lane turns sharp right at the cottages, go through gate on left and climb to the right across field to gate to woodland. ③ After track turns left and rises sharply, go right at top of rise. Continue about ⅓ mile (0.5 km). ④ The bridge has been wired off because with no parapet it is a danger to animals. Use felled trees to cross the wire. ⑤ Follow bridleway path to stream, step across – one long step – and rejoin outward path. At point ③ bear right, ignoring outward route. ⑥ Turn left when path joins cart track. Follow track to point ①.

🏠 These cottages are all that remain of a woollen-mill village of 1,600 people.

St. Nicholas's tower may have been part of a local landowner's hunting lodge.

🌿 Woodland spring flowers to be seen but not gathered include bluebells, wild garlic and delicate anemones.

🦅 Likely country for spotting green woodpeckers (an unmistakable, bright green), and jays with their scolding cries.

🏠 St. Nicholas's Church, built before 1131, has an unusual six-sided tower and round-headed windows that give it an Italianate look.

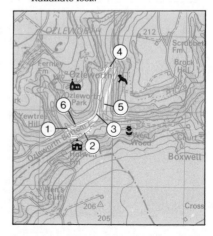

Edgeworth Manor
4 miles (6.5 km) Sheet 163 948059

Moderate Edgeworth, set in the high wolds at the head of a valley, is a beautiful and typical Cotswold hamlet. Not recommended in autumn or winter–mostly exposed. *Farmland, parkland; 2 climbs.*

Start Edgeworth, best approached via Sapperton, signposted from the A419, Stroud-Cirencester road. **Parking** near Edgeworth church.

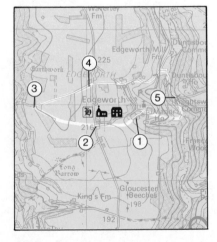

The stately Edgeworth Manor is said to have been built on the site of a Roman villa.

① Go down hill between houses opposite the church and into open fields. In fields climb to the right to a wide track. Follow this. ② Where the track meets the road cross to the track opposite and continue. ③ Where the track exits from the triangular section of woodland, turn sharp right on to another track. ④ At road, follow the road opposite. ⑤ After crossing the bridge, the road rises steeply. Take the first obvious track right (through gate) leading into woodland, continuing to ①.

🖫 Edgeworth lies close to the grass-covered Ridgeway, an ancient British track. From Roman times it was used to carry salt south from Droitwich, where the springs still rise from beds of rock salt. It was also a route for the drovers bringing sheep and cattle in great numbers to Cirencester and even to Smithfield in London, to the Christmas market.
The hamlet stands at the head of the valley of the Frome, also called Stroud's Golden Valley.

🛉 In St. Mary's the remains of an earlier Saxon church can still be seen in the W part of the nave.

🏛 Edgeworth Manor, a 17th C. building, was enlarged in the late 19th C.

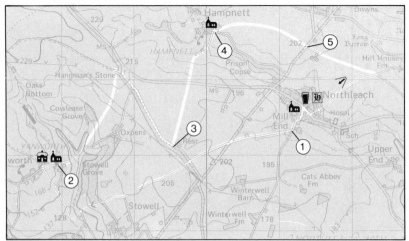

Northleach's Wool Church
8 miles (13 km) Sheet 163 115145

Moderate Wool was the Cotswold's wealth, and it paid for some superb churches and houses; the church at Northleach is certainly among the finest, and arguably the most remarkable because the village itself is so small. Yarnworth is especially delightful in spring. *Farmland; one climb.*

Start Northleach, on the A40 between Cheltenham and Witney. **Parking** in Northleach.

① Leave Northleach with the church to the right and turn right into lane. Follow this over the A429 and on into Yanworth. ② From Yanworth church follow lane between buildings and downhill into a valley. After the lane starts to rise, go through gate on left, continuing to small wood, right. Just beyond wood, go through gate into fields. Keep field boundaries to right and head towards the power cables. Pass beneath them and continue to lane. Turn right and continue to road. ③ At small District Council building take the bridleway left and continue to the A40. Follow track opposite downhill towards Hampnett, turning right at the track junction. ④ Turn left along track next to 3 large barns, and follow the fence to the A429. ⑤ Follow the lane to Folly Farm, but carry straight on where the farm lane bends right. At the road turn right for Northleach.

Northleach was one of the centres of the Cotswold wool trade, thriving from the mid-14th C. to the mid-17th C. The church is a 15th C. building with a tower and a noble porch in the Perpendicular style. Inside are the memorial brasses to many of the merchants of Northleach, their feet resting on the sheep and the woolsacks which gave them their wealth; the brasses are engraved, too, with their marks, which were stamped on the bales of wool. One brass is in memory of Thomas Fortey, a merchant who died in 1447. His epitaph speaks of him as a 'renovator of roads and churches' and he rests in the beautiful church which he did much to rebuild.

The Union Hotel.

In Yanworth, a Saxon wool village, the church has some Norman remains. Facing the church is a fine old barn with an entrance for the packhorses and carts which carried the fleeces.

Hampnett church, a neat Norman building, was oddly decorated inside with bright stencils late last century. Over 100 years earlier, the church got a name for having a rector who would marry couples without asking awkward questions.

An excellent view of Northleach church.

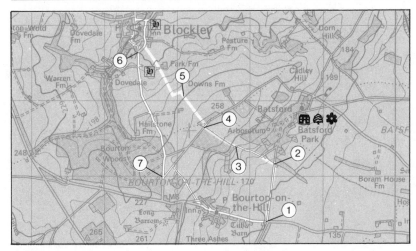

Bourton-on-the-Hill
5 miles (8 km) Sheet 151 175325

Moderate A route through 2 fine examples
of large Cotswold village; a wealth of
pleasing stone houses and cottages.
Parkland, farmland; 2 climbs.

Start Bourton-on-the-Hill, on the A44 W of
Moreton-in-Marsh. **Parking** in village.

① Leave the A44 towards Batsford
Aboretum. ② At the lodge go left through a
gate and cross field to blue gate. Go right for
10 yards (9 m), then left on to track. ③ At
obvious sharp left bend in track go right a
few yards to park wall and follow wall to
road. ④ Across road to path opposite
through copse. ⑤ Cross 2 fields, keeping
boundary to left. Go through gate on far side
of second field and turn left on to track. In
200 yards (183 m) go right through iron gate
and downhill through large field. Keeping
fence to the right, make for gate. Through
gate, keeping farm buildings to right. Cross
field, keeping pond to left. Over stile and
follow right edge of field to grass track.
Follow track to road at Blockley. Continue
through village. ⑥ Leave Blockley by B4479
(i.e. same road) and make for Bourton.
⑦ Take second lane on left (the last turn
before the A44). Along it take the first
obvious track to the right. Follow it, ignoring
track on right just after old quarries, to A44
just above Bourton.

*Smooth Japanese maple, seen among the
Arboretum's superb oriental collection.*

🏛 Batsford Park, late 19th C., was once the
🏠 family home of Lord Redesdale, whose
daughters were the famous Mitfords. Its
✿ Arboretum and Garden Centre are open
each day, 10 a.m. to 5 p.m., April-
November.

⑲ This is an ancient fish pond.

⑲ Blockley has an astonishing industrial
history. The Domesday Book recorded 12
mill wheels on the Blockley Brook, which
is fed by a number of unfailing springs.
These later powered silk mills, an iron
foundry, piano, soap and collar factories,
and made the village one of the first to be
lit by electricity. Now this quiet place has
no silk mills, and the mill buildings have
become pleasant houses with an
imposing old church at their centre.

St. Catherine's Brook

1½ or 3 miles (2.5 or 5 km) Sheet 172 778703

Easy Typical of the relatively unwooded, low valleys that are found in the Southwolds, the Cotswold area between Bath and the M4; reveals a straightforwardly excellent example of the Cotswold, and the English, country lane. *Farmland; in wet weather 150 yards (137 m) between ④ and ① is likely to be waterlogged.*

Start From the A46 between Cold Ashton and Swainswick take the road signposted St. Catherine's. **Parking** near St. Catherine's Court.

① From the Court go downhill along the lane. After Orchard Farm take the path to the left signposted Bridle Path. ② Follow the yellow arrows on a black background. ③ For a short-cut back to the start, cross the footbridge on the left. The right of way is across the lawn of the house, but it is more considerate to go round the edge. At the far side, cross the fence by the half stile and continue up the field. If continuing for longer walk, follow yellow arrows. ④ Continue on hedged track (waterlogged after rain) to meet a lane. Turn left, and left again when the lane from ① is reached.

▦ St. Catherine's Court, originally a 15th C.
monastery, was rebuilt in the 16th C. into
🏠 a fine, four-square Tudor mansion with a

Behind the strong bulk of the Tudor house is a small church, secluded among trees.

magnificent porch. The church, which dates in part from the 13th C., is reached through the walled garden of the house.

🌲 Some exceptionally fine larches.

↘ Ashwicke Grange, a mid-19th C. mansion.

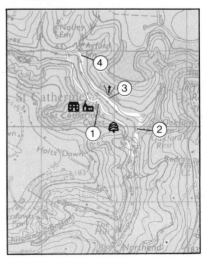

COTSWOLDS

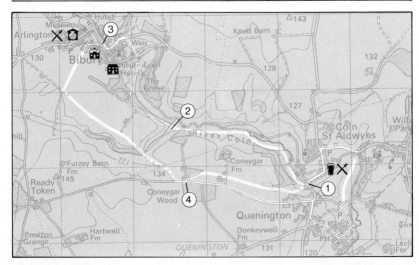

The Coln Valley
6 or 8 miles (9.5 or 13 km) Sheet 163 145053

Easy Follows a beautiful river from one lovely Cotswold village to another; some of the best walking in the area. *River meadows, farmland, parkland.*

Start From the A433 at Bibury, follow signs to Coln St. Aldwyns. **Parking** in Coln St. Aldwyns; alternatively Quenington or Bibury.

① Take the signposted bridleway/footpath across the bridge and then the signposted footpath to the right. Make for the tree ahead and continue to the wood. Take the obvious track in the wood. After emerging, keeping the wood to the left go towards the river. Follow the well-defined track along the river bank. ② Where the river bends right go across fields on well-defined path. Cross stone stile at corner of wood. Follow the wood edge to meet a broader track and follow this to the road beyond Bibury Court. Turn left, and left at the main road. Follow this into Bibury. ③ Cross the footbridge to Arlington Row, continue past cottages and uphill to Y-junction. Turn left between houses, on to path signposted to Ready Token. Continue to post with 5 footpath arrows. Go straight ahead through 2 fields. At the far corner of the second turn left on to a broad track and continue to road. ④ After

a lane leads off left take the signposted bridleway to left to return to the bridge. For the 8 mile (13 km) version, continue from ④ to Quenington and after going through the village take the path leading off the road which has a signpost requesting dogs to be kept under control. Exit from the park across a bridge to road. Turn left for Coln St. Aldwyns.

🍺 The New Inn, Coln St. Aldwyns, has a courtyard bar, a magnificent dovecote, ✗ and serves excellent food; a free house.

✗ Bibury Trout Farm has fish for sale.

◻ Arlington Mill Museum has many relics of a mill mentioned in the Domesday Book. The millrace, in which are rainbow trout, is lit by underwater floodlights. Open daily, 10.30 a.m. to 7 p.m., March-October.

🏨 Bibury Court, now a hotel, is a lovely building, dating in part from Tudor times, but mainly from the mid-17th C.

🏚 Arlington Row, originally a 14th C. sheep-house, was converted into weavers' cottages in the 17th C.

The River Coln winding through the water meadow at Bibury, described by William Morris as 'the prettiest village in England'.

COTSWOLDS

Cleeve Common
10½ miles (17 km) Sheet 163 023282

Energetic Includes the highest point of the Cotswolds, almost the last unenclosed section of high wold and a stretch of the Cotswold Way. The Common is open and bleak–dress warmly in cold weather. *Farmland, common; 2 climbs.*

Start Winchcombe, on the A46, Cheltenham-Stratford road; frequent buses from Cheltenham. **Parking** in Winchcombe.

① Leave Winchcombe along Vineyard St. following signs to Sudeley Castle. After Castle entrance, follow Cotswold Way waymarks to the TV masts on Cleeve Common. The route is waymarked by a combination of white arrows inscribed 'Cotswold Way' or yellow on blue painted arrows with a dot above. ② From the masts go left to the trig. point. Continue by following wall to right. ③ At the end of wall, ignore arrows pointing left, following instead those that point ahead to a track skirting the cliff of Cleeve Cloud. Follow the Way along the track to the head of Rising Sun Lane, and continue at the same level to the clubhouse of the golf course on Cleeve Hill. Alternatively, reach the clubhouse by crossing the Common–panoramic views (indicator) at the highest point. ④ At clubhouse take the well-signposted and well-worn track. ⑤ Turn right after just over ½ mile (0.8 km) to follow the wall of Postlip Hall. Keep the wall to the left and continue all the way round to a well-signposted path for Winchcombe. ⑥ At the far corner of a long (½ mile) field, cross the stone-slab bridge and take the indistinct track leading right towards Postlip Hall. (If doing the walk in the reverse direction this final track is difficult to find since it is the least obvious of three.) ⑦ Go through the mills by making towards 'Reception', then turn right past fire station and follow covered way to lane with houses. Follow lane until it bends sharp left. Cross the stile ahead and continue across the field to road. ⑧ At road, turn left for a short walk back to Winchcombe. Alternatively go right (signposted Belas Knap) for 200 yards (183 m) to two gates on left with stone stile between. Cross stile, go down to river, following it to gate. Turn left at road for Winchcombe.

The church in the grounds of Sudeley Castle.

🍷 The George was once a pilgrim inn for
✕ Winchcombe Abbey, long since gone. It serves excellent food.

🏬 Winchcombe Pottery, open during shop hours.

🏰 Sudeley Castle has strong Tudor links, especially with Katherine Parr, Henry VIII's widow. The gardens and lake are very fine, and there is an adventure playground for children, complete with wooden fort and dungeons. The castle is open every day, 12 noon to 5 p.m., March-October; the grounds open an hour earlier.

🏛 Wadfield Farm is an elegant 17th C. building in a splendid position.

🖼 Remains of Wadfield Roman villa, including part of a mosaic pavement.

🌾 Belas Knap is a huge, Neolithic long barrow (burial chamber). The dry stone walling at the lower part of the false entrance is original–some 6,000 years old. The barrow was first opened in 1863, and since then, excavations have produced 38 human skeletons.

〰 The Ordnance Survey triangulation point makes the highest point in the Cotswolds, 1,075 feet (326 m) above sea level.

Cleeve Cloud – the name comes from *clif*, a cliff, and *clud*, a rock or rock mass – is an exposed edge which shows the structure of the local limestone, the golden-coloured hallmark of Cotswold building for centuries.

Cleeve Hill is also the site of an Iron Age fort.

The Panorama Dial points out interesting views, including the Malvern Hills some 25 miles (40 km) distant and Sudeley in the valley to the NE.

Postlip Hall is 16th C.

The two paper mills at Postlip, which date from the 18th C., are still at work, making air and oil filter paper for motor cars.

The old Severn to Thames Canal is good walking. Take the Tarlton road from Coates to find the canal just past the railway bridge. Walk as far as the tunnel, where there is a pub.

Cooper's Hill – scene of cheese rolling – provides a climb (one part nearly vertical) that could be combined with some of the Cotswold Way.

A walk along the Thames runs from the A417 at 225 981. Follow the path to the pub at 247 986.

Cotswold Farm park, signposted from the B4077 at the A436, provides either short strolling to view its rare animals, or a longer walk along the River Windrush up to its head near the village of Ford.

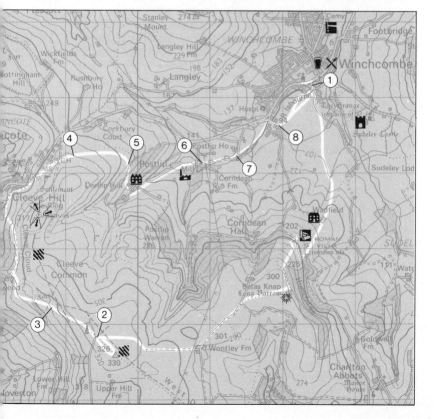

AROUND BIRMINGHAM

The Birmingham conurbation spreads and spreads, but at least its suburbs are infiltrated by countryside. The walks in this section all begin within 30 minutes' drive of the city's centre, some much sooner.

Indeed, one can walk right round Birmingham on the 162-mile (260 km) West Midland Way, which ingeniously links public footpaths and bridleways at an average distance of 12 miles (19 km) from the conurbation's outer edge. And a pleasant walk it is too, for this, to quote the novelist Henry James on Warwickshire, is 'midmost England', perhaps the purest expression of Englishness in landscape anywhere. Ambridge, the Archers' village, is supposed to lie somewhere between Warwickshire and Worcestershire.

To get the most from walking here requires some openmindedness. Industry is woven into the fabric of many parts, and it must be embraced. The canals are absorbing, gentle strolling; while some localities, considered industrial, or built-up beyond recall, offer pleasant surprises.

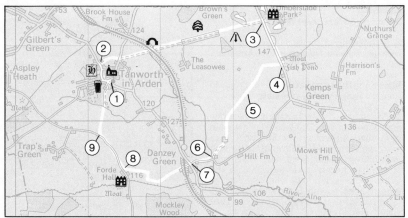

Tanworth-in-Arden
5 miles (8 km) Sheet 139 113705

Moderate Typical Warwickshire village and country; a spectacular, mile-long, tree-lined avenue, at its best in May. *Pasture and arable farmland; 3 climbs; mud after rain.*

Start Tanworth, off the A4023; weekday trains from Birmingham Moor St. to Danzey, near point ⑦. **Parking** at the Green, Tanworth.

① From the green, pass Ivy Stores into Vicarage Hill. ② Enter field on right immediately after Bellfield housing estate. Aim for lower end of estate. Cross road to join 'mile walk' (marked 'Private Road') to Umberslade Park. ③ At road, turn right. ④ Opposite lodge, follow 'Public Footpath' sign. After gate into second field, follow hedge round to fence in corner, then keep long hedge on left. ⑤ From gate at corner, keep same course across 3 fields, aiming for gate near electricity pole at hill top. Follow hedge on left to pass to left of Bickers Court Farm and join farm drive. ⑥ Turn right at road. ⑦ Cross Henley-Tanworth road and take track over railway. Where track turns left, continue with hedge on right. After gate, follow path as it curves around field boundary. At corner, turn left at farther gate and head for Forde Hall, passing to right of farm buildings. ⑧ Go right up lane, over crest of hill. ⑨ After slight right bend, go over fence on right. Following mature hedge on right, continue straight towards church,

over 2 bridges and up hill. After fence at top, turn left along beaten track and road to ①.

The balsam poplar's leaves and buds smell delightfully aromatic, notably in spring.

🏛 Tanworth's church is part 13th C. The village's name recalls that the area was thickly wooded by the Forest of Arden.

🍺 The Bell Inn is modernized, but retains some country pub atmosphere.

⌒ The landowner insisted the bridge was built to a special design, of grey stone – more to his taste than blue brick, like the other 63 on the line.

🌲 The mile-long avenue is of balsam poplars and chestnuts.

⇂ The Avon Valley, with the town of Broadway and the Cotswolds beyond.

🏢 18th C. Umberslade Hall, now flats.

🏢 Forde Hall dates from the 17th C.

AROUND BIRMINGHAM

Hartshill

3½ miles (5.5 km) Sheet 140 317944

Easy Reputedly an industrial area, but there is varied walking. *Hillside, woods, farmland, village; one climb; mud after rain.*

Start From B4114 in Hartshill follow signs to Country Park. **Parking** in Country Park.

① Leave car park by mound and continue across field to gate into wood. Follow main path down hillside to gate into field, then walk round right side of field. ② Go through gate half-way along field, then diagonally left up field to corner. Go through gate and follow hedge on left to ③ where go through gate, then left downhill on narrow track. ④ Go through farmyard and on to road. Turn right and continue over railway to T-junction. Turn right and in just over ½ mile (0.5 km) ⑤ follow the drive towards Spring Farm. ⑥ In field on left after railway, cross diagonally right to centre of opposite field boundary, then continue to bridge over canal. ⑦ Cross track, climb bank, then across to estate entrance. ⑧ Near road junction go down path by flats and into wood. ⑨ At T-junction go left, and in 15 yards (14 m) right. Climb twisting through woods to ①.

🔨 The quarries produce red granite and manganese ore, abundant in the area.

🏠 The Manor House, part 14th C., was the home of Robert Glover, put to death for his religious beliefs in 1555.

🏠 The almshouses S of the churchyard date from 1728.

⛪ The church has some fine 14th C. stained glass.

📖 Hartshill was the birthplace of Michael Drayton, the Elizabethan poet.

☀ A skeleton thought to date from Anglo-Saxon times was excavated here in 1824 – with a shield and spear.

🌳 The Country Park's woodland is a mixture of broad-leaved and coniferous trees, a classic habitat for great tits, blue tits and coal tits. In winter they may be seen feeding in company, working over branches with acrobatic movements.

🏓 The hilltop is a fine picnic site.

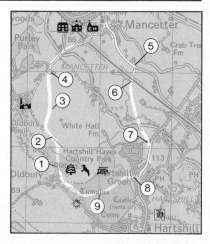

Fradley Junction

8 miles (13 km) Sheet 128 116114

Easy Satisfying walking country N of the conurbation, not in the much-used Cannock Chase; absorbing canal activity, especially in summer. *Farmland, woods, canal-side; mud after rain.*

Start Curborough Road, off the B5170, which is off the A51; frequent buses stop near end of Curborough Road. **Parking** in Curborough Road.

① Walk uphill along B5170 to the next road junction. ② Turn right and climb the bank at the footpath sign. Continue along the path straight ahead, crossing stream and passing through a wood. ③ Straight through the village and turn right at the post box in wall. ④ Where lane swings right, go left through gate into field. Walk up field and cross railway by stiles. Continue half left on slightly raised path, aiming to left of farm. Continue ahead along left edges of several fields to reach road by bungalow. ⑤ Turn left, then immediately right up a farm track. ⑥ At T-junction, turn left over bridge, then right, taking the track skirting the wood. ⑦ At road turn right, cross canal and follow canal towpath to Fradley Junction. ⑧ Walk back along towpath as far as first bridge. Cross, and go through gate on right into field. Follow this bank of canal to second woodland area, where bear left to road. ⑨ Cross road and down edge of field alongside wood. Cross dispersal bay of old Fradley airfield. ⑩ Cross stream by plank bridge and continue left along fence, then hedge. Pass left of disused farm buildings and join farm track, ⑪ where turn right down track. Cross road, follow edges of fields, crossing final one to cross railway again at stiles. ⑫ Follow edges of fields, passing to left of house ahead and continue to join made-up path. ⑬ Left down path, through kissing gate and cross field to start.

🛏 Fradley is the junction of 2 canals. One, the Trent and Mersey, was brought through Fradley in 1770. The other, the Fradley to Whittington Brook section of the Coventry Canal, was completed in 1782. Josiah Wedgwood, the famous potter, was hon. treasurer of the company that built both canals, and one of their main cargoes in the 19th C. was fine clay for the potteries at Stoke, including Wedgwood's own Etruria Works. The Trent and Mersey is linked, by a section of the Coventry Canal, with the Oxford Canal, and this in turn leads to London via the Thames.

The Trent and Mersey Canal Society is restoring the Trent and Mersey, and its ancillary workings, including the old mile posts. Some of the buildings at Fradley Junction are owned by the British Waterways Board, and some privately.

🍺 The Swan overlooks the canal.

🛏 There is a former boatmen's chapel at the canal junction, one of the few ever built, and now used as a garage. Bargemen were generally regarded as lawless outsiders, and had fewer welfare benefits.

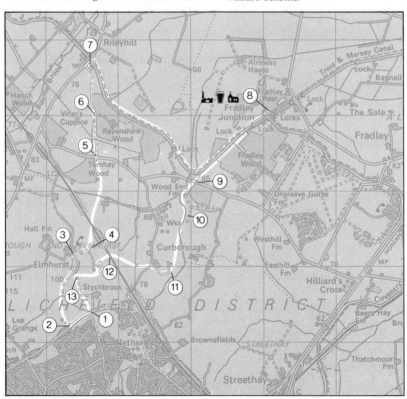

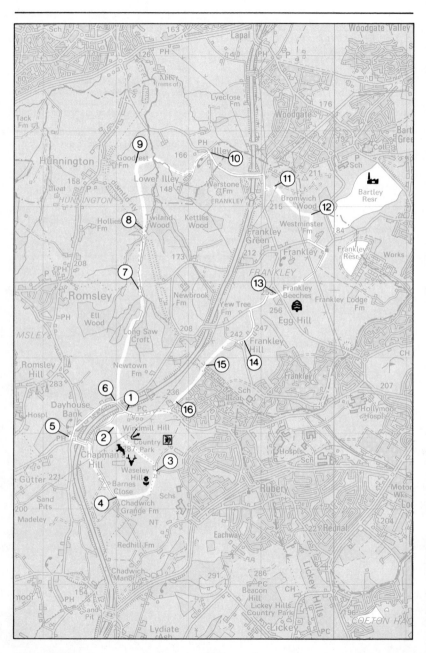

Frankley Beeches
9 miles (14.5 km) Sheet 139 972782

Moderate Pleasant walking, though almost encircled by conurbation; notable views of Birmingham. *Farmland, parkland, woods; 3 climbs; mud after rain.*

Start Waseley Country Park; from Birmingham centre take A38, turning right on to Frankley Beeches road. Bear left at unmarked mini-roundabout to Country Park. **Parking** at N end of Country Park.

① Leave car park and turn left along lane. Turn left at top of hill into field. Follow its left edge. ② Cross stile, turning right then left, climbing to top of hill. Continue along well-used track and path downhill to farm. ③ Turn right at farm track and in about 40 yards (36 m) follow field edge, hedge on left. Through gate, and follow second field edge, boundary on right. Through gate and continue with plantation on left, over stile, through gate and downhill, farm coming into view. ④ Turn right along lane, crossing motorway to road. ⑤ Turn right along road and after 100 yards (91 m) right again on to road towards Frankley and Country Park. ⑥ Turn left just before M5, then left at first gate into field. Follow right edges of 3 fields, cross next diagonally, follow right edges of 2 fields (crossing wire each time); right immediately on to path; left after 50 yards (46 m) on to track. ⑦ At cross-track, continue slightly right of ahead, along left edge of field. Then through gate into woods and left downhill. ⑧ Diagonally right over middle of field to stile (may be overgrown) at end of row of trees. Continue straight up hill past oak, then along right sides of 2 fields. ⑨ Turn right over fence after crossing second fence, then cross field to track, in sight from about 15 yards (14 m). Follow this past 'Gun Range' to farm; at farm, left up track on to road by pub in Illey. ⑩ Turn right along road, cross M5, right again, then left. ⑪ Through gate into field. Cross to edge of housing estate. Follow path crossing 2 metal stiles downhill towards reservoir. ⑫ Over stile, cross field over hill, to gate on to road. Left along road to church, where turn right up track to hilltop with Frankley Beeches. ⑬ Downhill to road, then along road passing farm on left. ⑭ Turn right along road to pass farm buildings, then left over stile. Down field to stile, then cross next field to bridge over disused railway. Cross. ⑮ Straight on with bank on left.

Foxes are an established feature of suburban areas – proof of the animal's adaptability and scavenging habits.

Where estate path crosses stream, bear right (through wire) to outside of estate and continue across mound, bearing right to join track to farm. ⑯ Along track to farm, then on to road turning right back to car park.

\↑/ Windmill Hill, 940 feet (286 m), has contrasting views – Birmingham and the Black Country to the NE, the Severn Valley and hills beyond to the SW.

➤ Kestrels, seen hunting over open ground.

ꚛ Foxes are seen occasionally.

🏛 Unlike the nearby Clent Hills, Wasely, made a Country Park in 1971, has reasonable visitor numbers. In Anglo-Saxon, 'waer' means sheep, 'ley' pasture.

🖿 Part of Birmingham's water supply.

🌲 Frankley Beeches were given to the National Trust by Cadbury Bros. Ltd.

The bridleways and footpaths of the Clent and Lickey Hills have long been the staple walking areas S of the conurbation. To relieve the pressure on them, try Hartlebury Common, ½ mile (0.8 km) SE of Stourport-on-Severn; Kingsford, one mile (1.5 km) NW of Wolverley or Nunnery Wood, 1½ miles (2.5 km) E of Worcester – more distant, but still accessible Country Parks.

Canal walking: the Trent and Mersey; the Stratford Canal; the Coventry Canal and the Grand Union.

NORFOLK

This is a county for artists, including, of course, all the great names of the Norwich School. Many people think, wrongly, that the landscape is featureless and flat; certainly the painters were not drawn to it for that. In any Norfolk view, the biggest single element is the sky, and it was the brilliant light which entranced Crome, Cotman and the rest, and still inspires the walker.

Choose where you go with care. Public paths are none too many. The coastline can be walked more or less continuously, and the mixture of long dunes, beaches, red-roofed villages, twisted pines and low cliffs is rewarding. Inland, the countryside rolls gently, but never quite enough to be described as hilly, although in Norfolk the merest bump is *called* a hill.

The walker sees more of the Broads than anyone in the nose-to-tail boats, for on land there are the wide vistas of the surrounding marshes. Breckland may disappoint those who find dense forestry plantations dull going. The best of inland Norfolk may well be the middle and eastern parts. Here are a mass of twisting lanes, churches, farms and hamlets – an ancient landscape compared with that to the west, which was much more strongly influenced by the dead straight divisions of parliamentary enclosure.

Burnham Market Town and Sea Marshes
5 miles (8 km) Sheet 132 832421

Easy A route with much of interest on it, or nearby: pleasant market town with Georgian houses, interesting churches, Scolt Head Nature Reserve, Holkham Hall and Burnham Thorpe, birthplace of Nelson. *Town, farmland, sea marsh; paths between ③ and ④ and ⑤ and ⑥ may be ploughed out.*

Start Burnham Market, off the A149. **Parking** in the market square.

① Opposite the war memorial take Herrings Lane uphill past track leading to church. After third electricity pole ② turn left through gap to field corner. ③ Follow left edge of field to track; turn right to road. Cross and continue through Burnham Norton to sharp left bend. ④ Turn right and bend left to double gates. Go through and follow track ahead to stile and more gates. Turn along left edge of meadow to brick building. Continue up to sea wall. ⑤ Turn right to end of bank. Cross field, making for windmill. ⑥ At road turn left, then right and follow track ¼ mile (0.5 km) to another road. Turn right to Burnham Overy church. ⑦ Follow B1155 back to Burnham Market.

✗ Fishes' Restaurant offers such delights as Pacific oysters, *scallops au gratin* and salmon fishcakes with crab sauce.

Low horizons, vast skies and the windmill – unchanging elements of Norfolk landscape.

🦅 Waders and marshland birds.

▧ Remains of Creake Abbey.

🏛 Holkham Hall, the great 18th C. Palladian house of white brick, seat of the Earls of Leicester.

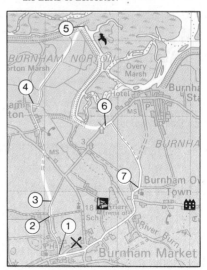

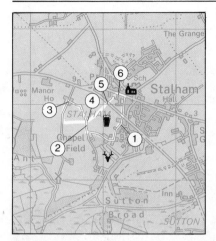

Stalham
2 miles (3 km) Sheet 133 373247

Easy Typical town and landscape of the Norfolk Broads, where the peak of boating activity is in spring and summer. *Broads, farmland, town; some paths may be ploughed out in early spring.*

Start Stalham on the A149; fairly frequent buses in summer. **Car park** (free) in Stalham.

① Facing away from Yacht Station, opposite the green, turn left and left again round dyke head to sharp right bend opposite track. Turn right to swing gate. ② Through gate, aim half left across field to road, where turn right to farm. ③ Turn right and follow lane for ¼ mile (0.5 km) to swing-gate. By it ④ turn left through wide gap and continue to road. ⑤ Cross into Stalham. ⑥ Turn right towards church, where turn right to main road and return to yacht station.

⋎ An excellent coarse fishing area: plenty of roach in the dykes; the reach past Wayford Bridge is noted for bream.

▮ The Maid's Head dates from the 15th C.

⛪ St. Mary's (late 15th C.) possesses, by accident, an extremely fine 16th C. font. During the last century it was found, covered in plaster, beneath the floor. Local historians assume it was hidden there to escape damage in the Civil War.

Great Yarmouth
9 miles (14.5 km) Sheet 134 522075

Moderate Stirring views of Burgh Castle, impressive remains of a Roman fort and, in season, the spectacle of migrating birds on Breydon Water. *Town, farmland, villages, banks of Breydon Water. Path between ⑥ and ⑦ may be ploughed out.*

Start Great Yarmouth; frequent buses and trains. **Car park** near the Two Bears inn.

① From pub cross Southtown Bridge and continue on A12 ¾ mile (one km) to Boundary Road into which ② turn right and continue through industrial estate to Coopers. ③ Turn left and in 100 yards (91 m) right to disused railway. ④ Follow the footpath ahead, then take track and grassy lane to ⑤ farm road, where continue

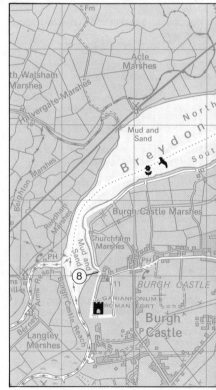

straight ahead to a kissing gate ⑥ in front of white cottages. Through gate continue over field to wooden rails, where ⑦ continue ahead to kissing gate then take farm track to road. Turn right, and continue to church where turn left to fort. Take path on left of fort to edge of marsh. Turn right along bottom of bank to stile. ⑧ Continue 3 miles (5 km) along Breydon Water, then on rough road to broken bridge. ⑨ Keep to river bank then take path to road. ⑩ Turn left, past transformer, and continue to ①.

Burgh Castle was a Roman fortress – Gariannonum – built in about A.D. 300. It commanded a large harbour: in those times the marsh that now surrounds the ruins and the sand bank on which Great Yarmouth stands were under the sea.

Around the mid-6th C. St. Fursey founded a monastery on the castle site,

but wisely removed to France when the Viking invasions began.

Breydon Water is either a large lake or mud flats, depending on the state of the tide. Its banks, covered with yellow flags – irises – are a blaze of colour in May-July. Iris is the Greek word for rainbow.

In late summer and autumn it is an excellent place to watch waders, large numbers of which arrive on passage to winter quarters. Winter brings various seabirds, such as cormorants, sheltering from the North Sea weather. In March there is the booming call of the bittern, whose plumage is camouflaged with vertical streaks.

The occasional Norfolk wherry may sail past. On narrower parts, where sailing is difficult, they are punted along with a pole called a 'quant' or 'spreet'.

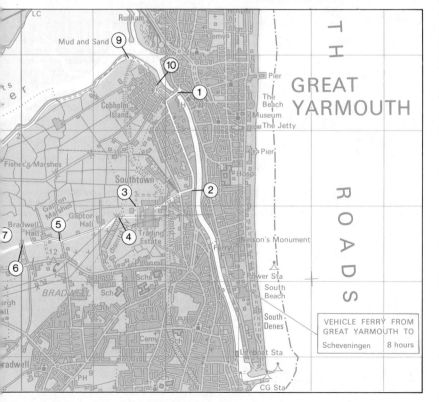

NORFOLK

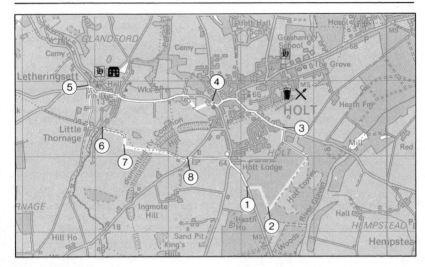

Holt and Letheringsett
6 miles (9.5 km) Sheet 133 082378

Easy Undulating countryside – to disprove the all-too-common belief that Norfolk is flat. In fact the route shows a fair cross-section of Norfolk landscape from attractive heathland to sheltered woodland rides; a walk for all seasons. *Heath, town, villages, farmland, woods.*

Start Holt Country Park, signposted from the B1149. **Car Park** (free) in Country Park.

① From car park turn left into grassy ride. Go over crossing track then bend right on track to a pond. Go left to cross ② a stile and join track, turning left and continuing ¼ mile (0.5 km), then left again into lane. Follow this as it bends right to road. ③ Turn left and continue ½ mile (0.8 km) into Holt. Continue through main street and curve right down Letheringsett Hill to ④ car park, where continue straight ahead to the dell. Keep to the higher ground, but then go downhill and turn right through ferns to road. Turn left, continue about one mile (1.5 km), the whole way on pavement. ⑤ Just past church turn left into lane and follow this. Just past cottages in Thornage turn left to ford. ⑥ Cross, turn left and immediately right on to track beside brick shed. Continue uphill, turning sharply right with track. Continue ¼ mile (0.5 km), then left at top to ⑦ iron gate.

Cross wooden rails, turn left and continue straight on ¼ mile to wooden gate, then road. ⑧ Turn left then in a few yards right on to track. Follow this to road, where turn right and continue ¼ mile on main road to ①.

🍺 The Feathers Hotel, fronting the market place, is a 17th C. coaching inn; food and ✗ real ale.

🏛 Gresham's School, Holt, the public school, was founded in 1555 by Sir John Gresham, one of the 4 brothers who became Lord Mayors of London. Among its pupils this century have been the poet W. H. Auden and composer Benjamin Britten. On a site close to the school was born a less enlightened celebrity, Alice Perrers, the hideous and calculating mistress of Edward III.

🏛 A humble, but remarkable local man is buried near the churchyard entrance. Johnson Jex, a blacksmith by trade, became obsessed with making clocks and watches, and developed into a master of the craft, but without gaining more than local recognition. His epitaph recalls this, describing him as a 'scientific anchorite' or hermit. Examples of his work are in the Bridwell and Castle Museums, Norwich.

🏠 The Hall is a Palladian manor house.

Peddars Way
4 miles (6.5 km) Sheet 144 934871

Easy Part of Norfolk's most ambitious unofficial long-distance path (see page 328-334) and an outstanding nature reserve. *Heath, woods.*

Start at Peddars Way sign on the A11, 5 miles (8 km) from Thetford and 23 miles (37 km) from Norwich. **Parking** on heath.

① Follow direction of Peddars Way sign ¼ mile (0.5 km) to level crossing. Cross and continue on Peddars Way to road. ② Turn left to second crossroads. ③ Turn left through army camp and continue ½ mile (0.8 km) to road junction, where ④ cross to track into forest and ⑤ go straight ahead for ¼ mile (0.5 km) to crossing of rides with field gate on right. ⑥ If visiting reserve, enter through gate. Otherwise continue left one mile (1.5 km) to level crossing and ①.

East Wretham Nature Reserve lies within the Norfolk area known as Brecklands. In contrast with the Broads, this is a landscape of pine forest, heath and boggy meres or lakes. It covers some 300 square miles (121 ha). The varied habitats are a haven for several notable species of birds and wild flowers:

The stone curlew is a rare visitor in March-Oct., identifiable in the air by its white wing bands and, at night, by its sharp 'coolee' call. Crossbills may be seen, or more likely detected, among the pines: they feed by extracting the seeds from pine cones with their sharp, 'crossed' bills, leaving a pile of debris on the ground below. They are not native to this area, but periodically, when the crop of pine cones fails in Scandinavia, they flock here across the North Sea in search of new supplies – a phenomenon known as irruption and an interesting contrast to conventional migration.

The meres used to puzzle observers because they seemed to fill and empty at whim, regardless of rainfall. It is now clear that their level is governed by the water table in the underlying chalk and not the height of the devil's sense of humour as local old wives have claimed. Rare plants include: Spanish catchfly (flowering June-Aug.); field wormwood (Aug.-Sept.); spiked speedwell (July-Oct.); and sickle medic (June-July).

Fly agaric, with its distinctive scarlet cap speckled with white is prolific in the East Wretham Nature Reserve area.

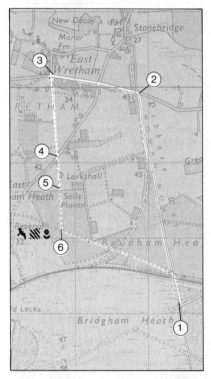

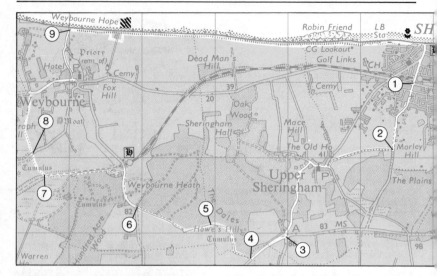

Sheringham and Weybourne Cliffs
10 miles (16 km) Sheet 133 158431

Moderate Along some typical Norfolk sand cliffs. Crosses high ground with good views, but sheltered enough to be an all-weather route. *Farmland, heath, shore, cliffs, woods; may be overgrown along railway between ⑥ and ⑦ – use field edge instead.*

Start Sheringham Station; frequent trains.
Car park Station Road Car Park.

① From Station Road Car Park turn right past roundabout into Holway Road. Continue uphill and opposite Beech Avenue turn right into grassy lane. ② Continue into Upper Sheringham, pass church and turn left for Holt. At crossroads ③ turn right for King's Lynn. In ¼ mile (0.5 km) ④ turn right into drive bordered by white rails. Follow drive, then perimeter track of camp, bending sharply left near end, but at next left bend continue few yards to stile and ⑤ into wood. Turn left to follow paths then track, continuing ½ mile (0.8 km) to road. ⑥ Turn right towards railway and before bridge left on to track, passing prefabs by left edge of rough ground then continuing on well-defined path. When close to railway get on to disused track and turn left to continue to cutting, where ⑦ turn right and descend bank. At bottom turn left into bracken, later

bearing right to road. ⑧ Turn right, then in a few yards left on to path between hill and field. At road turn right to church, where turn left to the beach. ⑨ Turn right and continue round cottages along beach or cliff top past lifeboat station, where turn right and continue to Sheringham. Continue through town to ①.

🚂 Sheringham flourished with the Edwardian vogue for seaside holidays.

🚂 The Poppy Line steam railway, restored voluntarily by enthusiasts, provides trips between Sheringham and Weybourne from Easter to October.

⚓ The deep water off Weybourne, unique to this coastline, has long been regarded as the prime place for a foreign invasion to land. No one has taken advantage of this, however, since the Angles came ashore here in the 7th C.

🌿 Samphire, the plant with fleshy, tubular shoots which grows wild on the cliffs and shingle near the sea, is sometimes available in the local shops. The fleshy parts can be boiled and eaten with butter or pickled in vinegar for a relish. Some say it tastes like asparagus; to go with it, fresh crabs and lobster are on sale in the shops on the sea front.

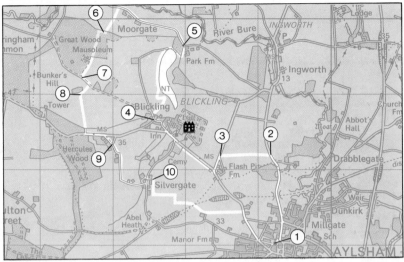

Blickling

6 miles (9.5 km) Sheet 133 192270

Easy One of the most interesting of Norfolk's great houses makes a splendid centrepiece for the route. *Farmland, parkland.*

Start Aylsham on the A140; frequent buses.
Car parks in Aylsham.

① From the church walk N over the railway, past Burebank School to double gate. ② Through gate, go half right towards corner of wood, then follow high hedge to road. ③ Turn left and continue to junction. Turn right and use parallel path on left, continuing to church. Continue past Hall and turn right past Buckinghamshire Arms to park gates. Go through and ④ continue to gate, then across to lake. Go round end of lake (lake on right), then left to ⑤ the road, where turn left and continue ½ mile (0.8 km). Pass farm and in 100 yards (91 m) turn left on to a well-defined path to a wood where ⑥ turn right, then bend left to mausoleum. Fork left to crossing track, where ⑦ turn left, continue a few yards then turn right to a wood and an iron gate. ⑧ Over gate, turn left to road, where turn left. Continue ¼ mile (0.5 km), where fork right downhill past cottages to road. ⑨ Turn right to Silvergate. Turn left then right into Weavers Way, where ⑩ follow signposts to 'Avenue', and follow this to road. Turn right, continue to crossroads, then left, past school, to ①.

In a manor house on the site of the present Jacobean house Anne Boleyn spent her childhood. She was the second of Henry VIII's wives, beheaded in 1536. Not only does she 'walk the Bloody Tower with her head tucked beneath her arm', but is said to commute to haunt Blickling.

From Holme-next-the-Sea, 2½ miles (4 km) NE of Hunstanton along the A149, there are excellent seaside walks with superb flocks of seabirds, especially in winter.

The wildlife centre at Blakeney Point can be approached by a path from Cley off the A149.

Several marked walks go from Cromer W along the coast to East Runton and inland to Beacon Hill Roman Camp.

Hoverton Great Broad Trail starts a short boat ride from Wroxham (just off the A1151) at the top of Salhouse Broad.

Near the sea at Bacton Wood, 2½ miles NE of North Walsham, are forest trails starting from a car park and picnic sites.

EAST MIDLANDS

Intensively cultivated, Lincolnshire has few public footpaths, and these often vanish beneath the plough, or barley, or potatoes. Moreover, the fields are long and rolling; daunting even to those most confident they know the line of the right of way. Leicestershire and Nottinghamshire have rather more paths. Often, they cut intriguingly across the neat, planned pattern of fields left by the Parliamentary enclosures, still the major influence on this landscape. The paths, of course, pre-date the enclosures.

The Lincolnshire Wolds (chalk) and Lincoln Heath (limestone), two modest features of the area, are part of the twin belts of chalk and limestone which swing right across England from Dorset to Yorkshire. Slightly elevated above the surrounding flatlands, they give surprisingly dramatic views.

To the north-east and the south lie the wistful immensities of the Lincolnshire marsh country and the Fens. West of the Trent, Charnwood and Sherwood Forests have lost most of their trees, but still muster echoes of medieval wilderness.

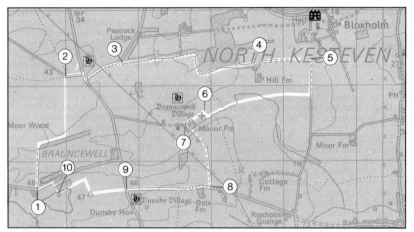

Lincoln Heath

7 miles (11 km) Sheet 121 025517

Easy Gentle walking, much of it with a peaceful air though close to the A15: wide horizons, a Roman road, 'lost' villages. *Farmland, woods; mud after rain.*

Start Brauncewell, ¾ mile (one km) off the A15 (Lincoln-Sleaford road). **Parking** on road verge in front of farm buildings just beyond limestone quarry.

① Cross road and follow signposted track alongside stone wall on left. Turn right on to the diverted path on far side of tree belt. Continue with trees on right for 500 yards (457 m). At gap in tree belt turn left across field – some 200 yards (183 m) beyond stone wall – and make for electricity pylon and clump of trees to its left. ② Turn right at lane and continue 250 yards (229 m) to main road. Turn right and in 100 yards (91 m) left down lane signposted B1191. Continue 600 yards (594 m). ③ Where road bends left enter strip of woodland on right following well-used path. Keep straight on across track towards Hill Farm, cross stone bridge and bear right along edge of Ten Acre Plantation, the Oaks and Spruce Covert. ④ Keep straight on along well-surfaced track where road to Hill Farm joins on right. At lane leading into Bloxholm ⑤ turn right and continue for 600 yards (549 m). Turn right over grass-surfaced bridge about 20 yards (18 m) past gate on left. Continue straight

ahead, keeping dyke on right. Cross grass-surfaced bridge by reservoir and make diagonally (reservoir to left) just to left of tree. This involves scrambling across the dyke, then aiming for the telegraph pole, near which is a grass-surfaced bridge. Cross the track to Hill Farm, keeping dyke on left. At bridge on left bear right for 20 yards and cross ditch to follow dyke on left up to gate in wire fence. ⑥ Go through gate and walk across paddock aiming for corner of stone building. ⑦ Turn left through double gates opposite wagon shed. Go left through farmyard and continue up the hill past stone house. ⑧ Turn right at lane and continue ¾ mile (one km) to A15. ⑨ Cross A15 and join signposted footpath, keeping hedge on right. Turn right at farm track. In 250 yards turn left off farm track along diverted path in line with edge of Hillside Plantation. ⑩ Turn right at Hillside Cottage to lane, and ①.

🏛 The A15 here follows the course of the Roman road King Street.

🏛 Site of a medieval village.

🏛 The site of the vanished medieval village of Dunsby: in the great house lived the Death family, one of whom was christened Welcome Death.

🏰 Bloxholm Hall and estate are much reduced in splendour from the time of one distinguished owner, the General Manners who served at Waterloo.

EAST MIDLANDS

Braunston and Launde Abbey
7½ miles (12 km) Sheet 141 832065

Moderate None of England's grandest
scenery, but this countryside has its own
quiet charm and some fine views. *Wooded
hills, lush valleys, village; mud after rain.*

Start Braunston, 2 miles (3 km) SW of
Oakham. **Parking** – with care – on church
green, Braunston.

① From Green walk along Wood Lane. ②
Near top of hill where the road to Lissington
bears left, continue straight on up road,
which soon becomes a stony track, then a
grassy lane. Ignore footpath to Lissington. ③
At end of grassy lane bear left to well-
defined track around edge of field. Go
through bridleway gate and follow track on
right towards top of hill. At reservoir on
hilltop turn right through gate. ④ Where
track bears left in field go straight on for 200

yards (183 m) to signposts showing
Braunston, Launde and Withcote. Continue
left along hedge towards Launde. Just before
end of field turn left through gate and
immediately right over causeway. Continue
down left bank of little valley to join another
bridleway. ⑤ By ruins of Cole's Lodge and
signpost follow bridleway over gully and
through gate. Continue by the hedge (river on
left) and cross bridge at other end of field. Go
through gate ahead and slightly right. Bear
half left into next field and make for top left
corner and edge of Launde Park Wood. ⑥ At
corner go through gap in hedge (not gate on
left). Follow faint track, keeping railings on
left. Pass Withcote Lodge. Go straight ahead
through wire fence and gate to climb
shoulder of hill. Follow track through gate
down to road. ⑦ At road turn left. In 60
yards (55 m), before cattle grid, turn half
right across field, passing to left of telegraph
post. Continue over rise and down far side of
gully to meet river again. Cross plank with

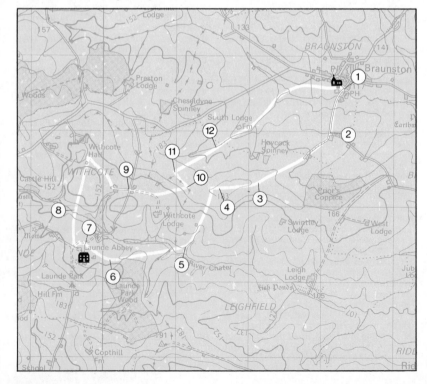

handrail. ⑧ Bear left round edge of field to Withcote Hall and lake. Just past barn turn right down avenue. Go through gate by cottages to the Launde road. ⑨ Cross road, keeping Dowry Cottage on left. In 300 yards (274 m) turn left off track by bridleway signpost. Follow hedge past horse jumps, go through gate on left and walk up field, keeping hedge on right. ⑩ At top right corner go through gate, turn left and continue 30 yards (27 m). Turn left through gate and continue along grassy lane. Go through gate at end of lane and turn right downhill on another grassy lane. ⑪ In 25 yards (23 m) turn right through hedge, over railings at foot of oak tree. ⑫ Braunston church can be seen 1½ miles (2.5 km) down the valley and this is the general direction for the next 13 fields. Follow dyke on left until the third field and cross stout bridge. Keep dyke and stream on right and after crossing stile and bridge keep hedge on left until stile; cross paddock to church.

By the belfry door of the church is a stone carving, more or less recognizable as a woman. It is probably a Saxon fertility idol. In the early days of Christianity, churches were often built on sites of pagan worship. For hundreds of years the carving served as a doorstep, until one day during the 19th C. it was turned over to reveal the carving and suggest the possibility that the earliest Christian converts hereabouts entered the church by trampling on the image of their former deity.

Launde Abbey is a house built on the site of a Norman Priory founded in 1125. Thomas Cromwell, the Tudor statesman who executed the Dissolution of the Monasteries came upon Launde in the course of his work and liked it so much he appropriated it for himself.

Launde Abbey.

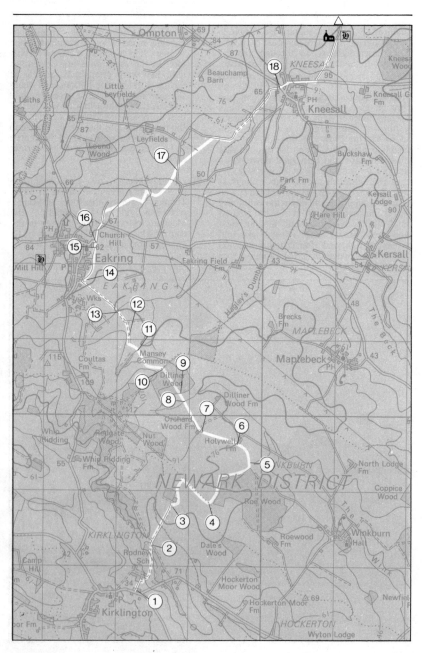

Kirklington to Laxton
4, 6½ or 9 miles (6.5, 10.5 or 14.5 km)
Sheet 120 682576

Easy A walk of contrasts through quiet woodland, grassy lanes and over Mansey Common. *Farmland, woods; mud; some paths under crops and ploughed over before and after Eakring. Point ⑱ to the end is simple to follow without map.*

Start Kirklington on the A617. **Parking** off the main road on the side road leading to Hall Farm – at foot of hill on Newark side of village; alternatively the Normanton lane, 50 yards (46 m) away. **Return** to start possible by car only from Eakring, Kneesall or Laxton.

① From parking continue up road in direction of Hall Farm for 170 yards (155 m). Turn right over cattle grid (waymark) and follow well-defined track around shoulder of hill. ② At hilltop cross cattle grid (waymark) and go straight on towards prominent barn. Continue on main track for 50 yards (46 m). ③ Turn right off track, keeping hedge to left. On entering strip of woodland turn right and follow meandering track to end of trees. ④ Turn left across ditch (waymarks) and go straight on, keeping Roe Wood on right for full length of wood. Turn right through wire crossing ditch and continue along edge of Roe Wood to end. ⑤ Twenty yards (18 m) beyond end of wood turn right over bridge and immediately left on to well-defined track. Where track bears left continue on footpath straight across field to hedge just left of barn. (It is permissible to keep on track round edge of field to point where footpath crosses.) ⑥ Turn left off track by end of hedge and aim just left of Orchard Wood Farmhouse, crossing hedge into another field on the way. ⑦ Turn right behind house and buildings on to farm road. At end of Orchard Wood farm buildings turn left across field to electricity pole 50 yards (46 m) distant. Go straight on towards Dilliner Wood, keeping hedge on right. ⑧ Go down slope and enter next field by tree. Go straight ahead across corner of field to bridge with 2 stiles. Cross and bear half left to 2 old telegraph marker posts and bridge to Dilliner Wood entrance. ⑨ Continue straight on ignoring cross-tracks. ⑩ Leaving wood turn left and follow horse-tracks across Mansey Common for about 120 yards (110 m). Turn half right off horse trail and follow meandering track through scrub. Go

down steep bank to cross footbridge. Climb bank to field. ⑪ Strike across field aiming for third electricity post from left. Keep line of wire about 80 yards (73 m) to left. Go over farm track to footbridge over dyke. ⑫ Cross and aim for electricity post on far edge of field. Cross rubble-covered bridge and aim for end of hedge just to left of double electricity post. ⑬ At end of hedge turn left then through or over gate. Walk down field, hedge on right. Turn right through hedge at bottom and follow remnant of grassy lane straight on. ⑭ Follow grassy lane along edge of field to 2 double electricity posts. Turn left through hedge and continue straight on along side of field. For Eakring (4-mile walk) turn left in a few yards and follow track to playing fields and Triumph Road, where there is access by car. To continue, go straight ahead keeping hedge, later stream, on left. Continue to Church Hill, then road. ⑯ At road turn right. In 200 yards (183 m) where road bends right go straight on along grassy lane for 170 yards (155 m). At beginning of second field on right turn right through opening. Walk uphill diagonally left across this and the next field, aiming just to the right of the electricity pylon. From the hill crest aim just to the right of the 2 trees below the church tower. Cross concrete bridge and bear left up farm track for 250 yards (229 m). ⑰ Turn right over fence (waymark) and continue diagonally left through 3 fields, going through gaps in hedges. At left corner of third field enter the grassy lane and turn right. Cross the field and continue straight ahead at the waymarked bridleway gate. Do not take the track to the right but go straight on along the line of poplar trees, up the hill to cross the A616. Continue straight on with Kneesall village triangle on right. ⑱ Pass post office and go straight up Ossington Road for 550 yards (503 m). Turn left up well-defined track through waymarked double gates. Follow grassy lane, ignoring all side turnings, for 1¾ miles (3 km) to the road. Turn right to Laxton.

🏛 Stone Cross marking site of Pulpit Ash.

⛪ St. Michael's Church, Laxton, once an exceptional medieval building, was spoilt
🏛 by Victorian rebuilding. A leaflet describing Laxton's fascinating project to preserve the medieval open field farming system, and other features, is available at the church.

EAST MIDLANDS

Tennyson Valley
9 miles (14.5 km) Sheet 122 334748

Moderate Fine views, lovely contoured dry valleys, remoteness and scattered communities unknown to many people who have lived in the area all their lives. *Farmland; section between ⑧ and ① may be ploughed out—follow directions carefully.*

Start Tetford, signposted from the A16 S of Louth. **Parking** by the church.

① From parking walk away from church, past post office and village hall. By sharp left bend turn right through kissing-gate on to signposted footpath and cross field to white footbridge. Cross and turn right along track and road by mill house. Turn right over road bridge at main road and continue past chapel and school. ② Where road turns right up Tetford Hill go straight ahead on well-marked bridleway and Roman road. Ignore farm track on left. After about 700 yards (640 m) ignore uphill track on right and continue along Roman road to white bridleway gate and bridge. ③ Cross bridge and turn right. Follow the *diverted* bridleway along edge of stream for 400 yards (366 m), turning left along signposted, stony track by earth bridge. Keep straight on at cross-tracks, continuing 300 yards (274 m). At end of trees turn right to follow headland and small dyke on right. Just past wood, by gate on left, turn left along old road. Turn right along concrete track and continue to road where ④ turn right up Belchford Hill. At T-junction turn left along Bluestone Heath Road. Just past abandoned quarry track on opposite side turn right through sparse hedge and fence. Go diagonally across field to gate by left edge of spinney. Turn right down tree-lined lane to Oxcombe. ⑤ Opposite postbox in house wall turn left down track immediately beyond cart shed. Aiming for Farforth, keep to track, with fence on left. Cross earth bridge over stream and keep straight on with fence on right. Turn right into stackyard and left to church. ⑥ At end of churchyard turn right along broad track behind church. Continue on well-defined track round valley edge by wood, through gate and across field to left of spinney. Ignore bridge into wood on right, leaving track and walking to the left to a broken gate in corner of field. Follow headland forward, keeping ravine and Jericho Plantation just below and to right.

Harvest mice, the most delightful occupants of the agricultural E Midlands' great corn-fields, at a typical nest site.

Cross stile to left of cattle trough and continue straight on along edge of field until possible to descend to drive of the Old Rectory. Continue to road and Ruckland. ⑦ Continue down road and about 150 yards (137 m) beyond bridge turn left along signposted track. In nearly one mile (1.5 km) cross cattle grid and follow track into Worlaby. Turn right at side of church and continue uphill, keeping dry valley on right. Climb stile at roadside. Continue uphill a few yards and ⑧ turn left up well-defined track marked by footpath signpost. In 300 yards (274 m) turn right to climb bank and stile by signpost. Over stile bear left through gap in hedge, over rise in hedgehill and across field to line of trees. Aim for fifth or sixth tree, where there is a waymark. Go straight on over shoulder of hill, keeping just to right of remnant of hedge line. At bottom of hedge go straight ahead into corner of field. Cross barbed wire and make for left side of cottage ahead. Cross track and go straight ahead along lane towards church.

⛪ The 14th C. church contains a conspicuous memorial to Captain Edward Dymoke. The Dymokes, who lived locally until the end of the 19th C., are champions of the crown: the head of the family used to attend all coronations 'well armed for war, upon a good horse'.

The White Hart Inn at Tetford boasts 2 literary connections, centring on its oak settle – the long, wooden bench. It supported Dr. Johnson when he addressed the Tetford Club in 1764; and Tennyson, who was born and raised at nearby Somersby, rested on it between bouts of skittles. Real ale; dining-room.

The cabinet-maker's workshop behind the pub is worth exploring.

Extensive views.

A few yards along the track is the county's smallest church, whose vicar runs no less than 15 scattered and isolated communities. Dedication to St. Olave reflects Viking influence.

To the coast.

The Lincolnshire County Council has created a series of first-class walks in the E Midlands area. All have efficient waymarking – arrow symbols on posts, stiles, gateposts and existing public footpath signs. They are described in a series of modestly priced leaflets.

One, on Lincoln Heath, takes in the Preceptory of the Knights Templar at Temple Bruer. Another, in the Vale of Belvoir, follows part Grantham Canal.

There is a fenland walk starting at Heckington, giving insight into the landscape's development, and another at Fishtoft, with a splendid section on top of the bank of Hobhole Drain.

The Grimsthorpe Estate walk is of interest to naturalists and a route at Bardney gives a glimpse of undisturbed remains of medieval strip farming.

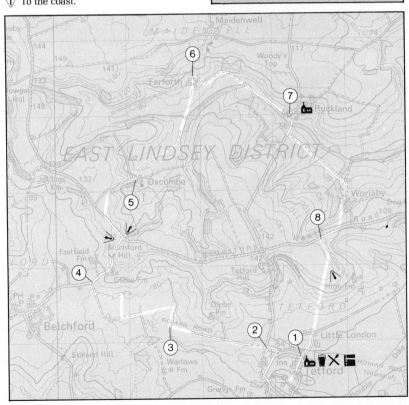

PEAK DISTRICT

There are few peaks: the name derives from that of an English tribe. The highest land, over 2,000 feet (610 m) around Bleaklow and Kinder Scout, is more or less flat-topped, though rough heather, peat and bogs make this true mountain terrain – dangerous to the unwary, especially when the weather comes down.

Here, at the southern tip of the Pennines, the Pennine Way starts its trail north, and here, too, in 1932, there were fisticuffs between ramblers and gamekeepers. Today there is free access to the moors under one of the Peak National Park agreements covering 70 square miles (28 ha). The Park also provides benevolent wardens, first-class information centres and gentle strolling on disused railway tracks.

South of Edale, the millstone grit of the Dark Peak gives way to a 20-mile (32-km) wide limestone dome, the White Peak. This is not such harsh country, decorated by stone walls and small beechwoods. Its rivers have worn the limestone into small chasms (notably Dovedale) as romantically picturesque as the Dark Peak is romantically wild. Both are beautiful.

Ilam, Thorpe and Dove Dale
4 miles (6.5 km) Sheet 119 136508

Moderate Takes in not only the popular Dove Dale with its Stepping Stones but also escapes the crowded places, exploring the lovely lower reaches of the Dove and its sister river the Manifold. *Riverside, village, limestone country; mud after rain.*

Start Ilam, off the A515; buses stop at the Ilam crossroads 2¾ miles (4.5 km) from ①.
Parking in the grounds of Ilam Hall, signposted at village centre.

① From Ilam centre cross the bridge, turn left over stile and follow the river downstream past series of waterfalls. ② Cross bridge and continue up lane to Thorpe village. ③ Cross the Ilam road and continue in direction of signpost to Lin Dale. ④ Enter Dove Dale at the Stepping Stones. Either cross over these and follow the road, or stay on same side using the path, crossing by footbridge lower down river. ⑤ At car park turn right and cross series of fields behind the Izaak Walton Hotel back to Ilam.

🏢 Ilam Hall, built in Victorian times by Jesse Watts Russell, a local manufacturer, now contains a youth hostel.

🏠 Ilam, a model village built by Watts Russell, is in a style with echoes of

Ilam Hall, Dove Dale; the beautiful grounds are worth exploring.

London and the Home Counties – a curiosity in these parts.

🔟 The River Dove's virtues were praised by Isaak Walton in *The Compleat Angler*. He stayed nearby with his friend Charles Cotton. Dove Dale is 'Eagle Dale' in George Eliot's *Adam Bede*.

🍺 Peveril of the Peak and Isaak Walton Hotels.

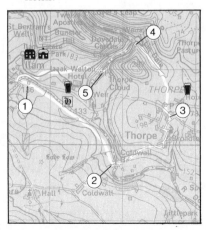

THE PEAK DISTRICT

Padley Gorge
5 miles (8 km) Sheets 110 and 119 251788

Easy A delightful woodland walk which leads easily to the gritstone edges above the Derwent Valley. *Gorge, woods, meadows, gritstone edges; one climb; mud after rain; in the early stages of the walk several alternative paths climb through the gorge; all join higher up – but if the stream is kept in sight, route-finding is simple. If inexperienced in hill-walking, avoid in poor visibility.*

Start Grindleford Station off the B6521; buses to Fox House Inn, from where walk can be joined at Longshaw Lodge, near point ③; trains to Grindleford. **Car park** at station.

① From station walk upstream on right side of Padley Gorge, following main path through the oak wood and on to open moorland beyond. Continue almost as far as the bend in the road below the distinctively shaped Toad's Mouth Rock. ② Turn right and cross to other side of the valley; enter the Longshaw Estate. ③ Follow the rough track past the front of Longshaw Lodge. ④ Turn right at the road and continue as far as the Grouse Inn. ⑤ Follow the footpath from behind the Grouse Inn and walk steeply down through the Haywood to join the B6521 at Grindleford. ⑥ Turn right and cross the riverside meadows. ⑦ At small stream on right (Burbage Brook) turn sharp right and climb gently through fields to cross the railway line by a bridge. Turn right on entering lane and follow it past Padley Chapel to the station.

🏠 Padley Chapel was once the gatehouse of a large manor house now demolished. During the persecutions of the Roman Catholics in Elizabeth I's reign, 2 priests who celebrated mass there were hung, drawn and quartered in Derby. A stained glass window commemorates the execution.

\!/ Carl Wark, ½ mile (0.8 km) away, and Burbage Rocks, ¾ mile (one km) distant.

※ Carl Wark is a Neolithic fort made of gigantic gritstone blocks. The walls are excellently preserved.

🍺 Grouse Inn.

\!/ Froggatt Edge and the Derwent Valley.

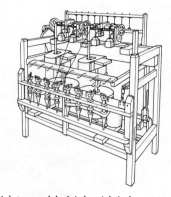

A later model of Arkwright's famous Water Frame, so-called because it was water-powered.

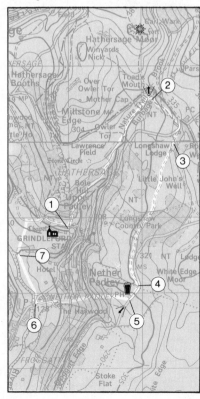

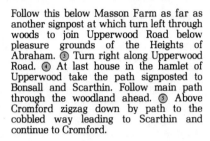

Matlock to Cromford
2½ miles (4 km) Sheet 119 297601

Easy A convenient escape from the crowds in this holiday area; fine views and peaceful woodland. *Farmland; woods.*

Start Matlock; frequent buses and trains. **Car parks** in Matlock. **Return** to starting point by bus or trains; buses leave from the square, Cromford.

① From the centre of Matlock follow the Snitterton road past Williams Deacon's Bank to lane on left signposted Bridge Farm. Follow this. At farm, climb short flight of steps into field. Follow path uphill and fork left to cross fields by stiles. Enter wood. ② Turn right by St. John's Chapel and walk up the lane to signpost for Matlock Bath. This points to a track to left of a large house.

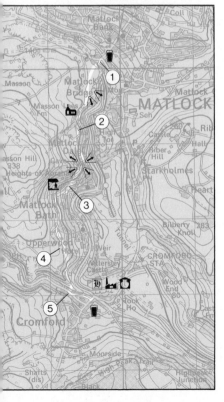

Follow this below Masson Farm as far as another signpost at which turn left through woods to join Upperwood Road below pleasure grounds of the Heights of Abraham. ③ Turn right along Upperwood Road. ④ At last house in the hamlet of Upperwood take the path signposted to Bonsall and Scarthin. Follow main path through the woodland ahead. ⑤ Above Cromford zigzag down by path to the cobbled way leading to Scarthin and continue to Cromford.

▮ A variety of pubs and cafés.

\\†/ Derwent Gorge, dominated by the limestone cliffs of High Tor. On the hillside above High Tor, about a mile (1.5 km) distant, is Riber Castle, built in 1852 by a local mill owner as a hotel. It now houses a European fauna zoo.

🏠 St. John's Chapel, a building with an almost Tyrolean appearance.

\\†/ Victoria Tower, on Masson Hill, is an excellent vantage point.

🗼 There are guided tours round the caves in the Heights of Abraham public recreation grounds.

⚒ Richard Arkwright, textile magnate and inventor of spinning systems, established ⏏ his first water-powered mill at Cromford. It is preserved as an exhibition centre.

19 Arkwright started his career as a wig-maker, turning his mind to spinning in the 1760s and beginning work on his first machine in 1764. It made thread strong enough to be used for the warp in weaving – the threads running length-wise on a loom, crossed by the weft. Earlier machines, such as Hargreaves' 'Spinning Jenny', produced thread suitable only for weft. Within a few years Arkwright was operating several factories. and had made cotton cloth manufacture Northern England's leading industry. The inevitable accolades, and wealth followed: he was knighted in 1786 and left a vast fortune. Horse-drawn boat trips can be taken on the canal that ends at the mill.

▮ Pubs and cafés.

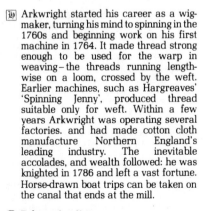

THE PEAK DISTRICT

Lyme Park and Bow Stones Moor
5 miles (8 km) Sheet 109 964823

Easy An introduction to much that is typical and dramatic of the Peak District. Excellent views of the Cheshire Plain from the moorland around Bow Stones. The gardens of Lyme Hall and the rhododendrons in West Park are at their best in spring and early summer. *Parkland, moorland, meadow, woods; one climb; slightly boggy in section* ⑤ . *If inexperienced at hill walking, avoid in poor visibility.*

Start Take the A6 to Disley and enter Lyme Park at signpost; buses and trains to Disley; transport in park from Parkgate. **Car park** at side of Lyme Hall.

① From car park follow path alongside Dutch Garden to lake in front of Hall. Turn right and walk through avenue of trees towards Knight's Low. ② Enter the pine woods on a wide track, turn right and walk through the wood to a stile over the boundary wall. Continue on path climbing open moor to Bow Stones Farm. ③ At Bow Stones turn right along lane. ④ At end of lane turn right through gate and follow rough path across open moorland of Sponds Hill. ⑤ Cross the lane and strike diagonally across field to a deep gully, then climb slightly into meadowland to a farm. Follow path to the chapel. ⑥ Turn right at the chapel and continue down the track to West Lodge. ⑦ At Lodge turn right into West Park woods and follow track to start.

♯ Lyme Hall – Elizabethan with some fine later additions – is the seat of the Legh family (Lord Newton) and is now maintained by the National Trust and Stockport Corporation. There are some superb Jacobean rooms. It is one of the several houses where Mary Queen of Scots was held captive; she visited nearby Buxton to take the waters for her rheumatism.

⩔ A large herd of red deer have lived in the 1,320-acre (534 ha) park for centuries.

⑂ Extensive views over the Cheshire Plain.

⁂ The Bow Stones are a pair of megaliths or monumental stones. Local legend holds that Robin Hood and his men used them for bending their bows.

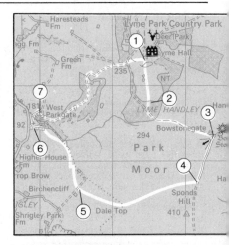

Elton and Gratton Dale
6½ miles (10.5 km) Sheet 119 223610

Moderate Gives insight into some of the area's contrasting rock formations and their interesting effect on the surface pasture; also passes a hermit's cave. *Farmland, dry limestone dales, gritstone outcrops; one climb; mud.*

Start From the A6 take the B5057 to Winster, then minor road to Elton; buses. **Parking** in Elton – do not block entrances.

① From centre of village follow the road opposite the church S as far as the speed de-restriction sign. Turn right along cart track between pastures. At junction with an overgrown track turn left – the way is easy to follow even if the track is overgrown. ② At end of track turn right over stile and cross a series of fields by way of a grassy path. Continue as far as the Cromford-Newhaven road. Turn right and continue about 150 yards (137 m). ③ At an indistinct style by side of a square field turn right over style and follow field wall around rear of Mouldridge Grange Farm. Turn right into Gratton Dale and follow it as far as Dale End Farm. ④ Turn left on to road at Dale End Farm and almost immediately right by a gate. The field here is marshy and the correct line of the path is impossible to follow. Instead follow gravel farm track to top of field above the swamp. Follow the wall around to the right as far as a stile. Turn left

THE PEAK DISTRICT

and cross several fields by stiles eventually reaching the Elton-Harthill road. ⑤ Turn left along the road and walk on until opposite the turning to Harthill Moor Farm. ⑥ Turn right and cross fields aiming to left of the distinctive shape of the rock formations of Robin Hood's Stride. ⑦ Go downhill to the road and turn right, walking uphill to the minor road to Dudwood Farm. Continue to farm. ⑧ Beyond the farm turn right on to a field path slanting upwards to Elton village.

🛕 Elton's church had a unique Saxon font, whose worth was unappreciated, and which was thrown out during rebuilding in the 19th C. It turned up, however, in Youlgreave church (see page 212), where it now stands.

🌱 Interesting orchids and other plants which thrive on limestone.

⛏ There are remains of lead mines on Elton Common, usually detected by grassy humps. They were small-scale, being worked by one or 2 men only.

🗐 This section follows the Portway, a prehistoric way running from near Nottingham to the hill fort on Mam Tor.

〰 The curious gritstone formation of Robin Hood's Stride is known locally as Mockbeggar's Hall because of the 2 'chimneys', which look particularly life-like at dusk. Rock climbers call them the Weasel and Inaccessible.

🖼 The hermit's cave has a crucifix carved in the rock at the rear.

〰 The rock strata can be seen changing from limestone (S) to gritstone (N).

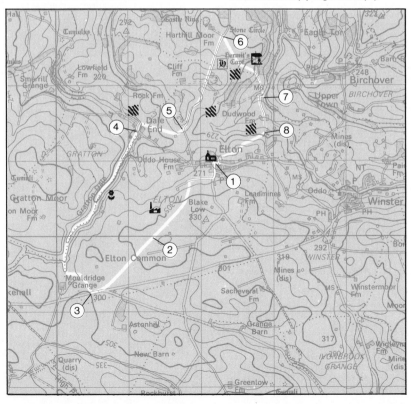

THE PEAK DISTRICT

Goyt Valley and Shining Tor Ridge
6½ miles (10.5 km) Sheets 118 and 119 012749

Moderate This is a safe walk from which to appreciate the solitude of wild moorland. The Goyt Valley is the first area of open country to operate a traffic-free scheme. Best in summer and autumn when the moor is dry. *Woods, moorland; 2 climbs; Cats Tor is boggy but avoidable.*

Start From the A6 Long Hill road (Manchester-Buxton) take the minor road into Goyt Valley from the summit; buses to Long Hill. **Car park** the Goyt Valley Car Park.

① From car park follow the forest trail to the stream below the ruins of Erwood Hall. Turn right, up towards the Hall. ② At Hall, follow track round the front and towards the far stream beyond the house. Follow this the whole way to the road. The lower reaches of the path are waymarked with white sticks: leave the waymarked route where the sticks turn sharp right and follow the path ahead. ③ At road turn left and walk almost as far as the Pym Chair Car Park at the highest part of the climb. ④ Turn off the road and walk forward on moorland following drystone wall or its remnants whole way to Tor. ⑤ At Shining Tor turn left and walk towards the far side of the valley. ⑥ Turn left down the smooth track back to the car park.

🖼️ Ruins of Erwood Hall, built by the Grimshawe family in 1830. The variety
⚓ of rhododendrons in the pine woods is a reminder that of this large plant group – over 600 species – about half are able to thrive in the U.K. Gardeners and landscape artists have found them useful material because their fine roots do not grow to great depths, which makes them easy to move without damage. Azaleas are abundant, too.

🏠 A circular shrine built in memory of a governess to the Grimshawe children.

\!/ Shining Tor opens up superb views of the Cheshire Highlands. The conical hill is Shuttlingslow, 1,659 feet (506 m).

✗ Café. About a mile (1.5 km) S on the road to Burbage is the Cat and Fiddle, one of England's highest pubs at 1,690 feet (515 m), from where views extend to the Mersey on clear days.

Our most familiar rhododendron, the so-called wild species (R. ponticum), with its purple flowers, was introduced in 1763.

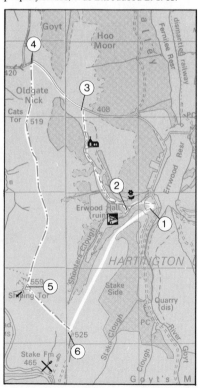

Castleton and Mam Tor
6½ miles (10.5 km) Sheet 110 151827

Moderate Interesting archaeological and geological features; fine views. *Dry dale, limestone moor, gritstone moor, grassy ridge; 2 climbs; take care on Mam Tor, which can be dangerously slippery if wet. Do not attempt in poor visibility.*

Start Castleton on the A625; buses to Castleton; trains to Hope, where there are buses to Castleton. **Car parks** in Castleton.

① From square in front of youth hostel enter Cave Dale by its narrow entrance between cottages. Climb up the dale and across the grassy moor on well-defined footpath. ② At crossing of 4 tracks turn right along the farm lane and continue past Rowter Farm. ③ Cross the road and enter the field opposite. Follow the track over Windy Knoll and cross the Rushup Edge road. ④ Climb the steep field opposite and at the stile turn right to climb the well-marked path across Mam Tor. ⑤ At Hollins Cross turn right and follow the path downhill. This eventually joins a walled lane which leads directly to Castleton.

🏰 Peveril Castle began in 1080 as a wooden stockade.

〽️ The brown, rounded rocks beyond the gate at Cave Dale's head are remains of an ancient lava flow.

🖼️ These are show caves.

❋ A Neolithic fort.

\!/ The Hope Valley.

\!/ Across Edale to Kinder Scout; down Hope Valley to the White Peak plateau.

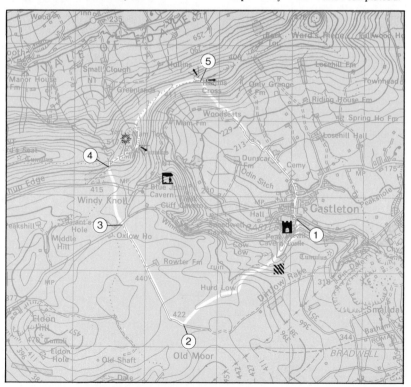

THE PEAK DISTRICT

Lathkill and Bradford Dales
12 miles (19 km) Sheet 119 210643

Energetic A route through some of the most interesting and attractive dales in the Peak. Well-blessing at Youlgreave is a charming spectacle, performed annually. *Farmland, limestone dales, villages; 2 climbs; mud after rain; Cales Dale is slippery when wet.*

Start Youlgreave off the B5056; buses. **Car park** at the sports ground, Youlgreave.

① From centre of Youlgreave walk up lane opposite the youth hostel as far as the car park beyond the old mineral workings. ② Leave road by stile marked with a footpath sign and walk across fields. The route is waymarked by posts painted with a yellow mark. ③ Go through Calling Low farmyard, following the signs, and cross a series of fields. ④ Descend steeply and cross Cales Dale on clearly defined path to One Ash Grange Farm. Continue on cart track. The walk may be shortened by turning right in Cales Dale and walking down it to join Lathkill Dale. ⑤ Where cart track beyond the farm turns sharp right at gate, go through gate and immediately turn left to follow wall up side of field. At top of field cross stile and follow path through series of fields. Eventually the path joins a walled, grassy lane; follow this the whole way to Monyash. ⑥ Follow the road through Monyash village, turning right at the green opposite the Bull's Head. Leave village on the Bakewell road. ⑦ In dip in road beyond Monyash turn right at the signpost 'To Lathkill Dale'. Follow the dale, keeping to the only path, which is on the N bank of the stream. Continue as far as the road bridge at Conksbury. ⑧ Turn right across bridge and walk up road as far as a footpath sign on left. Follow this path to the road at Alport. ⑨ Cross the road and enter Bradford Dale on wide farm track. Continue ¾ mile (one km). ⑩ Cross road and continue along the dale on path on N side of stream. At a clapper bridge, cross and continue up the dale, passing a series of trout pools. ⑪ Below the final pool turn right and cross the stream on wide stone bridge. Climb steeply through the woods to Youlgreave.

🏛 The church is one of Derbyshire's loveliest, with a fine 15th C. tower and a late medieval chest tomb. The centre of interest, however, is the Saxon font. It

has a curious side projection, the use of which is the subject of controversy; possibly it is a container for holy oil. More controversial still, to local people, is where the font belongs. During the 19th C. it was carried back and forth between here and Elton church, whose property it was: a saga of village rivalry. Elton makes do with a copy now.

✗ Calling Low Farm sells non-alcoholic drinks, including milk.

🏚 One Ash Grange Farm has a considerable main building, which in medieval times was a place of correction for erring monks.

🍺 The Bull's Head; Stone's ale and good pub food.

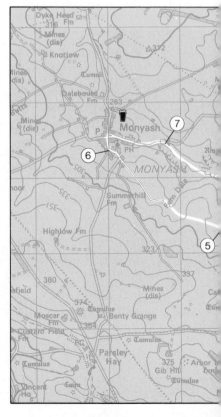

THE PEAK DISTRICT

🌊 The River Lathkill flows out of a cave here when it is wet. In dry weather the upper reaches run underground.

🎣 Clear trout pools in the Lathkill.

🏭 Ruins of a pumphouse which served Mandale Mine.

🌲 Lathkill Dale Nature Reserve.

🎣 Lathkill Dale.

🍺 The pub serves food.

🎊 The ancient local ceremony of well-blessing takes place in late June each year.

🍺 Several pubs and tea rooms.

The Delamere pine forest, off the B5152, has waymarked walks radiating from the car park and visitors' centre.

Edale is an excellent starting point for walks in most directions.

Longshaw, 3 miles (5 km) SE of Hatherage via the A625, gives access to paths with fine views leading to the Rocking Stone and Frog's Mouth Cave.

Congleton Edge provides a 3-mile walk with spectacular scenery. Approach on the A527 from Biddulph.

Well to the S there is Cannock Chase (lying SE of Stafford) with its network of secluded woodland paths.

Dove Dale's riverside and woodland paths deserve further exploration, preferably out of holiday season.

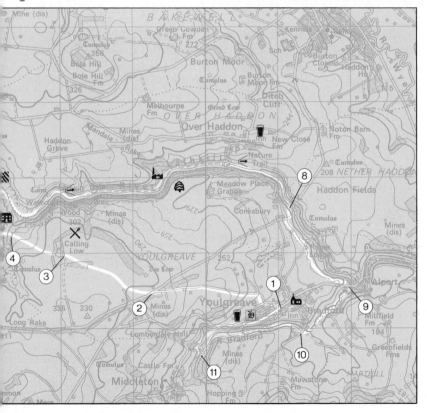

NORTHERN ENGLAND

LANCASHIRE, THE SOUTH PENNINES, YORKSHIRE WOLDS, YORKSHIRE DALES, NORTH YORK MOORS, CUMBRIA AND THE LAKES, NORTHUMBERLAND

LANCASHIRE

Some think that this county's charm was lost to the walker when its corner of the Lake District, Furness and Cartmel, went to Cumbria in 1974. At the same time, Lancashire gained a slice of Yorkshire containing the whole of the wild, fell-walking terrain of the ancient hunting Forest of Bowland.

The Forest is one of three hunks of the Pennines which thrust westwards into Lancashire. Next, to the south, is Pendle Hill, and then, across the Calder Valley, the fells of Rossendale. From both, the walker looks down on the milltowns. You do not, however, have to live in Burnley, Accrington, Nelson or Colne to feel the release of these uplands; the inhabitants of the intensively farmed flatlands behind Southport and Blackpool are thankful for them, too.

W. G. Hoskins, the great landscape historian, has noted that in the Ribble and Lune valleys ancient enclosures have produced almost Devonian scenery of winding lanes, stone farms and hamlets. These rivers debouch on the county's other great asset, a coast of wide strands and bird-haunted estuaries.

Wyresdale
5 miles (8 km) Sheet 102 551545

Easy Varied walking with excellent views of the fells. *Farmland, river, woods.*

Start The church (obscured by trees) 2½ miles (4 km) E of Dolphinholme on the road to Abbeystead. **Parking** opposite church.

① Go through churchyard to single gate on far side. Drop to footbridge and climb over double stile on right. Cross field on unploughed strip heading for farm. ② Turn left in yard through gate alongside barn. Continue keeping wood on left, and enter it over ladder stile at bottom of hill. ③ Over iron bridge, bear right, then left to footbridge over tributary. Leave wood over stile and turn right; climb track. Fork left beyond Catshaw Hall past Little Catshaw. ④ Track bends decisively right; leave it to follow reedy ditch. Bear slightly right after footbridge. Bear right in wood, descending to locate drained mill pond. Follow embankment, then descend to footbridge which points out of wood uphill to farm (not in view at first). ⑤ Follow farm track to tarmac road; turn left. ⑥ Leave road at first gate on left after farm. Descend through 3 fields on left of wooded stream. Track leads through wood, downhill to footbridge and then to minor road at bridge. Turn left over bridge and right over wall stile. ⑦ Track through riverside fields to road at Grizedale Bridge. ⑧ Leave road immediately at wall stile on left. Climb to footbridge and continue

until barn is 100 yards (91 m) to right. Keep to top of slope. Stiles waymark route straight ahead to road. ⑨ Cross stile opposite, then make for small gate. Turn right to ①.

🏠 The (18th C.) stone building once stabled churchgoers' horses.

🏛 Abbeystead House, formerly owned by Earls of Sefton, renowned for shooting hospitality: a record bag was 2,929 birds.

Wyresdale Church: shepherds probably hung their crooks on the porch's iron hooks.

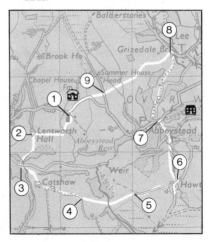

LANCASHIRE

Pudsay's Leap
10 miles (16 km) Sheet 103 778468

Moderate A refreshingly lonely stretch of the popular Ribble Valley. *Riverside, farmland, woods; mud; slippery in parts.*

Start Sawley, off the A59 NE of Clitheroe. **Parking** opposite Spread Eagle Hotel.

① Take minor road opposite Spread Eagle. Fork left. Go through gate on left just before gate to Sawley Lodge. ② After footbridge, cross 2 fields diagonally to stile and footbridge. Continue mainly by river about 1½ miles (2.5 km). ③ Climb track and fork right to go above riverside wood. Turn right at corner of fence and wood, heading for next corner, where look carefully for rail. Cross and head for barn, then Wheatley Farm. ④ Follow access road from farm, then go through gate on left of isolated barn. ⑤ After crossing steep-sided stream, head for farm on right. Straight ahead to road. Turn left and continue 1¼ miles (2 km). ⑥ Enter field on right of farm and descend to footbridge. Cross stile on left. Turn right, uphill. ⑦ After plantation, follow right-hand boundary to Fooden Farm. ⑧ Turn right at house. Leave yard at top end by building with curved roof. Bear left to gate in fence. In corner. ⑨ Cross 2 fields to join road to right of white house. ⑩ Cross stile on right at bend of road. Climb to stile to left of field corner. Leave next field at far left corner. ⑪ Continue ahead through kissing-gate and stile. Cut across bend of stream on right before crossing at footbridge. ⑫ Gradually close in on River Ribble (on left), then follow white stones. ⑬ Ford stream on right. Head for Sawley Bridge.

▷ The remnants of Sawley Abbey, a Cistercian monastery founded 1147.

🏛 Pudsay's Leap is the focal point of a fairy tale about William Pudsay, a 16th C. squire of Bolton. He jumped the river on a horse with a magic bit to escape arrest for (magically) minting silver from lead.

⩔ Deer seen at several points on route.

⛪ The church has a memorial to another, more down-to-earth Pudsay, Sir Ralph, his 3 wives and 25 children.

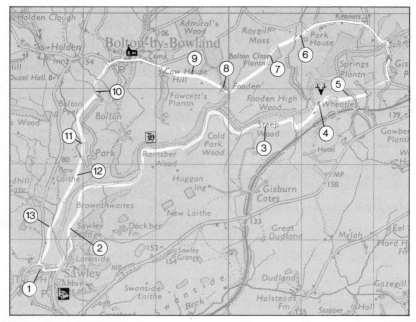

Chipping Fells
7 miles (11 km) Sheet 102 or 103 622433

Moderate Accessible, yet crowd-free at any season; constant changes of view. *Sheep and limestone country; 2 climbs.*

Start Chipping, N of Longridge and the B5269; buses from Preston to Chipping bus terminus. **Public car park** near the church, Chipping.

① From church, take the road N–the weather vane on the spire points the way. Then fork right. ② Midway along millpond, turn right to stile off track. Climb hillside with back to pond. Keep parallel to valley, then bear right of quarry ahead to stile. Aim to left of Birchen Lee through 2 reedy fields. ③ Follow track past Birchen Lee and turn left at first junction. At bridge in dip before next farm, walk a few yards upstream to join faint track at ford. Climb far bank to gate. Skirt to left of low hill and join rutted track; go right. ④ At Lickhurst Farm go straight ahead. Cross footbridge at bottom of hill. Climb to stile. Join faint, rutted track on left of limestone hill; follow it (winding course) to

Dinkling Green Farm ahead. ⑤ Pass right of building with carved face over door. Follow farm road for ⅓ mile (0.5 km), leaving it at end of wooded bank by gate on left. Climb over ridge and descend to stile-gate at road. Turn right, and left at telephone box. ⑥ Follow farm road for ¾ mile (one km), passing Higher and Lower Greystoneley (latter in ruins) to reach isolated barn. Go through gate, fork right past limestone mound, then continue to stile in tree-lined fence. Drop to footbridge, then follow right-hand boundaries of several fields straight ahead. At end of boundaries, straight ahead to farm road near wood boundary wall. Turn left, then right at road.

🔟 Chipping means 'market', which was the town's former role.

🏭 Berry's Chair Works, once a cotton mill.

🏠 The almshouses in Windy Street, founded by a local cloth merchant, are still used charitably, housing 2 needy persons.

🏠 Upland sheep rearing is taught here.

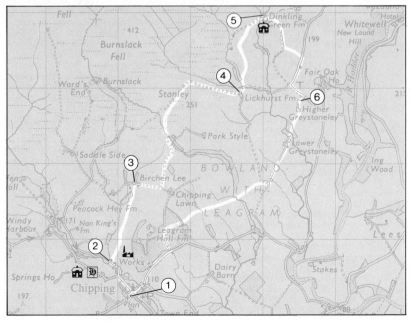

LANCASHIRE

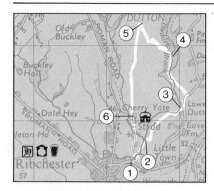

The Ribble Valley at Ribchester
3 miles (5 km) Sheet 103 653355

Easy A historically fascinating part of the Ribble Valley. *Farmland, woods; one climb; mud after rain.*

Start The New Hotel, outside Ribchester on the B6245 (Blackburn road); buses stop by the hotel. **Parking** near the New Hotel.

① Take minor road between New Hotel and bridge, but turn right after a few yards through gate with stile. Continue to follow stream after crossing stone bridge. ② Cross stile on right, then footbridge. Bear left and continue through 3 fields passing about 150 yards (137 m) to left of farm. ③ Cross stile in corner of field and stile on immediate left. Bear right to stile up bank on to road. Turn left and go to second gate on left (with stile). Cross middle of field to stile; follow trace of track to enter Duddel Wood. ④ Follow path through wood. Cross footbridge on left *after* passing ruins of comb mill. Path climbs to leave wood at stile. Cross stile on right after ruined barn. Leave next field in diagonally opposite corner. Make for summit of Duddel Hill. ⑤ Face across Ribble Valley. Descend to stile in short length of stone wall. Continue in same direction to cross gate, footbridge and stile in turn. ⑥ Pass through yard of Stydd Manor Farm. Follow lane to point ①.

🏛 Ribchester was the Roman cavalry fort, Bremetonacum; museum has relics .

🏛 The extraordinary Stydd Almshouses, 📿 with Roman pillars set into the porch, similar to those at the White Bull in Ribchester.

Dunsop Fell
12 miles (19 km) Sheet 103 659501

Energetic Insight into the wild beauty and enchanting softer aspects of Bowland. *Riverside, undulating sheep country; one climb; do not attempt in poor visibility – compass recommended.*

Start Dunsop Bridge, 2 miles (3 km) W of Newton and the B6478. **Parking** by riverside – clear with garage opposite.

① Take private road at war memorial. After 2 miles (3 km), cross first half of concrete and iron bridge. Continue on track uphill. At top of hill, fork right. ② Turn right on nearside of farm. Take rough track beyond barn to climb Dunsop Fell. After second elbow bend, path is indistinct, but the route is directly uphill, in direction of cairns and post on skyline. (Waymarked by green posts with yellow tops, and yellow paint on stones.) Approaching fell-top fence, follow path as it bears right to small gate in wall (waymarking stops). ③ Beyond wall, turn right, and gradually bear away from wall (beware of false tracks – made by sheep). When valley comes into view, descend on top of ridge on *right* side of valley. Turn right near bottom, and go through second gate in wall on left. Make for Burn Side (farmhouse), wall over to left. Follow access road to road. ④ Enter field from yard of Laythams (name on house). Then aim for farm ahead (Parrock Head), but bear partly right at first until gate in fence on left. ⑤ Leave Parrock Head farm yard on near-side of main building. Aim for Pain Hill Farm, reached over footbridge hidden in dip. ⑥ At Pain Hill Farm cross wall-stile on right of buildings, turn right then follow wall to left. Climb next field, looking carefully for stile in left-hand wall, 50 yards (46 m) before gate. *Do not cross stile*, but angle away, aiming to left side of tree-lined water hole. This puts you on target for a wall-stile 500 yards (457 m) distant. This stile is on right of kink in wall, hardly visible until wall is reached (the same applying to the next 2). Cross next field directly to wall-stile. Bear partly right in next to stile on to road (on left of pond). Continue about 250 yards (229 m) to ⑦ a walled, rutted track (Bull Lane). Follow it to end. Bear slightly right to gate that comes into view. Descending to Rough Syke Barn, note position of Back of Hill Barn beyond. Bear slightly right with track after Rough

LANCASHIRE

Syke Barn, down to bridge over stream. Pass through gate on left, ford a stream, and climb in direction of Back of Hill Barn. ⑧ At barn continue ahead, then bear right at track. Beyond Beatrix and deserted farm, leave track when fence on right stops. Continue parallel to overhead wires on right. Pass over hillside and descend to wall-stile 40 yards (37 m) to left of wires. Descend to river; turn left through yard to ①.

\ɫ/ Interior of the Forest of Bowland.

🔟 A superb, alternative approach to Dunsop Bridge is through the Trough of Bowland, a dramatic valley route.

Ideal for improvised walking in this area are the banks of the Lancaster Canal, one of the country's most pleasing waterways. Do not overlook the branch to Glasson, an attractive harbour on the Lune estuary.

Across the estuary there is a fine walk around Sunderland Point. Check time of high tide first – approach to Sunderland may be flooded.

Pendle Hill is a favourite climb, but not to be undertaken lightly.

A leaflet showing access areas in the Forest of Bowland is available.

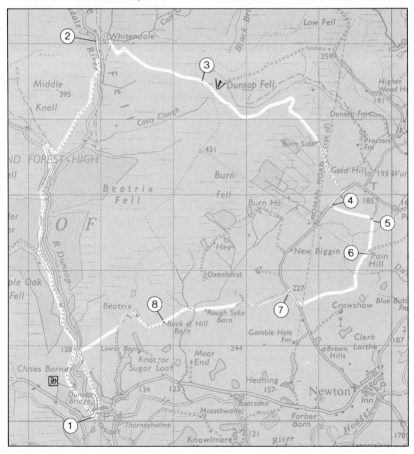

THE SOUTH PENNINES

Why should this end of the Pennines be despised? It often is and by walkers who ought to know better. They think of this region as a nondescript patch of largely industrialized hill country which intervenes between the northern boundary of the Peak District and the southern boundary of the Yorkshire Dales national parks. But attitudes are changing and these days ramblers are readier to see the charms of the country on their back doorsteps.

The landscape is seamed with canals, railways and now motorways which link the conurbations on either side of the Pennine chain. In fact the close juxtaposition of industry and nature makes for exciting contrasts. Huddersfield's centre, for instance, is within three miles of the moors and the nearby bluebell-filled Mollcar Woods. From Ainsley Top the walker has before him a sweeping view of the Calder Valley and Halifax.

The smaller textile towns and mill villages are living records of an industrial era now fading. Howarth was the home of the Brontë family and the surrounding moors provide a setting fully worthy of the great novels that were written here. Indeed, Withins Moor is supposed to be the model for Wuthering Heights. Through all this the Pennine Way weaves steadily northwards. Those who walk this first of our long-distance paths should pause to explore this robust, working terrain.

A lost village
3 miles (5 km) Sheet 109 911176

Easy Spectacular views across the Pennines, and over the Roch valley. *Pasture and rough grazing; one climb; mud after rain.*

Start From the A58 between Rochdale and Littleborough take road at Sandknockers Inn to Wardle. Continue through Wardle to Wardle Fold, and on to where lane ends below reservoir gates; frequent buses to Wardle. **Parking** by side of road in lane, not causing an obstruction.

① Go through the reservoir pedestrian entrance, following the main track around and to the right up to the reservoir dam. ② Continue along track around reservoir wall, through gate and around E side of reservoir. ③ Where track joins old, cobbled street, follow street N uphill. ④ Where lane bears right at ruined farm (gatepost on left), leave it left to descend to stream at head of reservoir. ⑤ Ford stream and follow line of old wall above little ravine ahead. Go through gap in crossing wall to next wall ahead. ⑥ Turn left along wall, keeping ahead across open pasture to join old, walled, grassy lane ahead. ⑦ Follow grassy way downhill curving right to ruined farm. ⑧ Cross open pasture above scattered trees, keeping about 100 yards (91 m) above reservoir and making for wall directly ahead and parallel with reservoir. ⑨ Descend to reservoir dam past old quarry – bear left towards gate. ⑩ Go through pedestrian gate and along top of reservoir dam. At end of dam turn right through reservoir gates.

🚶 Wardle Fold, a former weaving hamlet, has several 3-tiered cottages with the

Watergrove Reservoir: access around the edges is unlimited.

typical Lancashire weaving loft to accommodate the hand-weaving loom.

🏠 The weaving hamlet of Watergrove was drowned in 1935 to make the reservoir. The cobbled lane between Wardle Fold and Watergrove disappears beneath the dam, and it can be seen going under water at the reservoir's E edge. If the water is low, the hamlet's foundations are visible. The reservoir is Rochdale's principal water supply.

🏠 Small quarries and coal pits bear witness to this derelict area's former livelihood, as do the farms, emptied to avoid pollution of the reservoir.

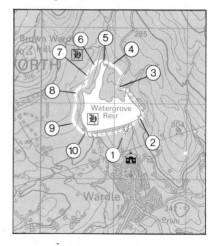

THE SOUTH PENNINES

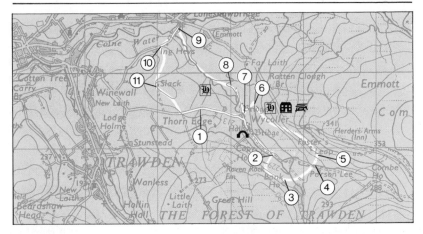

Wycoller
4 miles (6.5 km) Sheet 103 926395

Easy An attractive 'hidden' hamlet; views giving insight into typical local scenery. *Pasture; mud after rain.*

Start From Trawden, 2 miles (3 km) SW of Colne, follow signs to Wycoller; frequent buses from Keighley and Colne stop at Laneshawbridge – get off at crossroads and join walk at ⑨. **Car park** 440 yards (400 m) W of Wycoller hamlet on road from Cotton Tree and Colne – cars not allowed beyond.

① From car park walk down lane into Wycoller, keeping on lane through hamlet. ② Cross beck (stream), right, by ancient 'clam' footbridge, and follow wall uphill to crossing wall above. Follow track above this left to barn at Bank House. ③ Follow path round Bank House, then down slope on grassy way. Cross hurdle stile and footbridge below, then go uphill to gate and Dean House Farm. Walk between farm and barn to stile behind farm, over field and through gate to Parson Lee Farm. ④ Over stile to left of barn, cross lane, over beck at stepping stones and bear left uphill to white farm (Foster's Leap) ahead. ⑤ Follow path in front of farmhouse, then through series of stiles (some gaps) in narrow fields, keeping same height, then descending slightly to the left. ⑥ At gate, path joins sunken, metalled track; follow this downhill, through stile and down steps back to Wycoller Hall. ⑦ Keep right along track above Hall and behind hamlet, entering field

by gap on right. Over stiles to join track in front of old Pump House. ⑧ Follow track into fields, keeping same direction to junction of paths. Ignore stile straight ahead, crossing stile, left, and taking path between wall and beck. Cross stiles and take path on higher land above beck ahead to Covey Bridge. ⑨ At lane cross bridge and walk uphill. ⑩ Turn left at tall step stile, following wall for 150 yards (137 m), through stile on left, and at next stile bear diagonally right downhill across beck, going uphill, over stiles, to Slack Farm. ⑪ Follow track round outside of farm, go through gate on left beyond farm, then alongside wall and straight on through gates to lane just above car park.

🏠 Wycoller was a farming and weaving community which declined after the 1820s, the peak years of handloom weaving. The ruined Hall is reputedly the model for Ferndean Manor in *Jane Eyre*. Picnic site; refreshments at Oak House.

⌒ The hamlet was the meeting point for several cross-Pennine packhorse ways; the double-arched packhorse bridge may be 13th C. Nearby is the clapper bridge, made of 3 slabs, between 1,000 and 2,000 years old. The next upstream, a 'clam' bridge, is older still, the most primitive form of permanent bridge.

🏠 The unique walls of upright slabs were probably erected between 1100 and 1400 as enclosures for local cattle-rearing farms.

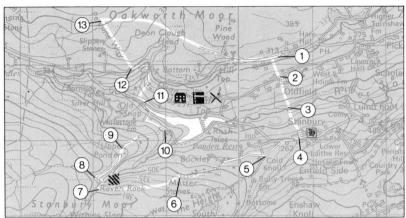

Ponden Clough
6 miles (9.5 km) Sheets 103 and 104 007382

Energetic An unusual walk on the fringe of the much-visited Brontë country, with superb views over the Oakworth, Haworth and Keighley areas. *Farmland, moorland; one climb; mud. Do not attempt in poor visibility.*

Start Unclassified road from Colne to Keighley. **Car park** at Hare Hill Edge, 1½ miles W of Oakworth.

① From car park walk W along road to signposted, enclosed path by water filtration works. Follow it to Oldfield School. ② Turn left in village, then first right along farm track. Below farm, continue along grassy way, which becomes a field path, going through gate and downhill to Griff Mill. ③ Cross beck (stream) at footbridge, turn right to go outside mill, climbing along enclosed, grassy track to Stanbury. ④ Through gate behind farm and into back lane, keeping right through village to Hob Hill (bus terminus); bear left up minor lane. ⑤ At junction of lanes, bear right above farms and cottages along quiet lane and track. ⑥ At last farm, keep left around outside wall on moor edge, through wicket gate. Where wall swings right, maintain height, keeping ahead to pick up faint track through heather. ⑦ As path nears end of short valley, bear right to path downhill to cross stream at small dam. Follow path downhill by beck, walk down rocky steps with handrail (extreme care

required if wet) and past waterworks retaining wall. Go left along clear path to next waterfall. ⑧ Continue along grassy footway, rising to Upper Ponden Farm. ⑨ Turn left immediately before farm, round farm and down to white notice by gate below. Turn right through gate and continue along track to junction. Right again for Ponden Hall. ⑩ From Ponden Hall retrace to junction, keeping straight ahead, then bearing right to track round reservoir, and climbing up to road. ⑪ Left along road for 100 yards (91 m), then right over stile (Pennine Way), climbing pasture to farmhouse, where turn left up farm track. Bear left along side of wall to road at Crag Bottom. Turn left along road. ⑫ Go 200 yards (183 m) along road, then right along track (Pennine Way) uphill. Continue ½ mile (0.8 km). crossing 3 substantial stiles. ⑬ At obvious junction of tracks, go right along path outside fell wall (avoiding boggy places) to wall corner. Follow track to pinewoods, then continue along well-defined farm track to road. Continue ahead to car park.

⒚ Timmy Feather, the last Yorkshire handloom weaver, worked in Stanbury.

〽 Ponden Clough – a steep-sided valley.

▦ Ponden Hall, dating from 1634, now a
▤ craft mill and shop, has changed little since the time of the Brontë sisters, who lived nearby at Haworth. It may be the model of Thrushcross Grange in
✕ *Wuthering Heights.* Tea shop.

THE SOUTH PENNINES

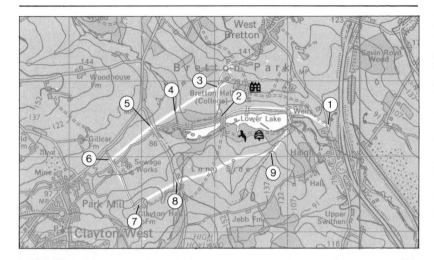

Bretton

5 miles (8 km) Sheet 110 296124

Easy Fine parkland surrounded by industry, close to the M1; an interesting contrast to other routes in this section. *Parkland, farmland.*

Start The Country Park one mile (1.5 km) S of West Bretton on the A637 – adjacent to M1 junction 38; frequent buses from Barnsley, Huddersfield and Dewsbury pass Park entrance; connections possible with Wakefield-Huddersfield service at Bretton roundabout and Wakefield-Holmfirth at West Bretton village. **Parking** by Visitor Centre at entrance to Park on A637. The Park opens at 10 am and the car park gates are locked at 6 pm. Alternative parking at W side of park on High Hoyland Road 220 yards (200 m) N of point ⑧.

① From car park and picnic site cross to entrance of Country Park, through gate and follow broad, well-defined path towards lake. Follow red posts of 'Red' trail downhill to Bretton Park Bridge (good view of lake from bridge). ② Follow bridleway uphill from bridge towards Bretton Hall. ③ To visit Sculpture Park and gardens turn right at junction of tracks, making for Sculpture Park car park behind College buildings, passing through car park to the drive with sculptures either side. Return by track leading left, at bungalow just S of main

entrance. Follow signposted path leading from track N of row of lime trees along edge of field to stile, then downhill to footbridge. ④ Over footbridge, then bear left around outside of field to gate and stile to reach Hoyland Road. ⑤ Go left for about 30 yards (27 m), looking for stile on right sunk low in wall. Cross and bear diagonally left towards stream and woods to cross 2 wooden stiles. Cross field to stile on to farm track. ⑥ Left at farm track, and climb past sewage farm to Clayton Hall Farm. ⑦ At NE corner of farm buildings, go through gate and keep fence on left. Go downhill through long field to stile and footbridge, crossing both to climb next field to stile on to road straight ahead. ⑧ Left for 20 yards (18 m) then right over stile before farm. Along field, over next stile and into Bretton Park. Descend towards lake crossing main track. ⑨ Cross stile into wooded area, go down slope to E edge of lake and back along 'Red' trail to car park.

⌂ Waymarked trails in the Country Park, with wildlife and botanical interest, are given in leaflets on sale at the Visitor Centre. Keep dogs on leads at all times in the Park.

🏛 Bretton Hall, built in 1720 in the classical style, was extended in Regency times. Now a college of higher education, it is not open to the public. The Sculpture Park features work by Barbara Hepworth, born in Wakefield.

The Towpath to East Marton
7½ miles (12 km) Sheet 103 932543

Easy Involves sections of 2 long-distance paths, the Pennine Way and the historic Leeds-Liverpool canal; plenty of activity on canal in summer. *Canal-side, pasture; mud after rain.*

Start Gargrave, off the A65 NW of Skipton; frequent buses; frequent trains to Gargrave station on the Leeds-Morecambe line. **Car park** in West Street, Gargrave (turn right by old Swan Inn); a second car park at junction of Broughton Road and A65.

① From the car park on West Street turn right up lane to the canal bridge. Follow towpath past moorings and wharves for one mile (1.5 km), crossing under A65 and railway. ② At Priest Holme Bridge, cross canal with towpath. Go along lane, then pick

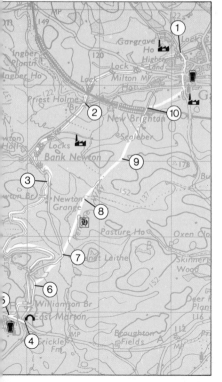

up towpath at wooden gap stile on left. Continue past locks and Bank Newton boat-yard. ③ At next bridge do not continue through stile on same side; cross canal, walk down lane and find entrance to towpath at wicket gate. Follow it for 2 miles (3 km) around deep bends to East Marton and double bridge. ④ Continue on towpath under A59, then take bridge on right to church. Follow path right alongside churchyard to main road at East Marton and make for Cross Keys Inn. ⑤ Follow lane beyond Cross Keys down to cross canal at Williamson Bridge. Continue on lane. ⑥ At stile (signposted) turn right to pick up Pennine Way into field. Continue past wood and back into lane. Follow lane. ⑦ Cross next stile, on right, and cross field to footbridge and stile. Bear left along beck (stream), crossing stiles. ⑧ One hundred yards (91 m) beyond wood, where beck bends E, keep straight on through gate and over bridge. Continue ahead along field edge, over stiles, across field corner and up Scaleber Hill. ⑨ Keep directly ahead to farm track below leading over railway bridge. ⑩ Over ladder stile on right. Follow path across fields and stiles to stile on left by old school.

🛶 Oldest and largest of the 3 trans-Pennine canals, the Leeds-Liverpool was built in 1770-1812, and remains the only one in working order. The old wharves, ware-houses and locks at Gargrave are fascinating, as are the boatyards at Bank Newton. This is a contour canal, preferring to use the natural lie of the land rather than locks, expensive to build. The canal follows an extraordinary loop S of Newton to avoid a climb and fall.

🍺 Cross Keys – real ale and good food.

⌒ The double-arched bridge was built this way for extra strength; 200 years later it is standing up to juggernauts.

🏛 Although only a linking section of The Pennine Way long-distance path (see pages 328-334), this is nonetheless green and attractive.

🍺 Gargrave is a former coaching village with a splendid coaching inn, The Old Swan. The village was also an important port on the Leeds-Liverpool canal, where lead from the Wharfedale lead mines on Grassington Moor was embarked.

THE SOUTH PENNINES

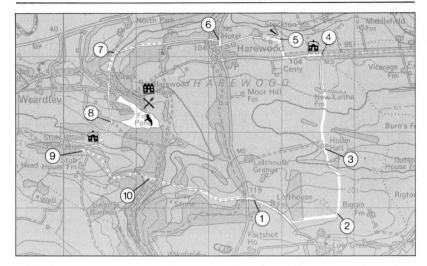

Harewood
7 miles (11.5 km) Sheet 104 326432

Easy A gentle but rewarding route; fine views over Lower Wharfedale and Pennine foothills. *Farmland, parkland; mud after rain.*

Start From the A61 between Leeds and Harrogate take the lane to Wike, making for SW gate of park; frequent buses to lane corner by start of walk. **Parking** on broad verge in lane between A61 and Lofthouse Farm.

① From parking walk along lane 700 yards (640 m) and take unsurfaced track branching left by wood. ② Turn left at field gate on to track alongside hedge. Continue along edge of fields to Spring Wood. Bear left with path downhill, past wood, then climb to Hollin Hall ponds ahead. Make for Hollin Hall Farm. ③ Go directly between farm buildings; leave farm track as it bends left to reach gate by hedge straight ahead. Cross bridge, and continue directly ahead along track to New Laithe Farm. Continue along farm drive to road. ④ Cross road with care, turn left, and walk 400 yards (366 m) to gate by edge of field on right. Follow path along edge of field to gate and stile. ⑤ Cross stile and join track to left, following it into village. ⑥ Cross A61, go along Church Lane ahead and slightly right. Continue for one mile

(1.5 km), past church to where lane descends; meet junction. ⑦ Turn left along farm road towards Stank–pass farm and rear of gardens. Where track turns left, keep on narrower track alongside wood to cottage ahead. ⑧ Follow path by ruined cottage (Carr House) to track above. ⑨ At junction, turn left into wood, bearing right and ignoring track on right to Stub House. Keep ahead into woods. ⑩ Follow main track to beck (stream), and cross at bridge. Follow track uphill to Lodge gates.

🏠 John Carr stayed at Carr House while Harewood was being built.

⚲ To ruins of 14th C. Harewood Castle.

🏛 Harewood, one of the greatest of Yorkshire's great houses, was designed ✕ by the York architect John Carr and built in the 1760s. Interiors by Robert Adam; park landscaped by Capability Brown; home of the Lascelles family (Earl of Harewood); art treasures; bird garden; refreshments. Open April-November.

🦆 Best views of waterfowl on lake are from the gardens, via official entrance.

🏠 The village stood in the park until a Lascelles had it removed and rebuilt to designs by Carr as a 'model' village on the present site.

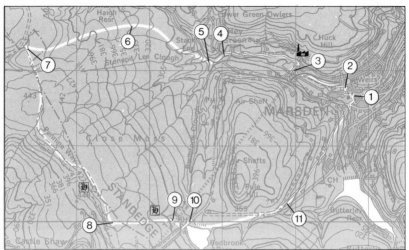

Stanedge
7½ miles (12 km) Sheet 110 047116

Energetic Involves one of the most spectacular stretches of the Pennine Way and some generally underrated walking country, rich in industrial and cultural history. *Canal-side, moorland; one climb; mud. Do not attempt in poor visibility.*

Start Marsden, on the A62 between Huddersfield and Oldham; frequent buses; frequent train service from Leeds. **Parking** in Marsden, near the church.

① From Marsden church, follow lane N of church, over packhorse bridge and up narrow, enclosed way. ② Turn right at top and cross to gate on left giving access to towpath of Huddersfield New Canal. Follow canal to canal basin and entrance to Marsden Tunnel. ③ From tunnel entrance climb to Junction Inn and left along lane past canal reservoir to Hey Green hamlet. ④ Where road bends left, look for iron gate, left, leading to narrow path between wall and river. Follow this to Eastergate packhorse bridge. ⑤ Cross bridge, do not take obvious paths left or right by beck (stream), but follow way up steep tongue of land between the 2 becks. This climbs to open moorland, and a more obvious track marked by stone pillars (most fallen) which bears right to cross beck and then climbs

open moorland ahead. ⑥ Keep clough (steep valley) and stream to left, and follow path due W to join A640 at layby S of the distinctive shape of March Hill, half right. ⑦ Do not reach A640, but turn S along Pennine Way up steep and (often) muddy track, marked by cairns. ⑧ Go past trig. point and last of fallen walls (with road in sight) and bear left on sheep track to find broad, shallow, grassy track over moor. ⑨ As track nears wire fence, turn right along top of reservoir culvert (channel) to reach A62 just E of Great Western Hotel. ⑩ Cross road, and enter Red Brook Reservoir by gate; follow path along embankment and over white footbridge, keeping same direction, then slightly left to join road by shallow clough. ⑪ Bear left at junction and follow lane with broad, verge down to Marsden centre.

🚇 The canal tunnel cuts through 5,416 feet (1,651 m) of Stanedge at 644 feet (196 m) above sea level; built 1798-1811.

🏠 The line of crags gives Stanedge its name – 'stan' means stone in Anglo-Saxon. Until the work of Metcalfe and others, it was a major barrier to E-W Pennine communications.

🏠 The grassy way is a survival of Jack Metcalfe's road over Pule Hill and Stanedge. The great road-builder, born 1717, was blind from childhood.

THE SOUTH PENNINES

Hebden Bridge and Heptonstall
7 miles (11 km) Sheet 103 993272

Moderate Includes a section of the Calderdale Way and 2 famous Pennine spots. *Canal-side, farmland, woods; 2 climbs.*

Start Hebden Bridge, between Halifax and Todmorden on the A646; frequent buses; frequent trains stop at Hebden Bridge (Manchester-Bradford-Leeds line). **Car parks** signposted at centre of Hebden Bridge, and one just E of point ①.

① Cross the small park on the main road in the centre of Hebden Bridge, go over the canal bridge and turn right alongside the canal. ② Cross bridge back on to canal towpath, and follow towpath across aqueduct over river; continue along towpath for nearly 2 miles (3 km). Continue past millpond. ③ After waterworks, where road comes in from left over canal, turn right over river and past mill to main road. Turn left at road. ④ Follow lane on right which goes under railway arch – signposted Calderdale Way, and Great Rock. It becomes a stony track, climbing zigzag through woods and past Eastwood Old Hall to Great Rock. ⑤ Follow path left of Great Rock, alongside wall and descending over ladder stile to Hippin Bridge. ⑥ Cross bridge and take track forking right in front of Hippins Farm. Follow it between buildings to stile. Continue ahead to farm. Cross track to stile on right and go along path by wall to more buildings. Continue along track, bearing left to gate into Blackshaw Head. ⑦ Take path over stile opposite post office, bear right to stile and keeping same direction descend diagonally across fields, over stiles, to Shaw Bottom. Turn left along metalled track, then sharp right along another metalled track which soon becomes stony. ⑨ At Pennine Way turn left down steps and right over Hebble Hole Bridge and Colden Water. Climb bank and continue along paved way to stile at corner of wood. Cross to next stile, then right over a third stile and cross several fields to broader track. ⑩ Turn right at junction, go past cottages and along paved way. Keep ahead at next junction on wide track to road at Lumb Bank. ⑪ Where road bends left, turn off right on to path which follows edge of Eaves Wood above crags, soon alongside wall. ⑫ Turn left at corner of wall into narrow lane which leads into back of Heptonstall village. Cut through churchyard,

The Great Rock near Hebden Bridge, landmark and stopping place for walkers, is millstone grit – coarse sandstone – like limestone, highly characteristic of the S Pennines. Stoodley Pike, seen across the valley, is a famous local landmark commemorating the Battle of Waterloo.

past ruined church. ⑬ From Heptonstall follow main road downhill towards Hebden Bridge. After 250 yards (229 m) take steps on left to road below. Keep ahead past track on left to where steep, paved way with handrail leads down to centre of Hebden Bridge.

🏠 Hebden Bridge is regarded as the capital of the S Pennines. The 'double-decker' houses are built one 'on top of' the other to take advantage of the steep hillside and minimize waste of space.

🚤 The Rochdale Canal, running from Manchester, Rochdale and Littleborough to Sowerby Bridge, was opened in 1804. A superbly engineered waterway, it is one of 3 trans-Pennine canals. Competition from the railways forced closure in 1952, but there are hopes of having it re-opened for pleasure use.

🏁 A section of the Calderdale Way, the 50-mile (80 km), unofficial long-distance route in the S Pennines (see pages 328-334). The route is a focal point for the revival of interest in the landscape of the area.

🏠 This is a good specimen of late 17th C. or early 18th C. Pennine farmhouse. 'Hippins' means stepping stones.

🏚 Blackshaw Head was an important meeting point of several packhorse ways crossing the Pennines.

🏠 Lumb Bank House is the former home of the poet Ted Hughes. The house now belongs to a foundation and is used for courses in writing and the arts.

🏚 Heptonstall was the focal point of the surrounding weaving community. The 🏛 13th C. church, dedicated to St. Thomas à Beckett, fell to ruin after suffering storm damage in 1847; it stands in the graveyard of the 19th C. church which replaced it. The 17th C. grammar school is a museum, open at weekends.

The Leeds-Liverpool Canal towpath provides splendid walking all the way from the centre of Leeds, through the Aire Valley and into industrial Lancashire. Though the towpath is not a public right of way, walkers who wish to make use of it have the full support of the waterways board.

There is more excellent canal walking in the Calder Valley beside the Rochdale Canal. Most of the canal can be followed from Rochdale to Sowerby Bridge. Parts of the Huddersfield New Canal can also be walked.

The Eccup Reservoir, north Leeds, is yet more easy waterside ambling, with paths mostly smooth and dry enough for prams or wheelchairs.

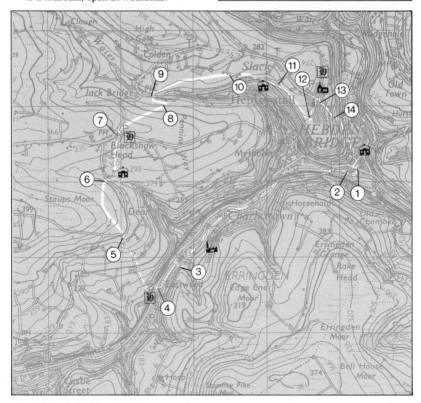

YORKSHIRE WOLDS

These hills are the quiet ending of the chalk lands which cross Britain from Dorset, via Wessex and the Chilterns, marching on through Cambridgeshire and Lincolnshire. At last, north of the Humber, the chalk expires in this crescent of low hills which reaches the sea with some drama at Flamborough Head. They lie mostly between the 400- and 600-foot contours (122 and 183 m), but top 800 feet (244 m) at Garrowby Top.

Until the end of the 18th century, the downs and their dry valleys were mostly sheep-walks, but today the land is nearly all arable. At best it is an airy, upland landscape, at worst, bitterly cold. When the wind is from the North Sea, it comes unobstructed by any higher ground between there and central Russia.

Public paths are sparse. Despite limited recent progress, much of the area suffers because the old East Riding County Council dragged its feet when making the required map of rights of way. The Wolds Way is some compensation, but would be better if farmers and landowners had not opposed its proper route. At the north, the Way joins the Cleveland Way and at the south, walkers can cross the footway of the impressive new Humber Bridge to join the Viking Way.

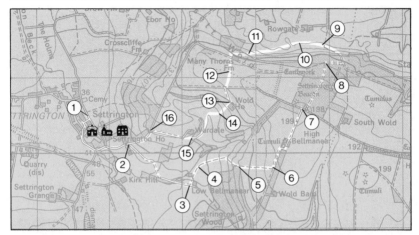

Settrington

6 miles (9.5 km) Sheets 100 and 101 836704

Moderate Follows some relatively recently agreed 'new' rights of way and a typical stretch of the Wolds Way official long-distance path. Excellent views of the N York Moors and the Dales. *Village, wooded hillside, woods, farmland; 2 climbs. Around ⑫ path crosses field, which may be cropped. Follow directions carefully.*

Start From Malton take the B1248, turning left for Settrington in about 1½ miles (2.5 km). **Parking** in village.

① From the village walk S, crossing the footbridge near a ford, and at road junction keep left to T-junction. Here turn left uphill, past Settrington House. ② At first farm track turn right and continue to Low Bellmanear Farm, going through 3 gates. ③ In front of Dutch barn turn left, soon following a track past a building on left to reach a gate. ④ From gate follow track up hillside to right. Keep to the right-hand track and head towards the wood edge. ⑤ At end of wood cross stile and follow field edge to the wood ahead. ⑥ Turn left and walk along the well-defined track. ⑦ At road turn right and in 20 yards (18 m) left through gate to forestry track. ⑧ Follow track as it turns right (signposted Wolds Way) and at its next right turn, turn left along a grassy track to emerge on Thorpe Bassett Brow. Continue on this track to bottom of Brow. ⑨ Turn left

and follow the track along the hill bottom, soon going through bridle gate, after which the track is less distinct. ⑩ Follow faint track up the hillside diagonally, heading for building between 2 woods. Track becomes more obvious before reaching a gate. ⑪ At gate make for ruined farm, turning left and right at the end of the building to follow field edge path (hedge on left). ⑫ Cross stile and follow waymarked route across the field to entrance of Wold House Farm. ⑬ Just in front of farm, turn right, then left just past a shed. Continue down the valley to the left. ⑭ At gate bear slightly right, soon crossing stile in field corner. Bear left and gradually climb the hill. ⑮ In corner at top of field cross stile to left of gate and follow the field edge to pick up a track. Follow this to the road, where ⑯ turn left and walk downhill into Settrington.

🏠 The village owes its attractiveness and uniformity to being purpose designed (in 1800) as an estate village. Most of the stone cottages stand well back from the stream, and are built on the blueprint of 2 windows and a doorway at ground level, and 2 more windows above.

⛪ Though much restored, All Saints retains its 13th C. character.

🏛 Settrington House, designed by Francis Johnson about 1790 as a 3-storey mansion, was partially gutted by fire in 1963.

YORKSHIRE WOLDS

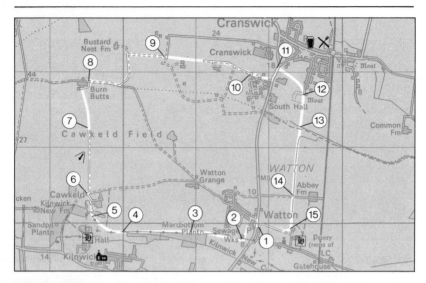

Watton Priory
6 miles (9.5 km) Sheet 106 018500

Moderate A walk for savouring wet places – springs, streams and a small lake – with attendant flowers and birdlife. Also, pleasant views of the Wolds, and a sense of history at Watton Priory. *Streamsides, woods, farmland; mud; some sections tend to be overgrown in summer, especially near ③ and ⑩.*

Start Watton, on the A164 between Driffield and Beverley; frequent buses. **Parking** on lay-by to E of Watton village. Walk can be shortened by catching bus back to Watton just N of ⑪.

① From lay-by cross A164 into village and turn left past the first pair of council houses, down a track and across the meadow ahead. ② Go through gate and past the old mill cottage, turning right along the beck (stream) bank after the stile. ③ Once in woods, turn right over the first bridge and then left to follow the other bank, still going W. Pass one bridge on left and cross a small plank bridge and stile. ④ Cross bridge and continue along stream (on left) until stile and bridge are reached. To visit Kilnwick, cross these and follow path. To continue, bear right across meadow to far corner. ⑤ Cross stile and turn left following path which turns left at

'Private' sign. Reach gate and continue ahead, following field edge to road. ⑥ At road turn right and in 10 yards (9 m) left up farm track, climbing steadily. ⑦ Where track finishes, continue ahead across fields to Burn Butts. After the gate turn right along the gravel track to the road. ⑧ At road turn right and at first junction left, soon turning right at the entrance to Bustard Nest Farm. ⑨ At bend continue ahead along field path with hedge on left, soon following farm track. ⑩ Where track leaves the hedge, continue ahead up edge of industrial area to main road. Turn left and in 100 yards (91 m) right. ⑪ Turn right across bridge and follow path along field edge into second field, where turn right when stile is reached. Continue across the meadow diagonally. ⑫ Cross stile and turn right along road, soon continuing ahead along field edge path until bridge. Cross. ⑬ After bridge turn to walk E and after gateway turn right, following the dyke to stile. Cross on to a farm road. ⑭ Cross road and after stile walk straight ahead to Watton Priory. ⑮ At the abbey buildings turn right and from the end of the building continue to white gate, where 2 stiles give access to track. Follow this back to lay-by.

⛪ All Saints is substantially Norman with a fine font and an interesting monument to the Grimston family.

234

🏛 Site of 18th C. Kilnwick Hall, seat of the Grimston family. All that remains of the old house is the huge brick wall that enclosed the kitchen garden, and a colonnaded well-head.

\↑/ Towards Middleton (946504) and South Dalton (967464).

🍺 White Horse – hand-pumped ales and ✕ bar meals.

🏛 The site of Watton Priory, founded in 1150 by Canon Eustace Fitzjohn. Among monastic communities it was unusual in that it had male as well as female members. They lived separately, prayed in separate churches and their grounds were divided by high walls so that they never saw each other. The only visible remains of the priory are the barn, the grassy mounds and the Prior's House, which has been incorporated in the private house E of the church.

Thixendale High Wolds

4 or 6½ miles (6.5 or 10.5 km) Sheet 100 844610

Moderate Offers a true feeling of the high Wolds, fine views and an extension to visit a deserted village. This part of the Wolds receives some considerable snowfalls, which transform the landscape. *Hillside, valley, farmland; 2 climbs.*

Start From the B1248 at Wharram le Street take the minor road past Bella Farm and access point to Wharram Percy. At Burdale pond turn right to Thixendale. **Parking** at edge of road near Cross Keys.

① Walk to the W end of the village and 100 yards (91 m) past the telephone box turn right up chalk track signposted 'Wolds Way'. In 40 yards (37 m) go through gate. ② Before farm buildings take the left fork soon crossing stile next to a gate and when fence is reached cross by the stile; turn left and walk around 2 sides of this field. ③ At fence cross stile and follow the path down the valley side. Just before the dale bottom, turn left over a stile in a small depression. ④ In valley bottom cross stile and follow path up the valley ahead to an ancient earthwork. Follow this along side of field. ⑤ Join the Aldro bridle road and turn right. ⑥ At end of wood on right opposite a farmstead across

the valley turn right heading towards ruined farm. ⑦ To visit Wharram Percy, continue along side of valley, soon bearing left and down to site of village. Otherwise ⑧ about 50 yards (46 m) past Wold House Farm (dated 1870) turn left along the track which soon bears right. ⑨ Where the track turns left and right (near a pond), turn right and follow the hedge on right. ⑩ Go through the bridle gate and turn left following the valley top. ⑪ At gate and fence, turn right and in 20 yards (18 m) go through the bridle gate and continue along the valley bottom ahead. ⑫ Cross fence near a hunting jump and continue across the field to a gate, entering village near Cross Keys.

🍺 Cross Keys – hand-pumped ale.

🏛 Wharram Percy is archaeologically the most interesting deserted village site in East Yorkshire, although apart from the restored Norman church there is little above ground to show for this.

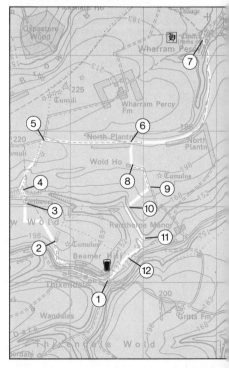

YORKSHIRE WOLDS

Pocklington Canal
12 miles (19 km) Sheet 106 803487

Moderate An absorbing towpath walk over heathland, with the remains of 7 locks. The last mile (1.5 km) across an airfield has the entertainment of gliders taking off, and there is a *Good Food Guide* restaurant on the route. *Pasture, streamside, canal-side, farmland, wooded common, heath.*

Start Pocklington on the B1246; frequent buses. **Car park** next to old station in Pocklington (now used as sports hall).

① From car park walk E and turn right opposite fire station along a narrow path to a lane, where turn left and continue to the cemetery entrance. ② Go up a grassy path to cross a stile and continue to cemetery corner. Cross stile and bear nearly half left aiming for stile in the far corner. ③ Cross stile and go through gate opposite to walk up centre of field to a stile. ④ Cross stile, then bear right and after a field follow the streamside, crossing several stiles until reaching a farm. Go through 2 gates to the main road. ⑤ Turn right on to the A1079 and in 50 yards (46 m) left into the canal head area. Walk along the canal towpath past 7 locks and 3 canal bridges. ⑥ At the second farm bridge after road bridge number 3, turn right across meadow to dyke. Cross by plank bridge. ⑦ After crossing stile walk up field to gate, where turn right on to a sandy track. Track soon bears left. ⑧ Follow track over a road to Thornton Grange. Walk through farmyard and continue in same direction on another farm track. ⑨ After passing 3 fields on right, turn right and follow the field edge (on left) to the road. Turn left towards the wooded Allerthorpe Common. ⑩ Through bridle gate (next to a large gate), bear right, soon taking the right-hand track to walk along the S edge of the common. ⑪ Where track reaches edge of wood turn left, entering trees again. ⑫ After 2 tracks have joined from left, continue ahead through gateway at crossing of tracks. ⑬ At end of wood, follow rough road as far as Allerthorpe village, where turn right then left to walk up main street. ⑭ At main road turn right, continue 250 yards (228 m), then left along road. In another 250 yards take track leading to old airfield. ⑮ Turn right along the perimeter track, following this across a runway, soon joining well-defined path on right which leads left of

a cream building. ⑯ At road turn right and in 200 yards (183 m) right along metalled path following the dismantled railway. At the road turn left and right back to car park.

🍺 Feathers Hotel, a former coaching inn, ✕ serves bar food.

❀ The gardens of Burnby Hall are renowned for their collection of waterlilies. The house, open Easter until May, contains a collection of memorabilia assembled from world travels.

🍺 Wellington Oak – hand-pumped ale.

⚓ Opened in 1818, at a cost of £35,000, the ✕ canal carried traffic up to 1934, then lay deteriorating until 1968, when

restoration began. Only 9¾ miles (15.5 km) long, with 8 swing bridges and 9 locks, it was one of the smallest commercial waterways. Birdlife along the banks includes herons, swans and many species of duck. Fish include pike, perch, roach and trout.

🍺 Cross Keys.

❀ Allerthorpe Common is a boggy heath harbouring, among other plants, the rather rare marsh gentian (flowers July-Sept.) and the carnivorous sundew (June-Aug.) with sticky red hairs for catching insects. Nightjars, curlews and whinchats may be seen.

\↑/ The Wolds.

✕ The Plough has a *Good Food Guide* entry.

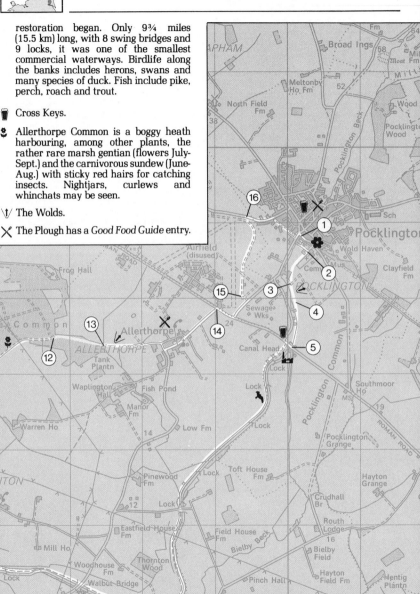

YORKSHIRE WOLDS

Welton Dale

7½ miles (12 km) Sheet 106 957273

Easy A happy mixture of dales, woods and field edge paths: Welton Dale is peaceful and unspoilt. The route passes a church in an exceptionally beautiful situation. *Valley, woods, farmland; one climb.*

Start From A63 take turning marked Welton and follow signs into village; frequent buses – alight at the Green Dragon. **Parking** on roadside opposite Green Dragon or by church 50 yards (46 m) away.

① From the church walk up Cowgate, then Dale Road, passing old mill buildings on right. ② At entrance to Dale Cottage continue on track past cottage and over stile next to white gate. Walk up the dale. ③ At the waymark bear right off the track and through the woods. ④ At end of woods, cross the road using the 2 stiles and turn left along the bridleway to the road. ⑤ At road turn left and enter the woods at the footpath signpost. ⑥ At the junction of paths turn right, following the path downhill to the road. Turn left. ⑦ Just before some untidy buildings turn right, soon turning left up short, steep hill. ⑧ At the track cross over and follow the well-defined track through the woods. ⑨ To visit Brantingham church, village and pub, walk down the hill. Otherwise, at the road turn right, continuing ahead after it has become metalled. ⑩ At the junction, follow the rough track ahead into the woods. ⑪ At the junction of paths turn right through the hand gate and follow the field edge ahead. ⑫ Just past the farm cottages turn left and in 20 yards (18 m) right at the pond, walking ahead with first pond, then wood, on right. ⑬ At junction of paths turn left and in 20 yards right over a concrete road and into trees ahead. Follow field edge path. ⑭ At quarry gate turn right and follow road into Welton.

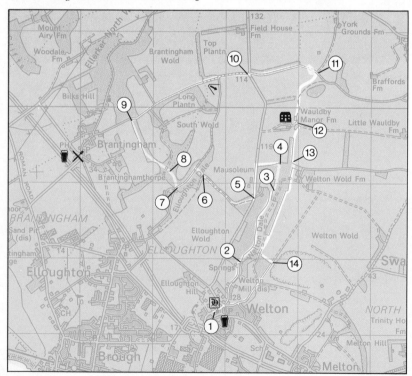

The white-fronted Green Dragon Inn was a favourite haunt of John Palmer, alias Dick Turpin, who was arrested here in 1739 and taken to York Prison, later to be executed.

St. Helen's churchyard is the resting place of a local 18th C. philanderer, Jeremiah Simpson, who, as his headstone records '. . . hath eight times married been but now in his ould age he lies in his cage under the grass so green'. The church's chancel is 13th C.

Triton Inn – hand-pumped ales and a restaurant serving good, plain food.

As far as the Humber Bridge, largest single-span suspension bridge in the world.

Wauldby Manor, and its chapel dated 1844; site of lost village S of church.

The disused railway from Beverley to Market Weighton is a 'walkway': access from Molescroft near Beverley.

The 23-mile (37 m) Holderness Way from Hull to Hornsea divides into 3 short sections, Hull-Beverley, Beverley-Leven and Leven-Hornsea.

There are short linear and circular walks incorporating sections of the Minster Way (Beverley Minster to York) and the Hull Countryway.

The Beverley 20, 20 miles (32 km) from Hessel to Beverley, has extensions forming the E Riding Heritage Way.

Leaflets and guidebooks describing these routes, mostly fully waymarked, are available from local officers of the Ramblers' Association.

All Saints, Brantingham, in its wooded setting; inside is an early 13th C. font.

YORKSHIRE DALES

No other English landscape so closely unites the wild and the domestic. The peat and the bent grass of the sheep-dotted fells butt directly on to the enclosed beauty of the dales them-selves.

The most exhilarating moment of a typical dales route is when starting to descend from the 'tops' into the next dale, spread below like a map. Towards its head are just scattered farms, with, it seems, grey-walled barns at the corner of almost every field. Further down, the dale widens to accommodate villages and meadows. Further still a great castle or abbey such as Richmond or Fountains may well command the broad skirts of the valley. Linking all will be a tawny river, possibly with dramatic falls and rapids – of which Aysgarth Falls on the Ure and the dangerous Strid at Bolton Priory on the Wharfe are only the most famous.

The tops themselves are criss-crossed by paths and green lanes – grassy tracks once used by drovers and packhorsemen. Around the Three Peaks (Ingleborough, Penyghent and Whernside) especially, the limestone of the area forms immense 'pavements', a stark landscape, but with the occasional rare plant growing in its 'grykes', crevices a few inches wide and many feet deep.

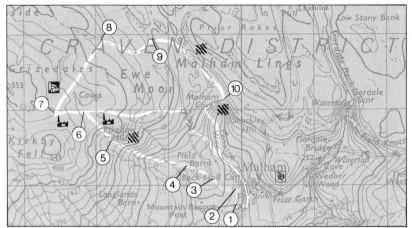

Pikedaw Hill and Malham Cove

5½ or 3½ miles (9 or 5.5 km) Sheet 98 900627

Moderate An unusual, richly interesting walk taking in famous Malham Cove. Rewarding in winter when the ancient field patterns are revealed after light snow, and Malham not overcrowded. *Moorland, limestone terraces; one climb. Do not attempt in poor visibility.*

Start Malham, N of the A65; frequent buses; frequent trains. **Car park** opposite Information Centre.

① From car park entrance turn right on to a stony track, then first right along track behind car park. ② Left at junction, following track uphill. ③ Left at next junction uphill past barns, then drop to stream. ④ Just past stream and footbridge, go through gate (with signpost) on right; follow path across field to stile to right of barn seen ahead. Then follow line of stream through gate and uphill. ⑤ Climb ladder stile over wall. Bear right through limestone outcrops, continuing ¼ mile (0.5 km) uphill, reaching grassy track at signpost. ⑥ Turn left along grassy track past mineshaft to gate in wall ahead. (For 3½-mile version, turn right along green lane down to Cove Road for Malham village.) ⑦ Follow wall past cross-shaft, through the gate on right, then continue on left through 2 gates through 2 fields. After second gate, cross field to grassy track. ⑧ Turn right along track to cattle grid on road. ⑨ Cross road, through gap, downhill to stile and along the 'Dry Valley' to Malham Cove. ⑩ Cross limestone pavements with care, bearing right to stile leading to steps down side of Malham Cove. Take well-defined path through kissing-gates back to village.

🏛 Today, the limestone scenery brings Malham's visitors; in the Middle Ages, it was the monastic settlement, later the sheep fair, then the lead and zinc mining.

〰 The beck (stream) down Pikedaw follows roughly the line of the Mid-Craven Fault, a major shift in the earth's crust.

🏭 A 'level', or entrance to part of Pikedaw lead mines, busy from the late 18th to late 19th C., now exhausted.

🏭 New Calamine Shaft, 60 feet (18 m) deep, covered by a manhole, was access to the calamine (zinc) mines.

🏴 The shaft of Nappa Cross, raised by monks of Fountains as a guide-post.

〰 The Dry Valley, carved by melting waters of the most recent Ice Age.

〰 The limestone face of Malham Cove, 300 feet (91 m) high, was the site of a great waterfall, fuelled by melt-waters of the Ice Age. The water now flows in many underground streams. The black marks on the face are produced by lichens.

241

YORKSHIRE DALES

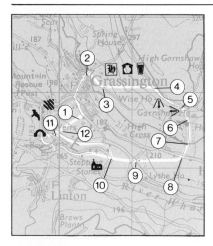

Watching a dipper feed underwater is as absorbing as any of the sights of a fast-flowing river. The bird looks silvery-grey underwater, and uses pebbles as anchors.

Grassington
3 miles (5 km) Sheet 98 003637

Moderate A short but varied walk from one of the most interesting Dales visitor centres; best in spring – clear, open views and possibility of snow on tops. *Farmland, woods, pasture; one climb.*

Start Grassington on the B6265 N of Skipton; frequent buses from Skipton; trains (Parklink through tickets available) from Leeds and other stations. **Car park** off the B6265, 220 yards (201 m) E of the Square.

① From car park walk along B6265 towards square. Walk up the main street, past square, to the Town Hall, where ② turn right along lane climbing past cottages. Take the first fork left past bungalow along walled track. ③ Look for a gap stile on left by a gate. Follow path over a second stile in wall on right. Continue on path, crossing a series of stiles, and diagonally over fields, climbing in same direction throughout. ④ Turn right where path meets track. Follow track uphill to point beyond radio mast at gate and ladder stile on left. ⑤ Cross stile and bear slightly right downhill above hospital towards pine woods. Make for wall. ⑥ Follow wall downhill, cross stile and continue alongside hospital. Continue straight on through woods to stile at end of woods. ⑦ Turn right over ladder stile, along edge of wood, then left at sign alongside tiny beck (stream) to ladder stile at road. ⑧ Cross road and pick up connecting path through fields, cutting diagonally across, over stiles. Cross track and head for left of barn (Ray Lathe) ahead. ⑨ Cross stile behind barn, continuing downhill. At second stile take path towards riverside. ⑩ Go through kissing-gate and along track by converted mill, through stile on left as track climbs, then follow field path, crossing stiles, to Tin Bridge. If river is low, cross stepping stones and go directly to Linton church. ⑪ Cross waterfalls by Tin Bridge; by mill bear left up to road. Left along road to church. Retrace to Tin Bridge. ⑫ Climb narrow, enclosed path to Grassington village and car park.

🏛 Grassington's history goes back to the Iron Age, with evidence of ancient settlements visible on the hillside terraces. The present village is mainly 18th and 19th C., when it was a mining centre, dependent on rich lead deposits of Grassington Moor. Museum; pubs.

\↑/ Across Wharfedale, and (clear days) as far as Pendle Hill, Lancashire.

⛪ This simple but fine Norman church ('the cathedral of upper Wharfedale') is on the site of an even older one.

〰 Linton Falls, with the limestone eroded into attractive shapes by the River Wharfe. The footbridge is known as Tin Bridge because of an earlier, tin-clad bridge on the site. Dippers; wagtails.

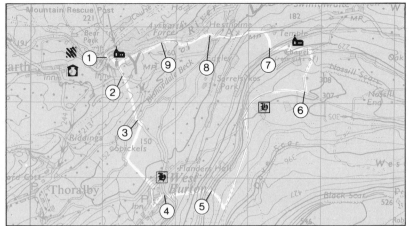

West Burton
6 miles (9.5 km) Sheet 98 011887

Moderate The typical limestone scar scenery of Wensleydale, with an outstanding village and fine waterfalls. *Farmland, riverside; one climb.*

Start Aysgarth Falls, signposted from Aysgarth, which is E of Hawes on the A684; frequent buses from Darlington; infrequent, seasonal service from Leeds via Ilkley. **Car park** at Aysgarth Falls.

① From W end of car park follow tarmac path to Aysgarth Bridge. Cross bridge and take steps by Carriage Museum past church to main road. ② Cross road and take path by stile ahead. It descends a shallow gill (valley). Continue in same direction through stiles and gates, aiming for Eshington Bridge, below. ③ Turn right through gate ahead, then left over stiles at top of field. Along field to road. Cross road and follow steps ahead into West Burton village. ④ Leave village by NW corner and follow path, passing waterfall to footbridge. Bear right, over stile, follow wall uphill, then cross pasture to wood. Follow path uphill through wood to stile at top. Follow path uphill to farther stile to right. ⑤ Keep straight on, bearing slightly right, to moorland wall ahead. Turn left along wall to gate which enters enclosed lane. ⑥ Turn left through gate to track. Take path which leads off at bottom of 'S' bend in track, making for gap between woods ahead.

Head for small, enclosed ruin (chantry). ⑦ Through gate, then right along field edge to road. Turn left and continue 250 yards (229 m). ⑧ Over stile at farm drive entrance, then follow stiles ahead to riverside. ⑨ Keep to top side of wire fence, then bear left to stile into plantation.

Aysgarth's Victorian church, serving a scattered parish; notable Tudor screens.

Aysgarth Falls are some of the Dales' finest; painted by Turner. Especially exciting when the river is in spate, the Upper Falls are the most spectacular – best view from the (Tudor) road bridge. Middle and Lower Falls are also worth seeing – best views from wood and riverside to N (path from car park).

Carriage Museum, in former cotton (later flour) mills, open daily in summer.

Picturesque West Burton was a manufacturing village, with a reputation for its wool combing.

This moorland track is known as Morpeth Gate – 'gate' meaning road or highway. It is the ancient way from Middleham and East Witton along Wensleydale.

Remains of a 12th C. chapel of the Knights Templar, the medieval religious military order.

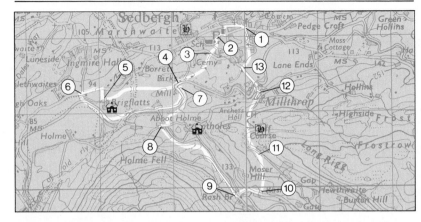

Lower Dentdale
6 miles (9.5 km) Sheets 97 and 98 657922

Moderate A comparatively unvisited area of the Dales, and a fine section of the Dales Way. Best in spring – possibility of snow on the tops – or autumn, for colouring on the fells. *Farmland, riverside; one climb.*

Start Sedbergh, on the A684; infrequent buses; Dales Rail Buses serve Sedbergh from Garsdale Station on certain weekends. **Car parks** (signposted) on Main Street (by National Park Centre), or on Dent Road.

① From car park walk W along Main Street to church. (From Dent Road car park cross road to church.) ② Follow metalled path behind church by school cricket pitch, following path left through school grounds and across playing fields. ③ Continue in same direction, crossing road at kissing gates. Follow path through stile downhill and around garden fence to lane. ④ Turn right over stile to follow signposted path, going straight on over 3 further stiles and crossing railway line. Then bear slightly left over 2 more stiles to Brigflatts Meeting House. ⑤ From Brigflatts follow lane to A683. Turn left along road to riverside path. ⑥ Follow riverside path back past disused railway line and meeting of rivers to Birks Mill. ⑦ Cross river at footbridge, follow path uphill to stile. Keep ahead through next 2 stiles, then bear left through stiles downhill to Abbot Holme Bridge. ⑧ Cross stile left and over bridge; follow path by river, then uphill above narrow gorge to stile into lane.

Straight ahead along lane. ⑨ Turn left over Rash Bridge, then right on to road. ⑩ At second gate on left (signposted) follow Dales Way uphill, bearing left along wall to join grassy track at stile. ⑪ Turn left along grassy track, continuing straight on over brow of hill and dropping past golf course to Millthrop. ⑫ Go through Millthrop and over Millthrop Bridge towards Sedbergh. ⑬ Turn right through stile and along path uphill to second stile. Take metalled path through kissing gates by playing fields into town for car parks.

🏠 Sedbergh, with the public school of the same name dominating the town, is equally noted as a fell walking centre.

🏠 Brigflatts Meeting House is one of the country's oldest and best-known Quaker meeting houses, dating from 1675. The town has close associations with Quakerism, and George Fox stayed in the vicinity before giving his famous sermon on nearby Firbank Fell to more than 1,000 people – generally accepted as the launching of the Quaker movement.

🏠 Catholes Bunkhouse Barn was converted to simple accommodation for walkers by the Countryside Commission as an experimental use for redundant barns which would otherwise go derelict. It is proving popular.

🏠 A section of the Dales Way, the 76-mile (122 km) long-distance path – see pages 328-334.

Hell Gill
9 miles (14.5 km) Sheet 98 787919

Energetic Some of the Dales', and Yorkshire's, most dramatic walking. *Farmland, fells; 2 climbs; do not attempt in poor visibility.*

Start Garsdale Station, off the A684 W of Hawes; infrequent buses; infrequent, seasonal trains from Leeds, Preston and Carlisle. **Parking** on verge (not causing an obstruction) of approach road to station.

① Cross A684 and follow path from stile and signpost uphill and slightly left to stile ahead. Follow path round above Rowan Tree Gill to farmhouse. ② Cross next stile, to right of farmhouse, and drop with path, crossing

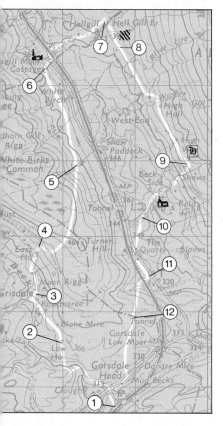

stile beneath Rowantree, and going through farm gate to join lane. ③ Follow lane along valley floor, past Moor Rigg farmhouse, then climb steeply on obvious track by East House. ④ At junction of tracks above East House, turn right. In 50 yards (46 m), leave track to climb directly up open fell over Turner Hill. Bear left at summit and drop to field gate below and left. ⑤ Through gate and follow walls, continuing straight on through gates to join road at Aisgill. ⑥ Follow track to right of Aisgill Moor Cottages to Hell Gill Force (waterfall); retrace and go uphill alongside Hell Gill beck (stream) to Hell Gill Farm. Beyond farm gate, make for Hell Gill Bridge. ⑦ Cross bridge, through gate and along grassy track. ⑧ Leave well-defined grassy track sloping down to West End, bearing left to ruined farm (High Hall) ahead. Pick up grassy track (High Way) above inclosure wall. In about ½ mile (0.8 km), ⑨ look for stile on right (with Y.H.A. sign) above Lunds. Follow path leading through ravine past Shaws Youth Hostel. Descend by gill, cross footbridge, drop by winding path passing Lunds church, and cross river by ford or footbridge. Follow hostel drive between pines. ⑩ Look for stile on left as drive climbs. Follow path across fields over stiles to road. Go left along road. ⑪ Opposite footbridge over railway look for indistinct path from stile leading to bridge (or use track). Cross footbridge and continue in same direction up fellside, bearing left over ruined wall to stile in wall ahead. ⑫ Cross stile, and stile in next wall ahead and to the left. Cross a third stile and drop to gate at road E of Garsdale Head; turn right to ①.

The Settle-Carlisle line, the highest mainline railway in Britain, reaches its summit at Aisgill.

Hell Gill has been described as one of the 7 wonders of Britain. The deep, limestone gorge is gouged by the waters of the River Eden, whose source is Hell Gill beck (stream). Here, in effect, is the watershed of England. The Eden flows N (unique among major English rivers) into the Irish Sea. The Ure, rising nearby, enters the North Sea.

The grassy track, known as the High Way, was in regular use from the Bronze Age to the 19th C.

The remote Lunds chapel is 18th C.

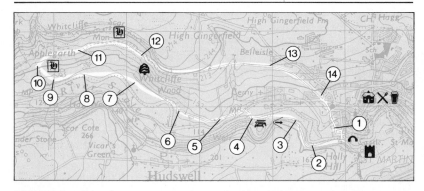

Richmond and Swale
7 miles (11 km) Sheet 92 168007

Easy The lovely old Dales town of Richmond, and a fine section of the Coast-to-Coast Walk. *Woods, farmland, riverside; one climb; mud after rain; walk single-file on paths through riverside meadows.*

Start Richmond, on the A6108; frequent buses from Darlington and Leyburn. **Public car parks** on Cravengate, above Richmond bridge, or in town centre.

① From car park walk down to bridge, cross and take opening on right down to river bank. ② Follow track into Hudswell Woods, soon climbing steps. Where path divides, take lower fork to right. Keep straight ahead at next fork to narrow path to bottom of wood. ③ Ignore wooded stile on right, looking for wooden stile directly ahead. Cross and continue with path over pasture, scar and between wooded knoll (Round Howe) and river. ④ At picnic site, cross river by footbridge and turn left along A6108. ⑤ Take first track on right, ignoring junction on left. Straight on to farmhouse. ⑥ In front of house carry straight on to find gate leading to grassy track through wood. At end of wood go through gate and keep along bottom of wood. ⑦ Follow path along beck (stream) to meet riverside beyond ruined wall and continue to stile. Continue straight ahead to edge of meadow, then right to stile. ⑧ Through stile keep straight along right edge of meadow to gate. ⑨ Follow waymarked path through gates, around and to left of farm, then uphill to join Coast-to-Coast Path. ⑩ Look for waymarked stile on right above farm. Then through 3 more stiles to join drive

to East Applegarth Farm. ⑪ Through gate, left before farm and around farm to join track leading towards Whitcliffe Wood. ⑫ Through gate and stile into woods. Carry straight on to far end of wood to join lane to Richmond. ⑬ Look for parkland (West Field) above Richmond – enter by stile and walk through it, parallel to road, into town. ⑭ Bear left across A6108 down Cravengate to car park.

🏰 Richmond is a fine old town clustered round the Norman castle started by Alan
🏠 the Red in 1071. The keep (12th C.) is well preserved. Interesting walks around
✗ castle walls. The town has some fine 18th C. buildings; military museum;
🍺 cafés; pubs.

⌒ Richmond Bridge (1879) may be the work of John Carr, the celebrated York architect and designer of Harewood House.

\!/ Hudswell Woods, beautifully situated along limestone scar above the Swale,
�"" give good views back to bridge, castle and town. Picnic site at W side near Round Howe.

🔟 This is a section of the 190-mile (306 km) Coast-to-Coast unofficial long-distance path pioneered by W. A. Wainwright, doyen of walking authors.

🔟 The memorial on the hillside commemorates Robert Williance's 'Leap' in 1606. His mare was killed, but he survived, and in gratitude he gave a silver chalice to Richmond.

🌲 Fine woodland, mainly larch and spruce.

Stean, Middlesmoor and Nidderdale Edges

8½ miles (13.5 km) Sheet 99 098734

Moderate Spectacular limestone features and first-class moorland views. *Farmland, moorland; 2 climbs; mud after rain.*

Start Stean, about 7 miles (11 km) NW of B6265 at Pateley Bridge; infrequent, seasonal buses from Skipton. **Car park** E of Stean bridge.

How Stean: the limestone here is soluble in water, and when the 2 come together natural sculpture follows.

① Follow 'scenic walk' through How Stean Gorge and Tom Taylor's Cave. ② Turn right at stile and sign to footbridge and steps. ③ Bear right after steps to wall and stile; then follow side of wall uphill. ④ Turn sharp right through gate at wood, downhill. ⑤ Bear left across stream, then over wooden stile by tree on right. Follow stiles downhill to lane. ⑥ Follow track across bridge left along river. ⑦ Follow track curving right up The Edge. ⑧ Fork left up Bracken Ridge, following track S over Lofthouse Moor. ⑨ From shooting lodge go downhill to gate; through it, turn left to pick up grassy track to wood where bear right downhill. ⑩ At Thrope Farm turn left through gates along grassy lane, then ahead through gates to Lofthouse.

≋ How Stean has been called Yorkshire's
▣ Little Switzerland. There are remark-
✕ able walks under the overhangs of the limestone ravine. Tom Taylor's Cave is 50 yards (46 m) long. The excellent café at the entrance serves hot meals; modest entrance fee to gorge.

⌂ Middlesmoor is a rare example of a
▮ Pennine hill village on the spur of a ridge.
⋁ Unspoiled pub; fine views down Nidderdale from churchyard.

🚲 The lane from Lofthouse to Angram and New Scar House follows the line of the former Upper Nidderdale Light Railway, built to carry men and materials to construct the reservoirs.

🏢 Lofthouse, a first-class grouse moor, has a typical Edwardian shooting lodge on the ridge.

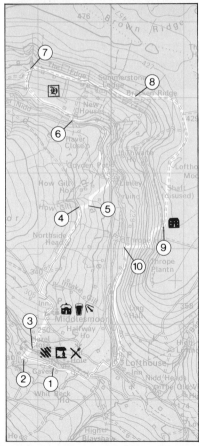

YORKSHIRE DALES

Ingleborough
11 miles (17.5 km) Sheet 98 693733

Energetic An unusual way of climbing this considerable English mountain; some fascinating limestone pavements. Best in spring and summer – clear views, possibility of snow on tops. *Fells, rough grazing, grassy slopes; 2 climbs; do not attempt in poor visibility – for experienced hill walkers – 1:25,000 map and compass recommended.*

Start Ingleton, on the A65 N of Settle; frequent buses from Skipton, Settle and Lancaster. **Car parks** (signposted) at Ingleborough Community Centre, Ingleton, or (fee) at entrance to waterfalls near bridge.

① From entrance to Falls (fee) go through kissing-gate and along path up gorge to head of Falls. ② At last fall, Thornton Force, follow path up steps, across beck (stream) and up further steps to join track (Twistleton Lane). Turn right. ③ Look for grassy track coming in from left, and follow it zigzagging uphill to limestone gap or 'nick' through Twistleton Scar End. Follow path straight ahead across edge of limestone pavements. ④ Do not follow wall, but keep slightly right over moor to pick up faint track, later turning to path. Follow it under steep side of hill and drop to Ellerbeck Farm. ⑤ Follow farm drive downhill by woodland to Chapel le Dale. ⑥ Cross road and follow path through stiles to Souther Scales. Continue with path through gate behind farm, uphill. ⑦ Follow well-defined path uphill through gate and along becks to saddle of Ingleborough. ⑧ On summit ridge turn right to summit shelter and trig. point. ⑨ Follow main track SW off summit, across area of large stones and boulders to broad track down fell. ⑩ Follow enclosed, stony lane directly back to Ingleton.

🏚 Ingleton was a coal-mining town.

〰 These are the most impressive series of waterfalls in England – 4½ miles (7 km) of gorges and glens filled with raging torrents. Ancient stone – pre-Cambrian rocks, Ordovician slates and Carboniferous limestone – are exposed at several points. The ravines are dangerous – keep to the hand-railed paths. A short-cut (4½ miles) runs back from Beezley Falls, below Beezley Farm.

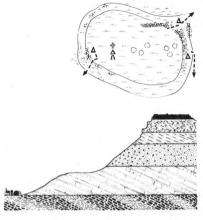

Ingleborough's geology: the base is ancient, coal-bearing rock. Then comes 600 feet (183 m) of limestone, then 3 layers of shale and sandstones, seen mainly as crag and scree. The cap is millstone grit. The summit reveals (left to right): the site of a hospice (triangle); a wind shelter (cross) with the view indicator and trig. point close by. Next are primitive hut circles, then remains of Roman walls. Arrows mark descents.

🏚 This ancient track, known as Kirkby Gate (gate meaning road or highway) was a prehistoric trading route, and in medieval times a packhorse way to Kirkby Stephen. The narrow nick through the limestone at Twistleton Scar End is a typical feature of ancient hill routes and may be partly man-made to indicate the line of the path.

🏚 The intriguing settlement of Chapel le Dale is close to 2 huge potholes – Hurtle Pot (seen from track) and Jingle Pot (seen from near track). Weathercote Cave, nearby (painted by Turner), is closed to the public. The sculpture by the road is intended to complement the natural, weathered limestone. More than 100 navvies, who died in epidemics when building the Ribblehead Viaduct, are buried in the graveyard.

〰 Ingleborough was long considered England's highest peak; in fact, at 2,372 feet (723 m), it is the second highest of The Three Peaks; Lake District NW.

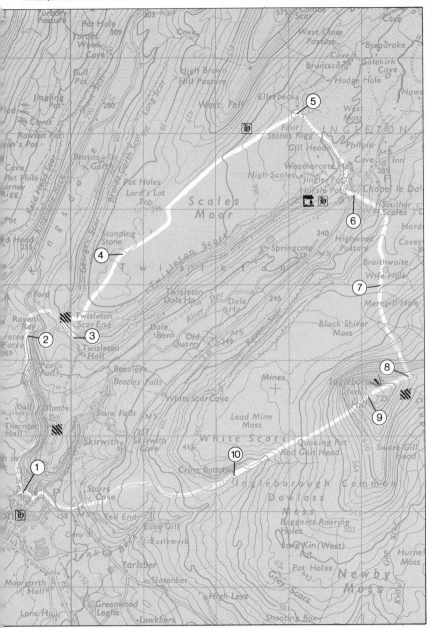

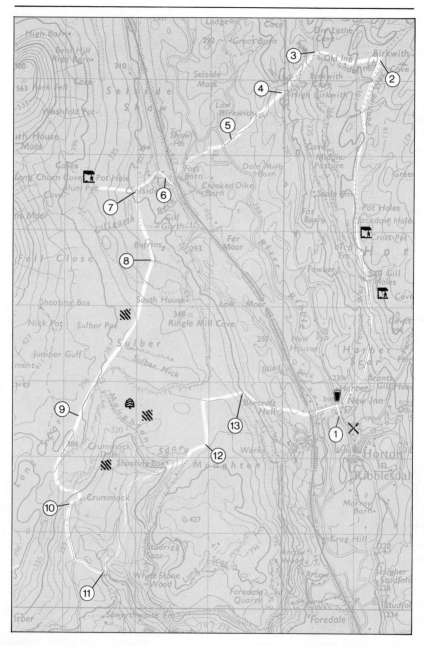

Alum Pot and Crummack Dale
14 miles (22.5 km) Sheet 98 808726

Energetic The Dales limestone country at its best – fell walking on the grand scale. Moorland, rough grazing, limestone 'pavement'; 2 climbs; do not attempt in poor visibility – for experienced hill walkers.

Start Horton, N of Settle on the B6479; frequent buses from Settle, infrequent seasonal service from Giggleswick station. **Public car park** in Horton; if full, use a verge.

① From car park walk NW to end of village and take track (Pennine Way) which starts at Crown Inn. Follow it N for 2½ miles (4 km). ② Follow Pennine Way (waymarked by posts) W to Old Ing – deserted farmhouse. ③ Leave Pennine Way at Old Ing, keeping along farm track down to High Birkwith Farm. ④ Turn right at High Birkwith through gap, cross stile by wood and 2 more stiles to reach Low Birkwith Farm. Keep same direction with Coppy Gill beck (stream) on right, crossing stiles to footbridge over River Ribble. ⑤ Cross bridge, ahead to ladder stile and into grassy lane leading to road at Selside. ⑥ Turn right through hamlet, taking first track left up to Alum Pot. (To visit Pot pay entrance fee at farm on right. Path to Pot through gap from lane corner ahead to clump of trees.) ⑦ Follow track to gate, then bear half left through gates to join track SW of Borrins. ⑧ Follow track uphill above South House to summit of Sulber and Sulber Gate. Continue on grassy track through limestone pavements. ⑨ At junction of tracks bear left downhill into Crummack Dale. Join farm track SW of Crummack Farm. ⑩ Follow lane downhill to next junction; bearing left along stony track to small ford and footbridge. Cross and continue to next junction. ⑪ Turn sharp left along Moughton Lane. Follow narrow, unsurfaced track to gate, then grassy path forming natural 'pass' over hillside. ⑫ Cross top wall at stile, then follow path left round outside of quarry fence, then right to join main path from Ingleborough. ⑬ Follow well-defined path N of Beecroft Hall to cross railway line at Horton Station. Straight on to village.

🔦 Jackdaw Hole and Sell Gill Holes, deep, natural shafts giving access to the area's underground cave system.

The limestone 'pavement' of this area makes stern, but fascinating walking.

🔦 Alum Pot's spectacular, spray-blown entrance, with the smaller potholes of Upper and Lower Long Churn above.

〽 Limestone pavements.

🌳 Moughton (pronounced Mooton) Scars has the remains of pre-Ice Age tree cover – the ancient dwarf juniper trees still clinging to the limestone pavement.

〽 Crummack Dale is one of the remotest dales, its upper reaches only accessible on foot.

✕ Horton in Ribblesdale, a popular walker's village, with a café, and the
🍺 Crown Inn, conveniently placed on the Pennine Way, Britain's original long-distance path, (see pages 328 – 334).

There are miles of easy tracks, mostly traffic-free, and many suitable for wheelchairs or prams, in the Studley Royal/Fountains Abbey estate.

A walk round the perimeter of Washburndale Reservoir is also a feasible expedition for those with young children. Other reservoirs in the Dales with paths or tracks and easy access are Nidderdale and Fewston.

York is not strictly speaking in the Dales, but its superb walls, many sections in an excellent state of preservation, are an intriguing circuit, or partial circuit, with convenient public transport.

NORTH YORK MOORS

'Grand' is the Yorkshire word for these moors. Once up on the flat plateau-tops, the heather stretches for miles. The Cleveland Hills, backbone of the region, rise to their summit at one and a half thousand feet (457 m) on Urra Moor. From Cringle Moor, on the Hills' escarpment, some have been able to make out Cross Fell, nearly 60 miles (97 km) away in the Pennines. The intersecting dales are more gently cupped than the Yorkshire Dales further west.

Expect some energetic walking. Off the beaten tracks, the heather stems make a stiff, calf- and thigh-straining barrier. Wind and rain penetrate icily; there is no shelter to speak of. The Cleveland Way offers superb cliff-walking, but watch for the sea frets – banks of fog rolling suddenly inshore. They are disconcerting and unpleasant.

The Moors carry the scars of digging for alum and jet, and the course of the railway that transported Rosedale's ironstone. Today's industry, despite the decline of small farms, is basically sheep, though the gloomy conifer forests have swallowed too much of the open land. The huge golf balls of Fylingdales early warning station are another intrusion, but at least they have their own eerie magic.

Rievaulx
3 miles (5 km) Sheet 100 575845

Easy Haunted by changing views of the centre of interest – the abbey ruins. *Woods, riverside, farmland; one climb; mud after rain.*

Start 1½ miles (2.5 km) from Helmsley on the B1257 bear left on to the road signposted Scawton and Old Byland. Continue downhill to river and turn right before bridge. **Parking** area on left in trees 300 yards (274 m) after right turn – do not use Abbey car park.

① From parking area turn right back to bridge. Cross and continue to next right turn where ② cross stream to Ashberry Farmhouse. Behind this cross stile and continue on path uphill along edge of wood. ③ Leaving wood keep to edge of open land near woods. Continue to ④, gate on to rough road. Through it, cross diagonally right, over stile and take footpath signposted Hawnby. Follow it (later beside river) to where fence obstructs progress. Turn left along fence to ⑤ gate on to road; turn left. In 750 yards (686 m) ⑥ fork left downhill on track. Soon cross outward route. ⑦ Cross bridge and continue uphill on farm road. After gate continue downhill. ⑧ In village opposite church turn right and continue to ①.

❀ Ashberry Nature Reserve fosters interesting plant specimens, including bird's-eye primrose and globe flower.

Rievaulx, the Moors' justly famous collaboration of lovely ruin and setting.

🏯 Monasteries owned farmland and these fields were probably worked by monks.

📌 Rievaulx (pronounced 'Ree-vo') fell into ruin after Henry VIII looted and shut down the Roman Catholic monasteries.

🏯 Rievaulx Terraces – landscaped hillside – and Twin Temples were created by a local landowner; views of the ruin.

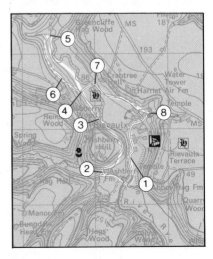

NORTH YORK MOORS

Lastingham and Hutton-le-Hole
4½ miles (7 km) Sheet 100 728905

Moderate Particularly fine views of the Tabular Hills – flat-topped, limestone headlands which are a major feature of the S edge of the Moors; visits 2 attractive and flourishing moorland villages. *Woods, farmland, village, moorland; one climb; mud after rain.*

Start From the A170 turn N at Keldholme for Hutton-le-Hole and continue to Lastingham. **Parking** in wider parts of village street.

① Leave village by steep road to Appleton-le-Moors and turn right to Spaunton. ② Left at end of village into lane between fields. Continue straight on for ¾ mile (one km), then bear right at fork. ③ At edge of wood; turn right through gate into wood; follow path along edge of wood and into lane. ④ Turn right on to road coming from farm at left and follow it through fields. ⑤ In Hutton-le-Hole find Public Footpath sign on wall opposite village hall and follow path across recreation ground. ⑥ Join road from Hutton-le-Hole to Lastingham and continue on mostly wide verges to ①.

🏠 St. Mary's church is unique among English parish churches for the scale of its crypt. This is almost a complete church below the main structure, with an apse (semicircular domed roof), chancel nave and side aisles. The first church on the site was built in the 7th C. by St. Cedd. It was reconstructed by Abbot Stephen of Whitby in 1078. A planned great church was abandoned in 1228 and the remains converted to a general parish church in the 13th C. The tower was added in the 15th C.

🍺 The Blacksmith's Arms.

🏯 Site of ancient manor house, home of lords of the manor of Spaunton.

✗ Tea shop.

🍺 The Crown Inn; restaurant.

🏠 The folk museum contains local archaeological finds and an impressive collection of implements, tools and household items made in the area; also ancient house reconstructions.

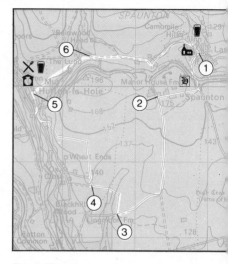

Broxa Forest
7½ miles (12 km) Sheet 101 965944

Moderate Views of the Moors without being on them; an unusual variety of landscaping for woodland, with a singular, remote, sheltered valley. *Woods, riverside, farmland; one climb; mud.*

Start From Scarborough, go through Scalby and steeply uphill; turn sharp right and continue on straight road through Silpho Forest. **Car park** on top of Reasty Bank at edge of Silpho Forest.

① From car park walk W on road along top of escarpment, following the blue hiker signs (Allerston Forest Walk). Shortly after turning the corner bear right down the steep slope towards the river, still following blue hiker signs. ② Continue downstream, keeping to the left bank. ③ At footbridge leave waymarked walk and bear left on uphill path. ④ Reaching level ground at top of slope, follow path at edge of wood to road. (Fifty yards [46 m] after ④ a broad forest ride joins from the left. This is the S end of the escarpment walk which was left at ①. After rain the riverside path is often severely muddy and this alternative route from ① to ④ is likely to be dry.) ⑤ Keep to top edge of wood for 100 yards (91 m) before going down through wood to reach road. (At ⑤ an alternative track leads downhill at the wood's edge. It is steep, and the last 200 yards [183 m] are rough.) ⑥ At road turn left. Cross stream, over stile and into field. Follow path towards farm. ⑦ Through farm, across stream and continue along valley of Whisper Dales, uphill about 2 miles [3 km] to ⑧.)

🦅 Birds include the tawny owl, the most familiar owl, with short, rounded wings and a head that looks oddly large for the body; also the sparrowhawk – broad wings with rounded ends, squared-off tail and a small head.

🦌 Roe deer may be seen.

▣ The ruins of Barnscliffe Castle. This is the approximate site, and the few remains are difficult to find.

🌲 The woods are an excellent example of modern creative forestry. Ten thousand to 15,000 years ago, there was woodland here, but Bronze Age man began its destruction in the quest for farming land. The soil seemed rich, but could only remain so if replenished with nutrients by the leaf fall each year. Clearance continued through succeeding centuries and the exposed soils became poorer and poorer. The soil became acid and a hard layer formed at about 24 inches (61 cm).

To make new woodland, deep ploughing was employed to break the hard layer. This allowed the roots of new seedlings to penetrate, and assisted drainage.

Conifers adapt best to the conditions here, and the present woodland is mainly larch and Scots pine, planted in the early 1950s. Some broadleaved (deciduous) trees have grown under the protection of the conifers ('nursing').

▣ A parish boundary stone: SIL is written on one side, marking the boundaries of Silpho and Suffield cum Everley.

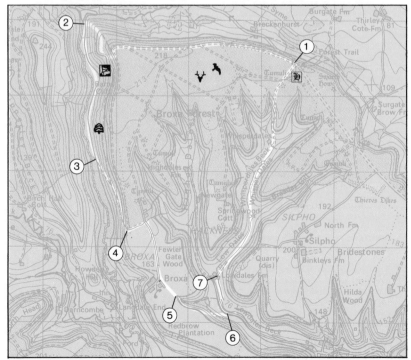

NORTH YORK MOORS

Kirkdale
4, 5 or 6 miles (6.5, 8 or 9.5 km) Sheet 100 676856

Easy The gentlest of walking: a winding, sheltered, secluded valley, fine woods, mellow buildings, an ancient church. *Farmland, woods, riverside; mud after rain.*

Start From A170 between Helmsley and Pickering about 1¼ miles (2 km) W of Kirkbymoorside, turn N and continue about ¼ mile (0.5 km) crossing disused railway, turning right at T-junction and almost immediately left before ford. **Car park** in 200 yards (183 m) by the church.

① From car park go through gate into meadow and cross stream. In about 600 yards (549 m) ignore track leading right and go left through gate into field. Follow path along valley. ② At mill do not cross river; go over stile or through gate to keep on track near river. ③ Cross stile beside gate and follow path into woods, soon climbing. In about 350 yards (320 m) ④ turn back sharply right on to well-constructed forestry path, first maintaining height, then descending, eventually joining outward route at ②. Retrace to ①. Extensions: from ④ continue 300 yards (274 m) uphill to level track and a further 250 yards (229 m) to meet road. Turn right, continue ¼ mile, meet road from Fadmoor to Kirkbymoorside, turn right and follow road for 1¼ miles (2 km) to ⑤ where follow path indicated by public footpath sign on right downhill. Continue bearing left into woods, eventually joining outward route and retracing to ①. Or, from ②, cross bridge, follow farm road to top, then to T-junction, and turn left downhill. At next T-junction turn left to ①.

🏠 St. Gregory's Minster has impressive claims to antiquity. A church stood on the site in the 7th C. (Saxon times), was destroyed by the Danish invaders in the 9th C. and rebuilt in about 1060.

🗿 The Hyena's Cave is the Moors' oldest archaeological site. Discovered in 1821, its contents included the bones and teeth of not only several hundred hyena but remains of rhinoceros, mammoth and other pre-glaciation animals .

⑲ Skiplam and Wether Cote are probably on the line of a medieval way.

St. Gregory's Minster, Kirkdale: there is an informative text on the Saxon sundial and a cross, probably Saxon, is carved on an outside wall near the tower.

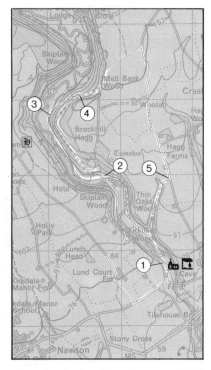

The Bridestones
8½ miles (13.5 km) Sheets 100 and 101 845899

Energetic Takes in some of the finest and most varied countryside in the region. *Woods, moorland, valleys; 2 climbs; mud.*

Start From the A169 5 miles (8 km) N of Pickering take the road signposted left into Lockton; 3 buses daily to and from Pickering. **Parking** between church and cemetery.

① From parking cross main road on to track. Continue through the wood and gates beyond to the farm road. Turn left and in about ½ mile (0.8 km) where it joins another turn sharp right through farmyard of Low Pasture Farm. Follow direction of National Trust signs for about ½ mile. ② At foot of hill walk behind isolated cottage and cross stream. Continue on track up valley, keeping left. Bridestones visible high on right. In about ½ mile ③ reach High Bridestones at top of steep shoulder. Curve right, descending towards Low Bridestones. Take left path through heather (NE) to join broad, cleared way – a fire prevention belt – between edge of heather and forest. Continue uphill by edge of woods and at top join well-defined track; follow it left, going NW to reach car park on A169. ④ Cross road at sharp corner and follow wide path out on to open moor. Do not follow path left down to valley. Eventually reach gate into lane and continue to Levisham, then Lockton.

🏛 Lockton's church has a 15th C. tower.

🞠 The Bridestones, an outcrop of sandstone of varying composition – hence the weirdly eroded shapes.

⟍⟋ Fylingdales early-warning system.

🍺 The Saltergate Inn, 100 yards N of ④.

🞠 The Hole of Horcum.

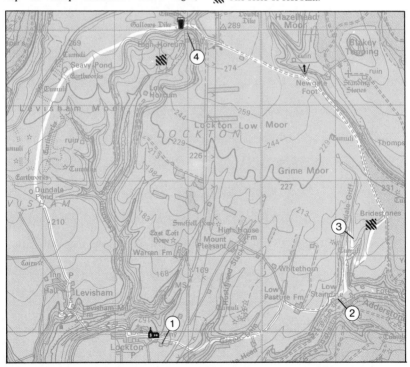

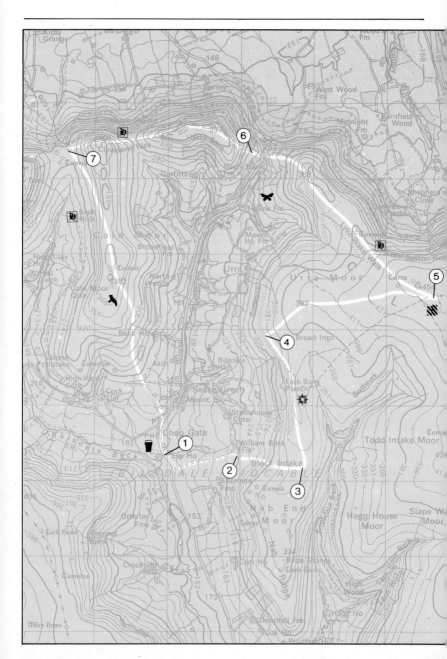

Above and Around Bilsdale
10 miles (16 km) Sheets 93 and 100 559994

Energetic A steady climb well up on to the Moors, from where most of the route can be surveyed; reaches the highest point on the Moors – superb views everywhere. *Farmland, moorland, craggy hills; mud.*

Start About 300 yards (274 m) S of Chop Gate on the B1257 between Helmsley and Stokesley. **Car park** 300 yards S of Chop Gate.

① From car park walk S along the B1257 to farm entry road with signpost 'Public Footpath to Bransdale'. Turn left and continue about ½ mile (0.8 km). ② Keep right in front of farmhouse, then left up lane between stone walls, continuing about ½ mile. ③ Turn left at T-junction of paths and after about 250 yards (229 m) sharp left. Then curve right, uphill, and follow contour. In about 1½ miles (2.5 km) ④ join track coming up from Bilsdale Hall and turn right. Continue about 1½ miles. ⑤ Near cairn turn sharp left to go downhill NW on well-defined track – the Lyke Wake Walk. Continue more than 2 miles (3 km). ⑥ After crossing road and climbing steps by wood edge, go left over fence and climb face of Hasty Bank. In about 1½ miles. ⑦ On descending steeply at W end of second hill crest turn left just before gate in stone wall; follow path beside wall for ½ mile, then take steep track left to join track on ridge of Cold Moor. Continue about 300 yards (274 m) S and bear left at junction. Continue about 1½ miles to Chop Gate.

🍴 The Buck Inn; restaurant.

🕸 The Moors' most impressive earthwork or dyke, which runs for 3 miles (5 km) along the E side of Bilsdale on the edge of Urra Moor: mostly in good condition.

🕸 At 1,489 feet, the Moors' highest point.

🔟 A section of the Lyke Wake Walk, which runs 40 miles (64 km) across the Moors.

🐝 In mid to late summer, beehives are seen dotted around Bilsdale and elsewhere on the Moors. Keepers bring them up to harvest the heather nectar.

🔟 A stretch of the Cleveland Way long-distance path; see pages 328-334.

Golden plovers in typical standing, flocking and flight attitudes: they look solid, with their rounded heads noticeable in flight.

🔟 Bilsdale hunt has a famous pack of hounds, based here. It is almost certainly descended from the 17th C. Duke of Buckingham's own pack, which he hunted after retirement to Helmsley Castle. Old people in the neighbourhood can remember when Hunt fixtures were announced from Bilsdale church pulpit.

🐦 Golden plovers are seen here during their breeding season, February to July. The mating song, heard in early spring, is a beautiful, trilling sequence.

Bridestones Moor Nature Reserve has marked trails.

Sutton Bank, on the A170, is a popular starting point for walks, including marked trails.

The Roman road on Wheeldale Moor, part of Wade's Causeway, is well defined for 1½ miles (2.5 km). A signposted path leads to it from the hamlet of Hunt House.

Goathland, 7 miles (11 km) SW of Whitby on the A169 is a starting point for exciting walks.

A geological trail starts from the Wildlife Centre on the unclassified road from the A171 into Ravenscar.

Paths round Robin Hood Bay 5 miles (8 km) SE of Whitby are waymarked as part of the Cleveland Way.

CUMBRIA AND THE LAKES

Writers – and no doubt walkers – long ago ran out of adjectives for the Lake District, this unique 900 square miles (1,448 square km) comprising the highest mountains in England and the long, deep lakes between them. Millions of words have been written describing the finest views. Wordsworth was by no means the first to do so, nor will Arthur Ransom be among the last. For the first-time walker here the best advice is to ignore other people's ideas of the 'best bits'. That way a reasonable chance can be gained of finding privacy by a tarn, a fell-side or waterfall, even in July and August.

The further east or west from the central Ambleside-Keswick axis, the lonelier the country. Treat it with the respect due to mountains. But do not neglect the rest of the county. What the locals call 'back o' Skidda' is a world of its own to the north of the lakes and there is the gentle Eden Vale to the east. The low hills of Arnside make excellent rambling and so do the tougher Howgills, a magnificent, miniature mountain range.

Mayburgh Henge Brougham Castle
5 miles (8 km) Sheet 90 519284

Easy A group of historical sites close to Penrith and the M6. *Minor roads, riverside; mud after rain.*

Start From Penrith head S on the A6. Cross Eamont Bridge (traffic lights) and take first right as for Pooley Bridge, then right on to narrow road. Follow it left and right. **Parking** at edge of this road, 150 yards (137 m) past henge, not obstructing houses.

① Walk back along road beside M6. ② Entrance to Mayburgh Henge is the signposted gate. Continue to A6, then right and first left. Follow road to castle. ③ Go down abandoned road N of Castle and continue to its end, where take riverside path back to A6. Retrace to ①.

☀ Mayburgh Henge, a ritualistic monument, is probably late Neolithic or early Bronze Age. One standing stone remains. A second henge, obscurely named King Arthur's Round Table, is close by.

🏠 St. Wilfred's Chapel dates from the 14th C. and has beautiful wood carvings.

▣ In the field can be seen the foundations of the Roman fort Brocavum. It guarded from the 2nd to the 4th C. A.D., what had

Primitive but powerful – the standing stone at the centre of Mayburgh Henge.

🏰 Brougham Castle grew with its successive owners from the mid-12th C. The last and greatest of them were the Cliffords; and of them the most formidable was Lady Anne, owner of vast estates, philanthropist and restorer.

been an important crossroads since prehistory. Around it there is evidence of a large Roman village.

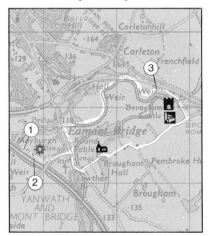

CUMBRIA AND THE LAKES

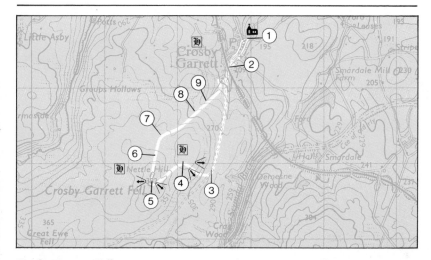

Crosby Garrett Fell
3½ miles (5.5 km) Sheet 91 729096

Moderate Gives a succession of outstanding views of the W flanks of the Pennines and of Cumbrian countryside; outside any tourist area. *Grassy hillside and plateau; one climb; mud after rain; some misleading vehicle tracks on the plateau – follow directions closely. Sheep country – control dogs.*

Start Crosby Garrett, W of Kirkby Stephen, signposted via Soulby on minor roads. **Parking** in village.

① From parking make for the railway viaduct. ② Go under viaduct and continue up distinct track. ③ When the track nears its highest point, look right, up the hill, where what appears to be a ruin or broken wall should be seen on the crest. This is in fact a limestone outcrop. Walk up to it over the steep grass slope – no path. Take this slowly – if too steep, take the gully near track's highest point; however this entails a trudge back to the limestone outcrop after reaching the plateau. ④ From the outcrop, look SW towards Nettle Hill and identify what appears to be a square ruin, with a central chimney, on the highest point. Make for this, choosing a route on higher places where the grass is shortest. ⑤ From the ruin – a heap of stones and trig. point – head acutely right from the line of approach. This is due N. There is no distinct path and

the easiest way through the tussocks is to follow sheep 'trods'. ⑥ Do not be diverted by vehicle tracks. ⑦ Head to the right when the vehicle tracks come together to run towards the village. ⑧ The track heads towards the corner of a wall; do not follow the wall round, but take the track descending in direction of village from the wall corner. ⑨ The track becomes better defined and surfaced with hardcore; follow it down to the viaduct.

Ancient records show the village was once called Crosby Gerard; who Gerard was is debatable, but Crosby means farmstead with a cross. In Christianity's earliest days, communities without churches made do with simple wood or stone crosses. Later, in Anglo-Saxon times, came a small church.

The limestone pavement is a good resting place and viewpoint. The hill here is common land, where the villagers had grazing rights. Sheep farming brought what wealth there was to the area.

Nettle Hill – and not a nettle in sight; but there probably was a nettlebed here once. Nettles, with various uses including dye for local wool, are a sign of earlier human settlement and these hills are covered with cairns and hut circles. N through E to SW are the Pennines; W and NW, the Lake District.

CUMBRIA AND THE LAKES

Long Meg and Lacy's Caves
5 miles (8 km) Sheets 90 and 91 566362

Moderate One of the finest Neolithic stone circles in the country, and a man-made cave in an idyllic situation; a beautiful river; all quiet. *Riverside, farmland; mud; may be overgrown between ④ and ⑥.*

Start From Penrith take the A686 in direction of Alston and turn left after crossing iron bridge over River Eden at Langwathby for Little Salkeld; infrequent buses. **Parking** in Little Salkeld without causing obstruction; alternatively NE of the village on grass verge in minor road leading to ⑭, starting the walk there.

① Walk W from centre of village to join surfaced track by railway. ② Continue on good-quality surface by railway line. ③ Go left on to concrete road. Turn sharp left by the transformer, then right at railway line to join narrow path leaving line, past old mine complex to riverside. ④ Watch carefully: Lacy's Caves can be overlooked. On reaching sandstone face, follow path on rock ledge to the left. After visiting cave, retrace steps to this point and follow the path up the bank onwards above the cave. ⑤ The path continues through lush growth and may be overgrown; some wet sections. ⑥ Follow the path beside river through fields. Make detours to avoid the worst of the mud. ⑦ Follow path through woodland to join minor road. ⑧ Follow road to Glassonby; look out for local drivers, who may not expect to meet anyone. ⑨ At Glassonby take the road right in direction of Little Salkeld. ⑩ Turn right on to unclassified road to church. ⑪ Go through churchyard following paved path through iron gate S, then take track to access road. ⑫ Cross access road and go through gate; follow fence, using sketchy track. ⑬ Follow fence alongside plantation. Cross crude stiles at end to join faint track following fences and field boundaries to stone circle seen ahead. After stone circle, continue on unclassified road heading S. ⑭ At this point an unclassified road joins from left, but continue heading S on track to join road again at Little Salkeld and starting point.

🖛 Long Meg mine produced anhydrite (for munitions) during the 1939-45 war.

\↓/ The River Eden can be approached here. It flows NW to the Solway Firth.

📷 The extraordinary Lacy's Caves are a mystery. The Lacy family arrived in the neighbourhood in the 18th C. and may have created them as a folly. Grottoes, preferably complete with a hermit's retreat, were fashionable then.

☀ Long Meg and her Daughters date from Neolithic or Bronze Age times – more than 4,000 years ago. Originally there were probably 60 stones. It is assumed they had religious and astronomical significance. Viewed from the centre of the circle, Long Meg is in position for the setting of the midwinter sun. The day when the sun 'turns back', giving promise of spring, must have meant much to the farmers who depended on this valley for their living long before recorded history. Wordsworth was much struck by coming on the stones for the first time feeling 'A weight of awe not easy to be borne . . .'

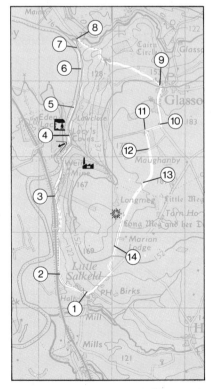

The Black and White Combes

5 miles (8 km) Sheet 96 153847

Energetic A neglected corner of the otherwise well-trodden Lake District; some regard the climb as a dull slog over featureless moorland – but this way it is not. *Valley, heather hillside; moorland, tussocky plateau; one climb; mud (avoidable). Do not attempt in poor visibility, or under snow.*

Start On the A595, 2½ miles (4 km) NE of Whicham. **Parking** in lay-by at Beckside.

① From parking cross road with care and go up lane opposite. ② Follow grassy path above cottage and cross stile. ③ At the apparent fork, keep left to go alongside the wood. ④ Through gate, across bridge and then follow well-defined track up into valley of White Combe. ⑤ After passing the crags above and to the left, follow track as it leads slightly away from beck. Watch for the waterfalls above and forward to the left. Walk up from track towards the falls. ⑥ Cross beck below fall and walk up steep bank alongside it (no path). There is a slightly easier route to the right in a wet gully – but either way it is steep. Above the falls, on a slightly easier slope, look upwards and identify gap in crags ahead. Head for this; to most people, it looks worse than it is. ⑦ As the beck forks, continue uphill towards gap in crags. Beware of loose stones. (Parties should keep close together to avoid being hit by stones loosened by leaders.) Also watch for bog – identified by level area of bright green moss. Scramble through the gap and out on to plateau, continuing upwards and bearing left (no path). ⑧ The plateau is hard walking on tussocky grass. As the higher parts are reached some sketchy paths and tracks are seen. Follow any of them towards summit. ⑨ Follow the more evident tracks going to the right of the summit of Black Combe. ⑩ The obvious summit is crowned by an untidy cairn and a trig. point. From here retrace steps to ⑪ pathless plateau above the White Combe. ⑫ To avoid worst of bog, pick a route near to the fence. Turn to follow summit ridge SE. ⑬ From here the subsidiary summit marked 'White Combe' on the map can be visited. Otherwise descend to ⑭ a distinct path which zigzags comfortably down into White Combe. ⑮ The 2 bogs can be avoided to some extent by climbing above the path. ⑯ The path bends back to a beck; descend on outward track.

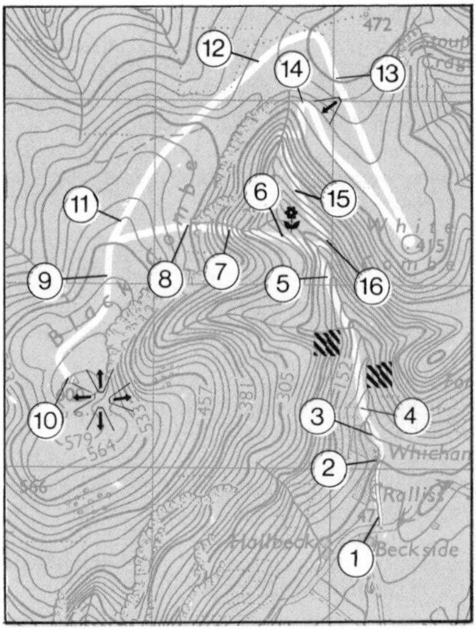

Supremely clear water in this stream, the colour enhanced by light grey rock.

The light grey rock gave the valley its name – White Combe – combe being the old word for a hollow. The rock is the oldest in the Lake District and known as Skiddaw slate.

A gardener would give much to reproduce the effect of the falls. The plant life is so profuse because the soil is enriched by minerals flushed to the surface by the water. There is a particularly large variety of mosses and liverworts. The dominant yellow flower is bog asphodel, flowering July-Sept.

The view is amazing; it is clear why mariners regard Black Combe as an important landmark. The Isle of Man is prominent; in best conditions one can make out the coasts of Ireland and the hills of North Wales and Galloway. All the higher central mountains of the Lakes are visible. Way out SE are the Pennines; S is Barrow and Walney Island with the Fylde beyond. Close to, the only ugly intrusion is Windscale Power Station. Wordsworth could truthfully write 'This height a ministering Angel might select . . .'

At last, the hollow of Black Combe.

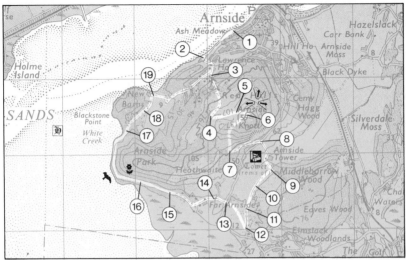

Arnside Knott, Tower and Cliffs
7 miles (11 km) Sheet 97 454786

Moderate A walk of contrasts – viewpoints, historical interest and natural history. *Sea promenade, cliff top, woods, farmland, beach; one climb; mud after rain; cliff path may be slippery after rain.*

Start Arnside, approached from Milnthorpe on the B5282. **Car parks** in Arnside.

① From road end walk along promenade and surfaced footpath on sea shore. ② Watch for the gateway (no gate) by lifebelt; go up lane between cottages. Climb steeply and at the road turn left. ③ At road junction climb steep road to left. ④ By car park and view indicator climb grass track to summit plateau. ⑤ Walk on terrace path for best views. Go to summit. ⑥ A number of paths lead off summit; descend SW – paths converge. ⑦ Join distinct track and continue left through woodland to descend to road. ⑧ Cross road with care and follow track towards ruined tower. Walk past this. ⑨ Take path on *right* through gate – woodland on left. ⑩ Ignore tarmac tracks leading left into caravan site. ⑪ When track reaches gate, go to its left and follow fence. ⑫ Go through wicket gate in fence and follow field paths towards road. ⑬ Cross road with care (blind exit) and go down surfaced lane

opposite. ⑭ Ignore caravan site service roads leading right. ⑮ Take track leading left, away from road towards shore. ⑯ Track becomes a cliff path; the surface varies. ⑰ Follow track as it turns left to White Creek; if conditions permit, continue on sands back to promenade. If the tide is too high, turn back having viewed White Creek and follow lane alongside caravan site to next bay. ⑱ Ignore service route into caravan site. ⑲ At bay, continue on beach round next headland; if tide is too high, go inland on lane to join roads into Arnside.

\t/ The best viewpoint is below the summit, slightly on the Arnside flank.

▧ Arnside Tower is 14th C.

❀ In midsummer the cliff face is a natural rock garden. The big show comes from the yellow rockrose. There are also bloody cranesbill (red) and centaury (pink).

➤ In winter, waders, ducks and geese feed at the water's edge.

▧ There is still a public road over Morecambe Bay from near Morecambe to Kents Bank, S of Grange-over-Sands, the town opposite. Once it was the only way into the southern Lake District and travellers needed guides.

CUMBRIA AND THE LAKES

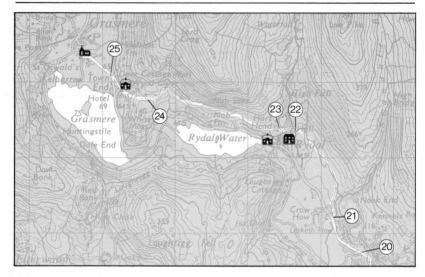

Windermere to Grasmere

9 miles (14.5 km) Sheets 96 and 90 414987

Moderate Famous views; opportunity to visit Wordsworth's home, the cottage where he wrote his best work, the museum there and the poet's grave. *Grassy hillsides, farmland; 2 climbs; mud.*

Start Windermere station; frequent buses and trains. **Car parks** in Windermere. **Return** to start by bus from Grasmere.

① From station walk across main road with care and continue about 100 yards (91 m) in direction of Ambleside. Turn up tarmac lane signposted Orrest Head. Join track at top going right by wall. Pass through iron gate to high viewpoint. ② From Orrest Head viewpoint continue on grassy path N towards farm. Path does not reach farm; follow it along wall to stile on to road. Turn right. ③ Turn left off drive to circumnavigate buildings. ④ Bear left with wall, through stile and continue direct to next stile on faint path. ⑤ Follow wall on right to next stile. ⑥ Follow wall round, then go left across corner to next stile. ⑦ After gate continue to cottage, then round it through 2 stiles at rear. ⑧ Do not continue forward, but go through gate towards barn and on behind it. ⑨ At farmyard corner bear right to follow tarmac lane. Cross minor road and ⑩ go through

gate beyond cottages and on to terraced, grassy path. ⑪ Join road, cross and continue on pavement. ⑫ Just *after* a road joins from right, go through gate on left and descend on track to cross 2 bridges. Continue uphill between walls. ⑬ Cross road and climb track opposite. Join another road and turn left; in about 80 yards (73 m) ⑭ climb track between walls. ⑮ Join level walled track. ⑯ Leave walled track by gate to follow path downhill. ⑰ Join track, over bridge and on past farm (High Skelghyll), following level track through woods. ⑱ Join surfaced lane and descend to minor road. ⑲ Follow road into Ambleside (Old Lake Road). ⑳ Leave Ambleside by Keswick road. ㉑ Join track through iron gates. Follow this fenced track about a mile through parkland. ㉒ Go between buildings behind Rydal Hall to join lane at T-junction. Turn right up slope. ㉓ Turn left on to walled track behind Rydal Mount. Later follow level path. ㉔ Join surfaced road to Dove Cottage. ㉕ Cross road with care and continue into Grasmere.

\t/ Orrest Head, one of the best vantage points in the district, takes in most of the central fells, but the glory is the long view over England's largest lake.

🏠 Town End is a worthwhile diversion: a 17th C. house belonging to a yeoman family, most of its interior is period, made

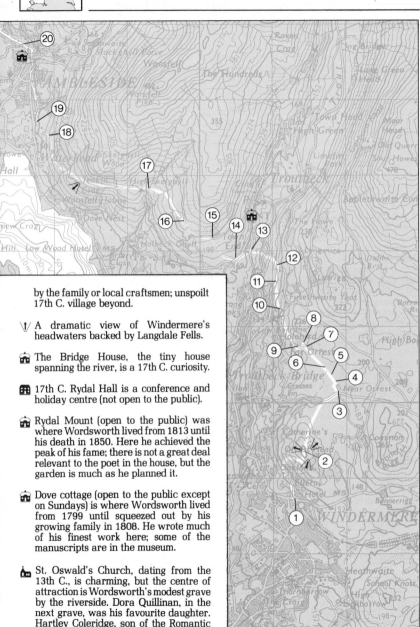

by the family or local craftsmen; unspoilt 17th C. village beyond.

\|↑/ A dramatic view of Windermere's headwaters backed by Langdale Fells.

🏠 The Bridge House, the tiny house spanning the river, is a 17th C. curiosity.

🏢 17th C. Rydal Hall is a conference and holiday centre (not open to the public).

🏠 Rydal Mount (open to the public) was where Wordsworth lived from 1813 until his death in 1850. Here he achieved the peak of his fame; there is not a great deal relevant to the poet in the house, but the garden is much as he planned it.

🏠 Dove cottage (open to the public except on Sundays) is where Wordsworth lived from 1799 until squeezed out by his growing family in 1808. He wrote much of his finest work here; some of the manuscripts are in the museum.

⛪ St. Oswald's Church, dating from the 13th C., is charming, but the centre of attraction is Wordsworth's modest grave by the riverside. Dora Quillinan, in the next grave, was his favourite daughter. Hartley Coleridge, son of the Romantic poet S. T. Coleridge, is close by.

CUMBRIA AND THE LAKES

Derwentwater and Lodore Cascade
3½ miles (5.5 km) Sheet 90 251213

Easy A delightful expedition, incorporating boat trips, and much opportunity for idleness; with a picnic lunch (the route is mainly on National Trust land) it could last all day. The ferry service operates between start of British Summer Time in March and the first Sunday in November. *Wooded lakeside, peat; parts flooded after rain.*

Start Hawse End, reached by regular boat service from Keswick boat stage; buses to Keswick. **Car park** in Keswick nearest the boat landing. **Return** to Keswick by boat (regular service) from Lodore.

① After picking up a timetable, board the Keswick Launch Co. boat going *anti-clockwise* for Hawes End – the first stop. ② Alight at Hawes End and go left along the shore path. ③ To avoid bog and scrub, the path continues through a stile and along a field edge. ④ Turn left with fence at end. Use the plank walk to avoid swamp. Follow the path along the shore again. ⑤ Ignore the path going steeply uphill to the right. Keep to the shore path. ⑥ Negotiate steps over rocky outcrop. ⑦ At the landing stage bear right. ⑧ At fork bear left and climb steps. ⑨ Go through kissing-gate and immediately left towards the land side of the boathouse. Continue between the boathouse and cottage; go through the gate. ⑩ At the fork, keep right (left track goes to a private house). ⑪ Enter Manesty Wood (National Trust sign). Go left with fence towards the shore. ⑫ To avoid worst of swamp, bear right, following path trodden by others for same purpose, to join a path sweeping down to the shore farther on. ⑬ Follow the path across the plank walk and over the bridge to the road. ⑭ Just .before Lodore Swiss Hotel Entrance, go up lane on right to Lodore Cascade (waterfalls). Retrace to ⑭. Go up road and turn left for the boat landing. ⑮ Join anti-clockwise boat to Keswick.

🔩 The lake was an important highway. Boats carried ore from mines about the
⑂ valley for smelting in Keswick, once a smoky industrial town. Friar's Crag, the viewpoint, is down the road and lane.

⑂ The shoreline's trees have particularly beautiful shapes. On St. Herbert's Island
🔟 lived the saint of the same name, a close

friend of St. Cuthbert; in fact they were so close they died, in sympathy, on the same day.

⑂ One of the shore's many viewpoints: opposite is Wella's Crag, with Great Wood below.

🔩 This is the easily overlooked waste heap of what was Brandlehow Mine. The hillside, mined from ancient times, contains galena (lead), iron, silver, manganese, even traces of gold.

⑂ N. the Skiddaw range; forward, Shepherds Crag – watch for climbers.

〰 Approach Lodore Cascade by paying a small fee at the hotel.

Opposite photogenic Derwentwater.

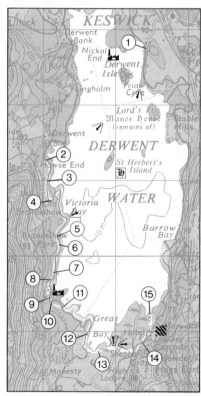

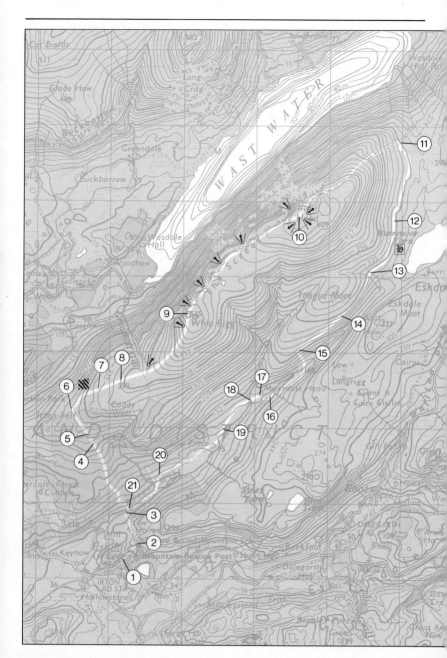

Wastwater Screes Top and Miterdale
10½ miles (17 km) Sheet 89 143003

Energetic Wastwater Screes Top ranks high among the Lakes' great vantage points and Miterdale, unknown to many Lake District addicts, is magically peaceful. In winter, the route should be attempted only by experienced walkers with appropriate equipment. *Forest, hillsides, fell top, valley; riverside; one climb; a hard descent; mud.*

Start Eskdale Green, signposted from the A595; frequent trains – the narrow-gauge railway service from Ravenglass goes to Irton Road station, from where turn right to village centre for start. **Car park** near public lavatories in Eskdale Green.

① Take the walled lane from the telephone box and public lavatories uphill beside the Outward Bound School. ② Bear left at fork, between walls. ③ At junction with road cross road into wood, cross bridge and climb stony track. ④ Ignore crossing roads and tracks, continuing straight on, climbing on stone track. ⑤ After crossing upper forest road, the track becomes a path through heather; follow this, and climb the rocky steps. ⑥ When path eventually leaves forest, turn right to follow wall and keep climbing. ⑦ Cross stile over wall, and escape the bog by going right. ⑧ The path is poorly defined on wet ground. A steep ascent approaches; follow path, now more obvious. ⑨ Only peak-baggers will make for the highest point direct; discerning walkers will follow the pathless route on the cliff edges to view the lake 1,700 feet below. ⑩ From the summit, Illgill Head, follow the track downhill NE as if for Wasdale Head. If fog is approaching, return to start by the same route, keeping away from cliff edge, staying on the path. ⑪ Follow indistinct level path. ⑫ Pick up better-defined level path seen ahead. (The 'bridleway' marking is optimistic.) ⑬ With care, the boggy sections can be by-passed. ⑭ The 'bridleway' climbs vaguely away; keep to the narrow path at present level and head towards plantation fence. ⑮ At plantation descend carefully on extremely steep path to river. Cross to path and descend with river on right. ⑯ Cross bridge to ruined farm. If the river is in spate (full and flowing fast) at this point, go back over bridge after viewing ruin and continue downhill on path to ⑲. This avoids a ford. ⑰ From farm continue up walled pathway and

soon go left through wall gap. Continue on grassy track across fields. ⑱ Cross the ford. ⑲ Follow track past footbridge (not across it) through farmyard by riverside. ⑳ Cross bridge to road. Follow this. ㉑ Turn left to rejoin outward path. Alternatively, go straight on to join village road, a more direct route to Irton Road Station.

Here the terrain changes from granite to the volcanic of the high central fells.

Obvious signs of the geological change – hard volcanic rocks, which resisted glacial erosion – rise ahead.

The lake, 1,700 feet (518 m) below is 258 feet (79 m) deep, with extremely clean water. The cliff (the 'screes') is unstable and sheds rock falls: it was undercut by the ice which ground out Wastwater over 10,000 years ago.

Towards the coast the contrasting geology is again evident: the sea plain is sandstone; the valleys are granite and the hills are volcanic.

Better a few yards W.

The more level area around Burnmoor Tarn is once more granite country. Pollen analysis of the tarn bed shows that some 3,000 years ago the area was well wooded. Neolithic man's stone axes, made from the volcanic stone, probably cleared away the forest.

Skiddaw can be climbed from Keswick by the side of Latrigg and up the public bridleway.

Take a bus from Keswick to Rosthwaite and walk back via Watendlath, Surprise View, Ashness Bridge and Walla Crag on public footpaths.

From Ambleside to Grasmere along the S side of Rydal Water and then by Loughrigg Terrace is a fine walk.

On Ullswater, take the service steamer from Glenridding to Howtown and walk back on the lake shore paths.

An ascent of Coniston Old Man can be made in *fine weather only* from Coniston via Low Water. Return by Goats Water and Walna Scar. The mountain is scarred by copper mines, but the view superb.

NORTHUMBERLAND

From its north-east to south-west corners, North-umberland measures 70 miles (113 km): a big county, full of interest for the walker. There is a coast of great beauty, complete with wide, firm beaches, islands, seals, history in the shape of massively romantic castles, and some splendid cliffs. Inland is a coastal plain of pure enclosure countryside, a range of noble river valleys, ranging from the Tweed in the north to the Tyne in the south, and the low swell of the Simonside Hills.

The county incorporates an entire national park at its southern end, of which the best bit is Hadrian's Wall. This marches, Roman-fashion, relentlessly across the contours. It demands to be explored on foot, the mode of transport employed by the legions who defended it.

Further north in the park, the Cheviots loom over the rest of the county. These are the northern end of the Pennine chain and quite unlike the rest. They are more smoothly rounded, and the grass covering them is of a kind better to reflect the changing light and shade. They bring a new character to the hills just when the walker who has slogged up the Pennine Way is nearing the end of the trek.

Hareshaw Linn
4 miles (6.5 km) Sheet 80 840834

Easy A pleasant stroll near an interesting town. *Woods; mud after rain.*

Start Bellingham on the B6320; frequent buses. **Parking** at centre of Bellingham.

① From Bellingham walk along the West Woodburn road and turn left along lane by stream. Continue beneath the disused railway towards a row of cottages. ② Follow

Magnificent Hareshaw Linn, at its liveliest after prolonged rain.

the path directly ahead and into the wooded ravine of the Hareshaw Burn. ③ The path follows the E side of the stream about 1¼ miles (2 km), then swaps sides; for another ¼ mile (0.5 km) 5 plank bridges switch the route from side to side. As there is no right of way past the linn (waterfall), return by the same route. This is no hardship – the views are different each way.

🛉 The principal church in Bellingham (pronounced Bellinjam) has a 17th C. stone vaulted nave.

🏛 The Pennine Way long-distance path (see pages 328-334) goes through the town.

🌢 The woodland plants growing beside Hareshaw Burn do not need strong light: many of them flower in spring before the trees in leaf cut off too much sunlight. Flowering plants to be seen include foxglove, the source of the drug digitalis, used for the treatment of heart complaints, and the greenish-yellow wood sage, a herbal 'cure' for rheumatism. The first flowers June-Sept., the second July-Sept.

🏛 Hareshaw Linn, cascading over sandstone, is one of Northumberland's most famous waterfalls.

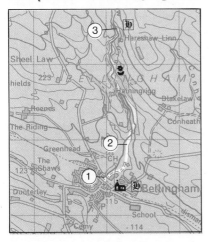

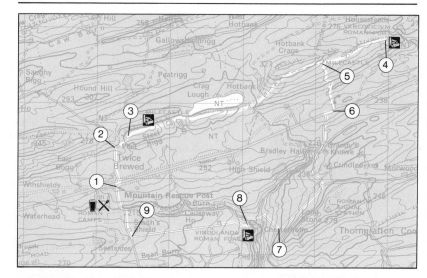

Along Hadrian's Wall

7½ miles (12 km) Sheet 87 753669

Moderate Follows the best-preserved and hence most interesting section of Hadrian's Wall, with a visit to Housesteads Fort and Vindolanda Roman Settlement. *Farmland, moorland, crags; 2 climbs.*

Start Bardon Mill, signposted from the A69; buses in summer. **Car park** at the Once Brewed Information Centre, signposted in village.

① From car park cross the B6318 and walk along the Steel Rigg road as far as the first cottage on the right. ② Immediately beyond Peel farmhouse turn right across a ladder stile and walk through the field as far as the Roman wall. ③ Turn right along Hadrian's Wall and follow it about 2½ miles (4 km) to Housesteads Fort (signposted at entrance). ④ Retrace steps from fort as far as Rapishaw Gap (pronounced dip in ridge) (the Pennine Way, clearly signposted, turns away from the wall at this point). ⑤ Turn left and walk downhill on faint path later becoming a track bearing slightly right through 2 fields to the road. ⑥ Turn right, cross and then left down the minor road towards Bardon Mill. In 1¼ miles (2 km) ⑦ turn right at Vindolanda car park, follow the lane past the museum and information

centre and ⑧ enter the ruins. Walk through Vindolanda and leave by the lane beyond the upper (W) car park. ⑨ At road right for ①.

▷ The Romans built this great wall between A.D. 122 and 126 as a fortification, a raised military patrol route and a base for raids against the barbarians to the N. The Wall stands 15 feet (4.5 m) high and over 7 feet (2 m) thick, with 'milecastles' – patrol points – every 1,620 yards (1,481 m) and smaller turrets every 540 yards (494 m).

▷ Housesteads (Vercovicium), probably the finest example of a Roman fort to be found in all Europe, includes barracks, granaries, a hospital, a mess-room with baths, and a latrine. The small museum contains interesting finds from the site.

▷ Vindolanda (Chesterholme) was both a Roman fort, with a small garrison of 500, and a civilian community, a *vicus*. Excavation has already revealed houses, taverns, workshops, baths and temples, stone-built and well drained.

▯ The 'Twice Brewed' pub, according to
✗ legend, got its name many years ago, when a customer complained that the ale wasn't strong enough and asked for it to be brewed again.

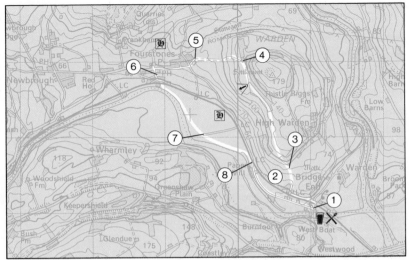

The Tyne Valley
4 miles (6.5 km) Sheet 87 910661

Easy A pleasing short walk through a little known area near Hadrian's Wall with excellent views of the S Tyne Valley. *Pasture, woods, riverside; one climb.*

Start Bridge End signposted from the A69; frequent buses; trains to Hexham, nearly 3 miles' (5 km) walk or bus ride from ①. **Parking** beyond the railway bridge near the Boat Inn.

① From the Boat Inn walk along the Warden road under the railway bridge and in about 60 yards (55 m) turn left along the path signposted to Quality Cottages. ② Turn right at the cottages and climb gently up through a small wood. Cross a series of fields on obvious track close to hedge, making for the wood ahead. ③ At the wood turn left and follow track past 2 sections of woods to a cottage. ④ Turn left at cottage and walk downhill (changing sides of wall) through a series of fields along track to Fourstones village. ⑤ Continue through the village and turn left at the crossroads. ⑥ Walk down the lane, over the level crossing and continue to the river bank. Turn left and follow the river. ⑦ In about a mile (1.5 km), ignore a stile leading left into a field and then continue ¾ mile (one km) along the river bank to the paper mill. ⑧ At mill turn right along the road and walk back to the Boat Inn.

🍴 The Boat Inn serves food. The road from the inn leads to Warden, where the N and S Tynes meet.

\†/ The S Tyne valley.

🏛 This country, through which the N Tyne flows, had a violent past. In the 12th C. Henry II agreed to the land passing into the care of the kings of Scotland, in return for their giving up a claim to inherit the earldom of Northumbria. A century later, nominees of the English crown, including Piers Gaveston, held the lordship of N Tynedale, and the resulting confusion between English and Scottish territorial power and influence made the area a lawless one, where outlaws could find sanctuary, protected by custom from arrest by law officers.

🏛 In the Middle Ages the king's judges were met by the Sheriff of Northumberland at Fourstones when they travelled north. In those days the village was on the borders of N Tynedale and Hexamshire. The judges could well have used the Roman road Stanegate on their journey.

There is a pub in the village.

NORTHUMBERLAND

By the Pennine Way to the Border
9 miles (14.5 km) Sheet 80 764027

Energetic An exciting section of the Pennine Way, clearly marked by a fence, with incomparable views of the Cheviot hills. Path may be overgrown between ② and ③ but the firebreak is easy to follow. *Forest, moorland; one climb; mud.*

Start Byrness, on the A68; frequent buses. **Car park** in Byrness (signposted near Information Centre), or parking in lane parallel to A68.

① From car park walk along the lane parallel to the main road as far as the chapel – about ½ mile (0.8 km). ② Cross the A68 and walk along a drive opposite, then turn right at a gate to climb steeply up a firebreak (gap in trees). ③ Above the forest the path is well defined, and becomes less steep after a short scramble through a boulder field. On Byrness Hill turn slightly left to follow the path the whole way across the moor to the Border Fence. ④ At the fence, climb a stile close by the forest and turn left. There is no path on this section, but the route is easy to follow by keeping close to the fence. Follow the fence 1¼ miles (2 km) to a pronounced depression. ⑤ In the depression, turn left, crossing the low fence, and walk into firebreak (gap between trees). ⑥ Descend the firebreak to forest track. Turn left and at the junction with another forest track, turn right and follow it downhill through the forest, ignoring side turnings, to the main road. ⑦ Cross and return to Byrness.

🔟 The second-longest footpath in Britain, the Pennine Way runs 250 miles (402 km) from Edale in Derbyshire to the tiny village of Kirk Yetholm, once a gipsy settlement, just over the Border. (See page 328-334.)

\ʇ/ The view SW takes in Kielder Forest, part of the 145,000-acre (58,681 ha) Border Forest Park created by the Forestry Commission in the last 50 years. Great plantations of trees, mainly sitka and Norway spruce, cover what was once sheep-grazing country, although the whole Border had been a forest in earlier times, before the Romans came.

\ʇ/ To the NE is Cheviot Hill, 2,676 feet (816 m) high.

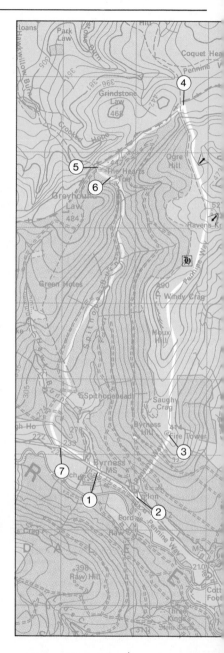

Craster and Dunstanburgh

4½ miles (7 km) Sheets 75 and 81 259198

Easy A coastal walk with a magnificent ruined castle as its focal point; interesting geological features; can be exhilarating in winter. *Sea shore, farmland, craggy outcrops.*

Start Craster, on minor road signposted from B1339; frequent buses. **Car park** in old quarry signposted on outskirts of Craster.

① From the car park walk towards the harbour and turn left; continue along road past cottages through gate on to coastal path. Follow the coast to Dunstanburgh Castle. ② After visiting the castle, leave by the main gate and turn right to follow the path around the golf course to Dunstan Steads Farm. Turn left through the farmyard and ③ follow the farm lane to Dunstan Square where, ④ turn left and walk downhill through a field towards the conspicuous crags – The Heughs. ⑤ Turn right and follow the path beneath the crags back to the car park.

✗ Craster's delicious kippers are reckoned the best in England: herrings from the North Sea are smoked over a fire of oak chips, and the results can be tried in the restaurant by the curing sheds.

🌢 Various seaside plants.

🏰 Largest of Northumbria's castles, Dunstanburgh was begun in 1313 by Thomas, Earl of Lancaster (and much altered in 1380-84 by John of Gaunt) for use as an outpost on the Lancastrian side in the Wars of the Roses. Turner included the castle in 3 of his paintings, and it is a magnificent spectacle, standing high above the sea on outcrops of the Whin Sill, the rock system which carries Hadrian's Wall.
Best preserved of the ruins are the gatehouse/keep and the Lilburn Tower.

🏠 This 14th C. tower house was titivated in the 18th C. Seat of the Craster family, it may once have been a watch-tower for Dunstanburgh Castle.

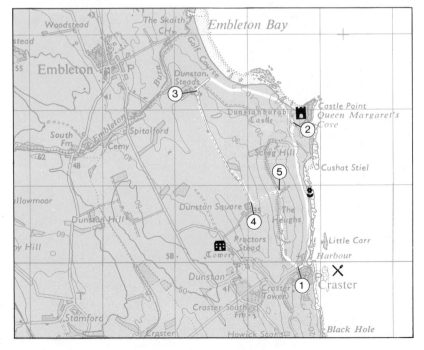

NORTHUMBERLAND

The Cheviot Foothills
12 miles (19 km) Sheet 75 992279

Energetic A solitary walk through contrasting countryside; some exposed moorland – avoid in poor visibility or bad weather. Superb views to the Tweed Valley and Scottish border country. *Moorland, valley, farmland; 2 climbs.*

Start Wooler, signposted from the A697; frequent buses. **Parking** in Wooler.

① From the Market Square walk up Ramsey's Lane. After about ¼ mile (0.5 km) its name changes to Common Road. Almost at the last house on this lane turn left on to a rough track to Waud House Farm. ② At the farm a stile by a gate leads to open country. Cross and turn sharply right to climb a small hill ahead on gradually improving path. Pass ramparts of a prehistoric settlement. Cross stile and walk through the young plantation. Continue towards Wooler Common Farm, seen ahead. ③ Go round the farm to the right and climb towards obvious gap between the 2 forests. Cross moorland – about 1¾ miles (3 km) – and descend to Carey Burn (stream). ④ Follow Carey Burn and at the junction of 2 streams follow the track climbing steeply above the stream on left. When the buildings of Broadstruther come into sight, follow path which veers slightly left and towards them. ⑤ Keep slightly left beyond the ruins of Broadstruther and continue on faint path across moorland towards the dip in the ridge ahead. ⑥ At the fence cross a stile, continue uphill about 100 yards (91 m) then descend by an improving path to Hawsen Burn and the Langleeford road, where ⑦ turn left and continue to Langlee Cottage. ⑧ Cross the burn (stream) by bridge on right; pass in front of Langlee Cottage and climb steep hill beyond. ⑨ Descend Brands Hill by a path which joins a farm track past the deserted farm at Middleton Old Town. Continue to North Middleton. ⑩ Turn left along the road and cross ford in Happy Valley. Follow road for about 1¾ miles and take the second turning right beyond the Happy Valley. ⑪ Follow lane to Earle Mill and then signposted path behind the mill to Wooler.

📖 Until 1251 Wooler was the seat of a barony with a castle (now in ruins). It was known for its sheep and cattle fairs and still holds the Trinian Fair, on September 27th.

🍺 There are plenty of pubs and cafés from
✗ which to choose in the spacious main street.

🏔 The granite Cheviots are ancient: they were high ground before the ice ages, and when the glaciers came, the hills blocked their movement. Forced to change direction, the ice marked out the river courses – and therefore the lines of communication – that have made and influenced the history of Britain.

📖 In the Cheviot foothills, the first settlers in Northumbria built their round huts and struggled to make a living from the land. The highest hill of the Cheviots is The Cheviot, 2,676 feet (816 m). It can be climbed in about 2 hours, starting from Langleeford.

Attractive, waymarked forest walks start from a picnic site near Stonehaugh. Follow the signpost off the B6320 N of Chollerford.

A forest track over the Simonside Hills, by Lordenshaw 2 miles (3 km) S of Rothbury off the B6342, leads to the dramatic vantage point of Tosson Hill.

Nature trails on the beautiful Farne Islands – with their superb seabird populations – can be reached by a short boat trip from Seahouses, 15 miles (24 km) N of Alnwick.

The secluded paths of Coquetdale, across the bleak moorland of the Cheviots, can be reached from Alwinton, 10 miles (16 km) NW of Rothbury.

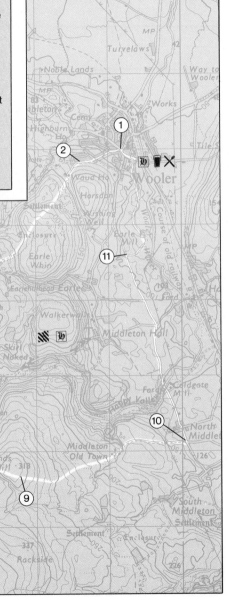

SCOTLAND

SW SCOTLAND

Somewhere in this region, Richard Hannay, fleeing London for his life, got off the train and took to the moors implacably pursued by the German spy-ring of *The Thirty-Nine Steps*. John Buchan was not the first romancer to set a tale here. Sir Walter Scott did so in *Guy Mannering* and *Marmion*, and those who explore the region on foot can still taste the romance, even if the mountains have not quite the drama of the Highlands.

Merrick, the highest point in southern Scotland, is quite an easy climb from the car park near the Bruce Stone. With the parallel Rhinns of Kells, it forms a granite complex geologically allied to the Highlands. In the area round Glentrool, the Forestry Commission caters elaborately for walkers, but the best bits of the Forest Park are the central, untamed hills which have been left unplanted.

There is an excellent coast which is perhaps finest along the Solway Firth. A small mountain called Criffel gives the best views across the shining strands of the estuary to the peaks of the Lake District. Further west along the coast is Burrow Head and the peninsula where Christianity was first established in Scotland.

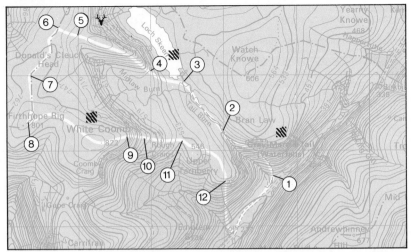

Loch Skeen and White Coomb
6½ miles (10.5 km) Sheet 79 185145

Energetic One of the most dramatic walks of Scotland's SW, with a superb waterfall, moraines and expansive upland views. The route passes through a gorge, best lit in May-June. *Gorge, heather moor, moraines, ridge, grassy slopes; 3 climbs; mud after rain. Do not attempt in poor visibility – for experienced hill walkers only – 1:25,000 map and compass recommended.*

Start Take the A708 from Moffat or Selkirk to **car park**, conspicuous about 7 miles (11 km) NE of Moffat.

① Cross bridge at car park. Uphill on path with waterfall on left. *It is dangerous to stray from the path.* ② Keep on E bank of burn (stream) until near loch. ③ Cross burn by stones below loch. ④ Climb Prominent ridge. ⑤ Head for higher ridge (with wall on it) to W. The path is indistinct. *If cloud is low, and you are not equipped with a compass, or uncertain of capability, retrace steps.* ⑥ A wall and ridge lead off at right angles to route from ⑤ – difficult to miss. Turn left at wall, following ridge and wall SW, S and SW to Donald's Cleuch Head. ⑦ Continue by wall S to Firthhope Rig. ⑧ Go E following wall down to col and climb by wall to White Coomb. ⑨ Descend from ridge ENE by wall. ⑩ Go ESE then E past Rough Craigs by wall.

The slope is steep, but there are grass/heather routes on either side of the broken ground. ⑪ Continue by wall SE, E, SE and S to top of steep slope above road. ⑫ *Avoid dangerous slopes on left.* Bear right all the way down on edge of forest until flat ground is reached. Return along road.

The Grey Mare's Tail Waterfall is a 200 feet (61 m) cascade of water, the Tail Burn pouring down a sheer cleft into Moffat Water.

Loch Skeen (or Skene) lies at a height of 1,750 feet (533 m), surrounded by 2,383 acres (964 ha) of land acquired in 1962 by the National Trust for Scotland. At the end of the Loch are moraines – shale and rocks left behind in the wake of glaciers. The lonely country behind it is grazed by wild goats and sheep. The sheep (whose stone fold is called a 'stell') are not aggressive, but the goats should be left well alone. The hinterland of the Loch gave the Covenanters sanctuary, but in later days, when Sir Walter Scott was riding through it in a thick mist, he and his horse fell into a bog and only got out of it with difficulty.

On White Coomb, 2,695 feet (821 m) high, the crescent of snow under the crest of the ridge generally survives well into May.

SW SCOTLAND

Craiglee
5 miles (8 km) Sheet 77 484949

Moderate Sensational views into the wild country of the Galloway Hills to the S. Best avoided in April-May as the route passes through a sheep farm. *Grassy slopes; heather and grass, rocky hilltops; 2 climbs; mud; coarse grass with boggy patches between* ⑦ *and* ⑧. *Do not attempt in poor visibility: 1: 25,000 map and compass recommended.*

Start One mile (1.5 km) SW of Dalmellington on the A713, take road signposted to Loch Doon Castle and continue to castle. **Parking** beside castle, but not in turning place.

① From castle go to gate nearby at foot of slope. ② Follow burn (stream) uphill and go through gate at top of field. Climb with plantation on right. ③ Turn corner and follow edge of plantation. ④ Leave plantation at its highest point and climb to summit. Continue along ridge and when convenient ⑤ descend to the col (pass) below Craiglee. Climb Craiglee to the trig. point. ⑥ Continue about 350 yards (320 m) along ridge. ⑦ Descend to left down prominent, grassy gully to head of burn (stream) and follow this to forest. ⑧ Follow forest edge to road. ⑨ Walk left along the road to the castle and point ①.

▉ Loch Doon Castle, built in the 13th C., was first called Castle Balliol. In 1290 the throne of Scotland was empty and Edward I of England chose John Balliol, an Anglo-Norman with lands in Scotland, to fill it as his vassal, favouring him rather than Robert Bruce. The castle, a Balliol stronghold, first stood on an islet in Loch Doon; it was moved and rebuilt when the level of the Loch was raised in the creating of the Galloway Hydro-Electric Scheme, Scotland's first large power scheme.

▣ Loch Doon, 5½ miles (9 km) long, a reservoir for the Hydro-Electric Scheme.

\†/ From Wee Hill the view N takes in 3 lines of hills: the Dungeon, Kells and Merrick.

\†/ Craiglee looks NW to the distant Island of Arran. Here Robert Bruce landed in 1306 on his way to begin the war to gain Scotland's freedom from England.

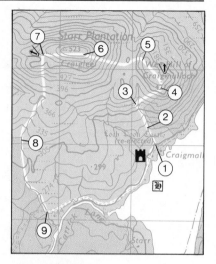

Rhinns of Kells
12 miles (19 km) Sheet 77 553863

Energetic Substantial, varied rambling in central Galloway, best in spring when the weather tends to be driest and insects fewest. *Farmland, woods, grassy slopes, boulder-strewn slopes, grassy ridges; 4 climbs; mud after rain. Do not attempt in poor visibility. For experienced hill walkers only. 1:25,000 map and compass recommended. Point* ⑦ *is difficult to leave in mist.*

Start Two miles (3 km) N of (St. John's Town of) Dalry on the A713, take road signposted to Forrest Lodge. **Car park** near end of road where it crosses burn (stream).

① Walk through gate beside car park into forest. Follow road past Burnhead. ② Keep straight on. Avoid right fork. ③ Follow firebreak out of forest. ④ Climb slope from edge of forest. ⑤ Follow crest of ridge and descend to lochans (small lakes) in col. ⑥ Climb ridge from lochans and follow crest to Corserine. ⑦ A difficult summit to leave in mist (wide and bare). Go right along top of scree cliffs until ridge narrows. ⑧ Avoid descent by Polmaddy Gairy by keeping right along ridge towards the forest and lochs. ⑨ Descend towards right bank of Loch Harrow, looking for guide poles above forest. ⑩ Descend between guide poles to firebreak which leads to forest road and start.

A golden eagle normally nests on a cliff, or in a tree. No other eagle soars on raised wings. Its size and obvious power set it apart from other comparable predators.

🏰 The Rhinns of Kells, rising to about 2,600 feet (792 m), form the SE side of Galloway Forest Park. They stand on the W of The Glenkens, the desolate country through which Mary Queen of Scots fled after the Battle of Langside in 1568 to Kenmure Castle.

⋎ Galloway Forest Park, 150,000 acres of forest, bog, loch, burn, moor and mountain, has much of the finest scenery in S Scotland and plentiful wildlife, including roe and red deer and wild goats. ('Galloway' comes from the Gaelic word *Gallwyddel* – 'stranger Gaels', the name given to the Celts who, until 1060, refused allegiance to the Scots crown.)

🦅 Among the Park's many birds is the golden eagle, the most magnificent of Britain's birds of prey, with legs fully 'trousered' by feathers and a wing span of 6-7 feet (1.8-2 m).

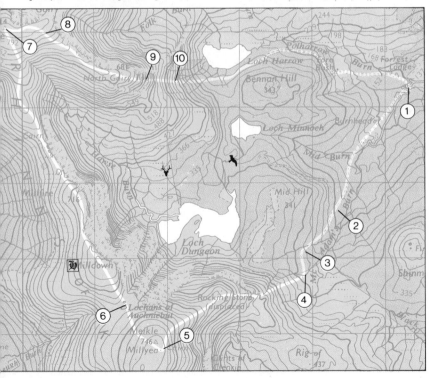

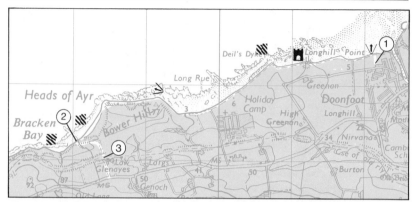

Heads of Ayr
3 miles (5 km) Sheet 70 322193

Easy A seaside walk near Ayr, with dramatic seascapes and views of the islands. *Sand dunes, rock 'platform', pebble beach, track; one climb; mud after rain.*

Start From roundabout at Doonfoot on the A719 2 miles (3 km) S of Ayr, take Earl's Way towards the sea; frequent buses between Dunure and Ayr. **Car park** on shore at foot of Earl's Way, frequent buses back to start.

① From car park follow shore line left to ②, where a path leading away from the shore starts just E of a small waterfall. Follow path. ③ Pass under old railway (site of bridge) and follow road past caravan site to A719. Buses back to start pass road end near Low Glenayes. Get off at Earl's Way roundabout to return to car.

🏰 Greenan Castle was one of the strongholds of the Kennedy family, who dominated the lands along the Firth of Clyde for some 30 miles (50 km) S of Ayr from the 12th to the 17th C. On 11th May, 1602, Sir Thomas Kennedy was murdered on the Sands of Ayr, and the bloody feuds between the Kennedys and other powerful families, in which he had taken a leading part, came to an end. The space for the Kennedy coat of arms is beside the first-floor doorway into the castle and not, as was customary, above the basement door, since this was on the N face of the cliff and very difficult to approach. There has been a castle on

Greenan Castle (Ayr beyond), a stronghold of the Kennedys and scene of predictably bloody clan warfare.

this site at least since the 15th C. The present building – now a ruin – is a mixture of dates: the first work on the tall, stern tower probably began in 1603.

🗾 Deil's Dyke, standing above shore level, may be followed seawards at low tide for several hundred yards.

\ʇ/ The view W takes in Greenan Castle, high on its cliff top, and in the distance the Island of Arran.

🗾 The Heads of Ayr are volcanic rock formations.

🗾 Bracken Bay, 25 feet (7.6 m) above shore level, an example of a raised beach.

Criffel
6 miles (9.5 km) Sheet 84 957655

Energetic Fascinating views over the Solway Firth, where the tide comes in at remarkable speed. *Farmland, heather hillside, woods; 2 climbs; mud. Do not attempt in poor visibility; 1:25,000 map and compass recommended. In June-Sept. the firebreaks from ⑤ to ⑨ are overgrown and extremely wet. It is advisable to divert back to ① by following the burn (stream) right. Visit the monument by climbing directly up firebreak from close to ①.*

Start From New Abbey take road W from The Square, past hotel to mill pond. Fork left past pond and continue to where road divides by Public Water Supply sign (ignore track leading right). **Parking** on left.

① From parking walk left over bridge. Pass left of shepherd's cottage and through small gate. In 15 yards (14 m) turn left on to well-defined track. Follow this, ignoring branches. It is generally well defined, becoming greasy. Go through gate by corner of plantation and *bear left* (skirting bracken if overgrown) alongside plantation, making for stone wall ahead. At wall turn right and follow it along ridge uphill. Over half-way to summit ② carry straight on where wall turns left along edge of forest. ③ From first summit (Knockendoch) follow path round ridge to summit of Criffel. Return from summit to col between the 2 summits. ④ Leave ridge and descend slope to valley to W, noting the firebreaks (gaps between trees on opposite hillside). The route eventually goes up the straightest of them, but now head for the foot of the one to its immediate left. ⑤ Cross burn at corner of forest by stepping stones if river not too high; otherwise a long stride is enough. To reach the correct firebreak (whose start is hidden by the trees to the right) begin ⑥ up the firebreak immediately in front. Go right when a clearing opens out on right and join correct firebreak. Continue up hill to summit of hill and ⑦ follow it down other side and as it bends right. Continue until it loses height in this new direction and ⑧ follow new firebreak which opens up to the left. Continue uphill to the monument. ⑨ From door of monument take the right of 2 firebreaks running downhill to ①.

🏠 Sweetheart Abbey was founded in 1273 by Devorguilla Balliol, mother of John Balliol, England's candidate for the Scottish throne. She was buried here with her husband's heart, which she had kept with her for 16 years. She also founded Balliol College, Oxford, which in 1966 set up a memorial stone to mark the original site of her tomb.

🏠 Kirk Kindar, is an ancient church built on a crannog: an Iron Age, man-made islet made of a pile of stones on a wooden base, reached by boat or causeway.

\!/ The views from Criffel, 1868 ft (569 m) high, reach to the Solway Firth, the Lake District and the Isle of Man.

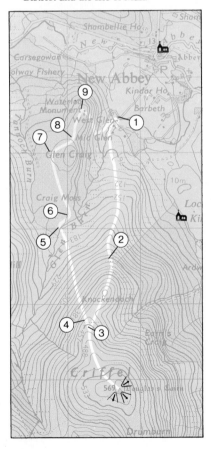

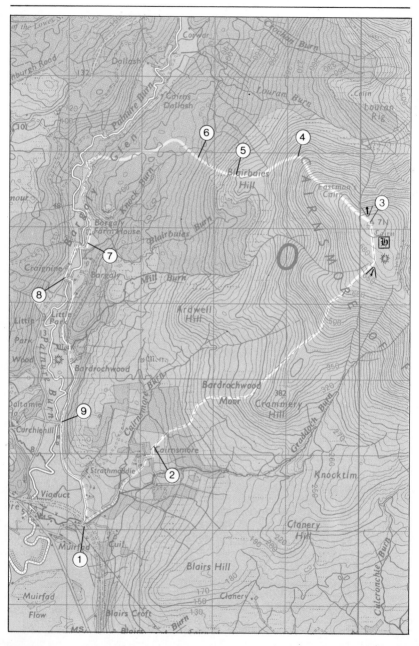

Cairnsmore of Fleet
10 miles (16 km) Sheet 83 462631

Energetic Some wild country within easy reach of the coast; remarkable variations of scenery: the walk climbs through several zones. *Woods, farmland, heather and grassy slopes, granite hillside, riverside; one long climb; mud. If inexperienced in hill walking, it is advisable not to attempt in poor visibility, certainly not to continue from ③ (the summit) if unsure of capabilities.*

Start About 2 miles (3 km) SE of Newton Stewart, leave A75 road 50 yards (46 m) S of bridge. Continue to remains of viaduct; buses stop on A75 near bridge. **Parking** on verge beside viaduct.

① Take track marked 'Cairnsmore Estate' in gap in viaduct. Later ignore private road leading left. Continue to white house. Follow track around it, then left (sign to car park). Enter field, and ② cross field diagonally to gate at field corner. Continue from here to summit, following well-defined path whole way (towards top, marked by cairns). ③ From summit descend to NW, staying on crest of ridge. ④ Once off steep ground, contour to Blairbuies Hill above the young plantation. ⑤ Descend to firebreak (gap in trees). ⑥ Join forest road to Bargaly Glen. ⑦ Cross bridge. ⑧ Re-cross river by bridge. ⑨ Keep straight on past bridge.

\t/ Views from Cairnsmore of Fleet take in the estuary of the River Cree, the sandy bays and beaches of the Solway Firth, and beyond the Firth, to the SE, England. To the N can be seen the Merrick, at 2,766 feet (843 m) the highest peak in S Scotland, and Murray's Monument. This is an obelisk in honour of Alexander Murray (1775-1813), a local shepherd boy who became Professor of Oriental Languages at Edinburgh University.

The cairn on the summit of the hill is a Stone or early Bronze Age building. Cairns – the oldest form of building to be found in Scotland – are piles of stones covering burial chambers, often with a number of side cells, reached by a long, low passage.

🔟 Cairnsmore of Fleet rises up out of the Cairn Edward Forest, which mainly consists of varieties of conifer. The hill itself has grassy slopes to the SW, and a steep, rocky face, strewn with granite boulders, to the N and E. On its summit is a cairn, an O.S. pillar and the ruins of a stone building. The pilot of a Tiger Moth is said to have landed his plane on the summit and safely taken off again. Wreckage from another plane, strewn about the summit and on the rocks to the N, is said by local people to be from a German Heinkel bomber which crashed in 1941. There is a recently erected memorial to 25 airmen killed in a number of crashes on the hill.

The motte of a feudal castle. The castles built in Scotland by the Normans in the 11th and 12th C. were at first an earth mound, supporting a 'imber tower and ringed by a ditch. The mound was the 'motte' or 'moat', the same word covering both the ditch and what had been piled up out of it.

There is all but endless scope for walking the great network of tracks and paths in the Galloway Forest Park. If overwhelmed by the choice, try the head of Loch Trool as a departure point.

The most famous walk in the area is the ascent of Merrick, highest peak in S Scotland. Start from the Bruce Stone, reached from the A714 by forking right at Bargrennan. Go past Glentrool Forest Village and then turn right to follow the edge of the Water of Trool, continuing to where the road ends at the Bruce Stone. From the Stone, cross the road and follow Buchan Burn's Falls to the house named Culsharg. From here climb the slopes to the top of Benyellary, then follow the easy ridge to Merrick's summit. Do not attempt in poor visibility; map and compass essential.

Waymarked (or fully described in leaflets) elsewhere in SW Scotland:

Two circular moorland walks of about 8 miles (13 km) starting from Whithorn Priory, 10 miles (16 km) S of Wigtown on the A746.

From Stinchar car park on the unclassified road from Straiton to Bentroot, 8 miles S of the B741, 2 imaginative walks of 4 and 6 miles in the Carrick Forest area.

SOUTH OF THE FORTH

Edinburgh's setting is as magnificent as the city itself. The Forth widens slowly but surely into a great estuary as it joins the North Sea. The coast offers ever-changing interest. There is the start of the Antonine Wall, the two great bridges, a variety of industry, fishing ports, sandy beaches and the port of Leith.

Inland there is just as much variety of scene. Immediately south of Edinburgh lie the city's own special hills, the rounded Pentlands, 16 miles (26 km) of elevated pastures intersected by wooded ravines. Further south are the equally appealing Moorfoots and the windswept Lammermuirs. None of these ranges are startling in height or rugged in character, but up here on the heights the walker can find a real sense of being away from it all.

Beneath, the lower land is as fertile and well-cultivated as any in Britain. It has been long settled and its place between Scotland's densely populated central belt and the border means that it is packed with history. Across it the drovers pushed their cattle on the way south from the great tryst at Falkirk to markets in England. Some of the old drove roads can still be traced, leading down to where the Cheviots rise to the border.

Tinto Hill
4½ miles (7 km) Sheet 72 964374

Moderate Arguably the grandest hill in the SW part of this section; its relative isolation means the views from the summit are truly extensive. The clear, cool air of winter and spring give the best visibility. *Hillside, moorland, streamside; one climb.*

Start From Lanark, follow the A73 SE towards Biggar and in 3 miles (5 km) cross Hyndford Bridge (traffic lights) and turn left. In 4 miles (6.5 km) turn right to Fallburn Farm (signposted); infrequent buses. **Car park** on left ¼ mile (0.5 km) after right turn.

① From the SW corner of the car park head towards the summit of Tinto Hill – a broad track is soon picked up. ② Follow the broad track E towards the lower summit of Scaut Hill. ③ Descend the N slopes of Scaut Hill (no path) to the valley of the Kirk Burn, then continue to Park Knowe. ④ From Park Knowe turn left after ½ mile (0.8 km) reaching the original track back to the car park.

🏔 The red felsite of Tinto seems to glow in sunlight, which may be why the lonely mountain is called 'hill of fire'.

🔆 Tinto's summit cairn is the remains of a Druid settlement.

\!/ The famous view from Tinto takes in 16 counties, from Bass Rock in the E to

The Pentlands, looking from Carnethy Hill towards Scald Law.

Goatfell on Arran in the W.

▶ The remains lower down the hillside (marked on the map as a tower) bore the curious name of Fatlips Castle, home of a local laird and reputedly haunted by a brownie.

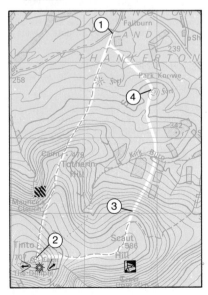

SOUTH OF THE FORTH

Bonaly and Flotterstone
7½ miles (12 km) Sheet 66 212675

Moderate An ideal introduction to the gentle Pentland Hills, and their lonely valleys: remoteness within 6 miles (9.5 km) of Edinburgh. *Woods, hillside, moorland; 2 climbs.*

Start From Edinburgh take the A70 to the Juniper Green crossroads and turn left. At Colinton post office turn sharp right, then second left (Bonaly Road); buses to Colinton post office, one mile (1.5 km) from ①. **Car park** at end of Bonaly Road.

① From car park follow track upwards through trees and on to open hillside. ② Cross stile and keep to track on right around the W side of Capelaw Hill. ③ The track becomes indistinct, but crosses gradually from the E to the W side of the valley. ④ On meeting road at gate, turn left and continue around the NE corner of Glencorse Reservoir. Follow the road down its E side to the pub at the main road. Turn left and continue. ⑤ Turn left off main road to Castlelaw Farm. ⑥ At Castlelaw Farm, turn right to Castlelaw Hill Fort (signposted). ⑦ Cross over to the E flanks of Capelaw Hill (no path), then keep around N flank of hill to regain the original track near Bonaly Reservoir. Do not stray N – a ravine bars the way back to the Bonaly track. It is not difficult or dangerous to negotiate, but may be tiresome.

🏠 Bonaly Tower, close to the route, was the home of the Scottish legal figure Henry, Lord Cockburn (died 1854).

\!/ Capelaw Hill looks N to the W parts of Edinburgh and across the Forth to Fife. All the coastline from the Forth Bridge to Leven can be seen – a stretch of about 25 miles (40 km) – with the hill ranges of the Ochils, the Cleish Hills, Benarty and the Lomonds behind.

\!/ The view up the Logan Valley is of the 5 hills of the Scald Law range: Turnhouse Hill, Carnethy Hill, Scald Law, and East and West Kip.

🚰 Glencorse Reservoir, capacity 368 million gallons (1,672 million litres), was constructed in 1822 by flooding the valley of the Logan Burn. The waters

cover the ancient church of St. Katherine in the Hopes (built in the 14th C.).

❋ Castlelaw Hill Fort or Soutterain was occupied in Roman times by a tribe called the Goddodin. Skilfully restored, the underground chamber is much as it must have been 2,000 years ago. (Key and information board at the farm at the bottom of the road.)

🍴 Flotterstone Inn and Restaurant perhaps took its name from the large, flat stone, once at the entrance, on which ladies alighted from their carriages. Full meals and bar snacks are available.

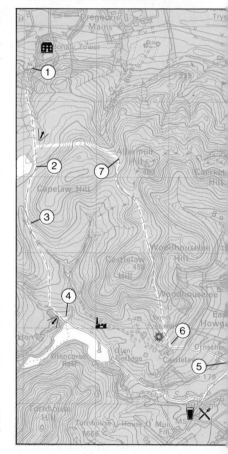

SOUTH OF THE FORTH

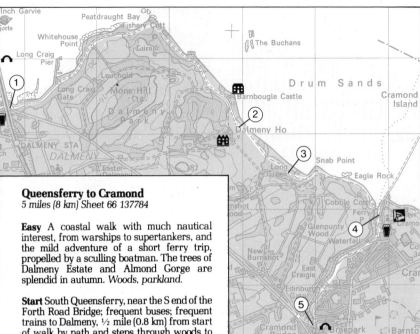

Queensferry to Cramond
5 miles (8 km) Sheet 66 137784

Easy A coastal walk with much nautical
interest, from warships to supertankers, and
the mild adventure of a short ferry trip,
propelled by a sculling boatman. The trees of
Dalmeny Estate and Almond Gorge are
splendid in autumn. *Woods, parkland.*

Start South Queensferry, near the S end of the
Forth Road Bridge; frequent buses; frequent
trains to Dalmeny, ½ mile (0.8 km) from start
of walk by path and steps through woods to
the N of the station. **Car park** on the sea front,
South Queensferry. **Return** to start by bus.

① Beneath for Forth Railway Bridge, bear
left, away from the main road, and keep to the
unsurfaced road along the shore. ② In front of
Dalmeny House, keep along the seaward edge
of the golf course. After passing the golf
course, keep to the right (landward) side of a
clump of trees on the water's edge, and
reaching stream, follow it inland about
100 yards (91 m) to reach a footbridge.
Continue on path through trees. ③ At Long
Green Cottages (on left), where path divides
into 3, keep straight ahead on the centre path
as it climbs through a tunnel of trees. ④ At
Cramond, keep to the road and path along the
E bank of the River Almond. ⑤ At the
landward end of the River Almond path, turn
right to cross the old Cramond Bridge behind
the Cramond Brig Hotel. The bus stop for the
return to South Queensferry is on the other
side of the main road, opposite the hotel
(½-hourly on weekdays, hourly on Sundays).

🍷 Hawes Inn, dating from 1683, was once
the ferry-boat inn. The ferry itself was
founded in the 12th C. by Queen
Margaret – hence the name 'Queensferry'.

⌒ Forth Railway Bridge, designed by Sir
John Fowler and begun in 1813, is 361 feet
(110 m) high.

🏰 Barnbougle Castle was the home of the
Rosebery family until the building, in the
🏰 early 19th C., of Dalmeny House. The
latter is open on summer weekends.

▧ Cramond – 'Caer-Almond' ('the fort on the
Almond') – was a Roman garrison town
and the foundations of the fort have been
excavated. There is a helpful display plan.

🍷 Cramond Inn was a haunt of Robert Louis
Stevenson, author of *Treasure Island*.

⌒ Cramond Bridge, known as Jock Howie-
son's Bridge, in tribute to a peasant who
rescued James V from attack by some
medieval muggers.

Traquair House, built by the 1st Earl of Traquair, and in its long history host to no

less than 27 monarchs. It is reputed to be the oldest inhabited house in Scotland.

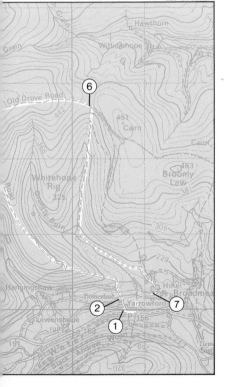

The Minchmoor

12½ miles (20 km) Sheet 73 407299

Energetic One of the best-loved and most outstanding of the Border drove roads: not only a cattle-driver's track, but a historic way, used by armies, highwaymen and monks alike. Offers the delight of walking on bright green, springy turf. *Hamlet, hillsides, moorland, woods, farmland; 2 climbs; mud.*

Start From Selkirk, cross the River Ettrick and turn left on to the A708. In 4 miles (6.5 km), at Yarrowford, look for Minchmoor Track signposted on right. **Parking** on roadsides at both ends of the walk. **Return** to. starting point possible by the infrequent Border Courier minibus service between Yarrowford and Traquair (details from Eastern-Scottish Bus Co.).

① The starting point is 100 yards (91 m) W of the telephone box in Yarrowford village. Follow the street N, past houses, to its end. ② Go past the right end of the garages, and continue uphill, through trees, on stony track. ③ Continue straight across wide forest road. ④ Again, continue straight across wide, forest road. ⑤ If making the return journey, look carefully for junction of paths. The path is wet and eroded here, and the old drove road running off to the left is not immediately apparent. If in doubt, continue downhill on Minchmoor Road, then strike steeply uphill to the left at small stone marking Wallace's Trench. Then turn right, on to drove road, at N end of the trench. In ½ mile (0.8 km) ⑥ descend track on right into the valley of the Gruntly Burn. ⑦ Bear right on road back to main road.

※ Wallace's Trench, close to the route, takes its name from Sir William Wallace, but may be part of the Catrail, a Pictish defensive earthwork.

\ȴ/ The view S is to the valley of the River Yarrow and the hills beyond.

🄱 At the Cheese Well, travellers used to leave cheese and other food to placate the local fairies and goblins.

🏠 Traquair House is, in part, 1,000 years old, but the main section, in the style of a French château, is 17th C. In the grounds are craft workshops and a brew house, with the excellent strong ale on sale.

SOUTH OF THE FORTH

Scald Law Ridge
12½ miles (20 km) Sheet 66 164636

Energetic Of the many fine walks in the Pentland Hills, this is the most dramatic, with its high, undulating section along the broad, grassy ridge connecting 5 hills. Best in early spring, when there is some snow on the hills: in cold conditions the air is clearer and the views longer. *Moorland, hill tops; 2 climbs.*

Start From Edinburgh take the A70 towards Lanark and turn left for Balerno. In ½ mile (0.8 km) turn left at Balerno for Marchbank Hotel. Just past hotel, turn left on to minor road; frequent buses from Edinburgh to Balerno stop a mile from ①. **Car park** on right ½ mile from turning at hotel.

① At top of avenue of trees, turn right, then first left, through a gate and on to the wide track which climbs across the moor. ② Leave track, striking left on the short, steep climb to summit of West Kip Hill (narrow, faint path). ③ In the dip between Scald Law and Carnethy Hill, cross over track and climb to summit of Carnethy Hill. ④ From Turnhouse Hill descend SE towards the long, narrow clump of trees, keeping them on left. Make for monument on SE edge. ⑤ Descend from monument to road running past Rullion Green Farm, then turn left on to A702. ⑥ From the pub/restaurant at Flotterstone, follow road past Glencorse Reservoir. ⑦ Just past the farmhouse (known as The Howe) the road becomes a footpath. Follow this through gap between Hare Hill and Black Hill. ⑧ At top of avenue, turn right and descend road back to car park.

🌸 Redmoss Nature Reserve – an area of raised bog.

\!/ From Scald Law the view stretches from the Broughton Heights and Tinto Hill 20 miles (32 km) to the SW, to Largo Law 35 miles (56 km) to the NE. Beyond the Ochils and Lomonds to the N the mountains of Perthshire and the Cairngorms are visible nearly 80 miles (128 km) away. Nearer, to the S, are the Moorfoot Hills and the rolling hills of Tweeddale. The 2 Forth Bridges can be seen 15 miles (24 km) to the N.

🔟 The Kirk Road, which crosses the route at right angles, is an ancient footpath,

dating from the days when the parish of Penicuik took in much of the surrounding hill country. The church – or Kirk – was in Penicuik on the S side of the hills, and parishioners from the N side crossed the Pentlands by this pass.

🗡 The Battle of Rullion Green was fought on the SE slopes of Turnhouse Hill on 28th November, 1666. About 900 Covenanters making their way home from a gathering in Edinburgh were attacked and overcome by troops under the command of General Tam Dalyell, whom Charles II had, at his restoration, recalled from service with the Czar of Russia. Many of the Covenanters were slaughtered on the spot, others were hunted into the Pentland bogs, or taken to Edinburgh to be publicly hanged. Among

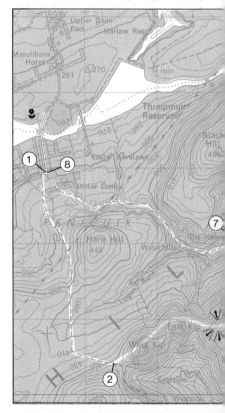

those killed were women and children, shot out of hand, against the General's orders. So ashamed was he about the outrage that he retired from the army and was never again seen in public.

Glencorse Reservoir is one of 16 in the Pentlands which supply Edinburgh.

St. Katherine's chapel, covered now by the waters of the reservoir, was built in the 14th C. by Sir William St. Clair, who was given an estate in the district by King Robert the Bruce, in settlement of a wager. The submerged building lies at the dog-leg of the reservoir. The forbear of another ancient local family, the Clerks of Penicuik, won a grant of land from Robert the Bruce by rescuing him from a hunting accident.

All of the 32-mile (51 km) Union Canal (Edinburgh-Falkirk) is pleasant, level walking; outstanding is the 9 miles (14.5 km) from Linlithgow to Falkirk.

The Eildon Hills give fine views over the Border countryside.

In Glentress Forest, 2 miles (3 km) E of Peebles, there are 4 waymarked walks starting from the Forest Office.

There is a waymarked nature trail along the cliffs W of Dunbar harbour.

The Water of Leith Walkway is a pleasant walk through Edinburgh city and suburbs.

Aberlady to North Berwick is a superb coastal walk. At the end, climb Berwick Law for grand views of the Forth Estuary.

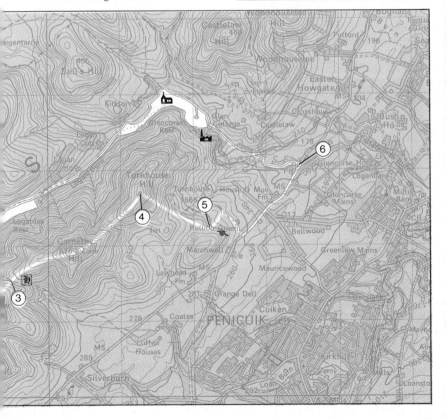

HIGHLANDS AND ISLANDS

Off the coast of Scotland are 610 islands and on those not unknown blue August days they dot a sea which looks more like the Aegean than the Atlantic. In this region, too, are Britain's only remnants of true wilderness, and its toughest mountains. There is, for instance, no easy way up the Cuillins of Sky. They are the preserve of experienced climbers. But any fit person can walk up Ben Nevis (at more than 6,400 feet (1951 m) Britain's highest mountain) by the bridle path from Achintee. Even so, it is a six- to eight-hour trek, not to be tackled in dirty weather or if ill-prepared. Alongside the lochs are days of comparatively gentle going.

One is generally free to wander at will on these moors and mountains, though it is a fallacy that there is no such thing as trespass in Scotland. Walkers are likely to be thrown off during the deer stalking season (roughly August to mid-October). Your main enemy, however, will be the dreaded Highland midge, which appears of a summer evening to torment human beings. There is no known defence.

The Lost Valley, Glencoe
2½ miles (4 km) Sheet 41 171568

Moderate, strenuous sections One of the easier short walks in Glencoe – the others being well-publicized nature trails. *Glen, gorge, valley; 2 climbs; mud after rain.*

Start The Pass of Glencoe, ½ mile (0.8 km) W of Allt-na-Reigh on the A82. **Parking** at the viewpoint in the Pass.

① From parking descend to the grassy, disused military road and continue about 250 yards (228 m) to where ② a path leads down to the river. Follow this to the bridge, cross, and continue on path leading up and into glen. ③ At large (bungalow-sized) boulder cross burn towards waterfall and continue along foot of rock face. ④ From the Lost Valley retrace steps. ⑤ Take path by trees towards burn (stream). Cross and walk downstream. Keep high to avoid wet sections. ⑥ Descend to join original path near mouth of gorge. Retrace to ①.

🐦 The pools below the car park are visited by black-throated divers. Alarmed, they submerge, heads only protruding.

🏠 Glen Coe itself – wild, brooding – explains much of the notoriety of the massacre of the MacDonalds here in 1692. Forty out of 150 adults were killed; more fled, to die of exposure.

The walk's lonely but rewarding goal – Coire Gabhail, or the Lost Valley.

\↑/ Into Coire Gabhail – the Lost Valley, where MacDonalds hid stolen cattle.

\↑/ Bidean nam Bian, highest in the glen.

⋰⋰ The gorge is a good example of hanging valley, created by a glacier.

🏠 Ossian's Cave, the 'home' of a 3rd C. bard: unlikely, as the floor is at 45°.

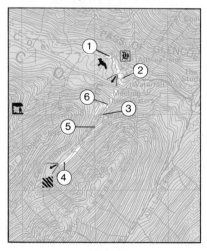

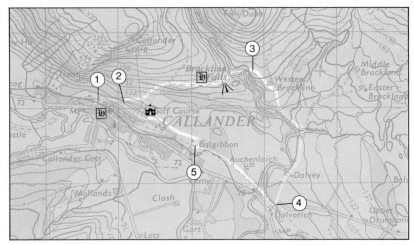

Bracklinn Falls
4 miles (6.5 km) Sheet 57 626081

Moderate Some typical, wild gorge scenery in the Trossachs; Callander is busy in the tourist season, but unspoilt. *Woods, upland pasture, gorge, golf course; one climb.*

Start Callander; buses. **Public car park** in Station Road behind the Dreadnought Hotel.

① With car park on left follow road over old railway bridge then ② take path on left beside wooden shelter. Continue round fence and uphill to main track which leads to road. Walk up to car park then follow signposted track to Bracklinn Falls. On the far side of the gorge the path follows the river for a few yards then leads up to an old stone dyke, where ③ go through the iron gate, over the rail then through the wooden gate towards the farm. By-pass the fence at the back of the farm, then follow the right-hand wall to drop to the gate at the road. ④ At the cutting which carried the old railway bridge climb the embankment to the old railway track and follow this to Balgibbon Cottage. ⑤ Take the path by the cottage; this leads to the golf course; turn left and the path finally emerges on a side road just before the club house. Cross into Ancaster Road which leads to ①.

🏠 Callander, pleasantly situated near the foot of Ben Ledi, overlooks a once-

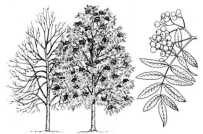

Rowan or mountain ash lines the gorge of Bracklinn Falls. Its bark is russet when wet, grey when dry.

important road junction. The scenery was immortalized by Sir Walter Scott in his epic poem, *Lady of the Lake*. The rounded mound by the Roman Camp Hotel is now known to be natural. The camp was at Kilmahog, 2 miles (3 km) W.

🏠 Rhoderick Dhu, in *The Lady of the Lake*, was 'brave but wild as Bracklinn's thundering wave'.

\†/ From Dumgoyne on the Campsie Fells to Stirling Castle.

🏠 Looking right, the second house was 'Arden House' in the TV series *Dr. Finlay's Casebook*. Callander was 'Tannochbrae'.

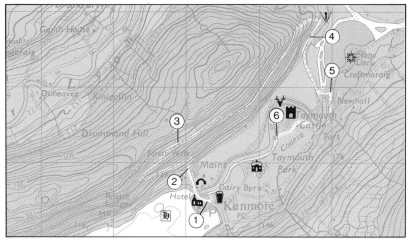

Kenmore

5 miles (8 km) Sheet 51 773455

Moderate An attractive village and varied walking country by one of Scotland's largest lochs, of which there is a famous view from the bridge. *Woods, riverside; one climb.*

Start Kenmore, on the A827 at the E end of Loch Tay. **Public car park** near the village square.

① From village square follow main road past church and over river. ② A few yards along the Tummell Bridge road turn left on to footpath which leads up to forest road. Turn left and continue on this, turning right at first junction, ½ mile (0.8 km) from gate. ③ At crossroads bear right to follow lower road for 2 miles (3 km), rejoining Tummell Bridge road. ④ Turn right then enter lane on left opposite cottage. Fork left to cross river by wooden bridge. ⑤ Turn right and follow old driveway which later joins main drive. Continue on this past Taymouth Castle. ⑥ From iron post keep to river bank path whole way to jetty. Take steps up to village.

The 3rd Earl of Breadalbane gave the town its church in 1760, and in 1774 built the bridge, which bears a double-edged tribute to George III. He donated £1,000 towards its cost, but the money came from the estates he won in the 1745 Jacobite uprising.

The nearby island in the loch is Eilean nan Bannoamh, 'the Isle of the Lady Saints'. Alexander I, King of Scotland, founded a priory on it after the death of his wife, Sybilla, daughter of Henry I, King of England. The nuns were allowed out once a year to visit Kenmore Fair.

Walk clear of the trees for a view NW up the Glen of Keltney Burn to the conical peak of Schiehallion.

Beyond the bridge on the left is Croftmoraig stone circle, whose origins and date are ancient, and uncertain.

Red deer come down to the river from Drummond Hill, especially in winter.

The enormous Taymouth Castle, now a boarding school, was built in the 19th C. to replace the 16th C. Castle of Balloch. From here the warlike Campbells of Glenorchy, later Earls of Breadalbane, ruled over one of the largest clan estates, with lands extending up to 100 miles (160 km).

The model dairy, Dairy Byre, is made of white quartz.

The Boar's Head; also the Kenmore Hotel, where Robert Burns pencilled a poem extolling the view from Kenmore Bridge on a chimneypiece.

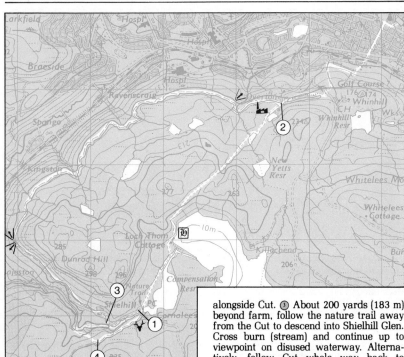

The Cut
8 miles (13 km) Sheet 63 247721

Moderate The popular Renfrewshire Hills and a historic waterway. *Lochside, moorland; one climb.*

Start Leave the A742 W of Greenock and follow signposts to car park; frequent trains to Greenock Central. At rear of station take Lyndoch Street under railway bridge and join path; follow disused mineral line to steps on right, then path uphill to road. Join Cut at right side of filter station. **Public car park** at Cornalees Bridge.

① From Information Centre by car park follow road by Loch Thom Cottage to Iverton. (Those starting walk from Greenock join route here and from Cornalees Bridge continue to Overton, then retrace to Greenock.) ② Turn left over bridge (with '1827-1927' fountain) to follow path alongside Cut. ③ About 200 yards (183 m) beyond farm, follow the nature trail away from the Cut to descend into Shielhill Glen. Cross burn (stream) and continue up to viewpoint on disused waterway. Alternatively, follow Cut whole way back to Cornalees Bridge.) ④ Turn left and follow path to Cornalees Bridge.

Cornalees Bridge marks a corner of the Clyde-Muirshiel Regional Park.

Loch Thom is named after Robert Thom, the engineer who built the Cut.

The Cut was built in 1827 to carry water 5½ miles (9 km) from the Loch Thom Reservoir to Greenock. Superseded by a tunnel in 1971, it is now protected by a conservation order.

Greenock, the Inverclyde town famed for ships and sugar, is also the birth-place of James Watt, improver of the steam engine. *The Comet*, Britain's first passenger steamboat, was built at nearby Port Glasgow in 1812. A replica is on show near Port Glasgow railway station.

Cowal Hills; NNW, Bute and Arran.

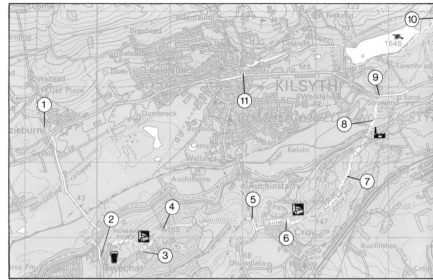

The Antonine Wall

4 or 8 miles (6.5 or 13 km) Sheet 64 693774

Moderate A few miles from Glasgow, this area of extensive Roman remains has a surprisingly remote atmosphere; may be bleak in winter. *Farmland, woods, rocky outcrops, canal, parkland; 2 climbs.*

Start Queenzieburn on the A803, 4 miles (6.5 km) NE of Kirkintilloch; frequent buses. **Parking** spaces on N side of A803. **Return** to starting point by bus from ⑨ or ⑪.

① From Queenzieburn follow side road towards Twechar. Cross canal bridge and continue to war memorial. ② Follow farm road left. ③ Just before drained water filter, enter field across stile and make for Bar Hill Fort. Take the path at the NE corner which leads to Castlehill. ④ Follow path alongside ditch to lane, then continue downhill to road. ⑤ Turn right, then left, then left again. Follow the lane by the lock-ups to rejoin ditch. ⑥ Follow the path uphill, then as it curves left alongside ditch by Croy Hill. ⑦ From uncut section continue to large boulders on higher ground, then follow edge of wood downhill and cross old mineral cutting. Descend by path through trees to Forth and Clyde Canal. Cross bridge, turn

right and follow bank for a few yards, then take path along far side of feed waterway. ⑧ Turn right in front of old stables; follow wall to stile. Cross and continue on path across disused railway, then follow stream to ⑨ the A803, where turn right, then first left along road and follow this as it curves right. ⑩ Just beyond cottage on left, take the path along the S bank of the reservoir. At far end turn right, then first left to follow feed canal whole way to Tak-ma-doon Road, Kilsyth. This leads to ⑪ the A803 – return to Queenzieburn by bus.

▉ The Quarry Inn; real ale.

▩ Bar Hill Fort, built by Agricola about A.D. 80 was one of the regularly placed strongholds on the Wall. Spanish, Balkan, even Syrian troops served here.

▨ The defensive ditch on the N Side was dug out despite the rock.

⌐ The Forth and Clyde Canal, completed in 1790, had a major role in industrializing central Scotland.

☞ Under the water is the site of the Battle of Kilsyth, 1645. Remains of an armed, mounted trooper were found in the bog.

HIGHLANDS AND ISLANDS

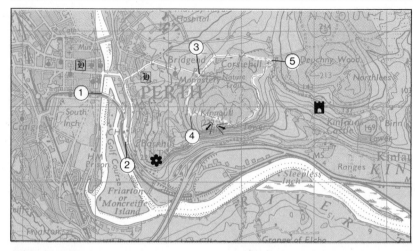

Kinnoull Hill
4½ miles (7 km) Sheet 58 120231

Moderate A country walk in the Tayside area only a few minutes from Perth City centre. Crosses the Tay by a narrow catwalk beside the railway. *Town, woods, cliff top; one climb.*

Start Perth; frequent buses and trains.
Public car park at riverside across road from Tourist Information Centre.

① Walk under railway bridge and climb steps to footpath alongside railway line. ② A lane on the opposite bank joins Dundee Road, where turn right if visiting Branklyn Gardens (signposted); to continue, turn left and just before the hotel take Manse Road, which leads up to Hatton Road; follow this. ③ Where Hatton Road veers left, take the path on the right by the signpost. ④ At the first viewpoint, leave the path for a smaller one on the left. Follow this as it climbs to Kinnoull Hill and the view indicator. Follow the path along the cliff, down to a gate, then as it climbs gently to the tower or folly. Continue through the wood. Ignore the path to the left and continue on track as it winds round a glen overlooking Kinfauns Castle. ⑤ At Jubilee Car Park, the track curves back into the wood. Fork right at the T-junction, descend to a wicket gate, then join the road. Continue straight ahead, forking left, then going down Hatton and Manse Roads to

Dundee Road. Turn right then left over Queen's Bridge for ①.

🏦 The district where Perth now stands was known to the Romans, and later, in 846, the first joint capital of Picts and Scots under Kenneth MacAlpine was established at nearby Scone. Perth dates from the foundation in 1210 of the royal borough by William the Lion, King of Scotland from 1165 to 1214.

    Sir Walter Scott's novel *The Fair Maid of Perth* is set partly in the house of his heroine's father, on the site of the present 'Fair Maid's House', off Charlotte Street at the N end of the town.

✿ Branklyn Gardens contains a fine collection of plants, notably alpines. The garden is open from 10.00 am to dusk, March-Sept., and at other times by appointment.

⚔ Kinfauns Castle was the seat of the Earls of Moray. James Stuart, Earl of Moray, the illegitimate son of James V, became Regent of Scotland when Mary Queen of Scots, his half-sister, abdicated.

🏰 Fine views over Perth, S across the Lomond Hills and E of the Tay winding towards the sea.

Worth the climb: the view from Kinnoull Hill is superb, and it opens out suddenly.

HIGHLANDS AND ISLANDS

Above Whiting Bay
4½ miles (7 km) Sheet 69 045262

Moderate The Island of Arran has been described as Scotland in miniature; this route, with its delightful variety, covers Arran in miniature. *Shore, glen, forest, hillside, farmland; one climb.*

Start On the A841 8 miles (13 km) S of Brodick; buses. **Public car park** at centre of Whiting Bay village.

① With car park on right take shore road through village. ② Just beyond bowling green, follow road uphill, ignoring side roads, past the houses of South Kiscadale. ③ Go through gate to join track winding up Glenashdale to join another forest track. ④ Turn right taking the track leading towards Lambash to large, cleared area with viewpoint overlooking Holy Island. ⑤ From

viewpoint retrace steps a few yards to signposted path descending through forest to join narrow road, where ⑥ turn right, then take first left before the farm to join a rough track leading down to a narrow road. ⑦ At road turn right for ①.

\↑/ Over an Iron Age fort to Glenashdale Falls, the island's largest with a vertical drop of 148 feet (45 m).

\↑/ Holy Island is associated with St. Molaise, a follower of St. Columba, supposed to have lived there after the discovery of ancient Runic inscriptions in the 'Saint's Cave'. Also to Goat Fell, towering above Brodick. This granite outcrop was once the molten margin of a now sunken volcano.

⬛ Arran Gallery, selling local handiwork, is housed in a former church.

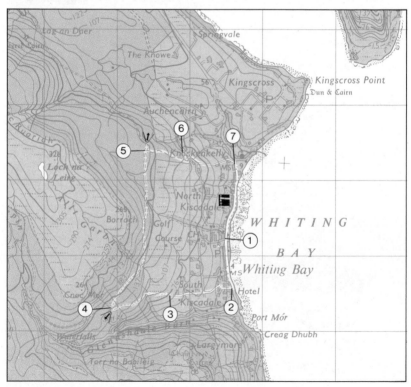

Mull's Grass Point
5½ miles (9 km) Sheet 49 728332

Moderate Dramatic island scenery and varied points of interest easily reached from Mull's principal ferry port. The flowers are best in spring and early summer. *Rough pasture, estuary, cliff tops, woods; boggy between* ⑤ *and* ⑧.

Start From Craignure take the Iona road S for 5 miles (8 km) and stop at head of loch Don estuary by telephone box; infrequent daily buses from Craignure stop at Loch Don. **Parking** on old road by telephone box.

① Facing S (as if walking from Craignure) turn left off 'main' road opposite telephone box on to track passing in front of houses. Continue on track to cross bridge in distance. ② Follow metalled track for ¾ mile (one km) past Ardnadrochir Farm. ③ About ¼ mile

(0.5 km) past Ardnadrochir Farm turn left at gate in deer fence to follow path downhill through bracken. ④ Emerging from trees at sea inlet, walk to shore and follow its line to the right, making for cottages at Grass Point. ⑤ Where the track runs right, away from shore, strike off left along faint path to top of grassy outcrop seen from road. ⑥ At top of knoll cross fence to take in view of Sound of Mull. Return over fence and keeping fence on left follow it downhill to ⑦ where fence ends, dipping steeply into dell. Skirt the dell, crossing the deer fence. A broad shelf now opens up: follow this above cliffs into bay. ⑧ Take care finding path out of bay: face inland, and look for where crags on right end and trees begin. There is a path here which should be followed up the bank, out of the bay and a few yards to meet track. Turn right on to track and follow it to Auchnacraig Farm. ⑨ Continue through farm to rejoin metalled track. Turn left and follow it to ①.

🏠 From Craignure, reached by car ferry from Oban, there is a pleasant drive through the valley of Glen More to Grass Point. The stretch of road between Lochdonhead and Grass Point is in part the oldest road on Mull: it was first an early pilgrim road and later, when Grass Point was the port for shipping cattle to the mainland, a drovers' road. Mull has good-quality grazing for cattle, and could be fertile enough to support many of them, as it did, until the introduction of sheep farming in the last century. This impoverished the land, and the rough-grass burning drove out 85% of the population.
Glen More formed the boundary between the Kingdoms of the Picts and the Scots.

🏠 Grass Point has a cottage museum and craft centre.

✕ Tea and biscuits available at Grass Point.

⚡ There are wild goats in the area, and the occasional sea-eagle. Also called the 🦅 white-tailed eagle or erne, the bird looks enormous in flight, moving with an exceptionally slow wing beat. It hunts on the wing, and will sit still for hours, watching for fish to snatch.

✳ The site of a prehistoric burial ground.

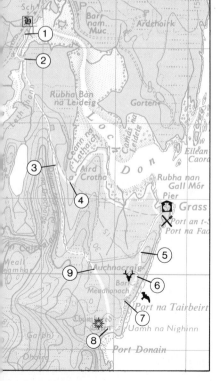

HIGHLANDS AND ISLANDS

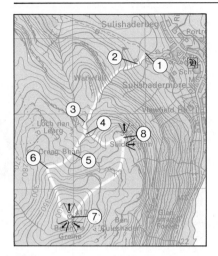

Portree is the capital of Skye and its finest harbour. The name is a version of Port Righ–'King's Harbour'–the name given it when James V of Scotland landed there. The inn where Flora MacDonald said farewell to Prince Charles Edward Stuart–'Bonnie Prince Charlie'–is now part of the Royal Hotel.

☀ Panoramic views from Beinn na Greine–'Hill of the sun'; but remember that Skye is known as the Misty Isle, and its evocative Norse name, *Skuyö*, meant Isle of Cloud.

☀ There are wide views N and E over Portree and the sea from Fingal's Seat. ('Fingal' comes from Fionn na Ghal, meaning Chief of Valour, the title given to the Celtic warrior Fionn MacCoul, who died heroically in battle against the Norsemen in 283.)

Beinn na Greine and Fingal's Seat
4½ miles (7 km) Sheet 23 472438

Moderate Superb panoramas within easy reach of Portree. *Moorland, peat; one climb; boggy; well landmarked, but do not attempt in poor visibility–the views are the point of the walk.*

Start Leave Portree by the A850, turn on to the B885 (signposted Struan). Continue steeply uphill about 550 yards (503 m) to a cattle grid; less than half an hour's walk from centre of Portree. **Parking** on track to left of cattle grid.

① Head for bothy (hut) on hillside to right of stream. ② Pick up path 10 yards (9 m) to left of bothy, and follow it about ¾ mile (one km) keeping to right bank of stream. ③ Just below meeting of the streams, the path leads off to the right. Leave it and continue along streamside to meeting of streams. ④ Follow the right-hand stream uphill. ⑤ When the stream finally disappears into the ground, head for the skyline in front, aiming for the left end of the line of peat hags–exposed outcrops of peat which encircle the hill. ⑥ At the saddle turn left and make for the summit of Beinn na Greine. ⑦ Return to Portree by following the hill's N spur (i.e., not the one used for the ascent) to Suidh Fhinn–Fingal's Seat–from where ⑧ turn away from the sea and descend hillside to rejoin stream and follow it downhill to ①.

The Falls of Glen Brittle Forest
6 or 8 miles (9.5 or 13 km) Sheet 32 384271

Easy Spectacular waterfalls; a useful alternative to the Cuillin Hills when the weather is bad. The extension opens up superb views of these hills. Waterfalls best after rain; much of the route is sheltered –suitable for winter, even a rainy day. Occasional views of Loch Eynort. *Forest, moorland.*

Start From Dunvegan turn on to the B8009 at Drynoch; continue to Carbost and follow signs to Glen Eynort. **Parking** by telephone box near bridge.

① From parking walk back along road and turn right at T-junction, crossing stream by bridge. Continue over cattle grid. ② Turn left off road on to track up hill. ③ Where track crosses stream, follow stream uphill a few yards to see waterfall. Retrace to track and continue. ④ At T-junction, turn right and follow around loch side. ⑤ At T-junction, turn right over stream. ⑥ At bridge over stream, turn right off track for view over edge of waterfall–but keep clear of the cliff edge. ⑦ At T-junction either follow track left up Bealach Brittle shoulder to view the Cuillins; or, go right, following track downhill to follow edge of Loch Eynort. It is about 2 miles (3 km) to ⑧ Forestry Commission buildings, through which follow the track to ①.

♣ It is worth coming here for the foxgloves alone in July-August.

\t/ The Cuillins: these peaks take their name from the Old Norse *Kjöllen*, meaning 'keel-shaped ridges'. They are notoriously dangerous, precipitous and subject to some of British Isles' most changeable weather. The pale brown crystalline rock is magnetic, making compass readings unreliable. But for all its starkness and danger, it has what seems an almost magical power to reflect sky colour, from black and purple to blue, grey and fiery red.

🏛 Glen Brittle, broad and fertile, is flat enough in parts to have been used as an airstrip before World War II.

🏠 A village of well-designed houses for Forestry Commission employees.

A 3-mile (5 km) walk through the wild Nevis gorge starts at the car park where the road ends 6 miles (9.5 km) inside Glen Nevis. Access via the signposted turn-off from the A82 N of Fort William town centre.

From the lay-by on the B829 near Ledard Farm, take the path from the farm through the wood, then uphill. The remains of an iron fence at the base of the SE peak can be followed to the top of Ben Venue.

Opposite the Rowardennan Hotel on the West Highland Way NW of Balmaha there is a path easily followed to the summit of Ben Lomond.

From Lochearnhead, try walking the former Oban railway line above Glen Ogle, returning by the drove road through the glen alongside river.

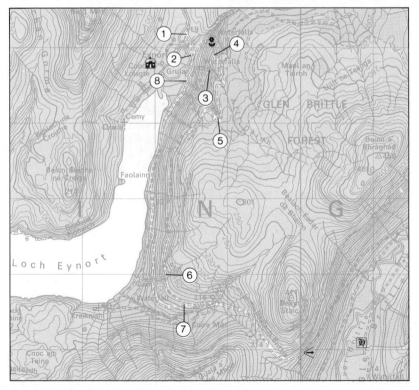

FIFE REGION

Cut off by the sea to the east, the Firths of Tay and Forth to the north and south and by the Ochils to the west, the so-called Kingdom of Fife was essentially self-contained until the coming of modern transport. Walkers looking for dramatic scenery will be disappointed, but this is countryside in which to saunter and enjoy the lingering atmosphere of hundreds of years of Scottish life.

The towns and villages are exceptionally well-endowed with native architecture, especially so the burghs and fishing villages of the East Neuk ('East End'), though only Pittenweem still has a working fleet. They are set in rich farmland, which rolls gently, with a pleasant scatter of woods, except by coast.

The interior of the peninsula does not have much off-road walking, but there is more than adequate upland tramping (and vistas to match) on the three main hill ranges – the Lomonds, the Cleish Hills and the Ochils. The last are the chief of the three, a free-standing group which marks the limit of lowland Scotland. West and north is essentially highland territory. From the Ochils' highest point, Ben Cleuch, they say one can see 21 (old) Scottish counties on a clear day.

The Cleish Hills
4 miles (6.5 km) Sheet 58 100955

Moderate Hills which tend to be ignored because of their closeness to large towns: consequently they offer unspoilt, pleasant walking. Best in summer: the hollows between the hills are excellent for picnicking. *Loch-side, hills, moorland; 2 climbs; mud.*

Start From the B914 take the unclassified road N towards Loch Glow. In 1¾ miles (3 km) stop by gate on left, near highest point of road; buses to Gask, 1¾ miles S of point ①. **Parking** on roadside (anglers' car park at loch is private).

① At junction in Land-Rover track bear right towards Loch Glow and the hills. ② A quarter of a mile after crossing small dam on Loch Glow, leave track and climb to top of small hill on right. Keep going N over the hummocky terrain to reach the rocky top of Dummiefarline. ③ From Dumglow head back towards W end of Loch Glow. There is no track until the loch-side is reached, and it improves along the S shore.

⩔ Deer are seen S of the loch.

⩗ The lands round Loch Glow shelter many birds, including grouse, lapwings, owls and herons. Bewick's swans are winter visitors to the loch itself, while among its most common residents are coot, mallard

Benarty near Loch Leven – not Fife's wildest walking, but grand and remote nonetheless.

and eider.

⩔ From Dummiefarline the view E and NE is to Loch Leven and the Lomond Hills; to the S it takes in the Pentland Hills and the S side of the Firth of Forth, as far as the Bass Rock, nearly 40 miles (64 km) away at the entrance to the Forth.

Dumglow, 'the fort of the tumult', was the main Pictish hill fort in the area. From its summit the view W stretches, on a clear day, to Ben Lomond and the 'Arrochar Alps' in Argyll, 50 miles (80 km) distant.

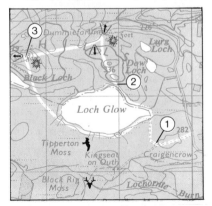

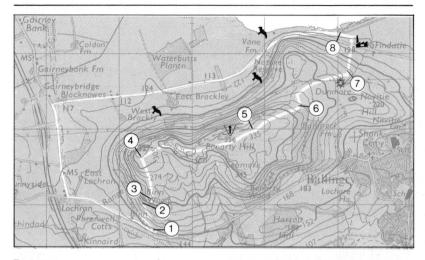

Benarty
7 miles (11 km) Sheet 58 144967

Moderate Shows the 2 faces of Fife: to the S, the grimy former mining towns; to the N, the waters of Loch Leven, the clean lines of the Lomond Hills and the farming land around Kinross. Best in autumn for colour – purple (heather), orange (dead bracken) and greens; or in early winter for the thousands of migrating duck and geese. *Woods, hillside and ridge, pasture; 3 climbs.*

Start From the B996 S of M90 junction 5, turn on to the unclassified road towards Ballingry. Stop in ¾ mile (one km); buses to Lochran Farm, 1½ miles (2.5 km) N of Kelty. **Parking** on road, and at start of forest road.

① From road double back up wide, forest track. In 100 yards (91 m), track divides, and a noticeboard warns of firing on range below. (A barrier is drawn across if firing is in progress.) Follow the main track as it zigzags uphill. ② The forest road ends in a clearing. On the right (E) side, the embankment is worn by walkers' boots. Clamber up here and pick up path through bracken to wall. ③ Cross wall, turn left, and follow wall along side of forest. At end of forest, keep straight ahead towards 2 posts on hilltop. ④ On summit of first hill, turn right (E) and follow dry-stone wall. Beware of straying too far N of wall – the hillside ends in sheer crags. Make for Benarty

summit, marked by a white trig. point pillar. ⑤ Keep to right (S) side of wall. ⑥ Follow wall to where it ends, then continue 300 yards (274 m) until almost reaching the forest. *Do not* descend at end of wall as the crags are dangerous. When almost at forest, descend to left down steep, grassy slope and head towards electricity pylon ahead. On reaching wall in front of pylon, turn right and follow wall. ⑦ At end of wall turn left and follow fence down to main road at Findatie car park and picnic site. ⑧ At W end of car park go through gate giving access to loch-side. Follow path until it regains road, then continue W along road.

\↑/ The Cairngorms, 50 miles (80 km) away.

※ Dunmore, 'the big fort', is one of the Pictish hill forts in the area.

⌂ The buildings below Loch Leven car park house the sluices, installed in 1826, which control the loch's water level.

🦆 Loch Leven is one of Britain's major wildlife centres. Wintering wildfowl include the whooper swan, pinkfooted and greylag geese, teal, wigeon, pochard, goldeneye and shelduck.

🦆 Vane Farm Nature Centre has static displays, a shop, an observation gallery (with binoculars) overlooking the loch and a nature trail.

Forth Bridges and Ferry Hills
4 miles (6.5 km) Sheet 65 129828

Easy For industrial surroundings, a surprisingly rural walk; magnificent views for little effort, sudden panoramas and impressions of immense space. *Town, hilltop, village, coastal path, industrial area; 2 climbs; mud; may be overgrown between* ① *and* ②.

Start From M90, junction 1, follow A92 (signposted Kirkcaldy). In ½ mile (0.8 km) turn right on to road leading to Inverkeithing square; frequent buses (stopping in square); frequent trains – station close to ①. **Parking** in Inverkeithing town square.

① At S end of lay-by on dual carriageway (A90), 35 yards (32 m) past R.A.C. box, turn sharp left and follow track uphill to top of road cutting. ② Cross open hilltop to meet tarmac path. ③ Turn right on to path and follow high fence to top of steps. Descend steps to bridge level, then continue downwards to road. ④ At road turn left and walk into North Queensferry. ⑤ In village, a steep road joins from left. At the bottom of this, and on opposite side, follow track as it climbs under the N approach viaduct of the Forth Railway Bridge. ⑥ Road alongside ship-breaking yard joins minor road. Continue on minor road until reaching railway bridge. Turn right at road, pass under small railway bridge, then turn right at road back to Inverkeithing.

🏭 Rosyth Naval Dockyard, one of whose roles is to refit, refuel and re-arm nuclear submarines.

⌒ Forth Road Bridge, the third longest suspension bridge in Europe. Walking its footpath is a worthwhile experience.

🌻 At least 40 species of wild flower are identifiable on the Ferry Hills.

🏭 Whinstone Quarry produces stone for road bottoming and other building work.

\↓/ W and E, right across Scotland.

⌒ Forth Railway Bridge (always being painted) is the largest bridge of its type.

🏭 Much of the North Sea's oil is shipped from Hound Point Oil Terminal.

The Forth Railway Bridge, built for the North British Railway Co.; opened in 1890.

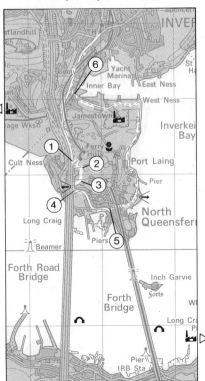

East Fife Coast

13½ miles (22 km) Sheet 59 613077

Energetic A taste of Fife's unspoilt coastline, well away from the tourist routes, with a picturesque fishing village and the town of St. Andrews, its golf courses and university. Best in summer for bathing, birdlife and delving into rock pools. *Cliffs, rocky shore, sandy beaches, dunes.*

Start Crail, on the A918 SE of St. Andrews: frequent buses. **Parking** in Crail. **Return** to starting point by bus from City Road bus station, St. Andrews, at 25 minutes past the hour; journey time to Crail, ½ hour.

Waymarked by posts with white tops; but some are missing, and some are not easy to spot. In general, keep to the seaward side of obstacles, or if in doubt about the path, near the shore. ① From Crail's main street, go down Shoregate to the harbour (signposted). ② Retrace from harbour to bend in road. At bend keep straight on up steps to Castle Terrace (sea-front walkway with viewpoint and indicator). ③ At E end of walkway, descend over grass to tarmac shore path and follow it E through caravan site. ④ Where fence crosses path, keep to seaward side of compound. ⑤ After coastguard station and lighthouse, keep to seaward side of golf course, following red posts. ⑥ At Cambo Sands car park, follow the road inland to Kingsbarns. (This diversion is necessary because it is impossible to cross the river up to ¾ mile (one km) W of Babbet Ness.) ⑦ Turn off road and go through village of Boarhills. ⑧ Just past the post office (on right), turn sharp right and follow farm roads back to shore. ⑨ Route climbs steeply to top of cliffs to avoid ravine. ⑩ At The Rock and Spindle go up steps to left. ⑪ Cross footbridge at harbour, then turn right. Go round seaward end of buildings, then turn right on path towards tall, square tower. ⑫ Follow railed path past castle on right, then along street for ¾ mile (one km) to golf clubhouse with flagpole. ⑬ Turn left towards road. Cross road and take first left (signposted Kirkcaldy). Bus station is at junction of first street on right. Buses for Crail (Dundee and Leven service) leave 25 minutes past the hour.

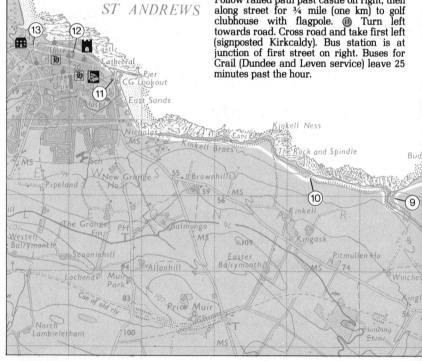

🏛 Crail Harbour, one of the loveliest old harbours in Scotland.

\↑/ To the SW is May Island, one of whose uses is as a tracking station for birds.

✳ Dane's Dyke was built over 1,000 years ago as a defence against Danish raiders.

\↑/ On Fife Ness there is an ultra-modern lighthouse and offshore, one mile (1.5 km) to the NE, is the beacon which replaced the lightship driven off station by a storm in the 1970s.

🍺 The Cambo Arms, tiny and friendly.

🪨 Buddo Rock is sandstone, hence the weird shapes carved by the elements.

🖼 The beautiful ruins of St. Andrews Cathedral, founded in 1160, long the religious capital of Scotland.

🏛 St. Regulus's Tower was built in the cathedral grounds more than 800 years ago to house relics of St. Andrew brought to Scotland by St. Regulus.

🏰 St. Andrews Castle, started in about 1200, and famous for its bottle-shaped dungeon.

🏛 St. Andrews University, founded 1411, the oldest in Scotland.

🏢 The Royal and Ancient Clubhouse, mecca of the golfing world.

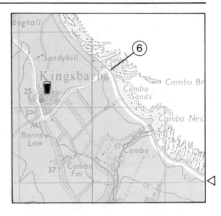

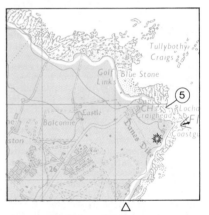

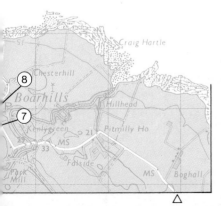

Dollar Glen and Ben Cleuch
11 miles (17.5 km) Sheet 58 963979

Energetic Uses the popular, and striking, Dollar and Tillicoultry Glens as access to more remote country. At best in spring – waterfalls at their most dramatic, clearer air giving longer views. *Wooded gorge, valley, hillside, ridge, town, disused railway, riverside; 3 climbs; mud. Advisable not to attempt in poor visibility.*

Start Dollar, on the A91; infrequent buses.
Car parks at top and bottom of road to Castle Campbell (signposted), or street-parking in Dollar.

① At top of Castle Campbell road go through gate marked 'Castle Campbell' and follow stream through picnic area. ② After entering woods, look for low building with blue door beside the stream. Take the upward path on right before reaching this building. ③ Path descends (look for chain handrail set into rock on right) to stream, then divides. Double back down and cross long, wooden footbridge which passes through gap in cliffs. ④ After climbing out of gorge, follow path across Burn of Sorrow by footbridge. Bear uphill towards Castle Campbell (on right). ⑤ Retrace from Castle Campbell to point where path at ④ joins the road in front of castle. Turn left off road and climb NW. Shortly join track which leads through upper part of gorge and into the open valley behind King's Seat Hill. ⑥ At head of valley, where streams meet, climb the grassy spur between the streams. From the top, look ahead (W) to a pointed hill and make across trackless moorland to the summit. (This is Andrew Gannel Hill, not named on the 1:50,000 map.) ⑦ From summit follow the fence towards the radio beacon (no path). ⑧ Pass radio beacon and continue along line of fence to the flattish summit of Ben Cleuch (indistinct path). Retrace from Ben Cleuch to radio beacon, bear right and ⑨ follow fence over summit of The Law. Pick up downhill path on S side of summit. ⑩ Cross the Daiglen Burn near where it joins the Gannel Burn, and pick up path running downhill through Tillicoultry Glen. There are a number of paths in the gorge, all eventually leading down to the town. ⑪ On A908 look for railway line crossing road, just before reaching the large, white, furniture warehouse. Turn left and follow the railway walkway E to Dollar. ⑫

Where B913 crosses old railway at Dollar, climb embankment to road – easiest ascent is on E side of bridge.

▦ Dollar Academy, a private school, was given to the town by John McNab (died 1802), a poor local boy who went to London and prospered in shipping.

〴 Kemp's Score, a high, narrow fissure where a long footbridge passes through the cliffs to a spectacular waterfall.

▮ Castle Campbell, once the seat of the Earls of Argyll.

〵 From Ben Cleuch, the highest peak in the Ochils, the view SW takes in the Wallace Monument and Stirling Castle. The winding River Forth is plainly visible, and so are the Pentland Hills to the SE.

Cairngorm peaks, to the N, are seen in good weather.

🚣 This wooden dam is a reminder that towns such as Tillicoultry were once thriving textile centres. Dams controlled the flow of water from the hills to provide constant power for driving machinery, washing cloth and so on.

🍺 The Woolpack is a free house, serving a range of beers, including the excellent local brew, McLay's.

✕ There are 2 tea rooms in Dollar's main street, one each side.

🚣 Devon Valley Railway, opened in 1871 and axed by Beeching in the 1960s, linked Alloa and Kinross. Now it is used by walkers and riders.

The Lomond Hills' moorland and tracks offer much improvised walking. E and W Lomond are Fife's highest points. Access from car parks at 228062 or 252058.

An easy hill climb, with views right across Scotland, is Saline Hill. Start from Saline on the B913.

Tulliallan Forest has a variety of easy walks on forest roads.

Aberdour to Burntisland is a short walk around Hawkcraig Point, then along coastal path beside the railway.

Kincraig Point has a dramatic walk on 200-foot (61 m) cliffs, returning by chain walk along the cliff face.

A popular track runs through the Ochil Hills from Dollar via Dollar Glen and Glenquey to Glendevon.

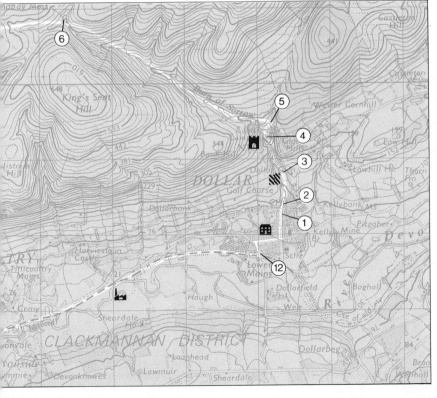

DEESIDE AND CAIRNGORM REGIONS

As spectacular and dangerous as any mountains in Britain, the Cairngorms, with their sub-Arctic climate, can and do kill the inexperienced and ill-equipped.

Here, the granite forms great humps rather than peaks – some mountaineers find them disappointing – and there is endless loose scree. But between the great bulges run the 'mounths', the old public paths linking the settlements. Longest of these is the Lairig an Lui (Abernethy to Braemar, 37 miles [60 km]). Its name means calves' pass, and it was once used for cattle-droving. Other trails spread out from Loch Morlich and Glen More. With the climate go flora and fauna as near Britain can offer to the Alpine.

Despite the sprawling pressures of holiday and ski complexes around Aviemore, escape to near-wilderness, especially on foot, is easy. Above Glen More, for instance, lies Rothiemurchus Forest, a remnant of the primeval Scots pine forest once part of the Great Wood of Caledon.

The Cairngorm massif is the source of three main river systems: the Avon, the Spey and the 'snow-fed Dee'. The last starts in wild grandeur, descends in majesty, but never quite forgets its birth, for high ground hugs it almost to the sea at Aberdeen – providing marvellous, accessible walking for that city's inhabitants.

Bruar Falls
2 miles (3 km) Sheet 43 823661

Easy A short walk passing spectacular waterfalls, ideal as respite from the A9. *Woods, riverside; one climb.*

Start On the A9 between Perth and Inverness 5 miles (8 km) W of Blair Atholl; frequent buses. **Car park** signposted on A9.

① Walk the few yards W across the bridge and turn right up the path between the bridge and the adjoining hotel. ② In 300 yards (274 m), at junction, take the right branch. In a few yards go through tunnel under railway line, then over stile at fence, immediately taking the left-hand path. ③ In about 600 yards (549 m) note the point where the river bends right (gap in trees for spectacular view) and 100 yards (91 m) above this ④ take the left branch to the upper bridge, passing through rhododendrons and pine trees. ⑤ Follow path across stone bridge just above the Bruar Falls; at other side turn left up slope. Follow path as it turns right. ⑥ Follow path downhill to where forestry road joins from left. Ignore the road, go through gate and continue downhill with care – exposed tree roots and slabs of stone. ⑦ At the lower bridge re-cross the Bruar Water and descend by outward route to car park.

⌂ The Clan Museum tells the story of the local landowning families – Robertsons,

The best views of the main falls come between points ⑤ and ⑥.

Duncans, MacConnachies and others.

🏛 The banks of the Bruar Falls were first planted with firs in the late 18th C. by the 4th Duke of Atholl, in response to Robert Burns's poem, 'Humble Petition of Bruar Water'.

🏰 Five miles (8 km) to the E on the A9, is Blair Atholl Castle.

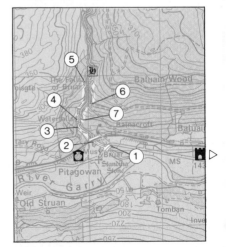

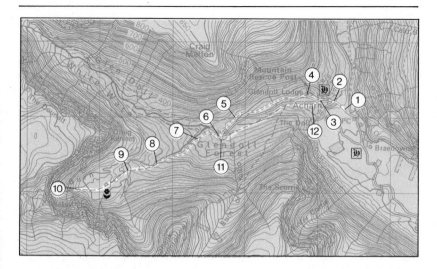

Glen Doll and Corrie Fee
5 miles (8 km) Sheet 44 284762

Moderate Getting inside a highland corrie (hollow) usually requires a long, hard walk; this is comparatively short. The area is famed for its alpine plants, at their best May-Sept. *Farmland, woods, grassy corrie; one climb; mud after rain.*

Start From the A926 take the B955 to Clova; continue 4½ miles (7 km) to Braedownie Farm, ¼ mile (0.5 km) beyond end of metalled road. Buses up the Glen from Kirriemuir. **Car park** (Forestry Commission) signposted near farm.

① From car park take the road leading to Youth Hostel and Glen Doll Forest. ② At Acharn Farm take the left branch of the 3-way fork (signposted 'Jock's Road' and 'Kilbo Path'). ③ In 300 yards (274 m) ignore the Kilbo Path as it branches off to the left and go straight on, through the gate. ④ In 200 yards (183 m) a track from the Youth Hostel joins from the right. Also ignore this. ⑤ In ¾ mile (one km) the drove road to Braemar – Jock's Path – branches off to the right. Ignore it and head down the gentle slope which leads, in a few hundred yards, to a concrete bridge over the Fee Burn (stream). ⑥ Just across the bridge take the right fork. ⑦ About ¼ mile (0.5 km) up the gentle slope a track goes off right. Ignore this

and continue straight on. In ½ mile (0.8 km) ⑧ the Land-Rover track ends but the route continues as a footpath. Follow it. Some sections may be muddy and careful footwork could be required. ⑨ At edge of forest climb high deer fence by ladder stile into Corrie Fee beyond. ⑩ The track is easy to follow for the next ½ mile up to the waterfall, where the ground is steep and sometimes slippery: take care. Return to ⑪, the concrete bridge over the Fee Burn, by the same route but instead of crossing it take the right-hand track. After about 500 yards (457 m) there is a bridge over the Burn of Kilbo and a junction of paths. Cross bridge and take the left branch, continuing downhill through trees. At the next junction do the same, turning left downhill. ⑫ At the crossroads turn left and cross the river by bridge. Turn right at the next junction and rejoin the outward route.

🏚 Jock's Road is an old drovers' – cattle drivers' – way.

♣ The floor of Corrie Fee is a habitat for alpine varieties of plants commonly found elsewhere, such as saxifrage, speedwell and cudweed.

🏚 The remote village of Clova, 4 miles (6.5 km) to the SE, and the rest of the Glen are worth exploring. It contains the 15th C. tower of Inverquharty.

Water of Ailnack

6 miles (9.5 km) Sheet 36 163174

Moderate One of the most spectacular walks in this locality, with a dramatic gorge. *Farmland, woods, moorland; 2 climbs. Do not attempt in poor visibility, or winter.*

Start At Tomintoul take the minor road in direction of Delnabo. Continue just past bridge over Avon. **Parking** in small area just beyond bridge: avoid obstructing the road.

① From the bridge take the road ahead towards Delnabo. In ¼ mile (0.5 km) ignore 2 junctions on the left. In a few yards also ignore road on right. Continue passing cottage on left and follow the Land-Rover track across bridge and as it climbs steeply to the left along edge of wood. ② Follow track along crest of small ridge with gorge on left and stream below on right. Continue towards wood, veer right through gate and after steep climb out emerge into open, flat country. In ¾ mile (one km) where the track turns left into a grassy field, walk to the edge of the gorge and follow a distinct sheep track. (Take care here, especially with children.) ④ At summit of a grassy rise (wooden pole at edge) rejoin the Land-Rover track and descend gentle slope towards lochan (small lake) on right. ⑤ About ¼ mile (0.5 km) past the lochan there is a small stream bed on the left and about this point the track becomes indistinct. It is advisable to cross the stream bed and join the sheep track near the edge of the gorge. ⑥ Follow path as it traverses edge of gorge and gradually descends towards the Water of Ailnack. (Short, muddy stretch here: because of the nature of the terrain, take extra care.) On rounding a corner of the river the path descends in a short, final steep section. ⑦ At the Ca-du Ford the water can be deceptively high: do not cross. Retrace to car park along outward route.

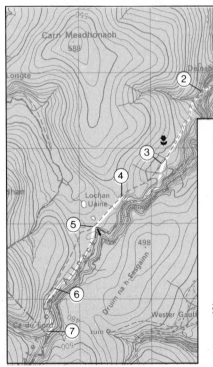

❀ In late summer and early autumn one of the pleasures of this walk is the sight of heather in bloom. Perhaps the most familiar species, properly called ling, has mauve, bell-shaped flowers and is distinguished by the quite substantial sprigs, which look like miniature conifer branches, sprouting from its stem.

The plant's scientific name, *Calluna vulgaris*, refers to one of heather's many practical uses. *Calluna* is the Latin for brush, and through the centuries, the plant has served for sweeping floors, thatching roofs, for bedding, fuel, basketry and making honey.

〵〵 The River Avon once formed a single river with the Don until the movement of ice carved a new valley for it.

\↑/ The gorge is all the more magnificent for being unexpected

DEESIDE AND CAIRNGORM REGIONS

Cairnwell Ridge
3 miles (5 km) Sheet 43 142776

Moderate Short enough for a family picnic expedition, but with some spectacular views; opportunity to watch skiing and hang-gliding. *Heather hillside and ridge, open moor; 2 climbs; boggy final section can be skirted; in winter miss out from end of ⑥ to ⑧ and return to start by the main road.*

Start The Cairnwell skiing complex on the A93 (Perth-Braemar road), 10 miles (16 km) S of Braemar. **Car Park** serving the Cairnwell skiing complex.

① From car park walk to fence which marks the border between the Tayside and Grampian regions. Follow the Land-Rover track which leads away from end of car park on left. It heads up a steep slope at right angles to the main road. In ¼ mile (0.5 km) ② at junction branch right. In about 400 yards (366 m) the path drops steeply to a watershed where ③ there are several huts connected with the skiing. Ignore paths leading to these and continue on track up steep section to crest of the ridge. ④ On top of rise the main track drops slightly into a small peat bog and then on uphill; do not follow this but turn right out along the obvious ridge. (If the main track is followed up the slope the summit of Meall Odhar is reached: only attempt in good visibility. ⑤ At end of ridge follow path as it runs right down an obvious spur to the junction of 2 streams and a small bridge. ⑥ Cross bridge and follow the track up to the main road. Walk downhill on road for about 200 yards (183 m), cross and go through metal gate on to section of former main road. In 100 yards (91 m) take the path which leads off parallel to the small stream entering from the right. ⑦ After ¼ mile (0.5 km) follow the path as it zigzags up the moderate slope to the top. The track may be difficult to find in places, but the flat ramp in the heather can usually be picked out. From the top follow the track as it contours easily back to the main road. (May be boggy.) ⑧ At road turn left to ①.

☷ Cairnwell Pass, 2,180 feet (665 m) high, is Britain's highest main road pass.

⚑ The chair lift climbs nearly 1,000 feet (305 m) to the summit of Cairnwell, 3,058 feet (933 m) high, from where there are views, and a dry-ski run.

Glen Lui and Glen Quoich
9 miles (14.5 km) Sheet 43 066898

Moderate Through an ancient Caledonian pine forest with mountain plants in plenty.*Woods, grassy and heather hillside, gorge; one climb.*

Start From the A93 in Braemar take the road for Inverey and Linn of Dee. Continue 6½ miles (10.5 km). **Car Park** ¾ mile (one km) beyond Linn of Dee, signed at edge of road.

① From car park walk E along the metalled single-track road for 300 yards (247 m). ② At gate turn left on to Land-Rover track (signposted 'Public Right of Way'), Walk up track beside Lui Water for 1¼ miles (2 km) to bridge. ③ Turn left to continue up the track. In ¾ mile (one km) where a stream crosses the track ④ turn right from track on to a footpath up a moderate slope. The path

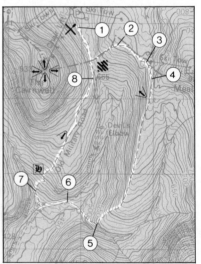

⚑ Hang-gliding during summer.

⒓ The track here was once part of a military patrol route.

⚑ There is a sweeping view of the Allt a' Ghlinne Bhig curving gently down.

✕ At the chair life a café provides snacks, tea and coffee.

is indistinct at first but better defined a few hundred yards up the side of the stream. Join the path and at the top of the slope follow it as it veers to the right away from the stream and contours round into another small valley, Clais Fhearnaig. ⑤ The sides of the valley become steeper with scree slopes either side of the path; reed-filled lochan (small lake) to the left. Soon enter Clais Fhearnaig proper, with crags on the left and boulder scree on the right. ⑥ Follow path past end of long loch and over large, grassy, 'island' in the heather. Continue on path down a gentle slope to the Land-Rover track. ⑦ At Land-Rover track turn right and follow it down the Quoich Water through pine forest. ⑧ About 300 yards (274 m) out of the woods turn left down footpath towards the Quoich Water. The path shortly drops to the river at point where river emerges from gorge. (The bridge is unsafe.) Walk back up the river about 100 yards (91 m) from

viewing Punch Bowl and Linn of Quoich and ⑨ join the Land-Rover track again which slopes gently through the trees on the left. At the top of the slope follow track as it veers right to join original track. Follow this to road. ⑩ At road turn right and follow it 2½ miles (4 km) to the car park.

\t/ The view takes in impressive Cairngorm peaks: Derry Cairngorm, Carn Crom and Carn a' Mhaim.

🌲 Plants of the locality include the butterwort (May-July), whose leaves can trap insects and alpine lady's mantle (June-Aug.), whose tiny flowers are green.

⋙ The valley is part of a fault system.

⋙ The cascading waters have worn cavities in the rocks. The almost circular one is 'the Earl of Mar's Punchbowl'.

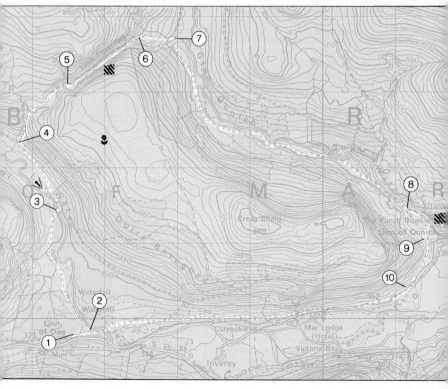

Views of Lochnager
12 miles (19 km) Sheet 44 215944

Energetic A safe and accessible route, but with a taste of remoteness; superb views of Lochnager and Balmoral Castle. Avoid in the deer-stalking season (Aug.-Oct.); spectacular in spring when the peaks are still snow-covered. *Woods, farmland, moorland; 2 climbs. Do not attempt route in poor visibility.*

Start From the A93 (Aberdeen-Braemar) take the unclassified road at the Inver Inn signposted Aberarder. Continue 1¼ miles (2 km) on metalled road, then about ½ mile (0.8 km) on unsurfaced road to Y-junction. Buses to Inver Inn. **Parking** area at Y-junction, on left.

① Turn right at the junction and walk out of the wood towards stream. ② Turn right at the junction, cross stream, then continue uphill towards Balmore Farm. ③ Turn right through gate and down across field to stream. Cross bridge, turn sharp left and continue up easy slope through birch woods. ④ Keep straight on at junction near edge of wood through fields by ruined croft and then through gate in deer fence. ⑤ At bottom of the steep zigzag another road joins from the right. Keep straight on. ⑥ At junction of paths turn left. The path – indistinct at this

Balmoral – on Scotland's relatively dry E side – a much-loved royal retreat.

point – runs between the 2 large posts forming a gate at an angle to the fence. In ½ mile (0.8 km) the path becomes a Land-Rover track again, descending long, gradual hill. ⑦ Turn left at the junction near the stream. ⑧ Cross ford (should present no problems) at Feardar Burn (stream), then climb easy slope before descending to Auchtavan Farm. Continue on track across fields out on to open moor, where rejoin original path at edge of wood at ④. Retrace steps to starting point.

\t/ A convenient point for pausing to view Balmoral and the River Dee; further on, they are obscured. Prince Albert, consort of Queen Victoria, bought the Balmoral estate in 1852 and had the house rebuilt in the 'Scottish Baronial' style. The Royal Family were, and are devoted to the place. Queen Victoria described it as this 'dear paradise'. Guests have christened it the Scotch House, because it seems to have more tartan yardage on display than the London shop of the same name. And of course, the interior is also festooned with hunting trophies.

\t/ Deeside and Balmoral again.

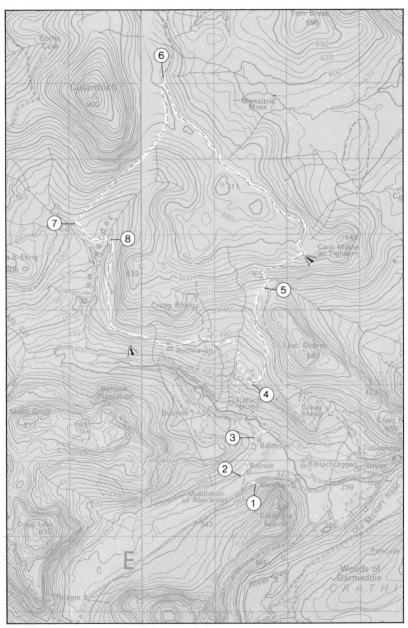

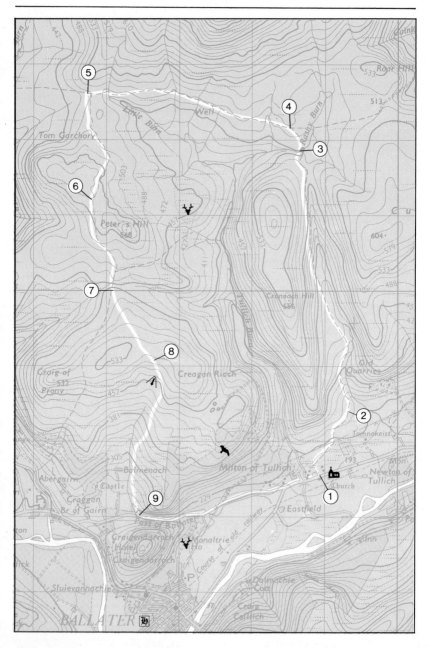

Tullich, Morven and the Pass of Ballater

12 miles (19 km) Sheet 37 391975

Energetic A walk for getting the feel of the Ballater area, and from which further routes may be planned from excellent views of the surrounding country. Avoid in winter: deep snow. *Woods, glen, moorland, hilltops, thin woods; 2 climbs; mud after rain. Do not attempt in poor visibility.*

Start On the A93 (Aberdeen-Ballater) 2 miles (3 km) E of Ballater; buses to Ballater. **Car Park** at Tullich Church.

① From car park cross road and take track to Braehead of Tullich Farm. Do not turn right into farm but go straight ahead and through gate at end of field. Turn right, go through second gate and follow track. ② Follow track through birch woods and in ½ mile (0.8 km) pass small loch on right. For the next 3 miles (5 km) the track is easy to follow. ③ At head of glen cross fence and then stream. The track becomes grassy; after a few hundred yards cross Rashy Burn (stream) by easy ford. For the next ¼ mile (0.5 km) the track is indistinct. ④ The track joins another forming a T-junction. Turn left along grassy track. ⑤ At junction of tracks turn left towards Peter's Hill. Follow track gradually uphill. ⑥ At top of rise follow track slightly downhill past several small bog lochans (small lakes) on right. Just past these a track joins from right: ignore it and carry straight on. In 300 yards (274 m) also ignore track on left. ⑦ Follow track down to watershed with rock outcrop on right, then climb moderately towards Creagan Riach. ⑧ Follow track downhill towards Balmenach Farm. ⑨ At main road turn left and walk through Pass of Ballater about 2 miles (3 km) to ⑩.

🏛 In the Kirk of St. Nathalan, built about 1400 and now a ruin, there are Pictish sculptured stones.

🌱 Red deer and mountain hares may be seen in the area.

\|/ Excellent views of the surrounding hills the Dee Valley and Glen Muick.

🌱 Monaltrie Animal Park.

The mountain or blue hare, so called because the mixing of its brown summer coat and white winter fur looks bluish.

🔟 Ballater's existence as a resort is due to an old woman who, about 1760, cured herself of a skin disease by heeding a dream and bathing in a nearby pool which was later made the spa.

🦅 Birds of the area include the capercaillie (the male looking like a shaggy turkey), red grouse and siskins, which are tiny (smaller than sparrows) with long wings and short tails – all noticeable in flight.

Kirriemuir is an ideal centre for exploring the surrounding hills; 12 miles (19 km) N of the B955, peaceful paths climb to Lake Brandy.

Paths around Carnoustie climb the local cliffs and traverse the heath round the international golf course.

Aboyne, 20 miles (32 km) W of Aberdeen has marked trails to Glen Mark and, 5 miles (8 km) NE, to Macbeth's Cairn.

Cullen Bay, 13 miles (21 km) W of Banff has cliff-top walks.

The Linn Trummel Nature Trail, near the Pitlochry Dam, takes in a salmon pass and Fastcally Reservoir.

Mountain walks, off the A951 near Aviemore, follow marked forest and upland trails. Advice on walking in the whole area can be gained from the Forestry Commission Information Centre at Glen More.

This is an introductory briefing to Britain's astonishingly large network of long-distance footpaths.

These are broadly classified as 'official' or 'unofficial'. Official means that the route is designated and maintained (often with substantial waymarking) as such by the Countryside Commission. Unofficial means, at one extreme, that the route is maintained and signposted by, say, a County Council, a local Ramblers' Association group or a private body. At the other extreme, it means a 'way' existing more in the mind of the walker who pioneered it than as a geographical entity; an imaginative linking of footpaths, not all in walkable condition or waymarked.

Here, all nine official paths, and the 2 most important unofficial paths are given long entries. The unofficial paths, with short entries, are a selection of those which are generally maintained to an adequate standard, or fully described in a guide.

To actually walk a long-distance path usually requires the relevant guide. These publications are almost always modestly priced, give detailed directions and generous amounts of relevant practical information, including accommodation and public transport links as well as general description. In the case of the unofficial routes they are mostly produced by enterprising private individuals, and do not enjoy wide retail distribution.

So rather than rely on what the shops have to offer, obtain the (regularly updated) Ramblers' Association Fact Sheet No. 2 covering long-distance paths from 1/5 Wandsworth Road, London SW8 2LJ. This lists the guides available for the paths, complete with prices and addresses from where they can be obtained by post.

As in the rest of the book, numbers are given of the 1:50,000 sheets needed.

The South West Peninsula Coast Path
518 miles (833 km)
This is the longest of the long-distance paths, and it is usually divided into four sections.

The Somerset and North Devon Coast Path: Minehead to Marsland Mouth
82 miles (132 km) Sheets 180, 181, 190.
This section is usually taken to be the start of the Coast Path, and considered the least arduous. It covers, however, as wide a variety of terrain as any. There are beautiful, picturesque villages. Parts lie in

the Exmoor National Park, and others within an Area of Outstanding Natural Beauty.

There are still several stretches where the waymarking is incomplete because public rights of way have not been obtained, or where it is inadequate, and it is therefore wise to carry maps and guides.

Between Porlock Weir and County Gate it is beautifully wooded.

There should be no lack of accommodation, but during the holiday season bookings should be made in advance. Trousers are recommended, rather than skirts or shorts, as well as windproof and waterproof clothing. Distance calculations should be increased by 25% due to the frequent changes of levels and direction.

Highlights Selworthy Beacon; Culbone Church, claiming to be the smallest in England; Lynmouth and Lynton, twin towns of great beauty; Valley of Rocks, below Hollerday Hill; Saunton Sands, which have dunes up to 98 feet (30 m) high; Clovelly, with its steep and cobbled streets, where donkeys instead of cars are used for transport.

The Cornwall Coast Path: Marsland Mouth near Bude to Cremyll on the Tamar
268 miles (431 km) Maps 190, 200, 201, 203, 204.

Like the Dorset Coast Path, this section of the Peninsula Coast Path goes mostly through an Area of Outstanding Natural Beauty. The walk goes across dunes, moorlands and cliff tops, often following the coastguard paths.

There is a wide variety of interest, from fascinating rock formations to the hunting ground of King Arthur at Tintagel; remains of tin mines; the artists' centre at St. Ives; the serpentine rock carving industry at the Lizard; and the china clay ports of Charlestown and Par, as well as the picturesque villages and beautiful views.

Conditions The path includes some sections regarded as easy and others as severe; the latter should not be undertaken unprepared. For example, Tintagel to Port Isaac, which includes one of the steepest parts of the whole Peninsula Coast Path; and St. Ives to Pendeen Watch, where there are 21 miles (34 km) without a place for rest or refreshment. There are some ferry crossings, and even wading at low tide. Beware when there is a heavy mist, or when there are strong off-shore winds.

Trousers, rather than skirts or shorts, are

advisable and distance calculations should be increased to allow for the changes in level and direction. Accommodation should not prove difficult, but this is a holiday area, and bookings should be made in advance. **Highlights** Many attractive villages and coves; Helford River Estuary, famous for its oyster beds; Looe, the shark-fishing centre.

South Devon Coast Path: Plymouth to Lyme Regis

93 miles (150 km) Sheets 192, 193, 201, 202. 1:25,000 Outdoor Leisure Map of South Devon, for the section between Bolt Head and Torbay.

Most of the walk comes within Areas of Outstanding Natural Beauty, and several sections have been defined as Heritage coast. Though walkers have to make their way around Paignton and Torquay, much of the route offers spectacular cliffs, wide estuaries and remote bays, together with charming Devon villages. The number of river crossings adds to the variety.

Conditions The path should not be difficult for most walkers with the exception of the landslip at the Dorset end – there it is tough going, and should be left to the experienced walker, as, once started, there is no way off it. A few sections are disappointing, but several are being improved.

Between Budleigh Salterton and Sidmouth there is a long diversion through lack of a bridge, and though in exceptionally dry conditions it is possible to wade the river Otter, this is not recommended. Ferries have to be used on several sections, and times should be checked.

Allowance of about 25% should be made when calculating distances, owing to the changes in levels and directions of the paths in some sections. Stout footwear and trousers, rather than skirts or shorts, are advised. There should be no lack of accommodation, but as this is a holiday area, bookings should be made in advance.

Highlights Burgh Island, a miniature St. Michael's Mount; Hope Cove, with its spectacular cliffs; Salcombe Harbour; Slapton Ley, a freshwater lake, rich in wildlife and an angler's paradise; Brixham, fishing port and yachting centre; The Landslip, caused by a vast cliff slide.

Dorset Coast Path: Lyme Regis to Bournemouth

72 miles (116 km) Sheets 193, 194, 195.

This is the shortest section of the South West Peninsula Coast Path. With the exception of Weymouth, the whole path is in an Area of Outstanding Natural Beauty.

The area is famous for the fossils to be found along the cliffs, and dramatic examples of folded strata can be seen.

Conditions In general the path is well signposted, but the alternative route between West Bexington and Osmington Mills will require a compass and good maps, and it should be noted that there is no accommodation or refreshment facility available for 12 miles (19 km) of this stretch. Otherwise these are readily available.

There are some problems in places with cliff slippage (for instance between Lyme Regis and Charmouth), and care must be taken to keep back from the cliff edge.

There is a badly neglected section between Abbotsbury and Weymouth. Firing takes place on Chickerell Range, and walkers must wait until given permission to proceed; and before setting out for the section between Lulworth Cove and Kimmeridge, a check should be made as to whether firing will be in progress; if so, the area must be skirted.

When calculating distances, allow an extra 25% for changes in level and direction. No special clothing is required other than strong footwear, but it is advisable to wear trousers because of overgrown sections.

Highlights Charmouth, a favourite town of Jane Austen; Golden Cap, the highest point of the South Coast, with spectacular views; Abbotsbury with its swannery; Lulworth Cove; St Aldhem's (or Alban's) Chapel, dating from Norman days; Chesil Bank.

The South Downs Way: Eastbourne to Buriton, near Petersfield

80 miles (129 km) Sheets 197, 198, 199. 1:25,000 OS Outdoor Leisure Map of Brighton and Sussex Vale shows route between Rodmell and Steyning.

The South Downs Way, as well as being a walk, is the only long-distance bridle way, so expect to see horseriders. In addition to the scenic beauty of this walk, with its superb views from such places as Beacon Hill, there is a profusion of wild flowers, birds and butterflies, and much to interest the archaeologist. Good public services make it ideal to walk in sections.

Conditions Even though the path is well signposted, maps are essential. Strong footwear should be worn for protection against sharp flints. Public transport is available all along the route, but services are not necessarily regular, so do consult the timetables. Accommodation can be found in nearby towns or villages, but other than a few youth hotels there is little on the route.

Highlights West Dean, a flint village; The Long Man of Wilmington, carved from the hillside; Alfriston, with its timbered inns; the Norman Church at Southease, with its 13th C. wall paintings; the prehistoric fort at Devil's Dyke; hang gliding at Soper's Bottom.

The North Downs Way: Farnham in Surrey to Dover, Kent, with a loop to Canterbury.

140 miles (225 km) Sheets 186, 187, 188, 178, 189, 179

The North Downs Way was officially opened by the then Archbishop of Canterbury, Dr. Donald Coggan, at the end of September 1978, and its route through South-East England offers plenty of variety–much of it along the crest of the North Downs, with its many beautiful and extensive views.

In parts it coincides with the Pilgrims' Way, so-called because it is supposed to have been used by pilgrims to the shrine of Saint Thomas à Becket at Canterbury.

There are many buildings of architectural and historic interest on or near the route, as well as attractive villages and major towns.

Conditions Being so near London, this walk has ample public transport. Special equipment is not needed, but walkers are advised to wear strong shoes and to take waterproof and windproof clothing. In several places negotiations are still taking place on rights of way, and the text of the guide books will indicate these.

In Surrey the route is marked by oak signposts, and in Kent by low stone plinths which are sometimes obscured by vegetation. Where there is some doubt, the acorn waymark is used to confirm the route. Finding accommodation should be easy.

Highlights The famous stepping stones over the River Mole; St. Martha's Hill, giving glorious views; Bluebell Hill, with fine views from its picnic site; the Crondale Nature Reserve; Chilham, claimed to be the prettiest village in Kent; Canterbury Cathedral; Dover Castle; and, on a clear day, France.

The Ridgeway Path: Overton Hill to Ivinghoe Beacon

85 miles (137 km) Sheets 165, 173, 174, 175

The Path was opened in 1973. It lies entirely within the North Wessex Downs and Chiltern Areas of Outstanding Natural Beauty, and goes through the 5 counties of Wilts., Berks., Oxon., Bucks. and Herts. Much of it follows the ancient routes of the Wessex Ridgeway and Icknield Way.

At the start you see 5 round and 2 long barrows. A long and beautiful section is the downland patch passing by Segsbury Camp, close to Grim's Ditch, and down to the River Thames at Streatley. Leaving the river after some 5½ miles (9 km), the path wanders through woods to join the Icknield Way, and skirts Beacon Hill. Here you can visit the Rowant Nature Reserve. After crossing the Chiltern Hills the path drops down to the Union Canal. Having crossed this, you come to one of the loveliest sections over wood and grasslands to the Beacon.

Conditions This walk is not hard going, but sensible shoes should be worn against the sharp flints, slippery clay and chalk. Youth Hostel accommodation is plentiful, but other types are limited, so book ahead.

Highlights Bronze and Iron Age relics; Avebury Stone Circle; the Iron Age fortifications of Barbury Castle; Ashdown House, tiny and beautiful, owned by the National Trust; Wayland's Smithy, a chambered long barrow, with a fascinating legend; Coombe Hill, the highest point of the Chilterns.

Pembrokeshire Coast Path: Amroth, Pembrokeshire, to St. Dogmaels, near Cardigan

168 miles (270 km) Sheets 145, 157, 158

The Pembrokeshire Coast Path gives magnificent views from the cliff paths of the beautiful coastal scenery. The coastline and the offshore islands are one of the greatest seabird areas, and there is much of archaeological and historical interest.

Conditions The path is well marked, but good maps are essential for enjoyment. Some sections are difficult and hazardous and should only be undertaken by the fit. Most stretches are however within the average walker's capabilities.

Sudden changes in the weather must be expected, and clothing should be appropriate. Altitude and direction changes during the walk should be taken into account when calculating distances.

Accommodation is available, but should be booked in advance during holiday times.

There is a stretch between Elegug Stacks and St. Govan's Head which is closed by the

Ministry of Defence when firing is in progress, and enquiries should be made before setting out – there are inland detours.

The estuaries at Pickleridge and Sandy Haven can only be traversed at low tide; at other times it is necessary to make detours. **Highlights** From Whitesands Bay there are views of Ramsey Island with its famous colony of grey seals; St. David's Cathedral, 12th C., said to be the resting place of David, the patron saint of Wales; the magnificent natural harbour of Milford Haven, now the largest oil port in the British Isles; Penally, noted for its old red sandstone rocks and carboniferous limestones; St. Govan's Chapel and holy well, dating from the 13th C.

Offa's Dyke Path

168 miles (270 km) Sheets 162, 161, 148, 137, 126, 117, 116
The Offa's Dyke Path takes its name from the 8th C. earthwork dyke built by King Offa to mark the boundary between England and Wales. It is unique among designated paths in that it follows an archaeological route rather than a geographical one, and is considered by historians as the most interesting survivor of the Dark Ages, but note that the Dyke itself is only followed for about 60 miles (97 km).

The walk has become one of the best used of the long-distance routes, offering a particularly wide variety from the rough and lonely hill country and the steeply wooded valley of the River Wye to the lowlands and wide valley of the River Severn. Though there is no rock work, the walk is strenuous in places.
Conditions Though nearly all the path is well signposted, in many places the route is not clear; directions are given in the guides.

A compass is recommended as the path covers some moorland stretches.

Improvements to the route have been accepted in principle, and it is hoped that there will be some re-signposting. Avoid the long ridge walk of the Black Mountains in bad weather and be prepared for no readily available accommodation or transport between Abergavenny and Hay-on-Wye.
Highlights Wintour's Leap; White Castle; Pen Twyn, an Iron Age fort; Telford's Aqueduct; Panorama Walk.

The Pennine Way: Edale in Derbyshire to Kirk Yetholm in Berwickshire

250 miles (402 km) Sheets 74, 80, 86, 91, 98, 103, 109, 110

The Pennine Way was the first of the long-distance walks to be established. It is the second longest in Britain, and remains the most challenging, passing through some of the remotest areas in the country.

There is much evidence of the past in the Roman remains, Norman churches and period houses. The Way goes through the heart of the Brontë country; there are splendid caves and potholes, spectacular views of rushing water. There is a profusion of plant life in the dales, and many varieties of bird can be seen.
Conditions This is a strenuous, high-level walk. It can be dangerous, indeed it presents some of the roughest walking in Britain. In bad weather it should only be undertaken by really experienced walkers, armed with maps and compass, and provided with correct clothing, equipment and supplies.

The frequent changes in level and direction make it necessary to add 25% when calculating distances.

Accommodation is obtainable in general – though it is advisable to check in advance; but there is a 27-mile (43 km) stretch at the end of the route, between Byrness and Kirk Yetholm, which must be accomplished in one day, unless equipped with tents.

Highlights Within's Height, with the ruined farmhouse – possibly the original Wuthering Heights; the Brontë Museum, Haworth 3 miles (5 km) off the Way; Pinhaw Beacon, giving panoramic views to all points of the compass; Pen-y-Ghent, offering fine views, and much loved by potholers; Hull Pot, where the Hull Pot Beck plunges spectacularly when in spate; Hardraw Force, and High Force waterfalls; Hadrian's Wall, and the forts of Birdoswall, Great Chesters, Vindolanda and Housesteads.

The Wolds Way: Filey Brigg to Herrle Haven on the River Humber

76 miles (122 km) Sheets 100, 101, 106
The Wolds Way is the latest of the long-distance routes to be designated by the Countryside Commission. Though it was approved in 1977 the official opening is in September 1982. The walk links with the Cleveland Way, running along the chalk hills of the Yorkshire Wolds, crossing some of the prettiest of the dry dales of the region, through farming country.
Conditions Waymarking is complete along all rights of way along the path. As new

sections are created they will also be waymarked. When the Way is opened in September 1982 it will be one of the easiest long-distance paths to follow.

The Cleveland Way: North York Moors and coast

93 miles (150 km) Sheets 93, 94, 99, 100, 101. The OS 1 inch to 1 mile Tourist Map of the North York Moors shows the whole route.

The Cleveland Way was the second long-distance walk to be opened in England and Wales. Its horseshoe shape is almost all contained within the North York Moors National Park, providing both moorland and coastal scenery – the latter being so outstanding that it has been defined as a Heritage Coast.

The path is well marked, but it is essential to carry maps and a compass on many sections. Accommodation is limited inland and it is wise to book well in advance.

Conditions There are frequent cliff slips, particularly in winter after rain, and the area is noted for its rapid changes in weather conditions, and for fog. Great caution is required, and suitable clothing must be worn. Always take an extra pullover and emergency rations.

Because of the climbs, and direction changes, distance calculations should be increased by as much as 25%.

This walk should not be undertaken alone, except by the most experienced – and even they would be ill-advised to do so.

Highlights The remains of the beautiful Norman Rievaulx Abbey; Botton Head, the highest point of the Cleveland Hills; Captain Cook's monument; the impressive remains of Whitby Abbey, at the picturesque resort; Robin Hood's Bay with its cliff-hanging cottages; the inlet of Cloughton Wyke, popular with geologists and photographers.

Two long-distance paths have become – by virtue of their popularity and excellent waymarking and condition – 'official unofficial' routes. They are:

The Cotswold Way: Chipping Camden to Bath

100 miles (161 km) Sheets 150, 151, 162, 163, 172.

A walk along the Cotswold Edge had been suggested as far back as 1953, and it was sponsored by the Gloucestershire County Council in 1970 in the hope that it would be taken over by the Countryside Commission

as another long-distance footpath.

The route passes through many places of interest, the villages are beautiful, and plenty of time should be allowed to enjoy them and, of course, the great City of Bath. Because much of the route follows the top of the steep Cotswold escarpment, it has similarities with a cliff-top coastal path.

Conditions There should be no problems with this path. In wet weather suitable footwear must be worn to deal with the deep Cotswold mud; and, of course, waterproof gear. The path is largely over cultivated land, and care must be taken to fasten gates and not to disturb livestock. Dogs must be kept on leads. The path is waymarked using the Countryside Commission's system of coloured arrows supplemented by use of the white spot. Where there is need for careful navigation, the guide gives special warnings. Even so, maps are strongly advised.

Highlights Broadway, with its beautiful houses and the Lygon Arms Hotel; Stanton village; Stanway House, with its Inigo Jones gatehouse; the remains of the abbey at Hailes; Barrow Wake, giving superb views; Cooper's Hill – cheese rolling on Whit Monday; Horton Court, a medieval hall.

West Highland Way: Milngavie *(on the outskirts of Glasgow)* to Fort William

95 miles (153 km) Maps incorporated in the official guide.

The West Highland Way is the first long-distance path to be designated in Scotland. It has taken many years to negotiate, and there has been some debate as to its value, since Scottish walkers already enjoy more or less free access to the countryside.

Conditions The route has been well though unobtrusively signposted with dark brown waymarks with a thistle symbol.

As the path progresses N, there are stretches through remote country with no shelter and some rough walking and scrambling. Scottish weather is unpredictable, and correct clothing and supplies should be taken. There is adequate accommodation, though bear in mind the remote stretches. In the tourist season it is wise to book in advance. Care should be exercised not to disturb livestock, and dogs should not be taken.

Highlights The whole route offers scenery second to none, but the shores of Loch Lomond and the rugged mountains of the western highlands are of course unforgettable.

Avon

The Avon Walkway *13 miles (21 km) Sheet 172.*
From Pill, following the River Avon, through the Avon Gorge, and the centre of Bristol, to Nethan Bridge. The walk can be continued to Bath, but this part is not waymarked.

Buckinghamshire

The North Buckinghamshire Way *30 miles (48 km) Sheets 152, 165.*
From Chequers Knap, through the Vale of Aylesbury to Wolverton. Here it joins the Grafton Way – *see Northamptonshire.*

Cheshire

Gritstone Trail *17 miles (27 km) Sheets 109, 118.*
From Lyme Park to Rushton, linking with the Staffordshire Way – *see Staffordshire.*
The Sandstone Trail *30 miles (48 km) Sheet 117.*
From Frodsham to Grindley Brook.
Wirral Way *12 miles (19 km) Sheets 108, 117.*

Cumbria

The Dales Way *81 miles (130 km) Sheets 90, 97, 98.*
From Ilkley to Bowness. This is a difficult path following the rivers Wharfe, Dee, Lune and Kent, and some of the Pennine Way.

Derbyshire

High Peak Trail *17 miles (27 km) Sheet 119.*
From Cromford to Dowlow, connecting with the Tissington Trail this walk follows the route of the old Cromford and High Peak railway, and gives fine scenery.

Devon

Two Moors Way *103 miles (166 km) Sheets 202, 191, 181, 180.*
From Ivybridge, Plymouth to Lynton, Barnstaple, linking Exmoor and Dartmoor.

Dorset

South Wessex Way – *see Hampshire.*
Tissington Trail *13 miles (21 km) Sheet 119.*
From Ashbourne to Parsley Hay, connecting with the High Peak Trail, following the old railway route, and offering fine and varied scenery.

East Sussex

The Forest Way *9 miles (14 km) Sheets 187, 188.*
From Groombridge to East Grinstead, through to the Forest Way Country Park.

Essex

The Essex Way *50 miles (80 km) Sheets 187, 188.*
From Epping to Dedham, in the lovely Constable countryside.
The Forest Way *20 miles (32 km) Sheets 167, 177.*
From Epping Forest to Hatfield Forest, the ancient tracks of the forests opening out to large attractive areas.

Gloucestershire

The Heart of England Way – *see Staffordshire.*
The Oxfordshire Way – *see Oxfordshire.*

Gwent

The Lower Wye Valley Walk *34 miles (55 km) Sheet 162.*
From Chepstow to Ross through the varied Wye Valley Area of Outstanding Natural Beauty.
Usk Valley Walk *22 miles (35 km) Sheets 161, 171.*
From Caerleon to Llanellen, providing both high superb views and quiet riverside walking.

Hampshire

South Wessex Way *117 miles (188 km) Sheets 197, 184, 185, 195.*
From Petersfield to Poole; links the South Downs Way with the South West Peninsula Coast Path.

Hereford and Worcester

Lower Wye Valley Walk – *see Gwent.*

Humberside

Viking Way – *see Lincolnshire.*

Isle of Wight

Bembridge Trail *15 miles (24 km) Sheet 196.*
From Shide to Bembridge Point, through marsh and woodland.
Coastal Path *60 miles (97 km) Sheet 196.*
Circling the coastline.
Hamstead Trail *8 miles (13 km) Sheet 196.*
Hamstead Ledge to Brooke Bay, meeting the Coastal Path.
Tennyson Trail *15 miles (24 km) Sheet 196.*
From Carisbrooke to Alum Bay – offering varied downland and forest walking, and fine marine views.
Worsley Trail *15 miles (24 km) Sheet 196.*
From Shanklin Old Village to Brighstone Forest, giving a wide variety of forest, downland and high countryside.

LONG-DISTANCE PATHS

Kent

Wealdway *57 miles (92 km) Sheets 178, 188, 198.*
From Gravesend to Uckfield.

Leicestershire

Jubilee Way *16 miles (26 km) Sheets 129, 130.*
From Melton Mowbray to Brewer's Gate, Nr. Woolsthorpe, linking with the Viking Way – see Humberside.
Viking Way – see Lincolnshire.

Lincolnshire

Jubilee Way – see Leicestershire.
Viking Way *140 miles (225 km) Sheets 141, 112.*
From Oakham to Humber Bridge.

London

London Countryway *205 miles (330 km) Sheets 165, 166, 167, 175, 177, 186, 187, 188.*
Complete circuit of London, with access by rail at several points.

Merseyside

Wirral Way – see Cheshire.

Northamptonshire

The Grafton Way *12 miles (20 km) Sheet 152.*
From Wolverhampton to Greens Norton, linking with the North Bucks Way and The Knightley Way.
The Knightley Way *12 miles (19 km) Sheet 152.*
From Greens Norton to Badby, linking with the Grafton Way.

Norfolk

Peddar's Way *50 miles (80 km) Sheets 132, 144.*
From Knettishall (Norfolk-Suffolk border) to Holme on the Norfolk Coast.

North Yorkshire

The Dales Way – see Cumbria.
The Ebor Way *70 miles (113 km) Sheets 100, 104, 105.*
From Helmsley to Oakley. This links the Cleveland Way long-distance path and the Dales Way and goes via York.

Northumberland

Hadrian's Wall *73 miles (117 km) Sheets 85, 86, 87, 88 and the OS Hadrian's Wall Map.*
It is not possible to walk the whole length uninterrupted, but there are some fine unspoilt sections.

Oxfordshire

The Oxfordshire Way *60 miles (96 km) Sheets 163, 164, 175.*
From Henley-on-Thomas to Bourton-on-the-Water. This walk links the Chiltern and Cotswold A.N.O.B's.

Powys

Glyndwr's Way *121 miles (195 km) Sheets 125, 126, 135, 136, 148.*
From Knighton to Welshpool, the walk, giving splendid scenic views, is divided into 16 strenuous sections.
The Wye Valley Walk *36 miles (58 km) Sheets 147, 148, 161.*
From Hay-on-Wye to Rhayader.

Staffordshire

The Staffordshire Way *32 miles (51 km) Sheets 118, 128.*
From Mow Cop to Cannock Chase, linking with the Gritstone Trail and divided into 2 sections, providing valley and hilltop paths.
Heart of England Way *80 miles (129 km) Sheets 127, 128, 139, 150, 151.*
Joins the Staffordshire Way at Cannock Chase with the Cotswold Way at Chipping Camden.

Surrey

Wey South Path *36 miles (58 km) Sheets 186, 197.*
Along the towpath of the former Wey and Arun Canal.

Thames

Thames Walk *150 miles (241 km) Sheets 163, 164, 174, 175, 176.*
From Putney to Thames Head.

West Midlands

West Midlands Way *162 miles (261 km) Sheets 127, 128, 138, 139, 140, 150, 151.*
Completely encircles the conurbations of West Midlands Metropolitan County.

West Yorkshire

The Calderdale Way *50 miles (80 km) Sheets 103, 104, 110.*
Making a circuit of Calderdale, by Ripponden, Todmorden, Heptonstall, Brighouse and Greetland.
Colne Valley Circular Walk *15 miles (24 km) Sheet 110.*
A circular path starting from Golcar.
The Dales Way – see Cumbria.
The Ebor Way – see North Yorkshire.

INDEX

Aberdaron, 153
Aberdovey, 155
Acharn, 320
Alfriston, 99
Amesbury, 90
Arnside, 265
Ashbury, 89
Aylsham, 195
Ayr, 286
Aysgarth, 243
Bala Lake, 156
Balerno, 296
Ballater, 327
Ballingry, 312
Bardon Mill, 274
Beckside, 264
Beddgelert, 162
Bellingham, 273
Betws-y-Coed, 152
Biggar, 291
Blackfield, 76
Blackheath, 109
Blair Atholl, 319
Bonaly Tower, 292
Bossington, 44
Bourton-on-the-Hill, 176
Bovey Tracey, 28
Brauncewell, 197
Braunston, 198
Brendon Two Gates, 53
Bretton, 226
Bridge End, 275
Bridgeham Heath, 193
Brockweir, 169
Brockenhurst, 75
Burghclere, 85
Burley, 76
Burnham Market, 189
Byrness, 276
Bwlch-y-groes, 107
Cairnsmore Estate, 289
Cairnwell Ski Complex, 322
Callander, 300
Camelford, 16
Carn Brea, 15
Castleton, 211
Cerne Abbas, 40
Chevening, 118
Chilgrove, 97
Chipping, 217
Chop Gate, 259
Clayton Green, 94
Coln St. Aldwyn's, 178
Colwyn Bay, 150
Conwy, 151
Cornalees, 302
Craignure, 307
Crail, 314

Craster, 277
Cremyll, 23
Crosby Garrett, 262
Crowfield, 141
Cwm-llwch, 146
Dalmellington, 284
Dalry, 284
Delnabo, 321
Disley, 208
Ditchling Beacon, 96
Dollar, 316
Dolphinholme, 217
Doonfoot, 286
Downs Ridge, 102
Dunsop Bridge, 221
Eamont Bridge, 261
Eartham Wood, 93
Edgeworth, 174
Errwood Reservoir, 210
Eskdale Green, 271
Farrington Gurney, 62
Flax Bourton, 56
Fovant, 83
Freshwater Bay, 69, 70-85
Friday Street, 106
Fritham, 79
Gargrave, 227
Garsdale Station, 245
Godshill, 67
Gomshall, 113
Goyt Valley, 210
Grassington, 242
Great Kimble, 125
Great Yarmouth, 191
Grindleford Station, 206
Grwyne Fawr Valley, 143
Gwaun Valley, 138
Horton, 251
Hare Hill Edge, 225
Harewood, 228
Harlech, 158
Hartshill, 184
Headley, 114
Hebden Bridge, 230
Hneley, 129
Higher Bockhampton, 38
Holford, 51
Holt, 192
Ilam, 205
Ingleton, 248
Inkpen, 86
Inver, 324
Inverkeithing, 313
Ivinghoe Beacon, 123
Kenmore, 301
Keswick, 268
Kirkdale, 256
Kirklington, 201

Lastingham, 254
Leatherhead, 105
Lichfield, 185
Linn of Dee, 323
Little Black Hill, 142
Little Hampden, 126
Little Malvern, 170
Littlebredy Farm, 36
Little Salkeld, 263
Lizard Village, 20
Llangollen, 154
Llwyncelyn, 144
Loch Don, 307
Loch Doon, 284
Loch Glow, 311
Lockton, 257
Love Pool, 168
Lucott Cross, 43, 49
Lullingstone Park, 118
Lydeard Hill, 50
Lydford, 26
Lyme Park, 208
Malham, 241
Marsden, 229
Matlock, 207
Meldon Reservoir, 30
Midsummer Hill, 167
Moretonhampstead, 27
Morvil, 136
Neuadd Reservoirs, 147
New Abbey, 287
Newborough, 157
Newlands Corner, 116
New Polzeath, 17
Newton Stewart, 289
Northleach, 175
North Wootton, 55
Oakworth, 225
Osmington, 37
Otford, 121
Ozleworth Bottom, 173
Pass of Glencoe, 299
Pengegin, 139
Perth, 304
Pocklington, 237
Poldue Downs, 19
Porlock, 48
Priddy, 57
Princetown, 25
Queenzieburn, 303
Reigate, 110
Ribchester, 220
Richmond, 246
Rievaulx, 253
Ringmoor Down, 29
Roche, 22
Rosebush, 135
Rostegue, 18

Rubery, 187
Rufus Stone, 73
St. Catherine's Court, 177
St. David's, 133
Shalford, 108
Sawley, 218
Sedbergh, 244
Settrington, 233
Sherringham, 194
Silpho Forest, 254
South Queensferry, 293
Stalham, 190
Stean, 247
Steyning, 94
Sticklepath, 33
Studland, 35
Symond's Yat, 171
Tanworth-in-Arden, 183
Tarpantan, 147
Tarr Steps, 44
Tenby, 134
Tetford, 203
The Hog's Back, 114
The Lee, 126
Thixendale, 235
Tintern Parva, 169
Tinto Hill, 291
Tollard Royal, 92
Trefriw, 160
Turville Heath, 124
Ty-i-saf, 156
Tywyn, 149
Upton, 46
Walbury Hill Fort, 86
Walderton, 100
Wardle Fold, 223
Watton, 234
Webber's Post, 47
Wells, 58
Welton, 238
Wenallt, 146
Wherwell, 84
White Coomb, 283
Whiting Bay, 306
Winchcombe, 181
Windermere, 267
Winkworth Arboretum, 106
Winscombe, 60
Woldingham, 117
Wooler, 278
Wootton Bridge, 71
Worth, 58
Worth Matravers, 39
Wycoller, 224
Yarmouth, 68
Yarrowford, 295
Youlgreave, 212

ACKNOWLEDGEMENTS

Christopher Hall is editor of *The Countryman,* former Nat. Sec. of the Ramblers' Association and Director of the Council for the Protection of Rural England.

David Platten Director, Say Yes to Adventure Liz Prince *Walks in the Dartmoor National Park* (Dartmoor National Park Department) Anne-Marie Edwards *New Forest Walks, More New Forest Walks, Discovering Hardy's Wessex, In the Steps of Jane Austen* (available from 2, Woodlands Road, Ashurst, Southampton); *The Unknown Forest* (Countryside Books) David Butler (pseudonym of one of the Exmoor National Park wardens) *Exmoor Walks for Motorists (Warne)* E. M. Gould Footpath Secretary, Mendip Ramblers' Association Ben Parkins *South Downs Walks for Motorists* (Warne) Janet Spayne and Audrey Krynski *Walks in the Surrey Hills, Afoot in Surrey, Walks in the Hills of Kent* Nick Moon *Chilterns Walks for Motorists, Southern and Northern Areas* – 2 vols. (Warne) Chris Barber *Exploring the Brecon Beacons National Park;* Originator of the Three Peaks Trail, organizer of the South Wales Seven Peaks Marathon Walk, mountaineering instructor, caver James T. C. Knowles *Snowdonia Walks for Motorists* (Warne) Donna Baker *Tracking Through Mercia* – 3 vols. (Express Logic) Richard Sale *A Guide to the Cotswold Way* (Constable) S. G. Wallsgrove Rights of Way Secretary, Midland Area Ramblers' Association Jeanne le Surf 'Rambler' of the *Eastern Evening News* Brett Collier walks columnist for the *Lincolnshire Evening Echo,* Secretary, Lincolnshire and South Humberside Area Ramblers' Association Brian Spencer *Dovedale and the Manifold Valley, The Derbyshire Wye, Matlock and the Upper Derwent, Castleton and Edale* (Moorland Publishing) Cyril Spibey *Walking in Central Lancashire, Walking in the Ribble Valley* (Dalesman); rambles contributor to *Leisure Post* and *Lancashire Evening Post.* Colin Speakman *Dales Way* (Dalesman); Footpath Secretary, W. Riding Area Ramblers' Association Geoff Eastwood *Walking in East Yorkshire* (from 60, Front Street, Lockington, Driffield, E Yorks); *The Minster Way,* with Ray Wallis and Alan Kilnwick (Lockington Publishing); Footpath Secretary, East Yorkshire and Derwent Area Ramblers' Association John Parker *Lake District Walks for Motorists* (Warne), *Observer's Book of the Lake District* (Warne), *Cumbria* (Bartholomew) Ken Andrew *Scottish Mountaineering Club Guide – Southern Uplands, with Thrippleton (Scottish Mountaineering Trust)* Dave Forsyth rambling contributor to *Dunfermline Press;* Angus and Fife section in *Walking in Scotland* Bill Brodie local walks leader F. C. A. Gordon Aberdeen Mountain Rescue Team, 1973-80.

PICTURE CREDITS

12-13 Janet and Colin Bord 15 Robert Roskrow 6, 21 Aerofilms Ltd 27 Jorge Lewinski 30 Janet and Colin Bord 35, 41 Mike Edwards 43 Jeff Haynes 67 British Tourist Board/Robert Harding Associates 73, 83, 84 Mike Edwards 87, 89 Aerofilms Ltd 98 Janet and Colin Bord 105, 110, 111, 113 Nigel O' Gorman 120 Allan Payne 124 Don Gresswell 130-1 Janet and Colin Bord 139 Roger Worsley 141 Glyn Davies 145 Chris Barber 149, 153, 161, 162 Mel Petersen 164-5 Nigel O' Gorman 167 John Bettell/National Trust 173, 174, 177, 179, 180 Nigel O' Gorman 189 Patrick Matthews/Robert Harding Associates 199 Janet and Colin Bord 205 Derek Widdicome/National Trust 217, 223, 230 Mel Petersen 239 Hull Daily Mail 247, 251 Colin Speakman 256 Janet and Colin Bord 261, 269 Janet and Colin Bord 273 Richard Wylie 291 Ken Andrew 299 Scottish Tourist Board 305 Bill Brodie 311 Ken Andrew 313 Dave Forsyth 324 Scottish Tourist Board.

The help of the Countryside Commission in compiling the long-distance paths section is gratefully acknowledged; also of the Countryside Commission for Scotland and the Gloucestershire County Council.